ATTITUDES AND ATTITUDE CHANGE IN SPECIAL EDUCATION:

Theory and Practice

A Product of the
ERIC Clearinghouse on Handicapped and Gifted Children
The Council for Exceptional Children

EDITED BY REGINALD L. JONES

Library of Congress Cataloging in Publication Data
Main entry under title:

Attitudes and attitude change in special education.

1. Handicapped children—Education—Addresses, essays, lectures. 2. Mainstreaming in education—Addresses, essays, lectures. 3. Attitude change—Addresses, essays, lectures. 4. Handicapped—Social conditions—Addresses, essays, lectures. 5. Teachers—Attitudes—Addresses, essays, lectures. 6. Public opinion—Addresses, essays, lectures. I. Jones, Reginald Lanier, 1931- . II. Council for Exceptional Children.

LC4019.A75 1984   371.9   84-12050
ISBN 0-86586-137-4

A product of the ERIC Clearinghouse on Handicapped and Gifted Children.

Published in 1984 by The Council for Exceptional Children, 1920 Association Drive, Reston, Virginia 22091-1589.

Development of this publication was supported by the National Support Systems Project, under a grant from the former Division of Personnel Preparation, Bureau of Education for the Handicapped, US Office of Education, Department of Health, Education, and Welfare. The points of view expressed in this publication are those of the authors and do not necessarily reflect the positions of the US Office of Education, and no official endorsement by the US Office of Education should be inferred.

This publication was prepared with funding from the National Institute of Education, US Department of Education, under contract no. 400-81-0031. Contractors undertaking such projects under government sponsorship are encouraged to express freely their judgment in professional and technical matters. Prior to publication the manuscript was submitted to The Council for Exceptional Children for critical review and determination of professional competence. This publication has met such standards. Points of view, however, do not necessarily represent the official view or opinions of either The Council for Exceptional Children, the National Institute of Education, or the Department of Education.

Printed in the United States of America.

Contents

Authors

John Adamopoulos is Assistant Professor of Psychology, Indiana University at South Bend.

David Brinberg is Assistant Professor, School of Management, Baruch College, New York, New York.

Constance Chiba is a lecturer at Sonoma State University, California and Research Educationist, Institute of Human Development, University of California, Berkeley.

Louise Corman is Program Analyst, Office of Health Planning and Evaluation, Public Health Service, Department of Health and Human Services, Washington, DC.

Richard Curci is a graduate student, Department of Educational Psychology, New York University, New York.

Robyn M. Dawes is Professor of Psychology, Department of Psychology, University of Oregon.

Jay Gottlieb is Professor, Department of Educational Psychology, New York University, New York.

Samuel Guskin is Professor, Department of Special Education, Indiana University, Bloomington.

Janet D. Jamieson is Governmental Relations Information Officer, California State Federation, The Council for Exceptional Children.

David W. Johnson is Professor, Department of Educational Psychology, College of Education, University of Minnesota.

Roger T. Johnson is Professor, Department of Curriculum and Instruction, College of Education, University of Minnesota.

Reginald L. Jones is Professor, Departments of Education and Afro-American Studies, University of California, Berkeley.

Donald L. MacMillan is Professor of Education, University of California, Riverside.

Gale M. Morrison is Assistant Professor of Education, University of California, Santa Barbara.

Barbara Wentz Reid is a teacher of emotionallly disturbed children, Board of Cooperative Education Services, Orange County, New York.

Jerome Siller is Professor, Department of Educational Psychology, New York University, New York.

Arthurlene Gartrell Towner is Associate Professor, Department of Special Education, San Francisco State University.

Harry C. Triandis is Professor, Department of Psychology, University of Illinois, Urbana-Champaign.

The late **William A. Watts** was Professor, Department of Educational Psychology, University of California, Berkeley.

Preface

A culmination of activities on behalf of handicapped persons in this country is to be found in landmark legislation: Public Law 94-142 and Section 504 of the Rehabilitation Act of 1973. We have, indeed, witnessed a considerable shift in legislation affecting handicapped persons in recent years, but the battle is far from won. A critical obstacle remains—attitudinal barriers. We can legislate physical access and the provision of educational opportunity as we have done, but we cannot legislate acceptance; and it should not be surprising to any informed observer that meaningful implementation of legislative acts will require that we give as much attention to attitudinal barriers as we have given to the elimination of barriers of physical access, barriers of employment access, and barriers of educational access.

A varied and rich literature is developing on attitudes toward handicapped persons, but this literature has not yet been synthesized for special education consumers and researchers. If we are to be as effective in removing attitudinal barriers as we have been in removing educational and physical barriers, much ground work is needed. First, we need states-of-the-art overviews of the literature on attitudes toward diverse handicapped persons. For example, based on extant literature, what do we know about the assessment and modification of attitudes toward handicapped persons? Second, we need a critical evaluation of this literature. Are extant studies sufficiently well done to enable us to confidently assess and modify attitudes toward handicapped persons? If the knowledge base is inadequate, we must then chart directions for further research and study.

The present volume has been developed to accomplish the above objectives by drawing upon the expertise of established and emerging scholars of attitudinal studies who have been invited to summarize and critically evaluate the

vii

literature in their special areas of expertise including, where appropriate, their own research and studies.

In the first chapter, Jones and Guskin highlight reasons for a volume devoted to special attitudes at this point in time. They call our attention to misconceptions about attitudes toward handicapped persons that exist, point to gaps in our knowledge, and present an overview of social psychological theories and approaches toward handicapped persons. Triandis, Adamopoulos, and Brinberg (in Chapter 2) provide an overview of issues and perspectives in the field of attitude definition, formation, and change. The authors define attitude, give a brief account of its history, discuss the relation between attitude and behavior, review the functions and organization of attitudes, discuss attitude formation, and, finally, present one approach to attitude change: the assimilator. Although this approach was developed to instruct people on how to understand social behavior in other cultures, it is demonstrated to be a useful method for changing behavior toward the handicapped.

Several theories of attitude change that have implications for special education are analyzed in Chapter 3, and a number of methods which have been employed to change attitudes (including the empirical support of these methods) are discussed. We are reminded that few of the theories and principles have been applied to special education concerns. The article concludes with discussions of methods which are believed to be especially useful in changing attitudes toward handicapped persons and of the generalizability of laboratory studies to the "real world." Its author was William Watts, my highly respected and admired colleague at the University of California, Berkeley, who died suddenly on April 10, 1980. The publication of this article now will, I hope, serve as some small memorial to his humanity and interests.

Almost every reviewer of the special education attitude literature (see chapters in the present volume by Gottlieb, Reid, Siller, Chiba, Jamieson, and Towner) has pointed to problems of instrumentation in measuring attitudes toward handicapped persons. Even the most rudimentary measurement principles and considerations, many reviewers noted, are ignored in the cited investigations. It seemed important, then, in light of this lacuna, to include a review of approaches to and principles of attitude measurement in this volume, an assignment performed most ably by Dawes (Chapter 4). His discussion begins with a definition of measurement and includes such topics as determining the usefulness of measurement, and types and examples of measures and their uses. Direct as well as indirect measures of attitude are discussed.

Much of attitude research in special education has involved sociometric methods. It appears highly likely, given the movement toward the integration of handicapped students with those in regular classrooms, that these methods will be extensively used in order to determine the degree to which handicapped pupils are accepted by their classmates. Review and critique of the special education sociometric literature at this point, then, is especially timely. In Chapter 5, MacMillan and Morrison discuss the elements of sociometrics, address the limitations of sociometric techniques, and review and critique the special education sociometric literature. A conceptual model for research on sociometric status in special education is also presented; using it as a guide, the authors review past and potential interventions. Finally, MacMillan and Morrison examine dependent variables used in sociometric studies and consider alternative approaches for studies of the dynamics of social acceptance of handicapped children.

The chapter by Johnson and Johnson (Chapter 6) represents an important attempt to use social psychological theory to develop programs for modifying attitudes toward handicapped children in classroom settings. Their program is unique in its emphasis upon instructional activities in ongoing classroom settings as the basis for attitude change, its grounding in theory, and the variety of settings in which it has been applied and tested. Participants have been learning disabled, emotionally disturbed, and severely mentally retarded children, working cooperatively (and competitively or individualistically) with their nonhandicapped peers. Anyone interested in developing programs for changing attitudes toward handicapped students in regular class settings would do well to read this chapter in combination with the chapters by Towner and Watts. As Towner's review indicates (Chapter 12), much of the special education literature on attitude change has not been informed by social psychological theory and research (see Chapter 3 for a review of this literature). Johnson and Johnson's chapter is an important and rigorous application of social psychological principles to problems of special education attitude change.

Gottlieb, Corman, and Curci (Chapter 7) draw upon social psychological theories and insights—and Gottlieb's extensive research—to delineate the formation and change of attitudes toward mentally retarded persons. These authors give attention to the impact of direct and indirect experiences upon attitudes toward mentally retarded persons as well as to an important methodological problem: the attitudinal referent, that is, the manner in which the concept of mental retardation is presented to the subject. Gottlieb, Corman, and Curci raise the important question of whether format (e.g., sketch, videotape, film, or simply the abstract label of mentally retarded) contributes to differences in attitudes which are found among the subjects of different investigations. The evidence they cited suggests that manner of presentation is indeed important and, moreover, that there is probably value in applying the concept of attitudinal referent to studies of attitudes toward other groups of disabled persons as well.

Articles by Reid (Chapter 8), Chiba (Chapter 9), and Siller (Chapter 10), on attitudes toward, respectively, the learning disabled, the emotionally disturbed, and the physically disabled also draw upon social psychological theories and insights. Commonalities as well as differences are found among these and other chapters. For example, Reid, Chiba, Jamieson, and Towner all adopt a tripartite approach—that is, they view attitudes as consisting of cognitive, affective, and behavioral components—and they use this schema for evaluating the attitudinal literature. Siller, on the other hand, draws upon his own research to introduce a model that includes eight components. Chiba focuses upon children, while Reid gives attention to the attitudes of both children and adults. Jamieson focuses upon the attitude of teachers and administrators, whereas Siller includes the attitudes of rehabilitation personnel as well.

The selection of topics and coverage has been more than representative but it is by no means exhaustive. Attitudes toward the gifted and the speech impaired, for example, are two conspicuous omissions. Nor is coverage comprehensive in specific chapters. Because of the nature of the available literature and its perceived importance, the focus is upon the attitudes of children in some chapters and upon children and adults in others.

Virtually all chapters give attention to methodological issues, some more than others. The size and scope of the chapters are influenced by several factors, not the least of which is the quantity and quality of research available on the topics; some topics have been well studied while others have received virtually no attention. The identification of gaps in our knowledge and, hence, areas needing study and investigation, has been emphasized in all chapters.

An attempt was made to keep the chapters discrete, but some overlap has occurred nevertheless. For example, teacher attitudes are a major focus of the chapter by Jamieson (Chapter 11) but they are also covered by Reid (Chapter 8). In their review of literature on attitudes toward the mentally retarded, Gottlieb, Corman, and Curci (Chapter 7) give attention to studies on attitude change, the topic that is the major focus of Towner's chapter (Chapter 12). Many contributors give brief definitions of attitude (as a preface to their expositions and to provide the framework for their analyses and discussions), although the nature of attitudes and attitude formation is presented formally and comprehensively in Chapter 2 by Triandis, Adamopoulos, and Brinberg.

Individual authors read and commented upon potentially overlapping chapters and suggested deletions or additions as appropriate. The remaining overlap was judged to be healthy and was retained because a single study or phenomenon can be interpreted in several ways depending on the context. Thus, Triandis, Adamopoulos, and Brinberg treat attitude-behavior relationships in a general way whereas Dawes emphasizes the associated measurement issues. Overlap among some sections of individual chapters, then, may be more complementary than redundant.

All contributors give attention to methodological issues, some more than others. Siller, for example, treats measurement concerns extensively while Towner gives particular attention to the empirical and theoretical underpinnings of attitude-change methods and procedures. Chiba and Jamieson pay particular attention to correlates of the attitudes. The reviews and studies, in toto, are a rich potpourri and our expectation is that the work reported herein will contribute significantly to future conceptualization, research, and study of attitudes toward handicapped persons.

I am indebted to many individuals who contributed to this volume. I must first acknowledge a special debt of gratitude to Maynard C. Reynolds of the University of Minnesota who unfailingly supported this undertaking—conceptually, intellectually, and financially—through the National Support Systems Project which he directed. Without his support and that of his associates Karen Lundholm and Sylvia Rosen, who gave unstintingly of their time and expertise, it is highly unlikely that this volume would have come to fruition. June B. Jordan of The Council for Exceptional Children has shown the highest level of professionalism in helping to reconceptualize the volume in order to maximize its value to the widest possible readership, and she has been equally helpful in seeing the volume through to production—under trying circumstances indeed. Bluma B. Weiner was also helpful in preparing the manuscript for publication, as were Margaret Brewton and Norma Coleman of the University of California, Berkeley. Each person listed has significantly contributed to the volume and deserves our sincere gratitude.

Reginald L. Jones
April, 1984
Berkeley, California

1

Attitudes and Attitude Change in Special Education

REGINALD L. JONES
SAMUEL GUSKIN

The basis of this book is our belief that, if the laws and service patterns providing equal educational opportunities for handicapped[1] children and youth are to be effective, school environments must be made increasingly receptive to the individuals who make up this population. Both the courts and Congress appear to have assumed that full integration into communities and schools would alter traditional views of handicapped persons, but such alterations appear to be possible only through a better understanding of the attitudes that determine the status and treatment of people with handicaps in our schools and other social institutions.

Why should we devote attention to this topic at this time? Is it more important for us to concentrate on changing laws, providing new services, getting people to behave more appropriately toward handicapped persons, and, in general, improving the lives and opportunities of the disabled population than to spend our resources on research? Our answer is no. It is based on our belief that the effectiveness of new laws and service patterns is integrally related to changes in the attitudes of communities, professionals, and handicapped persons and their families. The dramatic new laws, policies, and services directed toward improving the lot of the handicapped cannot be fully implemented without increased receptivity toward them as persons with individual differences. Despite the assumption that full integration into communities and

---

[1]Although a distinction is made sometimes between "disabled" and "handicapped" (the first referring only to the physical or psychological impairment, the second, to the limitation(s) resulting from the impairment), the terms are used interchangeably in this and all other chapters. When the terms are used as nouns, no depersonalization is intended; rather, the usage should be understood to be a kind of shorthand.

schools will alter traditional views toward the handicapped, the achievement of full integration appears to be possible only through a better understanding of attitudes toward persons with disabilities and of attitude change.

The attitudes of the nonhandicapped majority toward the disabled minority are of especial importance currently because handicapped persons are moving or being moved into the mainstream of society. Judicial decisions (e.g., Diana v. Board of Education, 1970; Pennsylvania Association for Retarded Children v. Commonwealth of Pennsylvania, 1972) and legislative enactments (e.g., Section 504 of the Rehabilitation Act, amended 1974, Public Law 93-516; and Public Law 94-142, The Education for All Handicapped Children Act of 1975) have clarified the right of each disabled person to necessary treatment (e.g., education) in a setting that is the least restrictive environment feasible in the light of her or his particular limitations. Thus, the principle of *normalization*, that is, providing disabled persons with opportunities to participate in activities, programs, and living arrangments that most closely approximate those of the nonhandicapped majority, including placements in regular classrooms or successive approximations thereto (mainstreaming), must be incorporated into the design of every treatment. With the integration of disabled persons into the larger society and disabled school children into general education, the attitudes of nondisabled individuals and even of the disabled themselves are of paramount importance in determining the ultimate success of these integrative efforts (Gottlieb, 1975b).

Let us look more closely at the relations between attitudes and new treatment approaches. What attitudes would seem to generate resistance to changes in services? (a) Certainly, fear or dislike of contact with handicapped persons would lead to resistance to mainstreaming and normalization. (b) The handicapped and their parents or other advocates are likely to distrust the nonspecial professionals and bureaucracy which were so unhelpful in the past but would now carry more direct responsibility for mainstream programs. (c) The handicapped and their advocates are likely to have realistic fears about the reactions of nonhandicapped members of the community with whom they will be forced to interact. (d) Professionals and administrators who for the first time have been given the responsibility for the handicapped may fear, more or less realistically, that they will not be able to cope with these new responsibilities in addition to the old ones and, in fact, that the presence of handicapped persons in regular classrooms or communities will lead to complications in their professional careers and personal failure or unhappiness.

How may attitudes be changed by new service patterns? First, there is some evidence that people tend to adapt to a fait accompli and to change their beliefs to justify the behavioral changes they make (Festinger, 1957). Thus, if keeping a job requires one to work with the handicapped, one will do so and soon think that it is appropriate. Second, contact with the handicapped may not lead to the anticipated discomfort; thus, one's attitudes may become more favorable. However, if the contact leads to greater discomfort than expected, one's attitude may become less favorable.

These potential links between changes in education and attitudes illustrate in part the importance of studying attitudes at this time.

2

BOUNDARIES OF THE FIELD OF STUDY

How do we define attitudes and attitude change in relation to special education? Although there are diverse definitions of attitude, the feature common to most is that an attitude is the degree of liking (or disliking) held toward a person, group, issue, or other object. In addition, many definitions include beliefs and actions related to the object and, often, stereotypes, expectancies, and prejudices.[2] Inasmuch as there is no particular reason to restrict the definition at this stage, our discussion focuses on the favorability of reactions, whether it involves holding beliefs that imply liking or disliking, showing approach or avoidance behaviors, or directly stating one's feelings.

Our discussion deals with the favorability of reactions. Reactions to what? Obviously, we must discuss existing attitudes toward handicapped individuals and groups. We also must look at current attitudes toward special education services and interactions with handicapped students. Despite this concern with immediate attitudes, it should be clear that we are even more interested in attitude change. During the period of rapid change in education, any estimate of momentary attitudes is likely to be out of date by the time results are disseminated.

KNOWLEDGE BASE

What do we know about attitudes which are related to special education? Answers to this question are treated in great detail in this volume but certain overview statements are appropriate here. Our knowledge, based on past research, has been heavily influenced by the availability and ease of particular research methods and populations and the popularity of techniques from certain academic and professional fields.

Types of Studies

Sociometric studies have been used extensively with "normal" school children. When the participants are asked to indicate with whom they like to play, for example, they generally show a preference for nonhandicapped playmates. Although the findings are consistent for some groups (e.g., retarded children), the magnitude of the relation is not great; that is, there is usually difference between the preference for handicapped and for nonhandicapped playmates, but there is also much overlap; a handicapped child rarely is the least popular in a regular classroom and, occasionally, is above average in popularity.

---

[2]*Stereotypes* refer to the set of beliefs, usually oversimplified, about the characteristics of a group; *expectancies* refer to the particular behaviors or competence anticipated of group members or individuals; and *prejudice*, to irrationally unfavorable decisions or actions one is prepared to take against group members.

College students, especially teachers in training, are the most common subjects for studies of attitudes toward physical disability and mental retardation. Often these studies focus on characteristics which are easy to measure, such as experience with the handicapped and major field of study. Another frequently used measure is the social distance scale; subjects are asked to indicate how close they are willing to get to different kinds of handicapped persons (e.g., Would you be willing to marry a blind person?). Generally, the results show greater avoidance of the most severely handicapped persons and a preference for physical disability over mental retardation.

A number of studies have examined teacher attitudes toward mainstreaming or the integration of handicapped children. Some studies have been concerned with changes in attitudes resulting from the introduction of services; others with identifying factors which are related to the favorability of such attitudes. Simple answers have not been forthcoming.

A few attempts have been reported of systematic efforts to modify attitudes, either by exposure to handicapped persons or specific educational efforts. The results have not been consistent.

Finally, a number of investigations have been conducted into the reactions of family members to the presence of a handicapped child. Generally, the findings demonstrate consternation at the initial discovery and concern with many chronic day-to-day problems. The willingness of parents to institutionalize handicapped children also has been studied and found to be related to both severity of handicap and certain cultural factors, such as the religion of the family.

Gaps in Our Knowledge

Although we know a great deal about the playmate preferences of nonhandicapped children for handicapped peers in the same regular classrooms, there are very few studies of preferences for nonintegrated handicapped individuals. The reason, obviously, is that a handicapped child must be known before he can be reacted to, and if he is never in a common environment with nonhandicapped children, playmate choice will be hypothetical rather than real. It is possible, however, to create situations in which reasonable exposure exists (Gottlieb & Budoff, 1973) or can be created (Gottlieb & Davis, 1973) to make such choices realistic.

Another gap occurs in our knowledge of playmate preferences for labeled integrated children. In most sociometric studies of mentally retarded children in regular classrooms, the children have not been so identified. Often, however, classmates know that an integrated child has been labeled "retarded" by the school. The results of sociometric studies in such situations are rare.

Despite the number of studies of children's reactions to handicapped classmates, few are developmental in nature; that is, little attention has been given to exploring the age at which children recognize handicaps or how their attitudes change with age. Attempts to study preschoolers' attitudes toward disabilities have met particular difficulty in assessing reactions to disabilities

4

which are less visibly obvious (Guskin, Morgan, Cherkes, & Peel, 1979; Jones & Sisk, 1970).

We know very little about the reactions of community members to the handicapped persons who live and work in their communities. We also know little about how the handicapped and their advocates react in these circumstances. In sum, there have been few studies of attitude change over time in the natural environment.

MISCONCEPTIONS ABOUT ATTITUDES

We suffer not only from a scarcity of systematic research on misconceptions but also from a readiness to think that we have the answers to what, in fact, are still open questions. Following are a number of widely accepted but inadequately validated assumptions about attitudes toward handicapped persons that are often found in popular and professional writings.

Assumption: *Others' attitudes and expectancies have powerful and negative effects on the behavior of the handicapped.*

Many writings suggest that if a person is thought to be a member of a group considered relatively incompetent (e.g., the retarded), such strong expectations will be aroused in others that they will invariably make the person behave incompetently, even if he or she has been mislabeled. This expectancy effect or self-fulfilling prophecy was popularized by Robert Rosenthal (see, especially, Rosenthal & Jacobson, 1968). Numerous attempts at replication (see Dusek, 1975, for a comprehensive review) have shown that the effect is elusive, demonstrable only under very special circumstances. Extensive reviews and critiques of the applicability of the assumption in special education, particularly in relation to mental retardation, have appeared in publications by S. Guskin (1978); MacMillan, Jones, and Aloia (1974); and Yoshida and Meyers (1975). This is not to say that attitudes and expectancies do not influence behavior but, rather, that they do so in a more complex and varied manner than is implied by the notion of self-fulfilling prophecy.

Perhaps the best way to illustrate the fallacy of oversimplified belief in the self-fulfilling prophecy is to examine one of its dramatic demonstrations (Beez, 1970). Just prior to a tutoring session, 60 tutors were given psychological reports on nonhandicapped preschool children with whom they were to work. By random assignment, half the tutors were given reports suggesting that the children had high learning ability while the other half received reports suggesting low ability. The tutors were given a list of 20 words which they were to teach the children to recognize within a 10-minute period. They were instructed to teach as many words as they could. The tutors who thought they were teaching "low-ability" children covered only half as many words as those who thought they were teaching "high-ability" children. On the word-recognition test that followed immediately, the "high-ability" children got twice as many words correct. These differences were highly significant.

The Beez study seemed to demonstrate clearly how the expectancy phenomenon works in schools: Teachers who think children are less competent

5

make fewer academic demands on these children; they give them less opportunity to learn and, therefore, encourage lowered performance, even if these children initially were equal to those thought to be more competent. However, this conclusion is valid only if one group received less teaching than the other, and Beez provided no such evidence. Instead of covering more words, the teachers in the Beez study spent more time on each word when they thought the children were less competent. They also spent more time explaining the meanings of words. The effect of this treatment was to reduce performance on the learning criterion (number of words correctly named immediately after the tutoring session), but it is far from clear that these children actually learned less. In follow-up interviews, some teachers felt that the children would perform better on long-term recall tests. Furthermore, it is possible that if all the children in the study had been mildly retarded, as the report for the low-ability children implied, rather than of normal intelligence, the performance of the "low-ability" group might have been superior to the "high-ability" group because of the intensive teaching. This possibility is suggested by findings (Vergason, 1964) that mentally retarded children perform as well as nonretarded children on recall tasks when overlearning is used.

The problem, then, is in our understanding of the learning needs of children and in our ability to make accurate educational predictions and prescriptions. In the Beez study, negative expectancies were inappropriate. Appropriateness can be tested empirically only by determining what works best for the individual or group. In other words, as has so often been stated, it is the realism or accuracy of expectancies, not whether they are high or low, that is critical.

Related to the misconception that low-performance expectations are always fulfilled is the belief that children who exceed such expectations are punished and pressured into lower performance. There is much evidence to the contrary; parents and teachers are constantly alert to signs that a child is more competent than he or she has been thought to be, and such signs encourage efforts to get the child to higher levels of performance. This striving is probably what leads professionals to complain that parents are unwilling to accept their child's handicap.

Assumption: *Attitudes toward the handicapped are negative.*

Perhaps the most widely accepted assumption is that attitudes toward handicapped children are unidimensional and largely negative. Only rarely (Efron & Efron, 1968; Gottlieb & Corman, 1975; Jones, 1974; Jones, Gottfried, & Owens, 1966; Siller, 1967) has the possibility been considered that attitudes toward handicapped children may be multidimensional rather than unidimensional, and that the attitudes may be influenced by the degree and kind of handicap, the nature of the interpersonal situation being responded to, and the personal characteristics of both the disabled and nondisabled persons. What the evidence tells us is that when little additional information is available about a handicapped person (i.e., nothing other than the handicap), people who are asked to state their preferences report less willingness to become close with a handicapped rather than nonhandicapped person. Even this conclusion must be qualified; in at least one study the investigators found that an obese person was rejected more often than an obviously handicapped person (Richardson,

6

Goodman, Hastorf, & Dornbush, 1961). Thus it would seem that a person is less likely to be accepted if he or she looks unattractive or different or performs less adequately and does not have the justification of a well-defined liability. The situation is different, of course, in personal interactions. Among nonhandicapped persons who interact with handicapped peers, as in school settings, the evidence indicates that some negative attitudes are reactions to the annoying personal behaviors of the handicapped persons (e.g., those of low ability who are labeled mentally retarded; Johnson, 1950). On the other hand, in the study of a group of peer-accepted, integrated blind children (a number of whom were identified as "stars"), teachers noted the absence of annoying personal characteristics and behaviors (Jones, Lavine, & Shell, 1970) as the reason for acceptance. These results should not be interpreted to mean that attitudes toward handicapped children are explained solely by their personal characteristics and behavior but that these factors obviously must be taken into account when we attempt to understand the variables influencing negative as well as positive attitudes toward the handicapped.

There is, undoubtedly, no question about the fact that handicapped persons, their parents, and their acquaintances would prefer that the disabilities not be present. The existence of practical problems that result from a disability is implicit in its definition (Wright, 1960). Awkwardness or mutual embarrassment in interacting with strangers is also fairly universal, at least initially (Goffman, 1963). When the disability is severe and/or the services provided by the community are very inadequate, the lives of the handicapped and their families may diverge greatly from the norm and generate considerable distress (Gorham, Des Jardins, Page, Pettis, & Scheiber, 1975). Under these circumstances, persons can be expected to hold unfavorable attitudes toward intimacy with the handicapped. This is not to say that they would necessarily dislike a handicapped person with whom they come into frequent contact.

There are also occasions when a disabled person's relatively normal behavior is seen as a sign of superior ability or motivation and, thus, the person is more highly valued than nonhandicapped persons who show the same behavior (e.g., Helen Keller). In short, we probably should not state simplistically that attitudes toward the handicapped are negative; instead, we should be specific about the context, object, and reality base of the expressed beliefs or feelings.

Assumption: *Negative attitudes are based on experience and/or misinformation.*

Related to the generalization that attitudes toward the handicapped are negative is the assumption that they are based on misinformation or inexperience. Support for or refutation of this assumption requires us to identify what kinds of information and experience lead to what kinds of beliefs and attitudes. Medical training in birth defects and experience with severely handicapped infants surely would lead to different attitudes than would experience in the vocational counseling of veterans with physical disabilities. Gottlieb (1975b) emphasized that under some circumstances exposure to handicapped individuals leads to less favorable attitudes.

One particularly important current assumption is that understanding or experiencing mainstreaming (or normalization) leads to more favorable attitudes both toward the handicapped and toward the mainstreaming process. This assumption is not supported by research findings (Corman & Gottlieb, 1978; Semmel, Gottlieb, & Robinson, 1979). One reason why attitudes may not become more favorable is that initially they may be unrealistically optimistic. To illustrate, one of the authors exposed teacher trainees to a simulation experience in which they played the roles of teachers, administrators, parents, and normal and handicapped children in a series of problem situations. The trainees were required to present and listen to arguments on both sides of the mainstreaming issue in different situations. Some trainees who, initially, had been highly favorable toward mainstreaming came to take a more balanced position as a result of participating in the simulation, whereas others, who had been very unfavorable initially, became more favorable (Guskin, 1973). Thus, it seems that initial attitudes may be based on misinformation, and experience may shift the attitudes toward an opposite direction, depending on the quality and intensity of the experience and the reality base of the initial beliefs and attitudes.

Assumption: *The handicapped hold low self-concepts.*

Another assumption widely espoused is that others' negative attitudes are internalized by the handicapped in the form of negative self-concepts.[3] There have been some attempts to dispel this belief (Gardner, 1966; Wright, 1960) but it seems to be so strongly rooted in common sense, everyday experience, and social psychological theory, that it must be examined systematically.

We all know that experiences of failure and rejection can lead one to feel inadequate. Why should not this truism hold for the handicapped who experience more than their share of both failure and rejection? One reason is that we all adapt to failure and nonacceptance in two ways: (a) by denying either the experience or appropriateness of the judgment, or (b) by removing ourselves from the source of the negative evaluation. For example, if we are good in creative writing and poor in mathematics, we choose to concentrate on those academic fields and occupational goals that accord with our skills; if sexy cheerleaders or handsome athletes find us unappealing as friends or dates, we do not keep trying to attract their interest and, thus, we avoid continual rejection. The modification of one's evaluative environment tends to keep most of us from having too favorable or unfavorable a self-concept. In the same way, a moderately retarded, unattractive 25-year-old woman living in a group home and working in a sheltered workshop may be an object of considerable interest to men of her age who work in the same place. Because they are the only men with whom she interacts regularly, their evaluation of her may be sufficient to foster her reasonably high self-esteem. In contrast, if she were living with her parents in the community and were employed scrubbing floors

---

[3]Similar beliefs are held with respect to racial minority groups. There is some evidence linking attitudes toward racial minority groups with those held toward the handicapped (Cowen, Bobrove, Rockway, & Stevenson, 1967; Harth, 1971).

in a local shop where she was the only handicapped person, we would expect her self-evaluation to be less favorable.

One of the difficulties often faced by the disabled is that they have not had the widest choice of evaluative environments. On the other hand, more often than not they have been placed in protected environments which, although initially mortifying to self-esteem (Goffman, 1961), actually present the possibility of self-aggrandizement (Edgerton & Sabach, 1962). This point raises the oft-heard debate between supporters and opponents of special settings and normalization or mainstreaming. The former believe that the special setting insures and protects self-esteem; the latter, that it labels the person and forces him or her into a low status that reduces both felt and actual adequacy. The parallel for us as professionals, if we are educators, is whether we feel more adequate because we are respected among our fellow educators or less adequate because we are held in lower esteem by society than are physicians.

Assumption: *Attitudes toward the handicapped are improving.*

It is thought that we are becoming more enlightened about handicapping conditions and more favorably disposed toward the handicapped. Handicapped persons are assumed to be better off as a result of these changes. Mainstreaming, deinstitutionalization, and normalization are assumed to illustrate and foster these trends. In turn, these changes are believed to be a function of our becoming more just and humane (or more civilized or advanced). Yet an examination of the history of reactions to handicapped children and adults does not support any long-term directional trend in favor of the disabled (P. Guskin, 1978).

An extreme example of the difficulty of verifying the existence of a continuing trend in the improvement of reactions to disabled persons is infanticide of the handicapped. It was practiced by the highly civilized Greeks (Langer, 1974); it was not a civil crime but an ecclesiastical offense during the early middle ages (Helmholz, 1975); it was favored by some individuals during the Protestant Reformation (Martin Luther, quoted in Kanner, 1964, p. 7); it has been practiced quietly by individual physicians in recent years; and now it is a publicly stated policy in the cases of certain disabilities (e.g., spina bifida children are allowed to die in some hospitals; Public Broadcasting Service, 1976). Certainly, infanticide is increasing dramatically if we include abortions after diagnoses by amniocentesis.

The lack of a simple trend is also illustrated by residential treatment in special facilities. Although we see deinstitutionalization as an improvement and a sign of favorable community attitudes, we must remember that residential settings were originally created to improve the education and treatment of the handicapped. Attempts to move the disabled back into or to keep them in the community have a long history. Even Bedlam, often seen as the symbol of inhuman treatment of the insane, attempted to return improved patients to the community (Plumb, 1973; Rosen, 1968). Furthermore, current normalization efforts are sometimes motivated by economic rather than altruistic objectives (Edgerton, 1975) and often they reflect a lack of sensitivity to the needs of the handicapped and their families (Gorham et al., 1975). We do not

9

mean to argue that we are becoming more unfeeling or negative in our attitudes toward the handicapped, but only that the matter is far from simple and requires careful examination, using a variety of criteria.

Assumption: *Handicapped persons and their families must learn to accept their disabilities.*

The assumption here is that coping requires recognizing the reality of one's limitations rather than fighting the facts. However, from the point of view of the disabled person, it may mean accepting a new and undesirable identity (Goffman, 1963). The person who is willing to accept a socially undesirable status may have less rehabilitation potential than one who refuses to consider himself or herself handicapped. The question is, who defines reality: the client or the professional? It may make life easier for public agencies if clients are passive and cooperative but passivity and cooperation may not achieve a client's ends. A client may, for example, be able to cope successfully in a more normal setting than the rehabilitation counselor or school psychologist believes. Similarly, a mother who takes her child from one doctor to another searching for a better diagnosis or prognosis may be justified, because many physicians do not have necessary specialized knowledge and are often incompetent in dealing with parents' concerns.

There is also confusion between rejection of the child and rejection of a disability label which professionals wish to assign to the child. The parent who refuses to think that his or her child is handicapped may be responding to the hopelessness of the offered treatment options rather than being unwilling to relate to the disabled child. Certainly, if professionals can argue publicly about the appropriateness of labeling handicapped children, a parent has the right to deny the label for his or her own child.

Assumption: *People working with the handicapped hold more appropriate beliefs and attitudes about them than others do.*

We are too ready to see the public as holding inappropriately negative attitudes because our perspective is so very different. For the special education professional, the presence of a handicapped person means a job; for the regular education professional or the public at large, it means a life complication, which may be a highly realistic view. Some professionals may feel that normalization requires parents to keep at home a severely handicapped child even if his or her hyperactive, destructive behavior leads the parents to quite another conclusion. In other cases, professionals (e.g., physicians) may assume that a handicapped child is unbearable for parents who, if given the opportunity and encouragement, might get a great deal of satisfaction from the child. Because professionals disagree considerably on what is best for a child, family, or classmates, it is hardly appropriate to use their beliefs and attitudes as criteria for persons in other roles.

Assumption: *People who hold more progressive views on other subjects are more favorable to the handicapped.*

We tend to think that enlightenment is generalized, and there is some evidence for this position (Chesler, 1965), but liberal or tolerant views on some matters may correlate with negative attitudes toward disability. For example, the person who argues for a mother's right to abortion when there is a high risk that she will have a deformed infant may be said to argue against the handicapped child's right to life. It also may be that the people who value intellectual performance most may hold the least favorable attitudes toward persons with cognitive or learning disabilities.

Assumption: *Negative attitudes lead to behavioral rejection of the disabled.*

We seem to hold the oversimplified belief that if we feel unfavorable toward the handicapped or to their integration into society, we will act accordingly. However, this belief neglects many other factors that influence our behavior. A mother may wish that her child were not handicapped but still she will love and nurture him as he is. A teacher may feel that a handicapped child will complicate his teaching job, but if such a child is placed in the classroom he may demonstrate effective effort in working with her. On the other hand, a teacher may express highly desirable values about integration and yet show unhappiness with and hostility toward a child who has serious emotional and learning problems. Behavior is determined by many factors other than beliefs and attitudes: social norms for more acceptable public behavior; more general values, such as justice and altruism; and specific responses in the momentary situation, such as a smile or hostile demand.

The preceding assumptions fail to exhaust the body of misinformation about the handicapped. They merely illustrate the range of significant unvalidated assumptions which are held by many of us. They have been presented here to stimulate a questioning and analytic response to popular comments on attitudes, the close examination of the research literature, and further research. The assumptions discussed are not necessarily invalid, only unvalidated. This section will have failed in its purpose if it merely leads to another set of diametrically opposed and equally unvalidated assumptions.

PROMISING AREAS FOR FURTHER WORK

It would seem that we are ready to delineate promising directions for future work, having identified areas of strength and weakness and having pointed out some widely held but insufficiently validated assumptions. However, future directions must be defined not merely by the adequacy of prior investigations and interventions but also by clear conceptualizations of the task. Although we can borrow concepts and methods from prior experience and from parallel fields, such as educational innovation, social psychological research on attitude change, and work on racial prejudice, it is essential to build systematically a distinct framework for thinking about, investigating, and intervening in attitudes toward the handicapped. To be useful, such a model should enable us to examine changes in attitudes paralleling or resulting from changes in services and changes following direct attempts to train or prepare personnel. The model should facilitate our examination of attitudes held by people in various roles, including the handicapped themselves and their advocates, professionals, nonhandicapped peers, and the public at large. It would be helpful if the framework allowed us to examine the relation between understandings and attitudes and the relations between both of them and behaviors. However, it is probably too much to ask that a single model cover this range of concerns. Throughout this volume, several formulations are explicated which move us in an appropriate direction. In Table 1, we have tried to list the main variables which should be considered in a model and suggestions for exploring their relations.

The first and second factors shown in Table 1 seem fairly obvious. We need to know whose attitude we are looking at and what the attitude is about. There is quite a difference between exploring the public attitude toward the physically disabled and regular classroom teacher attitudes toward mainstreaming educable mentally retarded pupils. Despite the obviousness of these two factors, certain groups tend to be forgotten both as subjects and objects. For example, how many studies can we find that explore the attitudes of the handicapped and their parents or advocates toward the services we provide?

The third factor requires further explanation. Judging how pleasant you find a handicapped person is quite different from comparing the pleasantness of nonhandicapped and handicapped persons. The latter approach tends to magnify differences which may be of little importance in daily living. We do not always choose to spend our time with the most pleasant person we know. However, we do avoid people we find unpleasant. Our preferences are also based on more than our knowledge of a person's handicap, yet most attitude studies provide only the disability label for evaluation. Studies by Gottlieb (1974, 1975a), Guskin (1962), and Jaffe (1966) indicate the relative importance of other information about a person in reactions to the disabled. A related point is the extent of prior contact with the handicapped persons involved in assessing the attitudes. Social distance judgments of hypothetic disabled persons require no contact; sociometric preferences for children in one's class are based on extensive exposure. The public nature of judgments is the final point made here. Comments made directly to handicapped persons are less open than anonymous check marks on an IBM sheet.

The fourth factor attempts to identify some important determinants of attitudes, ranging from generalized hostile feelings toward people who are different, and toward general intellectual immaturity, to specific training in working with handicapped persons. Extent of experience with the handicapped is frequently explored but the quality of the experience is rarely dealt with.

The fifth factor is implicit in all attitude studies. That is, we always assume that attitudes have consequences: More favorable attitudes lead to more desirable behavior. Yet, not only is there rarely a follow-up of consequences but we also find few attempts to analyze the range of possible consequences of attitude change. For example, what effect will observing a ward for severely handicapped infants have upon a prospective public school teacher's willingness to take a job in a school that emphasizes mainstreaming? Will an advertising campaign that emphasizes the need to invest in services for helpless disabled persons have a backlash effect on support for mainstreaming the mildly handicapped? Will a course introducing the special problems of handicapped children lead to greater self-consciousness in interacting with children who have special

TABLE 1
Factors to Consider in Exploring Attitudes in Special Education

Factor to Consider	Examples
1. Subject (who holds attitude)?	Public, professionals, children, adults, specialists; various handicapped groups, their advocates, relatives. Demographic (age, sex, SES) and personal characteristics.
2. Object (who or what is attitude about?)	Handicapped persons, groups, or labels; degree of visibility, severity, permanence of disability; degree of competence and attractiveness of group/person. Issues about services to handicapped, e.g., mainstreaming.
3. Context (under what conditions is the attitude expressed?)	Comparisons with other handicapped or nonhandicapped persons; availability of other information about person/group. Extent of contact with handicapped required. Extent to which behavior or judgment is public or private.
4. Influences (what are the determinants of these attitudes?)	Generalized attitudes toward differentness, understanding of handicap, general cognitive development. Experience with handicapped persons: extent and type. Specific training, attitude-change attempts, strategies.
5. Consequences (what effects do these attitudes have?)	On behavior with handicapped persons; on feelings when interacting with such persons; on willingness to work with or interact with them; on support for public policies requiring more services; on support for public policies requiring more integration.
6. Attitude measures and research methodology (how should we assess attitudes?)	Sociometric indices of acceptance or rejection; social distance measures; attitude scales and public opinion surveys. Observed interaction. Analysis of public laws, policies, institutional characteristics. Content analysis of mass media.
7. Theoretical formulations (what concepts, hypotheses, models can we use to guide our research or practice?)	Social comparison processes (Festinger, 1954). Ethnocentrism (Adorno, Frenkel-Brunswik, Levinson, & Sanford, 1950). Cognitive dissonance (Festinger, 1957).

Continued on next page

13

TABLE 1 Continued

Factor to Consider	Examples
	Communication analysis (Hovland, Janis, & Kelley, 1953). Modeling (Bandura & Walters, 1963). Reference group theory (Kelley, 1952). Attribution theory (Heider, 1958; Jones, Kanouse, Kelley, Nisbett, Valins, & Weiner, 1971). Social deviance labeling (Davis, 1970; Mercer, 1973; Scheff, 1966). Just world formulations. Social roles (Thomas, 1966). Altruism (Macaulay & Berkowitz, 1970; Mussen & Eisenberg-Berg, 1977).
8. Ethical considerations (what precautions must we take as we conduct attitude assessment and change studies?)	Informed consent. Privacy. Psychological harm to subject and object of attitude inquiry. Equity, justice, respect.

problems? Clearly, not all behavioral consequences are likely to be equally desirable.

The sixth factor asks us to look more critically at how we measure attitudes. Most studies use sociometric measures, social distance scales, or other traditional attitude scaling approaches. Although many writers call for behavioral or unobtrusive measures, most studies are limited to paper-and-pencil measures. However, the development of systematic observational methods has made observation more practical (Gampel, Gottlieb, & Harrison, 1974; Weinberg & Wood, 1975) although it is still more expensive and time consuming than paper-and-pencil methods. Also, we can analyze our laws and the characteristics of schools and institutions by using, for example, Wolfensberger's (1972) criteria for normalization; by using content analysis we can systematically evaluate newspaper and television accounts of disabled persons to determine how society characterizes the handicapped.

The seventh factor entails the search for theoretical formulations that may help us to conceptualize attitude studies and interventions. Extant research, writing, and theorizing in social psychology are advanced as the proper base for approaching the study of attitudes toward the handicapped and attitude change, but social psychology as a field is itself fragmented. Among its many theories, some hold promise for the issues of concern to special educators but have rarely been used for such purposes. Typically, the theories and studies have been developed for and carried out on adult populations, usually of college age and in college settings; studies of attitude formation, especially theories relating to special education concerns, are virtually nonexistent. Moreover, many theories still are undergoing development and refinement, and typically they explain limited phenomena. It should not be expected, then, that available social psychological theories can be adopted wholesale and applied to special education concerns. Rather, as noted, such theorizing, research, and writing can be expected only to guide our initial approaches and efforts.

Special education attitude researchers need not view themselves as mere adapters of existing theories; they are potential contributors to theory elaboration and refinement. For example, Morin and Jones (1974) applied Festinger's theory of social comparison processes to blind school-age children; at issue was Festinger's hypothesis that given a range of possible persons for comparison, someone close to one's own ability or opinion would be chosen.

In applying the hypothesis to the blind children, Morin and Jones predicted that manipulating the degree of relevance to blindness of a given ability would significantly affect the frequency with which the blind were chosen as a group for social comparison purposes. Getting around, reading, and earning money when one gets out of school were the tasks selected as highly relevant to blindness; paying attention to the teacher, remembering what one hears, and staying out of trouble were selected for their low relevance to blindness. The prediction was that the blind would be chosen for comparison on the tasks having high relevance to blindness.

A second and related hypothesis predicted that manipulating the level of difficulty of a given task would significantly increase the choice of the blind as a reference group. Counting 14 beeps which were presented very slowly was an easy task; counting 14 beeps which were presented very rapidly was difficult. It was reasoned that the choice of the blind on the difficult task would protect the self-regard of the blind persons by providing a less competitive group for comparison.

The results suggest the need to refine Festinger's theory: First, we must consider the degree of relevance of the question posed to the source of similarity between the individual and the reference group. Morin and Jones found that the blind were chosen significantly more frequently on those items that were of high relevance to blindness than on those that were of low relevance. The authors noted that an elaboration of Festinger's theory should clarify similarity to include the dimension of relevance.

Second, the Festinger model should be expanded to include the dimension of level of difficulty. It appeared that as tasks increase in difficulty, when two or more groups are available for comparison, the group that yields the more favorable comparison will be the one chosen. Morin and Jones found that as performance tasks became more difficult, the blind were chosen with greater frequency over any reference group, including the sighted, even though the task was not related to blindness. Although the results of the study as a whole were consistent with Festinger's theory, failure to consider similarity in relation to task relevance and level of task difficulty led to inefficiency in prediction.

It is quite probable that, when we begin to apply social psychological theories to other special education topics, similar adjustments in the theories may be necessary, thus enriching the theories as well as strengthening the foundation of special education theory, research, and practice. A few of the formulations which might be fruitfully applied or modified in attitude research on the handicapped are listed in Table 1.

Finally, but by no means the least important factor to consider in exploring attitudes in special education, is concern with the ethical implications of our research and interventions. The movement that has led to increased concern with the rights of the handicapped extends also to the study of attitudes themselves, especially with the impact of such study on the object of investigation as well as on the individual expressing his or her attitudes. It has been suggested that to inquire into the attitudes which one holds toward another is to infringe upon a person's right to his or her own mind and thoughts. Moreover, to presume to modify the attitudes uncovered without the consent of the individual studied may also be construed as infringing upon the rights of the respondent.

Within recent years, governmental regulations have been developed to ensure the informed participation of persons whose attitudes are surveyed, whose attitudes would be changed, or who serve as subjects in social, behavioral, biological, or other studies and/or experiments (DHEW, 1971; see also American Psychological Association, 1973). The concern is with the potential physical and/or psychological harm to the participants or to the class of individuals of whom the respondent/participant is presumed to be representative. Potential harm is obvious in some situations and subtle in others. For example, to expose an individual to his own negative attitudes toward the disabled by requiring him to respond to an attitude questionnaire or to interact with a disabled person, or summarizing public attitudes toward the disabled—emphasizing the negative tone of such attitudes—has been interpreted as harmful to the respondent and to the group which is the object of the attitude study. In the case of the respondent, potential psychological discomfort is associated with the individual's being forced to face the fact that his attitudes toward disabled persons are negative. The argument against reporting the results of public attitude surveys is somewhat more subtle and has rarely been given attention in the question of ethical issues in the study of attitudes. At issue is the possibility that the communication of negative societal attitudes may reinforce the perceptions of disabled individuals and/or groups as members of a suspect class, thereby compounding their difficulties in interpersonal relationships and general life adjustment.

Why, then, do we wish to study attitudes toward the disabled? Professionals in special education and related fields hold the view that we need to study attitudes in order to change them and, thus, to facilitate the adjustment of disabled persons. (The presumption, as noted earlier, is that we already know the attitudes to be negative.) The philosophy underlying this view is that all persons have a right to be respected as individuals, regardless of physical, racial, religious, ethnic, or other characteristics, and that the promotion of such respect is in the best interest of society. Hence, it is reasoned, it is better to integrate handicapped children into regular schools than to segregate them, and to educate school children, the general public, and educational personnel on the nature of disabled children (to the extent that differences exist) rather than to let each individual be guided by his or her own prejudices, preconceptions, and predilections.

16

Several practical concerns grow out of these more general issues which are likely to impact directly on research and generalizations about special education attitudes. The first issue focuses on permission to participate in attitude surveys. Many school districts will wish to assess student attitudes as the prelude to the initiation of programmatic changes to facilitate the integration of disabled children in regular classrooms, but they will have difficulty carrying out such assessments. For example, parental permission to participate in the studies will be required. Unless a majority and representative sample of students participate, it will be difficult to use the results either to understand the attitudes that exist in a given school building or classroom or, consequently, to structure experiences for the effective integration of disabled children. Thus, if too few children are permitted to participate in sociometric studies, the nature of the classroom structure will remain unknown and the best groupings of children to facilitate adjustment may not be possible.

There is also the matter of research into and generalizations about the nature of attitudes toward special education. Such studies require access to large and representative samples of subjects. Difficulties in random sampling arise not only from parents who refuse permission for their children to participate in attitude assessments but, also, from school administrators who refuse permission even to ask parents about such permissions. These limitations certainly make information about the nature of attitudes toward special education more difficult to obtain and our knowledge of such attitudes less certain.

It may seem that unobtrusive procedures can circumvent the difficulties of acquiring information on attitudes, but that is not so. Permissions must be obtained for collecting all data, with the accompanying requirement that the reasons for the study and expected uses of the data be given to the participants.

It is apparent as we approach attitudes and attitude change in special education that, in formulating questions and intervention strategies, we must give attention to several ethical issues, including informed consent, participant rights to privacy, and potential harm to the subjects and objects of our inquiry and intervention.

OVERVIEW OF VOLUME

Because changes in special education requiring the rapid adjustment of students, parents, teachers, and administrators have been mandated by Section 504 of the Rehabilitation Act and Public Law 94-142, attitudes toward children and youth with handicaps have assumed critical importance. Until this publication there has been no single source of information on the theory and effects of attitudes and attitude change in special education. The reviews of literature and syntheses of information which follow are organized with the special education consumer in mind. The approaches of the various contributors are sensitive to the theoretical and technical problems and issues attendant to the concerns of such consumers. It is anticipated that bringing the studies on attitudes toward exceptional children and related topics together with the perspectives on disabled children and adults, (See R.L. Jones' *Reflections on*

17

Growing Up Disabled published in 1983 by The Council for Exceptional Children.) and carefully and clearly describing the different theoretical and technical viewpoints and considerations will influence the quality of special education research and writing on attitudes and attitude change and, ultimately, influence the services provided handicapped children.

REFERENCES

Adorno, T. W., Frenkel-Brunswik, E., Levinson, D. J., & Sanford, R. N. *The authoritarian personality*. New York: Harper, 1950.

American Psychological Association. *Ethical principles in the conduct of research with human participants*. Washington DC: Author, 1973.

Bandura, A., & Walters, R. H. *Social learning and personality development*. New York: Holt, Rinehart & Winston, 1963.

Beez, W. V. *Influence of biased psychological reports on teacher behavior and pupil performance*. Unpublished doctoral dissertation, Indiana University, 1970.

Chesler, M. A. Ethnocentrism and attitudes towards the physically disabled. *Journal of Personality and Social Psychology*, 1965, *2*, 877-882.

Corman, L., & Gottlieb, J. Mainstreaming mentally retarded children: A review of research. In N. R. Ellis (Ed.), *International review of research in mental retardation* (Vol. 9). New York: Academic Press, 1978, 271-275.

Cowen, E. L., Bobrove, P. H., Rockway, A. M., & Stevenson, J. Development and evaluation of an attitude to deafness scale. *Journal of Personality and Social Psychology*, 1967, *6*, 183-191.

Davis, F. Deviance disavowal: The management of strained interaction by the visibly handicapped . In H. S. Becker (Ed.), *The other side*. New York: Free Press, 1970, 114-137.

Department of Health, Education and Welfare. *The institutional guide to DHEW policy on protection of human subjects*. Washington DC: DHEW Publication No. (NIH) 72-102, December 1, 1971.

Diana *v*. State Board of Education. C-70-37 (REP Dist. N. Calif.), 1970.

Dusek, J. R. Do teachers bias children's learning? *Review of Educational Research*, 1975, *45*, 661-684.

Edgerton, R. B. Issues relating to the quality of life among mentally retarded persons. In M. J. Begab & S. A. Richardson (Eds.), *The mentally retarded and society: A social science perspective*. Baltimore: University Park Press, 1975.

Edgerton, R. B., & Sabach, G. From mortification to aggrandizement: Changing self conceptions in the careers of the mentally retarded. *Psychiatry*, 1962, *25*, 263-272.

Efron, R. E., & Efron, H. Y. Measurement of attitudes toward the retarded and an application with educators. *American Journal of Mental Deficiency*, 1968, *72*, 100-107.

Festinger, L. A theory of social comparison processes. *Human Relations*, 1954, *7*, 117-140.

Festinger, L. *A theory of cognitive dissonance*. New York: Row, Peterson, 1957.

Gampel, D., Gottlieb, J., & Harrison, R. Comparison of classroom behavior of special class EMR, integrated EMR, low IQ, and non-retarded children. *American Journal of Mental Deficiency*, 1974, *79*, 16-21.

Gardner, W. I. Social and emotional adjustment of mildly retarded children and adolescents: Critical review. *Exceptional Children*, 1966, *33*, 97-105.

Goffman, E. *Asylums: Essays on the social situation of mental patients and other inmates*. New York: Doubleday, 1961.

Goffman, E. *Stigma: Notes on the management of spoiled identity*. New York: Prentice-Hall, 1963.

Gorham, K. A., Des Jardins, C., Page, R., Pettis, E., & Scheiber, B. Effects on parents. In N. Hobbs (Ed.), *Issues in the classification of children.* San Francisco: Jossey-Bass, 1975.

Gottlieb, J. Attitudes toward retarded children: Effects of labeling and academic performance. *American Journal of Mental Deficiency,* 1974, *79,* 268-273.

Gottlieb, J. Attitudes toward retarded children: Effects of labeling and behavior aggressiveness. *American Journal of Mental Deficiency,* 1975, *67,* 581-585. (a)

Gottlieb, J. Public, peer, and professional attitudes toward mentally retarded persons. In M. Begab & S. A. Richardson (Eds.), *The mentally retarded and society: A social science perspective.* Baltimore: University Park Press, 1975. (b)

Gottlieb, J., & Budoff, M. Social acceptability of retarded children in non- graded schools differing in architecture. *American Journal of Mental Deficiency,* 1973, *78,* 15-19.

Gottlieb, J., & Corman, L. Public attitudes toward mentally retarded children. *American Journal of Mental Deficiency,* 1975, *80,* 72-80.

Gottlieb, J., & Davis, J. E. Social acceptance of EMRs during overt behavioral interaction. *American Journal of Mental Deficiency,* 1973, *78,* 141-143.

Guskin, P. J. *Fools and madmen: The diversity of attitudes toward mental handicap before 1800.* Unpublished manuscript. Special Education Department, Indiana University-Bloomington, 1978.

Guskin, S. L. The perception of subnormality in mentally defective children. *American Journal of Mental Deficiency,* 1962, *67,* 53-60.

Guskin, S. L. Simulation games for teachers on the mainstreaming of mildly handicapped children. *Viewpoints* (Bulletin of the School of Education, Indiana University), 1973, *49,* 85-95.

Guskin, S. L. Theoretical and empirical strategies for the study of the labeling of mentally retarded persons. In N. R. Ellis (Ed.), *International review of research in mental retardation* (Vol. 9). New York: Academic Press, 1978.

Guskin, S. L., Morgan, W., Cherkes, M., & Peel, D. *Deafness and signing on Sesame Street: Effects on understanding and attitudes of preschoolers.* New York: Children's Television Workshop (One Lincoln Plaza, NY 10023), 1979.

Harth, R. Attitudes toward minority groups as a construct in assessing attitudes toward the mentally retarded. *Education and Training of the Mentally Retarded,* 1971, *6,* 142-147.

Heider, F. *The psychology of interpersonal relations.* New York: Wiley, 1958.

Helmholz, R. H. Infanticide in the Province of Canterbury during the fifteenth century. *History of Childhood Quarterly,* 1975, *2,* 379-390.

Hovland, C. I., Janis, I. L., & Kelley, H. H. *Communication and persuasion.* New Haven: Yale University Press, 1953.

Jaffe, J. Attitudes of adolescents toward the mentally retarded. *American Journal of Mental Deficiency,* 1966, *70,* 907,912.

Johnson, G. O. A study of the social position of mentally handicapped children in the regular grades. *American Journal of Mental Deficiency,* 1950, *55,* 60-89.

Jones, E. E., Kanouse, D. E., Kelley, H. H., Nisbett, R. E., Valins, S., & Weiner, B. *Attribution: Perceiving the causes of behavior.* Morristown NJ: General Learning Press, 1971.

Jones, R. L. The hierarchical structure of attitudes toward the exceptional. *Exceptional Children,* 1974, *40,* 430-435.

Jones, R. L, Gottfried, N. W., & Owens, A. The social distance of the exceptional: A study at the high school level. *Exceptional Children,* 1966, *32,* 551-556.

Jones, R. L., Lavine, K., & Shell, J. Blind children integrated in classrooms with the sighted: A sociometric study. *New Outlook for the Blind,* 1970, *66,* 75-80.

Jones, R. L., & Sisk, D. Early perceptions of physical disability: A developmental study. *Rehabilitation Literature,* 1970, *31,* 34-38.

Kanner, L. *A history of the care and study of the mentally retarded.* Springfield IL: Charles C Thomas, 1964.

Kelley, H. H. Two functions of reference groups. In G. E. Swanson, T. M. Newcomb, & E. L. Hartley (Eds.), *Readings in social psychology.* New York: Holt, Rinehart & Winston, 1952.

Langer, W. L. Infanticide: A historical survey. *History of Childhood Quarterly*, 1974, *1*, 353-363.

Macaulay, J. R., & Berkowitz, L. (Eds.). *Altruism and helping behavior.* New York: Academic Press, 1970.

MacMillan, D. L., Jones, R. L., & Aloia, G. F. The mentally retarded label: A theoretical analysis and review of research. *American Journal of Mental Deficiency*, 1974, *79*, 241-246.

Mercer, J. R. *Labeling the mentally retarded.* Berkeley: University of California Press, 1973.

Morin, S., & Jones, R. L. Social comparison of ability in blind children and adolescents. *Journal of Psychology*, 1974, *87*, 237-243.

Mussen, P., & Eisenberg-Berg, N. *Roots of caring, sharing, and helping.* San Francisco: W. H. Freeman, 1977.

Pennsylvania Association for Retarded Citizens *v.* Commonwealth of Pennsylvania. 343 F. Supp. 279 (E.D., Pa.), 1972.

Plumb, J. H. *Bedlam.* In J. H. Plumb, *In the light of history.* Boston: Houghton Mifflin, 1973, 25-36.

Public Broadcasting Service. NOVA, "A small imperfection." New York: Time/Life Multimedia, 1976. (TV film)

Richardson, S. A., Goodman, N., Hastorf, A. H., & Dornbusch, S. A. Cultural uniformity in reaction to physical disabilities. *American Sociological Review*, 1961, *26*, 241-247.

Rosen, G. *Madness in society: Chapters in the historical sociology of mental illness.* Chicago: University of Chicago Press, 1968.

Rosenthal, R., & Jacobson, L. *Pygmalion in the classroom.* New York: Holt, 1968.

Scheff, T. J. *Being mentally ill.* Chicago: Aldine, 1966.

Semmel, T. I., Gottlieb, J., & Robinson, N. Mainstreaming perspectives on educating handicapped children in the public schools. In D. C. Berliner (Ed.), *Review of research in education.* Itasca IL: Peacock, 1979.

Siller, J. *Studies in reaction to disability.* XII: Structure of attitudes toward the physically disabled; disability factor scales—amputation, blindness, cosmetic conditions. New York: New York University, School of Education, 1967.

Thomas, E. J. The problem of disability from the perspective of role theory. *Journal of Health and Human Behavior*, 1966, *7*, 2-13.

Vergason, G. *Retention in educable retarded and normal adolescent boys as a function of amount of original learning.* Unpublished doctoral dissertation, George Peabody College, 1962.

Weinberg, R. A., & Wood, F. H. (Eds.). *Observation of pupils and teachers in mainstream and special education settings: Alternative strategies.* Reston VA: Council for Exceptional Children, 1975.

Wolfensberger, W. *The principle of normalization in human services.* Toronto: National Institute on Mental Retardation, 1972.

Wright, B. A. *Physical disability: A psychological approach.* New York: Harper, 1960.

Yoshida, R. K., & Meyers, C. E. Effects of labeling as educable mentally retarded on teachers' expectancies for change in a student's performance. *Journal of Educational Psychology*, 1975, *67*, 521-527.

2

Perspectives and Issues in the Study of Attitudes

HARRY C. TRIANDIS
JOHN ADAMOPOULOS
DAVID BRINBERG

The term *attitude* is widely used by the public to denote a psychological state that predisposes a person to action. The scientific study of attitudes started in the middle of the 19th century in Germany with the use of a number of theoretical terms to designate a person's preparation to respond to a class of social stimuli. At that time, the word *set* was often used to refer to such a state. Later, in the 20th century, the concept was given a more restricted definition. For example, Thurstone (1928, 1931) emphasized the person's *feeling* or *affect* toward an attitude object.

People can feel good, pro, or favorable, or bad, anti, or unfavorable toward an attitude object. Many contemporary attitude theorists have used this restricted definition of the word. Others, however, have taken the view that the concept is widely used by the public and, therefore, when social scientists communicate with the public on attitudes, they should use the public's definition. This viewpoint favors defining attitude as having several components and restricted definitions of these *components*. Among the many major theorists who share this view is, for example, Allport (1935); he defined an attitude as "a mental and neural state of readiness, organized through experience, exerting a directive or dynamic influence upon the individual's response to all objects and situations with which it is related" (p. 810).

Triandis (1971), following many other theorists, used a three-part definition: "An attitude is an idea charged with emotion which predisposes a class of actions to a particular class of social situations" (p. 2). This definition has three components: the idea (cognitive component), the emotion attached to it (affective component), and the predisposition to action (behavioral component).

21

COGNITIVE COMPONENT

The cognitive component reflects thoughts about the attitude object. People give identical responses to stimuli that are quite diverse. For example, they may use the term "handicapped" to describe a broad array of persons. A *category* is inferred from comparable responses to discriminably different stimuli. People also use *critical attributes* to decide how to categorize experience. For example, to categorize a person as "handicapped," some individuals may consider those particular physical limitations of the person which make certain kinds of actions difficult; others may consider psychological limitations; and still others may use many criteria at the same time. In other words, the way the attitude object is defined is an aspect of the cognitive component. Numerous other thoughts may also be associated with the attitude object: for example, beliefs about the "cause" of the handicap and the "consequences" of being handicapped. Some beliefs about how human behaviors or traits covary (go together); for example, a person may believe that a physically handicapped person is dangerous or strange.

Beliefs about a category of persons are often called *stereotypes*. A stereotype is a belief that members of a particular group have a certain common trait or attribute. Some parts of the stereotype can be accurate, in the sense that a connection between a group of persons and the particular behavior or trait may be shown by careful research. For example, certain groups of people who "go to church" reliably are stereotyped as "pious." Stereotypes which have been validated by research are called *sociotypes*. However, in most cases, people do not form stereotypes on the basis of careful research; instead they react on the basis of a minimum of evidence. Often, all they know is what other people told them while they were growing up, which is usually inaccurate. So, most stereotypes have little or no validity.

People also have "implicit personality theories" (Schneider, 1973); that is, they think they know what kinds of traits "go together." Sometimes these theories appear to be so "obviously logical" that people are convinced that empirical examinations of them are unnecessary. For example, a person may hold the "theory" that the attribute "fat" is related to the attribute "low self-esteem," and then look for data to support this "theory" because it is "intuitively and obviously right."

AFFECTIVE COMPONENT

The whole network of thoughts about categories of people constitutes the cognitive component of attitudes toward people. Each element of this network has some affective value attached to it. Affect is attached to any category when positive or negative experiences co-occur with the category. For example, if "low self-esteem" is frequently associated with undesirable events or states, then the concept acquires a negative affective value.

An attitude object is at the center of a network of thoughts, and each element (thought) of the network has some degree of emotion, positive or negative, associated with it. In addition, the attitude object is connected to those elements with varying degrees of strength. So, the total affect or emotion attached to the attitude object depends on the strength of its connections with various cognitive elements and on the emotion that is attached to each element (Fishbein, 1961). In fact, humans cannot think of many things without feeling some emotion. We are evaluative animals; that is, we keep evaluating what is going on around us.

The importance of evaluation can be seen in the work of Osgood, May, and Miron (1975). These researchers worked in some 30 different language-culture communities spread all around the world. They worked with high school students, in the students' own languages, but used identical procedures. They started by asking the students to provide "qualifiers" to 100 easily translatable words (e.g., fire, mother, moon, truth, and adventure). Students filled in phrases, such as (in English) "The HOUSE is _____"; "The _____ MOTHER." The words that were elicited from this procedure were identified as "qualifiers." Osgood and his associates took the most frequently given qualifiers and constructed a questionnaire that required every student to indicate the extent to which each of the 100 words was connected with each qualifier (e.g., the extent to which MOTHERS are *active*). Then, using a statistical technique called factor analysis, which allows scientists to discover similarities and differences in responses given to such questions, the investigators found that evaluative qualifiers were highly intercorrelated in every part of the world. For example, *good* things are seen as generally *beautiful, just, wise*, and *intelligent;* bad things are seen as generally *ugly, unjust, unwise*, and *stupid.*

What was important, for our purpose, is that these evaluative judgments formed the most important (in the sense of variance accounted for) cluster of worldwide judgments. Universally, people indicated that when using words to qualify objects the most striking attribute is whether the object is good or bad. Incidentally, two other clusters of judgments are also universal: *potency* (whether the object is big, powerful, or heavy) and *activity* (whether the object is active, fast, and alive).,

It is easy to see how these qualities have become important. When early humans faced a hostile environment, many of the stimuli they encountered had to be evaluated: "Is this *something* good or bad for me?" Once the judgment was made, two other judgments were also important: "If it is bad and also small, I can afford to ignore it; if it is bad and dead I can also ignore it." Survival depended on making such judgments correctly. It is because we humans developed the skill to evaluate the world more or less accurately that we have survived.

BEHAVIORAL COMPONENT

An important set of beliefs attached to an attitude object concerns the behaviors that may occur toward the object. The options in the case of *social* behavior are limited: One can go *toward, away*, or *against* the attitude object. If the attitude object is good, approaching it makes sense; if it is bad, avoiding or fighting it may be good options.

When humans developed more complicated social systems, they added dimensions. Corresponding to evaluation is association (going toward) versus dissociation (going away or against); corresponding to potency is superordination (giving advice, criticizing) versus subordination (asking for help, accepting orders of); and corresponding to activity is overt action (e.g., hitting) versus covert action (e.g., silently hating). Finally, in relation to other people, humans have devised systems of action that reflect the quality of interaction (e.g., formality versus intimacy). These dimensions of social action appear to be universal and emerge in many types of data in both studies of personality and of social behavior (Adamopoulos, 1982; Triandis, 1977a). In short, our social behavior can be overt or covert, formal or intimate, superordinate or subordinate, and associated with liking or disliking the other person. Mixed dimensions are also common. For example, one may dislike the other but say or do nothing (covert action); one may like the other but still act very formally; one may act in a bossy (superordinate) way toward others whom one likes or dislikes. These more complex responses do not depend just on attitudes. They also reflect the kind of social situation and the history of the relationship between the persons.

In sum, one of the major theoretical issues in the study of attitudes is how attitudes are to be defined. One difference of opinion is between theorists who define them simply as evaluation, that is, as emotion for or against the attitude object, and those who use the three components. Another difference of opinion is between theorists who define attitude as a predisposition to respond and, therefore, by definition, assume that attitudes are related to behavior, and those who define it as just another response which may or may not be related to the behavior of interest. The next section presents the view of the first group.

How Are Attitudes Related to Behavior?

By definition, attitudes predispose toward action. However, some investigators have found no relation between their measure of attitude and their measure of action. One possibility for the lack of correspondence between attitude and behavior is the poor methodology used in these studies.

A measure has two attributes in which we are interested: *reliability* and *validity*. Reliability expresses the consistency of a measure across occasions or places. If a measure is reliable, we should get pretty much the same score when we use it on another occasion or in another place. If the measure consists of several responses, then there should be consistency across these responses.

Validity refers to the extent to which an instrument measures what it is supposed to measure. There are many kinds of validity (Brinberg & Kidder, 1982). For instance, *concurrent* validity is obtained when two measures which supposedly measure the same thing are, in fact, related. *Construct* validity is obtained when correlations emerge among variables predicted from a theory.

Because we define attitude as a predisposition to action, when we do not get a correlation between attitude and action we must show, through an in-

24

dependent study, that the attitude measures were, in fact, valid. If there is no additional information of this kind, we do not know why we did not get the expected correlation. It could be because (a) the attitude measure was unreliable; (b) the measure of the behavior was unreliable; or (c) the measure of the attitude was not valid. Each possibility can be checked with additional data. For example, a researcher can show that the reliability of the measures is high or that the attitude measure correlates with other attitude measures that supposedly measure the same thing. Typically, in studies in which the relation between attitudes and behavior was low, no such additional data were presented.

The most famous study of the relation of attitudes and behavior was published by LaPiere (1934). Methodologically, it was a weak study. However, since it is historically important and people still cite it, it is useful to indicate why it was weak. In the early 1930's, LaPiere traveled through a portion of the United States with a Chinese couple. They stopped in 66 hotels and 184 restaurants, and they were refused service only once. Six months after the trip, LaPiere sent letters to the establishments which had served them, asking if they would give service to Chinese guests. Only 128 establishments answered this letter; of those answering, 92% indicated that they would *not* accept Chinese guests. Thus, LaPiere claimed that there was little connection between attitudes and actions.

Why is the study a poor one?

1. We do not know whether the person who admitted the Chinese couple was the same one who answered the letter.

2. The letter elicited a "norm" (i.e., usual and appropriate action) rather than an attitude; it did not measure the particular respondent's attitude.

3. There is no additional evidence that the answers to the letter provided a valid measure of attitudes.

4. There is no information on the reliability of either the behavior or the supposed attitude measure.

5. The attitude objects were not the same: There is a big difference between "Orientals" (the wording of the letter) and *that* particular, pleasant-looking, smiling Chinese couple who arrived in an expensive automobile with a white professor.

Although this study was weak, it is very instructive. It tells us that we must pay attention to the total stimulus field surrounding the person who is responding to an attitude question or who is acting. Consider the difference between answering a letter which asks about Orientals in general and responding to a specific Chinese couple. The difference is immense.

The same point can be made on the opposite side of the argument. There are excellent predictions from attitudes to behavior in the case of voting behavior. Here, the researcher uses a sheet of paper that looks like a ballot, has the same names that will appear on the ballot, and may be used a few days before an election. After the election, people are asked how they voted. The latter answers can be cross-checked against actual voting frequencies across a sample of precincts. The typical results in such cases have very high validities (correlations between the attitude measures and the behavior). The explanation is simple: The two tasks are very similar and they occur rather close in time. It is almost like asking a person to vote twice, and the correlations are more like reliability measures than measures of validity.

Characteristics Associated with Behavior

All behaviors which we study have five characteristics associated with them: a specific *actor*, a specific *action*, in a specific *context*, at a specific *time*, and toward a specific *target*. Simply put: *"Who*, does *what*, to *whom*, *where*, and *why."* The attitudes which we generally study also will have these characteristics associated with them. All too often, researchers obtain behavioral measures that have a different set of characteristics from the attitude measures. For instance, a researcher may measure a person's "attitude toward handicapped people" and obtain a behavioral measure of whether the person will help a specific blind man across the street. Obviously, there is a lack of correspondence between the characteristics of the attitude and the behavior. The researcher will probably find a low relation between the general measure of attitude and the particular behavior, and may conclude that attitudes do not predict behavior. However, when there is a higher correspondence between the characteristics of the attitude and the behavior measure (e.g., the attitude toward helping a blind person across the street), attitudes will be fairly consistent predictors of behavior. It is important to note, then, that the greater the degree of correspondence between the attitudes and behavior measures, the more accurately attitudes predict behavior.

If we measure a very general attitude (e.g., attitude toward the handicapped), it should not be very surprising to find that this general measure does not predict very accurately any one specific behavioral measure. Multiple measures of behaviors that are associated with the attitude object are necessary. In this case, if we measure a person's attitude toward the handicapped and then obtain several behavioral measures (e.g., helping a blind person across the street, donating to a charity for the handicapped, etc.), it is likely that we will observe moderate to strong relations between the measure of attitude and the several measures of behavior. In short, if the researcher is interested in predicting behavior from a general attitude measure, it is important to obtain multiple measures of behaviors; however, if the researcher is interested in predicting a specific behavior, it is best to obtain a measure of attitude that corresponds to the specific behavior.

In conclusion, the argument about whether attitudes predict behavior is misleading. If the attitude measures are properly obtained, if the characteristics of the attitude object correspond to those of the behavior being measured, and if multiple measures of behavior are obtained to correspond to a general measure of attitude, then it is likely that a fairly high relation will be found between attitudes and behavior (Fishbein & Ajzen, 1975).

The argument just summarized does not imply that all the variability in behavior is predictable from attitudes. Far from it. Very often people do not do what they would like to do. This fact is so obvious that we tend to forget it. People often do what is legal, moral, or ethical or what has good consequences in the long run, rather than what gives them the greatest pleasure in the next minute. In fact, attitudes often control relatively small amounts of the variability (technically, the variance) of behavior. People sometimes learn how to act in different situations by being exposed to rewards and punishments. If some of these rewards are clearly connected with actions, a person sees good consequences for these actions. Other people also give information about what is correct behavior and act as models for correct action. Much of what we learn is, in fact, a result of observations of other people who are rewarded or punished for certain actions. Once we act a few times in a certain way, because of such social factors or because we expect good consequences, our behavior in a situation may escape self-instruction (conscious thought). It is like driving a car: We stop at the red lights without giving ourselves the instruction to do so. Our attitudes, then, may be shaped to conform to our behavior, and we can acquire attitudes that justify what we do. So, in a real sense, when we study attitudes, we are tapping established behavior patterns.

The relation between attitudes and behavior, then, is reciprocal. Attitudes predispose actions; actions shape attitudes. Viewed in a broad historical and cross-cultural perspective, individuals hold the attitudes that are most useful to them for effective social action in a particular historical period and a particular culture. These attitudes predispose their behavior, but when their behavior is shaped by contemporary events (e.g., new laws, social movements, travel to other countries, etc.), they acquire new attitudes.

Another perspective can be drawn from clinical cases. Many times our habits are inconsistent with social norms, roles, or even our self-concepts. For example, suppose a person has a particular sexual habit which is not socially approved, and we measure the person's attitude toward that sexual habit. This measure may reflect the social norm (social desirability). So, the person might indicate a dislike of, and opposition to, such sexual behavior. In many clinical cases individuals think that they disapprove of a behavior, except when they are "carried away" and do it in a "weak moment." What we have in such cases is an affective system, shaped by past pleasant events and personal experiences, and a cognitive system, shaped by social influences. Each system predisposes a class of actions, but the actions are incompatible with the attitude or are viewed by most members of a society as incompatible. Such persons may ask clinicians for help to bring their habits in line with their ideals of who they are and how they should behave.

A less extreme case, but parallel to it, is the situation in which a person has habits (e.g., smoking) which are known to be harmful. Here, the cognitions reflect probabilities of future events (cancer, death, etc.) but the habit is well entrenched. The person may then *like* to smoke but verbalize the *intention* to stop. In this case, too, there is a contrast between the habit-affective system and the cognitive system.

To sum up, when people have no established habits about a certain behavior they do what is socially desirable, consistent with their self-concepts, intrinsically enjoyable, and has good perceived consequences. Different persons weigh these factors differentially; some pay a lot of attention to what is socially desirable, others do what is enjoyable, and so on. In addition, the weights may be different for different behaviors (e.g., when we pray, we do what is socially desirable or what has good consequences; when we drink at a cocktail party, we may give more weight to what is enjoyable). Also, some social situations call for more of one or another of these factors. For instance, in a church, as opposed to a party, people are more likely to perform socially desirable rather than personally enjoyable behaviors.

When a behavior is under "habit control" (escapes conscious self-instruction), what we think, feel, or like to do (in short, our attitudes) may be irrelevant. So, in thinking about attitudes and attitude change, we must consider what *kind* of behavior we are trying to change. If we want to change a behavior that is under habit control, we have to use one course of action; if it is not under habit control, another course of action may be best.

The second big issue concerning attitudes, then, is whether they are related to behavior. The view just described is, by definition, that attitudes are related to behavior, although they may sometimes not account for very much of the variability of behavior. The opposing view is that attitudes are not *necessarily* related to behavior.

Another approach to the study of the relation between attitudes and behavior is the use of people's specific beliefs about a behavior in the prediction of the actual behavior. A belief simply links an action (or object) with a consequence, attribute, or another object. For example, one belief that may be associated with allowing handicapped students to take part in "normal" classes may be that "allowing the handicapped to take part in normal classes would mean that the nonhandicapped students will be slowed down in their learning." Each different belief associated with the behavior (in this example, allowing the handicapped to take part in "normal" classes) may then be examined in order to determine the relation of *each* belief to behavior.

An example may help to clarify how we can study the relation of a particular belief to a behavior. Suppose we are interested in finding out whether the belief that "allowing the handicapped to take part in normal classes would mean that the nonhandicapped students will be slowed down in their learning," is related to the behavior of voting to allow handicapped students in the classroom. We would ask a person two questions associated with the belief: (a) "Suppose that allowing handicapped students to take part in normal classes would mean that handicapped students will be slowed down in their learning. How likely is it that you would vote to allow handicapped students in the classroom?" (b) "Suppose that allowing handicapped students to take part in normal classes would *not* mean that nonhandicapped students will be slowed in their learning. How likely is it that you would vote to allow handicapped students in the classroom?" The difference between the responses to those two questions would indicate the psychological relevance of the belief to the behavior of voting. The greater the difference between the two responses, the more relevant this belief would be to the behavior. Conversely, the less the difference between the two responses, the less relevant this belief would be to the behavior.

This approach has a number of implications for the study of the relation between beliefs and behavior. For example, it allows us to determine the relevance of each belief. If we are interested in altering a behavior, the most efficient strategy would be to attempt to change the relevant, rather than the irrelevant, beliefs (Jaccard & King, 1977).

Why Do People Have Attitudes?

Attitudes help people in many ways.

1. Attitudes help people to understand the world around them by organizing the very complex array of stimuli in the environment. Imagine how difficult it would be to act if we had to develop our action patterns from first principles each time. By holding stereotypes and having predispositions to respond, we act more quickly. Of course, there is a price: To the extent that our stereotypes are inaccurate or our attitudes are unjustified, we also act more inaccurately or inappropriately.

Consider, for example, a person who dislikes handicapped people. Such a person may be "using information" given to him by others to the effect that the handicapped are parasites on society. This attitude predisposes a ready-made response, so the person has a set of actions immediately available when called for. For example, he or she may vote against government actions in favor of the handicapped.

2. Attitudes help people to protect their self-esteem. They make it possible for people to avoid unpleasant truths about themselves or to cover up uncomplimentary thoughts. In our example, the person who dislikes handicapped people can cover up extreme stinginess by arguing that the handicapped are parasitic (thus, the government should not support programs for handicapped children).

3. Attitudes help people to adjust to a complex world so that they will do the right (rewarding) things at the right time. For example, if a person's friends also dislike handicapped people, he or she will be rewarded for such attitudes.

4. Attitudes help people to express their fundamental values. In our example, the person may place his or her personal, financial condition ahead of a good society.

This analysis was developed by Katz (1960). He discussed the *knowledge, ego-defensive, adjustive-utilitarian,* and *value-expressive* functions of attitudes. The importance of the functional approach is that it directs us to examine the bases of a person's attitudes, which will suggest different courses of action for attitude-change purposes, depending on which basis is discovered. For example, attitude change is best achieved through information if the attitude basis is mostly informational; it is most effective through psychotherapy if the basis is mostly ego-defensive; it is most likely to work through changes in the person's social group if the basis is mostly utilitarian; and it is most responsive to an attack on the connection between attitudes and values if the basis is mostly value-expressive. In short, the functional approach implies that we do not change all attitudes the same way. We should tailor-make our attitude-change procedures to take into account the functional bases of the attitudes. Of course, some attitudes may have two or more bases, and more than one change procedure may be needed to change them.

Attitudes have additional functions. Since positive or negative emotions are usually associated with attitudes, they may be used as reinforcers. Reinforcers, of course, may be used to increase or decrease the likelihood of a behavior. The effectiveness of the attitude as a reinforcer depends upon how polarized (extreme) it is. For instance, if a person has a very strong positive attitude toward people in wheelchairs, this attitude may be used to shape a number of different behaviors, such as helping a person in a wheelchair, becoming friendly with someone in a wheelchair, or allowing people in wheelchairs to attend public schools. The use of the attitude as a reinforcer may increase the likelihood of these behaviors. The converse of this example would also be true; that is, if a person has a negative attitude, it would be possible to use the attitude to decrease the likelihood of a behavior.

Attitudes may also serve as stimuli to elicit behaviors which have been previously learned and associated with the attitudes. For example, if a person has a positive attitude toward handicapped people, behaviors (e.g., giving to charity) that were previously learned and associated with the attitude may be elicited when the attitude is made salient.

In sum, it is useful to identify the function(s) of each attitude. However, an important issue in the study of attitudes is how much weight to give to the functional bases of attitudes. One view is that the study of why people have particular attitudes is extremely important because only by designing change procedures specifically for these attitudes can we have real attitude change. Another view is that the study of why each person holds a particular attitude is too time-consuming and expensive; we must discover procedures that work for everybody, even though we admit that such procedures may work better for some people than for others.

How Are Attitudes Organized?

A central principle of attitude organization is consistency (Abelson, Aronson, McGuire, Newcomb, Rosenberg, & Tannenbaum, 1968). Cognitive elements (e.g., thoughts about attitude objects) are connected with one another positively ($+u$) or negatively ($-$). When we assign plus and minus signs to relations, consistency or balance implies that multiplying the signs algebraically will give us a positive sign. For instance, if Person B dislikes ($-$) Person A, and if Person A dislikes ($-$) attitude object X, then Person B's attitude toward

O would be balanced if B liked O, because then we would have $(-)$ times $(-)$ times $(+u)$ = $+u$. On the other hand, if Person B disliked O, we would have $(-)$ times $(-)$ times $(-)$ = $(-)$, which is not balanced. Unbalanced attitudes are more likely to change than balanced attitudes. A change could involve any of the above elements; for example, B may start liking A, or B may perceive A as liking O, or B may start liking O.

When a person does something positive toward an attitude object but feels negatively about it, there is imbalance or dissonance (Festinger, 1957). Imbalance is an unstable state that motivates people to change their attitudes. For example, suppose some people believe that the handicapped are poor workers and dislike them. Now imagine that a law requires these people to hire handicapped workers. Further, assume that they are law-abiding and therefore, do hire the handicapped. The cognition that they have acted in a positive way is in conflict with the cognition that they dislike handicapped people. When there is such conflict, some cognition must change to restore consistency. Inasmuch as it is difficult for people to think that they have not acted in a positive way, the cognition about the attitude (dislike for the handicapped) is easier to change. Such people simply may say to themselves, "Well, what do you know? They are not bad . . . I *like* the handicapped!"

Unfortunately, things are not always that simple. There are a number of things people can do when they are faced with inconsistency. Abelson (1959) has identified four such strategies:

1. They can *stop thinking* about the inconsistency; if the discrepancy between two cognitions is not considered, there is no reason to change.

2. They can *bolster* one cognition; for instance, they can argue that their behavior was due to their being a law-abiding citizens or their desire to please their supervisor, and has nothing to do with the way they feel about the handicapped.

3. They can *differentiate*. That is, they can argue that even though they like some kinds of handicapped people, they dislike most of them.

4. They can *transcend* the inconsistency by finding some higher level explanation, such as the general principle that one should act in a positive way even toward those one dislikes, or by arguing that it is a good principle of action in a civilized society.

Another complication is the freedom which people saw themselves as having at the time of the act. If they did not see themselves as free to act positively *or* negatively, then there is no inconsistency. That is, they had no choice so their behavior had no relevance to their attitude. Still another complication concerns the extent to which they feel committed to the action. Suppose that such people see very little reason for acting the way they did, other than that it was the right way to act. In short, they reason that they acted because they *felt* that that was the only way to act. In this case, the discrepancy between action and attitude becomes greater because there is commitment. So, the more free people feel to act or not to act, and the less reason they see for having acted, the greater the dissonance and thus the greater the discomfort from the discrepancy between action and attitude. The discomfort is reduced when they change attitude.

The various components of attitude (i.e., cognitive, affective, and behavioral) must be consistent with one another. If they are not, the person experiences dissonance. Thus, the person's ideas must fit the person's feelings and intentions to act. Furthermore, past behavior is one of the most important pieces of information used by the person to decide how he or she "really" feels about the attitude object.

These general points apply to everybody, but there are also individual differences in the organization of attitudes which are worth noting. First, there is the problem of categorization. Conceptual categories can be broad or narrow. Some people react to the world with broad categories, whereas others use narrow categories. For example, consider the idea of what is "legal." Some people categorize many acts of marginal legality as "legal," any act that does not land them in jail is seen as legal. Others have a very finely tuned conception of what is legal.

The way people react to handicapped persons will reflect, in part, such differences in categorization. Some will use a single broad category, but others will use several rather specific categories. Broad categorizers tend to be more tolerant of deviant behavior. They are less upset when a person who is supposed to act one way acts in a somewhat different manner. Narrow categorizers, by contrast, accept only a straight and narrow path of action.

An important aspect of categorization is the placing of stimuli into three categories: acceptance, rejection, and noncommitment. For example, consider opinions about the way people should act toward handicapped children. Some of these opinions would be acceptable to a person, others would be rejected, and finally there will be a group of opinions toward which he or she feels no commitment one way or the other. It turns out that people who are extreme in their attitudes (i.e., extremely favorable or extremely unfavorable toward the attitude object) have a large category for rejection and a very small category for noncommitment (Sherif, Sherif, & Nebergall, 1965).

An important issue in the organization of attitudes is how much emphasis to place on phenomena that apply to everybody, such as balance and dissonance, and how much attention to pay to individual differences, such as differences in categorization and in the bases of attitudes.

How Are Attitudes Developed?

Attitudes are learned. For instance, children may learn a new category when they compare two objects and are told, "This is not the same as that." Positive and negative events or positive and negative words are associated by parents with certain categories. The parent may say, "Blind people must be helped across the street," and reward the child for helping. After many such experiences, the child learns to feel good and to intend to be helpful in the presence of blind people. Thus, a positive attitude is born.

When a category of people or a behavior toward people is frequently associated with positive or negative events, the person learns attitudes toward the category or behavior reflecting these events. There are several kinds of events: direct experience, which may be positive or negative, or indirect experience, such as receiving information from others. A person may experience the positive event directly—for example, receiving candy in the presence of an attitude object—or may be told that one will receive candy in the presence of an attitude object.

People may start by evaluating a particular attitude object neutrally, but if they form new beliefs connecting the attitude object with particular attributes, consequences, or antecedents, then they will move away from neutrality. Some beliefs will be strong and some weak; some will connect the attitude object to positive attributes, others, to negative attributes. The sum of the products of the strength of these beliefs and the evaluative aspect of each belief is an index of the affect toward the attitude object. Fishbein and Azjen (1975) discussed this idea in detail. They pointed out that although a person holds many beliefs about an attitude object, only some of these beliefs are salient, and affect toward the attitude object depends only on the salient beliefs.

There is evidence that affect is positively related to exposure to an attitude object. In other words, repeated exposure to a stimulus leads to liking it. Harrison (1977), after a review of 10 years of research on this phenomenon, speculated that it may be related to the Solomon and Corbit (1974) opponent-process theory of motivation. This theory suggests that if the presentation of a stimulus triggers an affective reaction, the withdrawal of this same stimulus will trigger an opposite (the opponent) process which, in turn, results in feelings that have the opposite affective value. So, if a novel stimulus is threatening or annoying, the absence of the stimulus will produce positive affect. Repetition of this sequence leaves the initial process unaffected but strengthens the opponent process (Solomon & Corbit, 1974) so that the latter becomes conditioned to the stimulus and, as a result, a stimulus which originally was threatening becomes positive after many exposures.

The application of this finding to reactions toward handicapped persons suggests that if people are frequently exposed to handicapped persons, other things being equal, they will start to like them. However, this idea is also related to the so called "contact hypothesis," a hypothesis which has been shown by research not always to lead to greater liking.

In sum, attitudes are formed because the person is exposed to the attitude object, which can generate positive affect; the attitude object is observed to have particular attributes; the person learns from others that the attitude object has some attributes; and/or the person is rewarded for believing that the attitude object has certain attributes. The rewards may be of many kinds, such as money, goods, information, services, status, or love (Foa & Foa, 1974). Children, of course, are also receptive to these rewards, although the specific form of the reward may be different for them. When a reward is given consistently for a period of time, there is more learning but there is also rapid forgetting ("extinction" of response) when the reward is no longer given. On the other hand, when the reward is given only some of the time (intermittent reinforcement) extinction does not occur so readily. In short, learning is more likely to last if the reward is not always given. Many other factors are relevant, such as how big the reward is, how soon after the response the reward is given, and so on.

How do stereotypes develop? The preceding discussion is directly relevant. Suppose a person has some positive and some negative experiences with deaf people. If the positive experiences are more frequent or of greater magnitude, or are more clearly connected in time or place to deaf people, then the attitude toward the deaf will be positive. However, most people do not have direct experiences with all attitude objects. In fact, most people have limited experiences; the majority of their attitudes are formed in school, or at home, or are based on what other people tell them. So, one of the major determinants of stereotypes is what people are told in their formative years. Of course, reading and watching TV and the other mass media also impact on the formation of attitudes.

Does interaction with deaf persons have good or bad consequences? There is no simple answer. Interaction can have positive consequences, for instance, in seeing that one's conceptions about what the deaf can do are wrong (e.g., sign language can be used to communicate extremely complex and abstract concepts). Interaction can also have negative effects. One must analyze the total situation, the total flow of interaction, and the kinds of rewards and costs that this interaction entails for the individual. One must avoid simple formulas, such as the idea that mere contact is beneficial. In some situations interaction reinforces one's stereotypes and confirms one's worst expectations (Amir, 1969).

The *conditions* under which interaction takes place are very important. For instance, when a person is in competition with another group, the interaction is likely to have negative consequences if that group gets rewards the person had hoped to obtain. On the other hand, if cooperation with the other group makes it possible for the person to obtain desired consequences which would not be available otherwise, then the results will be positive.

When two groups differ on a given attribute, the greater the difference the more likely it is that this attribute will appear in their stereotypes of each other. Furthermore, they are likely to experience what is called "contrast"— to see a difference as larger than it really is. So, for example, the public is more likely to consider "deaf" people as completely deaf and is unlikely to realize that there are variations in the degree of auditory loss; or the public may perceive "blind" people as completely blind and not realize that some of them are able to read print under certain conditions. In such cases, interaction can change a stereotype, thus eliminating misperceptions and exaggerated contrasts between one's own and the other group.

Another influence on the formation of stereotypes and belief systems—the bases of attitudes—comes from various "implicit personality theories" (Schneider, 1973) about the way attributes, traits, and human characteristics are organized. For example, a person may think that fat people are jolly, an attitude that implies a learned tendency to see particular traits as "going together." Clusters of traits reflecting (a) extroversion, (b) agreeableness, (c) dependability, and (d) emotional stability often have been reported in the literature. In one such study, Tzeng (1975) found six dimensions which were characterized by the following clusters of traits:

34

1. Good, nice, pleasant, honest, just, sincere, polite, sensible, sympathetic, friendly.
2. Old, strong, heavy, large, clean, hard-working, courageous, cultured, rich.
3. Young, light, fast, nervous, beautiful, thin, lazy, joyous, amusing, greedy.
4. Optimistic, open-minded, happy, hot, simple, wholesome, rich.
5. Discreet, trusting, calm, sober, sincere, thin.
6. Cultured, nervous, complicated, intelligent, hard-working, active, curious, optimistic.

A related belief is that of a "just world" (Lerner, 1975), that is, the idea that good things happen to good people and that those who are suffering or deprived deserve their fate. Believers in a just world are more likely than nonbelievers to admire fortunate people, derogate victims, be more religious, be more authoritarian, and be more satisfied with existing institutions and political leaders (Rubin & Peplau, 1975). This belief has obvious implications for handicapped persons.

The explanation of the tendency toward this belief seems to be that people find it painful to see a victim of misfortune who has done nothing to deserve this fate. Observers are threatened by the possibility that the same thing could happen to them. Observers who derogate the victim feel more secure because this suggests that as long as they are "good" nothing "bad" will happen to them.

It is possible, then, that negative attitudes toward handicapped persons represent a "just world" phenomenon. This possibility has important implications because it suggests that emphasizing the merits of handicapped persons can increase observers' defensiveness.

What kind of evidence suggests that people have a "just world" viewpoint? In one experiment (Lerner, 1965), two students, one attractive and the other unattractive, worked on a task for which one, randomly selected, was paid. Observers rated the paid person as contributing more to the task, as predicted from the "just world" theory. In addition, people felt more comfortable when the attractive student was paid and less comfortable when the unattractive student was paid. However, subsequent research has questioned whether the "just world" hypothesis is necessarily supported by these data. In some studies, for instance, it has been argued that observers may feel guilty for participating in situations in which one person is treated better than another, and that this guilt leads to the derogation of the victim. However, still other studies have attempted to control for this possibility and found that derogation occurred even when the observers could not have felt personally responsible for the fate of the victim.

The issue of perceived responsibility for the victim's plight is important in applying the "just world" theory to handicapped persons because it is likely that most observers (teachers, other students, citizens) are not responsible for the condition of these individuals. The literature suggests that derogation exists when a person is powerless to help the victim. Thus, this theory may provide an explanation for the overly solicitous behavior often observed among persons who interact closely with handicapped people. When they perceive themselves as "helping others," they experience a reduction in the discomfort generated by the "just world" viewpoint.

The way the child is socialized is also relevant to the way attitudes are formed. Harvey, Hunt, and Schroeder (1961) argued that some children are socialized by getting very little information about the way the world is made up. On all available occasions they are told how to act, but they are given no explanations for so acting. When such children become adults, they are likely to conform to authority figures. Other children, who also are not given any information, are punished inconsistently. Such children are likely to reject authority figures; they may become rebels or delinquents. Still other children are consistently given a lot of information about the way the world is: "If you do X, Y will happen." Such children may become adults who like to do what other people, particularly their peers, consider correct. Finally, some children are given information inconsistently. This last group may become particularly inquisitive, often trying new ways of doing things.

According to the argument of Harvey et al. (1961), adults will react differently to particular attitude objects, depending on which of the four methods of child rearing was used during their socialization. For example, if school authorities say, "We must integrate the handicapped and the nonhandicapped as an experiment in this class," those in the first socialization pattern may conform without asking questions; those in the second may find many reasons for not conforming; those in the third may "check" with their friends to see what their friends are doing, and do likewise; and those in the fourth pattern may say, "Sure, let's try it," and then keep a critical eye on the "experiment," changing their attitudes if the experiment does not work.

Some child-rearing patterns result in some individuals becoming insecure. Highly punitive parents often have children who, as adults, suffer from chronic and generalized anxiety and low self-evaluation (Rohner, 1975). Such adults are more likely to change their attitudes than people who are secure (Triandis, 1971). Sometimes the attitudes themselves reflect insecurity. For example, a person who feels insecure may not want competition from handicapped peers since a loss in such a competition would be especially humiliating.

An important source of attitudes is our social group. We learn to look at the world the way our cherished social groups (e.g., family, friends) look at it. One way to analyze the sources of people's attitudes is to check on their friends. One way to change people's attitudes is to change those of the persons with whom they interact. Not only people's actual friends, but also the friends they aspire to have (the reference group) may be important in the formation of attitudes. If people aspire to join particular groups, say those of higher status, then their perception of the attitudes of others in those groups is very important in determining their attitudes.

Certain socialization influences are also responsible for more or less strong beliefs in a "just world." One of the consequences of socialization patterns that lead to a child's becoming authoritarian, dogmatic, very religious, and so on, is a strong belief in a "just world." This consequence is both desirable and undesirable: desirable because such people are more likely to do what they believe to be morally correct and consistent with social norms, and undesirable because such people derogate victims.

Rubin and Peplau (1975) examined the socialization practices that might lead to a reduction in the emphasis on the "just world." They pointed out that most children's television programs give the message that good guys always win and bad guys always lose. Parents often tell children that accidents are due to their having been "bad" in the past, teachers usually depict successful people as faultless, and religious leaders often tell stories about the punishments that have befallen those who did not follow God's orders. These socialization patterns tend to emphasize the "just world" cognitive bias. More sophisticated television programs might indicate that sometimes the bad guys get away (a reality which, according to the Justice Department, is statistically more probable than anyone wants to admit), that accidents are usually not punishments for some misbehavior, that successful people often have more faults than the average citizen, and that punishments occur to both "good" and "bad" people. The world is often unjust. Above all, the knowledge that we humans have a tendency to see the world as more just than it really is and to defend ourselves against information that shows it is unjust should help us to stop derogating perfectly innocent victims.

The issue here, as it is in the evaluation of the functions of attitudes, is the extent to which we should attend to individual differences and their sources. Some scientists argue that we should keep looking at the major common denominators and disregard individual differences, whereas others put great emphasis on such differences. A related controversy is whether the person's behavior is due to internal factors, such as personality or attitudes, or external factors, such as the nature of the situation (Endler & Magnusson, 1976). The view advanced here is that behavior is usually due to the interaction of both attitude and situation. Furthermore, the importance of the interaction depends on the kind of behavior, the kind of person, and the kind of situation which are involved (Triandis, 1977a).

A Partial Glimpse of Attitude Change

Inasmuch as attitude change is well covered by Watts in the following chapter, here we discuss only one aspect which is particularly related to our interests.

Consider a situation in which a person has negative attitudes toward handicapped people. What can we do to change them? Three broad strategies can be used: (a) informational, (b) behavior modification, and (c) experiential.

The informational approach exposes the target person to a variety of ideas, beliefs, and viewpoints about and possible insights into handicapped individuals. The range of ideas is broad: statistics about the contributions of handicapped persons to the gross national product, information on jobs which can be done only by handicapped persons (e.g., deaf persons are able to work comfortably in environments that have very high noise levels), or insights into one's motivations and the functional bases of one's attitudes toward handicapped persons.

The behavior modification approach would put the people in situations where they may make a positive response toward a handicapped individual, resulting in a reward. When people see themselves behaving positively, cognitive dissonance (Festinger, 1957) can lead to changes in their attitudes toward the handicapped which will "line up" their attitudes with the realities of their behavior.

The experiential approach would create conditions in which the experiences of the individual in the presence of handicapped persons would be positive. Repetition would condition the person to emit positive affective responses in the presence of the handicapped individual. Pleasant encounter groups, parties, or situations in which the person receives status or love in the presence of handicapped persons could be used also.

It is likely that each approach has a role in a program to change a person's attitudes. The combination to use is a matter of practicality or economics. Experiential and behavior modification approaches are expensive but effective, particularly when one wants to change behavior, rather than just attitudes.

One approach that combines the advantages of the informational with some experiential (at least vicariously) and behavior modification elements (by rewarding correct actions) is the "assimilator" used by Fiedler, Mitchell, and Triandis (1971) to instruct people on understanding social behavior in other cultures. This approach can be useful in changing behavior toward handicapped individuals.

The basic strategy is to present "episodes" of social interaction to people with two different perspectives and to ask each person to choose one of four explanations as the appropriate interpretation of each episode. The procedure for the development of such assimilators to change attitudes toward handicapped persons is as follows:

1. Take a sample of persons who have some experience interacting with, for example, deaf individuals. (The same procedure could be followed with any other handicap.) Call it sample A.
2. Take a sample of deaf people (sample B)
3. Interview samples A and B. Ask what "episodes" they can give you that describe interactions with members of the "other" group.
4. Edit the verbal episodes into descriptive paragraphs.
5. Present the paragraphs to new samples of A and B. Ask them to suggest *why* people in the episodes acted as they did. Each *why* is an *attribution*.
6. Edit the episodes and attributions so each episode has several different attributions which have been obtained from *both* sample A and sample B.
7. Present these edited materials to new samples of A and B. Present all the attributions as paired comparisons for each episode and ask, "In your opinion, which of these two explanations is the correct one?"
8. Analyze these data for differences in the chosen explanations; that is, identify situations for which sample A uses one explanation significantly more (or less) frequently than sample B.
9. Now rewrite the episodes with the statistically significant explanations found in step 8. The final item should look like the following: For the training for group A members, each episode should be followed by three explanations (attributions) frequently given by members of group A and one given by members of group B. When a trainee chooses one of the A explanations,

he is told in the "feedback" that it is "incorrect" from the point of view of the other group and to study the episode once more. When the trainee chooses the explanation of group B, he is reinforced and given more feedback explaining why group B looks at this episode that way.

For the training of group B members, each episode is followed by three B-preferred attributions and one A-preferred attribution, and the feedback is structured to parallel the feedback for A members.

The effect of the assimilator is to broaden the perspective of the trainee so that he or she will consider the point of view of the other group also. The trainee learns to empathize with and to appreciate the other group's point of view and, we hope, to change his or her attitudes also. One way to use the assimilator is to identify particular needed changes in behavior (as reflected in the various items) and, after the training, to provide rewards for such behaviors.

An important problem in the study of attitude change is whether to use a cognitive (informational), affective (experiences with pleasant and unpleasant events), or behavioral (positive events following specific desired behaviors) approach. There are also other issues and questions: How *much* to use each approach, in what *order*, *who* should be the source of attitude change, and how to modify the approaches for *different audiences*. Some new approaches to attitude change, such as the assimilator, may prove useful, but there is not enough research in the area of attitudes toward handicapped persons, using this approach, to allow a firm assessment at this time. Triandis (1977b) has discussed some of the methodological problems in assessing the effectiveness of such training programs.

To conclude: This chapter has examined attitudes as general phenomenon. Specific treatments of attitudes toward the disabled can be found in the literature, e.g., Thomas (1980).

REFERENCES

Abelson, R. P. Modes of resolution of belief dilemmas. *Journal of Conflict Resolution*, 1959, *3*, 343-352.

Abelson, R. P., Aronson, E., McGuire, W. J., Newcomb, T. M., Rosenberg, M. J., & Tannenbaum, P. H. *Theories of cognitive consistency.* Chicago: Rand McNally, 1968.

Adamopoulos, J. Analysis of interpersonal structures in literary works of three historical periods. *Journal of Cross-Cultural Psychology*, 1982, *13*, 157-168.

Allport, G. W. Attitudes. In C. Murchison (Ed.), *Handbook of social psychology*. Worcester MA: Clark University Press, 1935.

Amir, Y. Contact hypothesis in ethnic relations. *Psychological Bulletin*, 1969, *71*, 319-342.

Brinberg, D., & Kidder, L. *Forms of validity in research.* San Francisco: Jossey-Bass, 1982.

Endler, N. S., & Magnusson, D. *Interactional psychology and personality.* New York: Halsted, 1976.

Festinger, L. *A theory of cognitive dissonance.* New York: Row Peterson, 1957.

Fiedler, F. E., Mitchell, T., & Triandis, H. C. The culture assimilator: An approach to cross-cultural training. *Journal of Applied Psychology*, 1971, *55*, 95-102.

Fishbein, M. A. *An investigation of the relationship between beliefs about an object and the attitude toward the object*. Unpublished doctoral thesis, University of California at Los Angeles, 1961.

Fishbein, M. A., & Ajzen, I. *Belief, attitude, intention and behavior*. Reading MA: Addison-Wesley, 1975.

Foa, U. G., & Foa, E. B. *Societal structures of the mind*. Springfield IL: Charles C Thomas, 1974.

Harrison, A. A. Mere exposure. In L. Berkowitz (Ed.), *Advances in experimental social psychology* (Vol. 10). New York: Academic, 1977.

Harvey, O. H., Hunt, D. E., & Schroeder, H. M. *Conceptual systems and personality organization*. New York: Wiley, 1961.

Jaccard, J., & King, G. W. A probabilistic model of the relationship between beliefs and behavioral intentions. *Human Communication Research*, 1977, *3*, 332-342.

Katz, D. The functional approach to the study of attitudes. *Public Opinion Quarterly*, 1960, *24*, 163-204.

LaPiere, R. T. Attitudes and actions. *Social Forces*, 1934, *13*, 230-237.

Lerner, M. J. The effect of responsibility and choice on a partner's attractiveness following failure. *Journal of Personality*, 1965, *33*, 178-187.

Lerner, M. J. The justice motive in social behavior. *Journal of Social Issues*, 1975, *31*(3).

Osgood, C. E., May, W., & Miron, M. *Cross-cultural universals of affective meaning*. Urbana IL: University of Illinois Press, 1975.

Rohner, R. *They love me, they love me not: A worldwide study of the effects of parental acceptance and rejection*. New Haven: Human Relations Area Files, 1975.

Rubin, Z., & Peplau, L. A. Who believes in a just world? *Journal of Social Issues*, 1975, *31*, 65-89.

Schneider, D. J. Implicit personality theory: A review. *Psychological Bulletin*, 1973, *79*, 294-309.

Sherif, C. W., Sherif, M., & Nebergall, R. E. *Attitude and attitude change*. Philadelphia: Saunders, 1965.

Solomon, R. L., & Corbit, J. D. Opponent-process theory of motivation. *Psychological Review*, 1974, *81*, 119-145.

Thomas, D. *The social psychology of childhood disability*. New York: Schocken Books, 1980.

Thurstone, L. E. Attitudes can be measured. *American Journal of Sociology*, 1928, *33*, 529-554.

Thurstone, L. L. The measurement of social attitudes. *Journal of Abnormal and Social Psychology*, 1931, *26*, 249-269.

Triandis, H. C. *Attitude and attitude change*. New York: Wiley, 1971.

Triandis, H. C. *Interpersonal behavior*. Monterey: Brooks/Cole, 1977. (a)

Triandis, H. C. Theoretical framework for evaluation of cross-cultural training effectiveness. *International Journal of Intercultural Relations*, 1977, *1*, 19-45. (b)

Tzeng, O. C. S. Differentiation of affective and denotative meaning systems and their influence in personality ratings. *Journal of Personality and Social Psychology*, 1975, *32*, 978-998.

3

Attitude Change: Theories and Methods

WILLIAM A. WATTS

An overview of theories and research on the topic of changing attitudes toward handicapped persons is difficult because few studies have been carried out and most of those have been atheoretical. At first glance it would appear that virtually all the extant theories and research dealing with the dynamics of attitude change should be relevant to the topic, but a closer look raises many questions. The discussion here focuses on three categories of attitude change theory, several methods which have been used to change attitudes, and the persistence of attitude change. More comprehensive overviews of the topic of attitude change can be found in Fishbein and Ajzen (1975), McGuire (1969), Oskamp (1977), and Triandis (1971).

THEORIES OF ATTITUDE CHANGE

Information-Processing Theories

The information-processing views, best outlined by McGuire (1968, 1969, 1972) and Wyer (1974), call attention to the fact that persuasion is a frequent problem in communication rather than in overcoming active resistance to change. McGuire translated Laswell's (1948) analysis of the communication process (who says what to whom, how, and with what effect) into the components of *source, message, channel, receiver,* and *destination.* In his analysis of the attitude-change process, McGuire identified the components of attention, comprehension, yielding, retention, and action. Thus, attitude change is regarded as requiring a successive series of steps, each of which has only a certain probability of occurring but all of which must occur for a change in attitude to take place. For example, if the probability of a person's paying attention to the

41

message is .50 and his comprehension rate is .40, maximum likelihood of his yielding to the point of view advocated would be .20; in fact, in most cases, it would be much less, considering such tendencies as counterarguing while reading or listening to the communication. If behavior change, rather than verbal statements of opinion, is the ultimate dependent variable, two additional probabilistic steps are required: The person must retain the new opinion for some period of time, at least long enough to have an opportunity to modify behavior accordingly, and then he or she must modify the behavior. McGuire (1972) concluded "In the light of this analysis, the wonder is not that advertising campaigns have so little effect, but that they have any discernible effect at all" (p. 20).

It has been said of the analysis of variance that one of its most useful aspects is calling attention to otherwise frequently overlooked sources of variance; in the same way, the communication-persuasion matrix calls attention to important factors in designing attitude-change programs that otherwise might be forgotten. For example, the question might arise of how being distracted while reading a communication could affect attitude change; if one concentrated upon the yielding component, the prediction probably would be that opinion change is facilitated, inasmuch as the distraction interferes with the subject's tendency to counterargue. However, distraction also should lower the probabilities of attention and comprehension. The resultant effect on attitude change would then depend upon whether more was gained from interference with counterarguments than lost by poor reception of the message, yielding the prediction of a nonmonotonic inverted U relation over a wide range of distraction. That is, attitude change should increase with distraction up to some point and then decrease as distraction becomes greater. Furthermore, if the message were simple, the comprehension mediator would play a lesser role in determining the net relation between distraction and attitude change than in situations in which the communication was more complex.

To predict the effects of a particular independent variable in a given case, one must first estimate its effect upon each of the behavioral steps into which the persuasion process is analyzed and, second, examine the social influence situation (e.g., message complexity).

In other examples, McGuire pointed out that the multitude of studies investigating the effects of various personality variables (e.g., anxiety and self-esteem) upon attitude change have produced a conflicting array of results ranging from strong positive to strong inverse relations. If, rather than focusing upon attitude change or the yielding component, one considered the probable effect of each variable upon attention, comprehension, and, only then, yielding, the confusion might be clarified (McGuire, 1968).

Perhaps the most obvious individual difference variable with which to illustrate the application of the information-processing approach is intelligence. The layman asked to conjecture how intelligence is related to persuasability typically predicts a negative relation on the assumption that the more intelligence people have, the more difficult it will be to persuade them because they will have more arguments in support of their beliefs, will be better able to see the flaws in the opposition's arguments, will have greater self-confidence, and so on. Although all these conjectures may be true, they focus upon the yielding step in the process and ignore the others. When attention is turned to the reception components, it is clear that intelligent people should comprehend the message more adequately. The positive relation of intelligence and comprehension tends to enhance susceptibility to persuasion. Again, the net effects of a wide range of intelligence upon attitude change should be non-monotonic in the form of an inverted U with the greatest change occurring among people in the intermediate range. The point of the curve's inflection, the level of intelligence at which maximum persuasion occurs, depends upon the relative variance in reception and yielding in the particular situation. That is, if the message is very simple, maximum change is reached at a lower level of intelligence than in the case of a complex, difficult communication.

Situations also differ greatly in leeway for individual differences in yielding. If people understand the position being advocated in a physics lecture, for example, it is highly probable that they will accept it. On the other hand, if the issue is a heated political campaign, individuals may understand the arguments perfectly and still not accept the position; indeed, a boomerang effect would not be surprising. The more arguments presented and understood the more negative people would become (Dean, Austin, & Watts, 1971).

In one of the clearest confirmations of the theory, Zellner (1970) predicted and found that higher levels of self-esteem were associated with maximum attitude change as one went from conditions of suggestibility to conformity and then to persuasability. She reasoned that self-esteem would be positively related to message reception but inversely to yielding. Therefore, as the situation placed greater demands upon reception, going from minimum in the case of suggestibility, to maximum for persuasability involving relatively complex messages, the optimum level of self-esteem should increase. The results accorded with predictions, including the mediating variable—reception—which correlated with opinion change: $r = .22$ in the suggestion situation, .34 in the conformity induction, and .38 in the persuasion condition. Furthermore, reception was positively related to self-esteem.

Not all studies have shown the predicted relation with the mediating variable of reception. For example, Millman (1968) successfully predicted an interaction effect between levels of chronic and acute (manipulated) anxiety on opinion change, based upon their presumed influence upon comprehension, only to find that they had no effect. These results are disconcerting because the information-processing theories are based upon reception as a mediating variable in the opinion-change process. Yet, across many studies, the correlations between various measures of comprehension and attitude change tend to be weak and inconsistent (McGuire, 1966, 1968, 1972). This state of affairs led Greenwald (1969) to hypothesize that it is not comprehension of the factual material per se that is important but, rather, what he called "recipient generated cognitions"; that is, the idiosyncratic thoughts and evaluations that are aroused by the communication. It is clear that some degree of message comprehension is a necessary prerequisite for attitude change to occur; the questions are how much and which aspects of the communiqué are most important. These ambiguities need to be clarified, and further basic research should be done on the relation between comprehension and attitude change (e.g., Eagly, 1974) before one can apply this theory with confidence.

Although it is unlikely that in most programs concerned with handicapped persons such detailed information about the respondents' personality characteristics would be available to the investigator, the main value of this approach is to increase awareness of the complexity of the attitude-change process. This is not to say that it is impossible, for, as Lehman (1970) showed in a naturalistic setting, one can assess the personality characteristics of an audience and tailor the messages accordingly to maximize both attitude and behavioral changes in difference subgroups.

Theories of Consistency

Beginning with Fritz Heider (1946), a number of psychologists have developed theories that propose the basic tenet that people strive to maintain consistency among their beliefs, attitudes, and behavior. The drive for consistency is assumed to be a motivating factor, so that when inconsistency is introduced or made salient, people change one or more components to regain consistency. Although numerous consistency theories have been advanced (see Abelson, Aronson, McGuire, Newcomb, Rosenberg, & Tannenbaum, 1968), for the sake of space, only Festinger's (1957) theory of cognitive dissonance is discussed here.

Dissonance theory has probably inspired far more research than all other consistency theories combined. Dissonance occurs whenever an individual simultaneously holds two cognitions (ideas, beliefs, opinions) which are psychologically inconsistent. Because dissonance is an unpleasant motivational state, people strive to reduce it through a cognitive reorganization that may involve adding consonant cognitions or changing one or both opinions. To use Festinger's example, if a person believes that cigarette smoking causes cancer and knows that he himself smokes cigarettes, he experiences dissonance. Aronson (1968) discussed the range of tactics which the person might employ to reduce this dissonance. The most direct but difficult way to reduce dissonance in such a situation is to stop smoking. Barring this, there are several ways in which an individual might justify continuing to smoke. He might belittle the evidence linking cigarette smoking to cancer or associate with other cigarette smokers ("If Sam, Jack, and Harry smoke, then it can't be very dangerous"). He might smoke only filter-tipped cigarettes and delude himself that the filter traps the cancer-producing materials; or he might convince himself that smoking is an important and highly pleasurable activity and that a shorter but more enjoyable life is preferable. All these behaviors reduce dissonance, in effect, by lessening the absurdity involved in smoking when it has been shown to cause cancer. The numerous possible ways of reducing dissonance often create problems with testing the theory (see subsequent discussion).

Classic examples of research include postdecision dissonance in which, after making a choice between two or more objects to purchase, the person usually enhances the qualities of the chosen alternative and derogates those of the rejected one. In this case, dissonance arises from all the positive characteristics of the rejected alternatives which are lost; it can be reduced, however, by enhancing the chosen object, such as by reading advertisements that extol its virtues. Dissonance theory is differentiated from the earlier conflict theory in this case by predicting that changes in evaluation will occur after, rather than prior to, the decision.

Another common example of dissonance is liking something as a function of effort expenditure. For example, if persons work harder to accomplish something or undergo more severe initiations to gain admission to clubs or fraternities, they should evaluate the accomplishment more positively to reduce the dissonance that would arise from working so hard for something that is of little value (Aronson & Mills, 1959).

Similarly, if a person does something against his or her private beliefs, as in counterattitudinal advocacy, dissonance should occur; the magnitude of the dissonance should be inversely related to the degree of incentive or justification for acting. That is, the justification provides strong cognitions consonant with performing the counterattitudinal act and thereby avoids arousal of dissonance (Festinger & Carlsmith, 1959).

The range of dissonance studies greatly exceeds these examples (see Brehm & Cohen, 1962; or Wicklund & Brehm, 1976). Aronson (1968) and others (e.g., Chapanis & Chapanis, 1964) have pointed out a number of problems in the theory. It is psychological rather than logical inconsistency that is important; consequently, no clear, unequivocal rules can be applied in determining inconsistency. As a rule of thumb, Aronson suggested that dissonance is aroused when the cognition violates a strong expectancy.

Another problem is that a person may use multiple modes of resolving inconsistencies (e.g., smoking cigarettes), and the best attempts to block off alternative modes of dissonance reduction may fail. Thus, measuring one mode of reduction may be analogous to counting the people exiting from one door of a burning building.

Inconsistency is said to arise between two cognitive elements if, considering them separately, the opposite of one emanates from the other. However, in most situations, two cognitions are seldom evaluated by themselves. Consequently, two cognitions, when taken in the abstract, which would appear to arouse dissonance, may fail to do so because of the existence of a neutralizing underlying cognition. For example, a counterattitudinal position taken in the context of a formal debate would not induce dissonance because it is clearly understood by both the speakers and audience that the debaters' statements may not necessarily reflect their personal views on the topic at issue. Thus, the rules of debating provide an underlying cognition that prevents the arousal of dissonance.

Underlying most dissonance predictions is the idea that the person has a positive self-concept. Thus, telling a lie for a small reward would not be dissonant for a pathological liar or a person high in Machiavellianism who believes that lying is a central part of life (Epstein, 1969). Indeed, Aronson (1968) suggested that, in the Festinger and Carlsmith (1959) study, dissonance is not aroused between the cognitions "I believe the task is dull" and "I told someone the task was interesting"; rather, the perception that "I am a decent truthful human being" is dissonant with awareness of having misled someone.

Another problem with dissonance studies is that the variables manipulated have usually been quite complex. Thus, it is difficult to ascertain just what aspect of the manipulation produces the obtained effect. Furthermore, Chapanis and Chapanis (1964) criticized dissonance studies for their sloppy methodology. It is true that there is greater subject self-selection in these studies than in many areas of psychology, but it is probably unavoidable to some extent because the typical experiment involves "conning" subjects into doing something against their wishes while maintaining the illusion that they are doing it of their own volition. Indeed, the results of many studies may be due to the subjects' having their defenses aroused because they were being "conned," rather than their experiencing dissonance. For example, Yale students were requested to write essays arguing in favor of police on campus although they were adamantly opposed to the intrusion. In a high-choice condition, most students probably would have written against using police on campus. The experimenter's job was to convince the students to write the counterattitudinal essays while maintaining the perception of choice. Most students agreed to write in favor of police, but probably only after feeling very defensive and foolish for being conned into doing something against their wills when all they had to do was say no. This places a different perspective on Aronson's self-concept interpretation because now the "dissonance" results from the self-perception of actually being a person of principle who is relatively independent, and the cognition of allowing oneself to be conned into doing something against one's beliefs. In short, the question is one raised many years ago (Deutsch, Krauss, & Rosenau, 1962): Is it dissonance or defensiveness?

Functional Theories

In this point of view, best exemplified by Katz (1960) and Smith, Bruner, and White (1956), the position is that if you want to change attitudes or even understand them, you must know what function they serve. Different opinions serve various functions and the same attitudes may serve one or several, depending on the individual. On the basis of an intensive clinical study, Smith, Bruner, and White (1956) offered three broad functions served by attitudes and opinions: object appraisal, social adjustment, and externalization (or ego defense). Because Katz (1960) elaborated four functions that encompass the preceding ones in greater detail, they are discussed here instead.

Attitudes Serving the Instrumental, Objective, or Utilitarian Function

This function is based upon the utility of the attitudinal object in need of satisfaction; it is best exemplified in behavioristic learning theory. The attitudes are aimed at maximizing external rewards and minimizing punishments. To change such attitudes, one changes the person's evaluation of the goal to which they are instrumental or the person's perception of their instrumentality to that goal. Carlson (1956) demonstrated the effectiveness of these approaches to attitude change.

The Ego Function

This function refers to the case in which attitudes protect the person from acknowledging basic truths about himself or herself or about the harsh realities of the external world. Attitudes are developed as protection against internal conflict and external dangers. Mere presentation of new information about the attitudinal object, promising rewards, or invoking penalities would be relatively ineffective in changing these attitudes inasmuch as they frequently would further threaten the person and arouse anxieties, thus feeding ego-defensive behavior. The attitudes may be susceptible to change by removing the threats and providing catharsis and self-insight.

The Value-Expressive Function

The person derives satisfaction from expressing attitudes appropriate to his or her personal values and self-concept. Attitudes originate through maintaining self-identity, enhancing favorable self-image, self-expression, and self-determination. Two conditions are relevant to changing value-expressive attitudes: (a) Some degree of dissatisfaction with one's self-concept, or its associated values, is necessary. This dissatisfaction can result from failures or from the inadequacy of one's values in preserving a favorable image of oneself in a changing world. (b) Dissatisfaction with old attitudes which are inappropriate to one's values also can lead to change. The impetus to change may stem from new experiences or the suggestions of other people.

The Knowledge Function

The individual has a need to give adequate structure to the universe. Attitudes help people to simplify and understand the highly complex universe and to provide meaningful cognitive organization, consistency, and clarity to their views of the world. Attitudes serving this function should be particularly amenable to change when new information is communicated to individuals, or when they have new experiences with an attitude object.

Relatively few studies have been conducted specifically to test the functional approach; they have focused heavily upon the ego-defense function, which is probably the most interesting and nonobvious, and used racial attitudes and authoritarianism as the dependent variables. In all cases, the predictions were that subjects who were intermediate in ego-defense mechanisms would be more influenced by a self-insight approach than their counterparts who were high and low in this respect. It was assumed that subjects who were high in ego defense would be unaffected by the single treatment because it would threaten them and raise their anxieties; and subjects scoring low would hold their prejudiced views for other, non-ego-defense, reasons. Thus, for example, if low-defense subjects held their prejudiced views to conform to group norms, or because of a lack of information, providing self-insight on the relation between emotions and prejudice would be irrelevant.

47

The results of these studies (Katz, McClintock, & Sarnoff, 1957; Katz, Sarnoff, & McClintock, 1956; McClintock, 1958; Stotland, Katz, & Patchen, 1959; Stotland & Patchen, 1961) were disappointing in that the predicted relations were obtained in only two (Katz et al., 1957; McClintock, 1958), and, in the first study, only when using certain measures of ego defense. Four different measures were used by Katz et al. (1957): two TAT cards; a sentence-completion test; the Paranoia Scale of the MMPI, and items from the (California) F Scale; the expected relation was obtained only with the latter two. Furthermore, Stotland and Patchen (1961) later used the same F Scale items but did not find the predicted relation. It is quite likely that a major problem lies in the assessment of ego-defensiveness; thus Smith (1969) was led to conclude, "Here, difficulties in assessing motivation combine with those inherent in the study of attitudes to make clear-cut results difficult to obtain" (p. 95).

Despite the empirical problems in testing the theory, it is of considerable heuristic value and particularly relevant to changing attitudes toward handicapped students. Since many classes of handicapped persons are particularly distinguishable subgroups of the population, they would appear, as in the case of racial minorities, to be good targets for prejudice based upon ego-defense needs. Furthermore, teachers and students are likely to experience anxiety and to feel threatened in interactions with handicapped children; this state of affairs is one that presumably arouses ego-defense attitudes. Indeed, it is the dynamic quality of ego-defense attitudes that makes them particularly dangerous because they can be triggered by events that have no logical or direct connection (e.g., sexual frustration presumably can increase prejudice).

Belief in a Just World

One particularly interesting function served by attitudes toward the handicapped is what Lerner (1965, 1971) called the belief in a just world. Although this topic has been covered in Chapter Two in relation to attitude formation, its implications for opinion change are worth noting here:

> People have a need to believe they live in a just world—a world in which deserving people are rewarded and the undeserving are appropriately deprived or punished. Given this need, the awareness of someone who is suffering through no fault of his own creates a conflict for the observer. The observer can either decide that the world is not so just after all or go through the effort of persuading himself that the "innocent" victim actually merited his suffering. One relatively comfortable way the observer can resolve this conflict is by deciding that the victim, though innocent by deed, deserves his fate by virtue of his undesirable personal attributes. (Lerner, 1971, p.127)

It seems probable that the same process would operate in the observer's responses to handicapped victims who, in most cases, clearly have done nothing to deserve their fates. Thus, in many cases, negative attitudes toward handicapped persons may represent the "just world phenomenon"; and, if so, further information about the merits of the handicapped would simply threaten the observer to a greater extent inasmuch as it would increase his perception of injustice. Rather, it appears to be a case in which providing self-insight (in a nonthreatening manner) into the mechanisms operating would be more effective in reducing the negative attitudes. Incidentally, this theory also might explain the overly solicitous behavior that is often observed among people in close contact with handicapped individuals—because if they perceive themselves as "helping others," the "just world" discomfort is reduced.

TECHNIQUES OF CHANGING ATTITUDES

Persuasive Communications

No doubt the most common method of attempting to change attitudes is to present new information through persuasive messages. The literature on the topic is voluminous. Although the landmark text is Hovland, Janis, and Kelly (1953), the best resources probably are McGuire (1969) and Fishbein and Ajzen (1975).

Source Effects

Kelman (1961) suggested three components of source valence: credibility, attractiveness, and power. In turn, these components are associated with attitude change via three different psychological processes—*internalization*, *identification*, and *compliance*. Internalization is present when the person privately tends to manifest an attitude change in his or her verbal report or behavior even when the original source of the message has been forgotten or changed to a new position. Here, the credibility of the source is of major importance. Identification refers to the receiver's desire to establish a gratifying role relation with the source, either in actuality or fantasy; the motivation is primarily induced by the attractiveness of the source. Compliance involves public acquiescence to the attitude advocated by the source but without private commitment to it; dependence upon power over the receiver is a means to attaining desirable goals.

Of the three, source credibility has been most extensively studied and the results have been fairly consistent. When sources are purportedly expert on a topic, more attitude change is obtained, apparently because the receiver is more willing to yield to the expert's opinion. Messages from neutral or unvalenced sources are better learned than those attributed to high- or low-credibility sources but produce only an intermediate amount of opinion change. Perhaps it is only when a person is unable to evaluate the source that he must analyze the arguments himself.

49

Fear Arousal

In an early study, Janis and Feshback (1953) varied the extent of fear-arousing information on tooth decay in messages concerning proper dental care. With three levels of fear arousal, they found that the greatest reported change in tooth-brushing practices, a week later, was for the low-fear condition, and the least change was for the high fear condition. They interpreted these provocative findings in terms of defensive avoidance reactions in the high-fear condition. Subsequent studies seldom found this inverse relation (Higbee, 1969; McGuire, 1969) but, instead, generally showed that strong-fear appeals produced more attitude change than weak ones. McGuire (1969) proposed a nonmonotonic inverted U relation between intensity of fear arousal and attitude change based upon a two-factor analysis of anxiety. As a drive, anxiety should tend to increase the probability of the opinion-change response; as a cue, it should tend to elicit responses such as avoidance and aggression that would interfere with the opinion-change process. Therefore, an overall nonmonotonic relation between anxiety and opinion change should occur (assuming that one has varied fear levels over a wide range) with an optimal intermediate level of fear arousal. A nonmonotonic theory, such as that proposed, also implies a number of interaction effects with situational and individual difference variables. For example, higher levels of fear arousal should be optimal for subjects who are low, as compared to high, in chronic anxiety. Several studies (Leventhal & Watts, 1966; Millman, 1968) generally have supported this prediction. Similarly, higher levels of fear should be more efficacious in producing attitude change when they are highly specific and when detailed recommendations are made to reduce the fear (e.g., directions about where to go for a tetanus innoculation, Leventhal, 1970). There is also increasing evidence that various levels of fear have differential effects upon different dependent variables such as attitudes and behavior (Rogers & Thistlethwaite, 1970).

Fishbein and Ajzen (1975) criticized this research for confounding degree of fear with message content; hence, differential persuasion may be attributable to variances in the information provided rather than to levels of fear arousal. Similarly, Higbee (1969), in his excellent review of fear-appeals research, pointed out a number of problems, including ambiguities, in the sources of fear.

Discrepancy of Position Advocated

It is of considerable practical importance to know how discrepant the position advocated by the source should be from the receiver's initial opinion for the message to have maximum persuasive impact. We have two competing points of view on this issue: one is a straightforward discrepancy hypothesis that states that the more change requested, the greater the amount will be obtained; the other is a prediction of a nonmonotonic relation in which the greatest change occurs for intermediate discrepancies. The majority of studies indicate that the amount of obtained change is a negatively accelerated, increasing function of the discrepancy between the receiver and the messengers' positions, at least up to rather extreme instances (Brehm & Lipsher, 1959; Hovland & Pritzker, 1957). On the other hand, in the case of extreme discrepancies, a decline in opinion change, predicted by the nonmonotonic theories, sets in (Bochner & Insko, 1966; Fisher & Lubin, 1958).

Aronson, Turner, and Carlsmith (1963) reasoned, from the standpoint of dissonance theory, that the subject may make at least two responses in a persuasive situation: change opinion or derogate the source. They predicted, and found, as did Bochner and Insko (1966), that with highly reliable sources, the point of the curve's inflection comes at greater discrepancies, if at all, than for less reliable sources, which tend to be easily derogated when their positions appear too extreme. Unfortunately, Rhine and Severence (1970) and Eagly (1974) failed to find interactions between source credibility and discrepancy.

Subject involvement with the issue has also been used in attempting to reconcile inconsistent findings. To the extent that involvement refers to the subject's commitment to his initial opinion, there is some evidence that as involvement increases, the effects of highly discrepant messages decrease (Freedman, 1964; Rhine & Severence, 1970); but this finding has not been universal (Rule & Renner, 1968).

Drawing the Conclusion vs. Leaving it Implicit

A number of studies have sought to demonstrate that persuasive messages produce more attitude change if the conclusion is left for the reader or hearer to draw for himself. This hypothesis was inspired by similar views in psychotherapy. Paradoxically, most studies find the opposite: Explicitly drawing the conclusion leads to greater change than leaving the reader or hearer to infer the conclusion (Hovland & Mandel, 1952; Thistlethwaite, deHaan, & Kamenetsky, 1955). The problem appears to be that most subjects are insufficiently intelligent or motivated to draw the conclusion and, consequently, they miss the main point of the message.

Refuting vs. Ignoring Opposition Arguments

Hovland, Lumsdaine, and Sheffield (1949) found that for those members of the audience who were initially favorable, ignoring the opposition was more advantageous; for those who were initially opposed to the conclusion, mentioning and refuting the arguments was somewhat superior. There was also an interaction with intelligence, such that refuting the opposition was more effective for those with high intelligence and ignoring it better for people low in intelligence. McGuire (1969) speculated upon a number of conditions that would favor ignoring the oppositions' arguments: Mentioning the arguments in order to refute them might suggest to the receiver reservations about the conclusions that he or she would not otherwise have; rather than demonstrating the source's objectivity, it may indicate that the issue is controversial and the source has a persuasive intent; presenting the opposition's arguments, even to refute them, may put the receiver in a conflict situation; and, initially mentioning these arguments might cause the receiver to switch sides, thus producing defensive avoidance of the later supportive arguments.

Forewarning of Persuasive Intent

A number of studies have investigated various aspects of forewarning of persuasive intent. The effects of forewarning have been of interest from both theoretical and practical standpoints. With the recent rise in consciousness about the ethics of research, and the consequent concern about deception in studies of opinion change (e.g., saying that the study investigates learning, information processing, etc.), the question of the feasibility of simply telling subjects that one is studying opinion change has been raised.

There are at least three theoretical reasons for expecting forewarning to reduce the immediate impact of persuasive messages: (a) Forewarning may lead subjects to think of counterarguments either before or while reading the communication (McGuire & Papageorgis, 1962; Petty & Cacioppo, 1977). (b) Forewarning may arouse psychological reactance (Brehm, 1966; Hass & Grady, 1975): that is, the subjects' freedom of choice in evaluating the content is impinged upon, thus arousing reactance. (c) Finally, forewarning may cause the subjects to perceive the communicator as less fair and unbiased (Dean, Austin, & Watts, 1971; Hass & Grady, 1975). Although the majority of studies have found an inhibiting effect in forewarning, a few have found positive effects, particularly in cases of anticipatory belief change (McGuire & Millman, 1965), in which the subjects' opinions are measured after the forewarning but prior to receiving the persuasive messages.

Regardless of the immediate effects, Watts and Holt (1979) found in two studies that after a week's time the initial differences disappeared and forewarned subjects showed a delayed-action "sleeper effect" that brought them up to the same level as subjects who were not forewarned.

Distraction

One might conceive of distraction and forewarning as being at opposite ends of a continuum, ranging from the blatant announcement that the investigator is attempting to persuade the subjects to disguised persuasion in which the study is passed off as one of comprehension or some such thing in the general area and distraction at the other end. In the latter case, typically, not only is no mention made of persuasion, but subjects are also distracted in one way or another to minimize their tendencies to think of counterarguments. Whereas forewarning has been shown to facilitate the production of counterarguments, distraction apparently interferes with the subject's ability to think of them (Baron, Baron, & Miller, 1973; Petty, Wells, & Brock, 1976). Therefore, distraction should influence positively the yielding component in persuasion and make the person more susceptible, if the message is adequately comprehended.

However, there is considerable evidence that distraction interferes with comprehension (e.g., Haaland & Venkatesan, 1968; Petty, Wells, & Brock,

1976). Therefore, if distraction increases to the point where the loss in comprehension is too great, a decrease in opinion change should occur because, in the extreme case, one cannot conform to the position advocated in a communication without understanding the side taken. Hence, from a theoretical standpoint (McGuire, 1969; Wyer, 1974), a nonmonotonic relation should prevail with moderate levels of distraction facilitating opinion change. The majority of studies apparently have fallen into this "moderate" realm since most, but not all, have found an immediate facilitating effect of distraction. There is some competition between two theoretical interpretations of the positive effect (Baron, Baron, & Miller, 1973): the pre-mentioned inhibition of counterarguing and a dissonance theory interpretation that claims that the increased effort required to understand the message under conditions of distraction facilitates opinion change.

Indirect Effects of Persuasive Communications

In 1960, Katz claimed that one of the most necessary research areas was the generalization of persuasion. Stated simply, the question is the extent to which the persuasive effects of a message directed toward a specific topic generalize to similar or psychologically related, but unmentioned, issues. A number of studies have consistently shown an indirect persuasive impact of communications on logically related beliefs (Dillehay, Insko, & Smith, 1966; McGuire, 1960; Wyer, 1974) which, as would be expected, is usually considerably smaller than the direct effect. McGuire (1960) suggested that experimental manipulation of the salience of logical relations among beliefs should increase the indirect effects of persuasive communications by disrupting the equilibrium between wishes and reality that appears to characterize a person's cognitive system at any given time and to move it further into the logical reality oriented realm. Furthermore, to the extent that the relations among beliefs are salient, any change in a given belief requires some degree of corresponding change in the interrelated but unmentioned beliefs to maintain a given level of consistency. That is, increasing the salience of the relations reduces the chances of compartmentalization and resulting lack of change on the related beliefs. Several studies (Holt, 1970; Holt & Watts, 1969; Watts & Holt, 1970) have supported the finding by various manipulations of salience which consistently increased the indirect effects of communications. Furthermore, Watts (1978) found that distraction, which should interfere with the person's tendency to think of logically related beliefs, significantly reduced the indirect effects of communications and at the same time increased the direct effects.

Clearly, a person planning an attitude-change program concerned with handicapped persons should be aware of this research, not only to avoid unanticipated consequences in the form of possibly unwanted change in related beliefs, but also because of the anchoring effects that such related beliefs may have upon the target belief. That is, if the specific belief attacked in a persuasive message is interrelated with a number of other beliefs to which the person is committed or, for other reasons, the beliefs are resistant to change, they should serve as anchors for the attacked belief (Holt, 1970; Nelson, 1968) making it resistant to change. Thus, an attitude-change campaign, well designed in other respects, may fail because of the unmentioned anchoring beliefs.

Personal Contact

Most research on the effects of personal interaction upon attitude change has been directed to racial attitudes but there is no apparent reason for the findings not to be applied to handicapped persons. Amir (1969) summarized the conditions necessary for interracial contact to have a positive effect: (a) the members of each group must be of equal status or (b) the members of the minority group must be of higher status than the majority group members; (c) there must be a favorable climate for group interaction; (d) the interaction must be of an intimate rather than casual nature; (e) the interaction must be rewarding and pleasant; and (f) the two groups should have a mutual goal that requires interdependent and cooperative action.

Although the list is demanding and probably seldom met in real-life situations, Cook (1969) created similar conditions in a laboratory setting. Prejudiced White coeds were placed in the position of having to interact with a Black person over a 1-month period. When the White student agreed to participate, she was unaware that one of the other participants was Black. The game required a high degree of cooperation; it provided a basis for fairly close interaction for 2 hours each day on an equal basis, and it had a superordinate goal—winning and earning a bonus. Also, during each 2-hour session, breaks were planned that afforded opportunities for pleasant interracial interaction to allow the Black confederate to establish herself as an individual and, thus, to weaken the subject's racial stereotypes. A comparison of the subjects' racial attitudes before and after the experimental treatments indicated that approximately 40% showed positive changes in attitudes of one standard deviation or more, compared to 12% of an untreated control group of prejudiced women. Although these results are encouraging, it is important to note that 40% of the experimental women showed no change in attitude and approximately 20% became more prejudiced.

Foley (1976) suggested that perhaps 2 hours a day were insufficient to spend together since the subjects then returned to the conflicting norms of a southern city. Consequently, she conducted her study in a maximum security state prison where new inmates were randomly assigned to living quarters (two- and eight-person cells, and dormitories) with the exception of maintaining an equal distribution by race. The status of all participants was equal, and the study expanded on Cook's in that it examined changes in the attitudes of Blacks toward Whites as well as the reverse.

Different geographic locations within an institution tend to develop different norms, which are based on the attitudes of the individuals in the area; these norms should be expected to influence the attitudes of randomly assigned inmates. Indeed, normative data for the three living areas indicated that the regular inmates from the eight-person cells had the most negative attitudes toward interracial interaction, those from the dormitories the most positive, and the two-person cell inmates averaged somewhere in between. The new inmates were assessed on racial prejudice at entrance and again approximately 1 month later. Changes in prejudice over the month directly accorded with the normative attitudes of the groups to which the subjects were assigned. The results indicated a significant main effect for living area and a number of interaction effects involving personality variables.

In an early study of integrated housing that contained many of Amir's (1969) criteria for success, Deutsch and Collins (1951) reported decreased prejudice resulting from the interaction. However, it is difficult to interpret the data because of self-selection in moving into the integrated housing. Thus, the people who moved in voluntarily were probably more open to interracial experiences and more ready to undergo positive attitude change toward Blacks.

Siegel and Siegel (1957), in a naturalistic experiment, demonstrated the influence of group norms upon authoritarian attitudes. It was shown that students who lived in former sorority houses were considerably more authoritarian than their counterparts who lived elsewhere. A unique characteristic of the school was that all students who wanted to live in these houses drew numbers from a pool in a random selection process until the open places were filled. Thus, the investigators found a naturalistic setting, with the crucial random assignment to conditions built in, where the effects of living in different membership groups for a year could be examined. At the end of the year, the students who had not gained entry to the former sorority housing had decreased in authoritarianism significantly more than those who had lived in these houses. Furthermore, the effects of reference groups could be examined correlationally because, at the beginning of the following year, all students again had the opportunity of drawing for this housing. The investigators reasoned that those students who drew numbers again had maintained the same reference groups during the year that they had lived elsewhere, whereas those who no longer were interested in moving into the former sorority houses had presumably changed their reference groups. As expected, the data indicated that students who had changed their reference group showed greater reduction in authoritarianism than the ones who had maintained the original, more authoritarian, reference group. Numerous other studies have examined the effects of group norms upon the attitudes of their members and the results have generally been positive. Hence, we can hope that mainstreaming will result in more favorable attitudes toward handicapped students, providing the conditions are optimal.

Role Playing

Although much research has focused upon the attitudinal effects of role playing and counterattitudinal advocacy, one of the most directly relevant studies was conducted by Clore and Jeffrey (1972). It is described here in some detail to illustrate technique. Clore and Jeffrey used three conditions (role playing, vicarious role playing, and a control) to study changes in attitude toward handicapped persons. Students from an introductory psychology course were randomly assigned to the three conditions. The role players were told to imagine that they had recently been in automobile accidents which had severed

55

the lower part of their spinal cords, leaving their legs permanently paralyzed. They were asked to pretend that it was the first day back on campus after the accident. Each person was then asked to take a 25-minute wheelchair trip that included 100 yards of slightly uphill sidewalk, four elevator rides, several ramps and doors, and a complicated procedure for buying a cup of coffee.

Vicarious role players were instructed to walk behind the role players at a distance of 20 feet. They were fully informed about the roles the others were playing and they were asked to observe the role players' experiences but not to interact in any way, ride in the same elevator, or help them. Control subjects were asked to spend an equivalent amount of time walking around the campus and having a cup of coffee at a different location.

A number of dependent measures were taken, including affective and attitude scales; an attraction measure for the experimenter (who appeared to be confined to a wheelchair); volunteering a month after the experiment to help show handicapped prospective students around the campus; and a delayed attitude questionnaire given 4 months later. Role players had changed significantly compared to the control group on all measures except one of the four affective rating scales and volunteering to show a disabled student around campus. In the last measure, considerably more of the role players (63%) and vicarious role players (68%) volunteered than those persons in the group control (42%), but the difference did not reach significance. Interestingly, on most measures the vicarious role players changed almost as much as their role-playing counterparts.

The study demonstrates the dramatic effects of emotional role playing upon individuals' attitudes. The delayed effects are particularly impressive, inasmuch as they were obtained by telephone poll 4 months after the experiment, during a different semester, and in a context in which it was extremely unlikely that the respondents would connect the telephone poll with the previous experiment: the critical item was one of four directed to the expenditure of student funds. The authors favor an empathy interpretation of their data rather than dissonance reduction, because the vicarious role players responded so similarly to the actual role players.

In contrast to Clore and Jeffrey's findings of striking similarity between role players and vicarious role players, an earlier study by Culbertson (1957) found that a much greater percentage of role-playing subjects changed attitudes toward Blacks than of observers who merely listened to the discussion and were instructed to associate with assigned role players. It should be noted, however, that both role players and observers became significantly more favorable than untreated controls who only provided opinion data. As Fishbein and Ajezen (1975) pointed out, the discrepancy between the two studies may be due to the fact that in the Culbertson study role players actively generated information while the observers passively listened, whereas in the Clore and Jeffrey study, the roles of the two groups were more similar. Indeed, improvisation was suggested by King and Janis as early as 1956 as a necessary condition for active participation (role playing) to increase attitude change.

In a different context (cigarette smoking), Janis and Mann (1965), Mann (1967), and Mann and Janis (1968) reported that emotional role playing by a patient who had just learned that he had developed lung cancer and, consequently, could expect painful illness, hospitalization, and early death was much more effective in producing both immediate and delayed (18 months) reduction in smoking than merely listening to a tape recording of one of the experimental sessions.

However, Fishbein and Ajzen (1975) noted that different information was available to subjects in the role-playing and control conditions in these studies. For example, Janis and Mann exposed all control subjects to the same tape recording of a single role-playing session selected for its exceptional "dramatic and emotional quality." However, it is virtually certain that if another role-playing session had been recorded the control subjects would have been exposed to different information. A better procedure would have been to use Fishbein and Ajzen's "yoked" controls whereby each person would have observed a different role-playing session. It seems far more likely that Janis and Mann used a conservative strategy rather than one that would have maximized differences; that is, it appears that listening to "the best" role-playing sessions would have resulted in more change among the controls than if each individual had been exposed to a different session. At any rate, the importance of role players and controls having identical information cannot be overemphasized.

A possible source of bias in most of the studies, which would favor active participation, is the heavy use of introductory psychology students. It seems reasonable that psychology students, as a group, are more empathetic than the population at large; since empathic fantasy ability has been shown to facilitate opinion change through active participation (Elms, 1966; Matefy, 1972), the obtained results may be more supportive of role playing. Furthermore, the great preponderance of college students used as subjects probably indicates that the average IQ of the participants in these studies was well above the general population; this variable is positively related to opinion change through active participation when appreciable improvisation is required (Watts, 1973, 1977). Despite these criticisms, the technique appears to be valid; more interestingly, it has been shown to work in studies involving disabled persons.

Counterattitudinal Behavior

This area represents a reversal of the usual format in which information is presented in an attempt to change the recipient's attitude, with the hope that a behavioral modification will ensue. Festinger's (1957) theory of cognitive dissonance provided the impetus for a wave of studies on the effects of counterattitudinal behavior. According to this theory, if a person behaves in a manner inconsistent with his or her private beliefs or attitudes, a state of dissonance is aroused which is psychologically unpleasant and, in turn, provides the motivational impetus reduction through various modes, one of which is attitude change. Festinger reasoned that dissonance would be greater when subjects performed counterattitudinal behavioral tasks for small, rather than large, payments or under mild, rather than strong, negative sanctions, since each condition provided adequate justification for the behavior. In a classic experiment, Festinger and Carlsmith (1959) varied the incentives for telling lies. All subjects, male undergraduates, performed two boring and repetitive

57

tasks for approximately 30 minutes. Afterward, the control subjects were led to another room where a different person interviewed them on how interesting and enjoyable the tasks had been. In the experimental conditions, the subjects were told that the investigator's assistant could not come today and another student was already waiting to take part in the experiment. The experimenter then offered to hire the subjects to perform the role of assistant for either $1 or $20. The experimenter introduced them to the waiting female subject, who was actually his confederate, and, in accordance with instructions, the subject attempted to convince the confederate that the experimental tasks were interesting and enjoyable. Then the subjects, like those in the control group, were interviewed in a different context. As predicted, subjects in the $1 condition thought the tasks were more interesting and enjoyable than those who had been paid $20, presumably because of the dissonance aroused by the unjustifiable telling of lies.

Cohen (1962) extended the range of payments to $10, $5, $1, and 50 cents and, in an unpublished study, to 5 cents, causing McGuire (1966) to comment that there was room for one more dissertation in the area if green stamps could be used as incentives for counterattitudinal essays. Again, in accord with dissonance theory, an inverse relation was obtained between amount paid and the degree to which the subjects changed their beliefs in the direction of the position advocated.

Many similar studies have followed that examined a range of behaviors. For example, army recruits were induced to eat fried grasshoppers and they rated them as more tasty (Smith, 1961); children prohibited from playing with an attractive toy under conditions of mild threats devalued it more, following a temptation-resistance period, than the children who were severely threatened (Freedman, 1965). The somewhat mixed results led to the refinement and elaboration of different variables that should interact with reward or coercion.

Fishbein and Ajzen (1975) summarized a list of requirements, each assumed to be a necessary but not sufficient condition for the arousal of dissonance. Subjects must commit themselves to perform the counterattitudinal tasks with full awareness of the kind of reward they are to receive (if any); they must do so voluntarily with a maximum of subjective decision freedom; they must feel personally responsible for the aversive consequences of their behavior, which must violate an expectancy related to the self-concept; and it must be impossible for this behavior to be considered justifiable under any circumstances. They concluded, rather negatively, that even when investigators have attempted to meet all these conditions, the dissonance effect has not always been observed; more important, if all these requirements are accepted as necessary, it is doubtful that any situation can be found in which dissonance plays an important role in determining social behavior.

An exact opposite conclusion was reached by Varela (1971) who enthusiastically and, presumably, effectively applied dissonance theory principles to industrial situations (e.g., passing over a man for promotion; selling standardized window shades in Uruguay where no two windows are the same size). However, in Varela's work, it is somewhat difficult to separate the extent to which the results are due to dissonance theory or his own charisma. When Wicklund and Brehm (1976) reviewed the research in dissonance theory, they came out on a more positive note, perhaps because Brehm was one of the early disciples of the theory.

A number of problems arise in applying dissonance theory to any particular situation. One of the more difficult is selecting the appropriate magnitude of reward (or punishment): If too much of either is administered, no change can be expected; that is, the justification for certain behavior would be quite adequate if, for example, one's life were at stake. On the other hand, if too little reward is promised, a boomerang effect may occur as the subjects justify their decision not to perform the requested task.

One of the impressive aspects of the studies of counterattitudinal behavior is that the change appears to last for considerable time. For example, Freedman (1965) found that after time periods ranging from 23 to 64 days, virtually all the children's initial devaluations of the forbidden toy had persisted. However, in a series of studies, Nuttin (1975) and his colleagues found that the near-total persistence occurs only when the subjects have been post-tested immediately after the experimental treatment.

Bem (1967) argued persuasively and demonstrated, in several simulation experiments, that the obtained dissonance effects in the forced-compliance and role-playing studies can be interpreted more parsimoniously in terms of attribution theory. Thus, if a person observed another doing an onerous task for little payment, he would infer that for some reason the particular individual must find the task enjoyable. Bem argued that people basically make inferences about their own actions in the same way, that is, "I must like brown bread because I'm always eating it," or, to paraphrase H. L. Mencken, "I don't know what I think until I hear what I say."

Dissonance theorists have countered with the argument that an observer is in a very different situation in that he or she does not know the subject's original attitude, whereas, to the degree that it is at all salient, the subject has this advantage. Nisbett, Caputo, Legant, and Marcecek (1973) have shown that people make quite different inferences about the causes of their own behavior as compared to that of someone they are observing. Regardless of which interpretation is correct, from a practical standpoint, considerable research indicates that counterattitudinal behavior can be an effective way to induce attitude change.

Socratic Methods and Value Confrontation

McGuire (1960) and others (Henninger & Wyer, 1976; Holt & Watts, 1969; Rosen & Wyer, 1972) demonstrated the "Socratic" method of persuasion whereby a person's opinions are changed through the mere process of answering a questionnaire and, thus, becoming aware of inconsistencies. For example, a person might be asked to rate his belief in the three following statements: (a) "When traffic congestion increases there is a marked rise in the incidence of deaths caused by lung cancer." (b) "Traffic congestion in the Bay Area is becoming worse." (c) "There will be increases in death from lung cancer in the Bay Area." Once the inconsistencies have become salient they are resolved through changes in opinion. Although not all studies have found evidence for this process (e.g., Watts & Holt, 1970; Dillehay et al., 1966), the preponderance have; this fact is provocative enough to warrant serious consideration.

Whereas the Socratic method induces opinion change through subtly making people aware of inconsistencies among their beliefs or opinions in the process of answering questions, Rokeach's (1971, 1973) value confrontation approach exposes people to information designed to make them consciously aware of the states of inconsistency that chronically exist within their value-attitude systems, below the level of conscious awareness. When individuals become aware of previously existing contradictions or inconsistencies between their values and self-conception, they should reorganize their value systems. Furthermore, since values are presumably dynamically related to behavior, such reorganizations should lead to some form of value-related behavior change.

In a typical study, Rokeach had subjects rank 18 terminal values, such as freedom, mature love, and a world at peace, in terms of personal importance. Then the experimental subjects were shown the average rank ordering made by a large sampling of fellow students, with freedom ranked first and equality 11th. To arouse feelings of self-dissatisfaction, the experimenter interpreted these findings to mean that students, in general, are much more interested in their own freedom than that of others. Subjects were then invited to compare their rankings with those in the table. To increase dissatisfaction, subjects were asked to state their degree of sympathy with Civil Rights demonstrations. Immediately afterward, they were shown a table that displayed a strong positive relation between attitudes toward Civil Rights demonstrations and values given to equality. The experimenter interpreted the significance as follows: "This raises the question as to whether those who are against Civil Rights are really saying that they care a great deal about their own freedom, but are indifferent to other people's freedoms. Those who are for Civil Rights are perhaps really saying that they not only want freedom for themselves, but for other people as well" (pp.). Once again, subjects compared their own rankings with results shown in the table.

The results indicated long-term changes in the rankings of equality and freedom among experimental subjects but little change among controls. Attitudes of the experimental group toward equal rights for Blacks had improved significantly at the delayed testing (3-5 months and 15-17 months), but not for the short-term (3 weeks) testing. Finally, significantly more experimental than control subjects responded favorably to an unobtrusive mailed request to join NAACP, and they enrolled in an ethnic core program in the college. The results were much stronger for subjects who had reported dissatisfaction with their rankings. Using a path analysis of Rokeach's (1973) original data, Grube, Greenstein, Rankin, and Kearny (1977) argued that the primary source of behavior change, after self-confrontation, is awareness of inconsistencies between behavior and self-conception, rather than mediation through values. Rokeach's data revealed that the method primarily affected the behavior of participants whose previous values and attitudes were not inconsistent with an egalitarian self-conception but whose behavior might have been.

In a study directly concerned with education, Greenstein (1976) conducted an experiment in a field setting with teacher trainees at Central Michigan University. During the first week of the teaching program, he administered a pretest questionnaire containing Rokeach's value survey. Approximately 10 days later, during the experimental session, the subjects received a "results summary" containing their own rankings of the 18 terminal values and feedback from 308 student-teachers who had completed the same value scale the previous year. The trainees' attention was focused upon two target values, and they were told approximately the following:

> One of the most interesting findings shown is that the student teachers, on the average, felt that "A Sense of Accomplishment" (ranked a "4") was very important; but that "Mature Love" (ranked as "8") was considerably less important. Apparently, Central Michigan University student teachers value "A Sense of Accomplishment" far more highly than "Mature Love."

The experimenter then invited the student teachers to compare their own rankings with those of the former sample and, after a few minutes, continued by telling the group that the previous year's teachers had been divided into two groups, those considered "good" and the others, "mediocre," as evaluated by their supervisors. It was then pointed out that the rankings were reversed, with the better teachers rating mature love rather highly and placing much less emphasis on a sense of accomplishment. The statement was then made that these data raise the question of whether concern for the problems of others, and the placing of less emphasis on personal achievement, is essential to success as a public school teacher. These data could be interpreted to mean that good teachers value the problems of others above personal gains or advantages.

Students were then invited to compare their own value rankings with those of the "good" and "mediocre" teachers and to discuss the interpretations of the differences. Control subjects were asked to rank the values as they perceived professors of education might; they were then given actual composite ratings made by professors of education in another study and encouraged to take part in a 15-minute discussion.

Thirteen weeks after the treatment session, the post-test was administered and evaluations were made from the recently completed student-teacher rating forms. Post-test differences in the rankings for mature love were as predicted; the experimental subjects ranked it much higher than the controls ($p > .001$). There were no significant differences in the rankings for a sense of accomplishment between the two groups; but this finding appeared to be due to the fact that the pre-test ratings were already consistent with the values of good teachers and, consequently, there was no reason to change. Perhaps the most interesting finding was that teaching evaluation scores were much higher for the experimental than control subjects ($p > .008$).

It is impressive and, indeed, almost incredible that one brief self-confrontation period can have such pronounced and long-term effects. The study is commendable in that it was conducted in a naturalistic setting. The judges (teaching supervisors) were unaware that an experiment was in progress, which ruled out some sources of invalidity. When considered in conjunction with earlier studies (Rokeach, 1971, 1973), the findings show considerable evidence that self-confrontation techniques offer effective and practical means of modifying complex behavior in such areas as racism, smoking, ecology, police-community relations, locus of control, and teaching. Hence, one could reasonably conclude that this method should be effective in modifying behavior toward handicapped persons.

PERSISTENCE OF INDUCED ATTITUDE CHANGE

Assuming that attitudes toward handicapped persons have been successfully changed, temporal persistence becomes a topic of major importance. Ephemeral changes or "elastic shifts in opinion" (Cialdini, Levy, Herman, Kozlowski, & Petty, 1976) would be of little interest because mainstreaming is a relatively long-term procedure and continuous attitude and action sessions would be costly, if not impossible. Furthermore, it is imperative that changes in attitudes persist at least long enough to be reflected in behavioral changes. Of course, if behavioral changes were initially induced, their persistence would be equally important. The most comprehensive review of the literature on this topic is by Cook and Flay (1978).

In the process of discussing several theories and procedures for changing attitudes, comments have been made here about the persistence of the resulting changes. For example, in discussing Rokeach's (1973) self-confrontation method, the studies to date indicate remarkable persistence, in some cases up to 24 months. Similarly, studies of role playing and counterattitudinal behavior have shown long-term changes. Also, some of the research on the modification of ego-defense attitudes through self-insight procedures found a "sleeper effect" wherein delayed changes were greater than immediate ones. Although these studies used a variety of techniques and approaches, they all have one thing in common: personal, active participation. It appears that the one generalization which can be made is that actively, rather than passively, involving persons leads to more long-term attitude change. Watts (1967) specifically studied the persistence of opinion change under conditions of active, compared to passive, participation in a situation in which, through prestudy and alterations of the communications, the immediate effects of the two methods were virtually identical, thus providing ideal conditions for studying temporal persistence. In the active condition, subjects wrote essays arguing in favor of various attitudinal positions; in the passive condition, they read communications taking the same positions that had been modified to produce equivalent immediate change. Greater persistence was predicted for the active group on the basis of more involvement and subsequent thinking about the issues, reading about them, and discussing them with friends. The results showed a "sleeper effect" for the active group whereby the attitude change not only declined less rapidly over time but, also, showed an absolute increase from the immediate-to-delayed measures. This information was related to the extent to which subjects said they had discussed and read additional information about the topic.

In discussing the relatively strong persistence found in these types of studies (consistency-based and behavioral-observation approaches, including role playing), Cook and Flay (1978) enumerated four general factors that seem to have been present when total persistence resulted.

1. Most researchers seem to have presented the subjects with behavioral dilemmas (how do I justify not playing with a toy that I like?) in the resistance-to-temptation studies; discrepancies between values and behavior in Rokeach's studies.
2. Most experiments seem to have generated considerable emotional affect (e.g., Janis & Mann's, 1965, technique of emotionally role-playing a cigarette cancer victim).
3. Most experiments seem to have had a high degree of personal relevance for subjects.
4. There were usually rather obvious ways available for reducing the self-relevant dilemma and its related arousal state.

Before becoming too enamored with the persistence conferred by consistency manipulations, however, it is wise to remember Nuttin's (1975) position that total consistency is induced by forced compliance in dissonance studies of counterattitudinal behavior only when immediate post-tests are given to the same subjects. It would be premature to conclude that such is the case for the full range of consistency studies; indeed, Nuttin dealt only with the forced-compliance design. Nevertheless, caution should be exercised until further data are collected with designs systematically varying the presence or absence of an immediate post-test.

Research concerning the persistence of change induced by persuasive communications has resulted in less consistent findings ranging from complete persistence and, in some cases, sleeper effects, to complete loss over comparable periods of time. In one of the few studies specifically investigating this topic, Watts and McGuire (1964) examined persistence as a function of subject recall of various aspects of the messages immediately afterward and over periods of 1, 2, and 6 weeks. The findings were complex, indicating that ability to recall the most fundamental aspect of the message, the topic, was positively related to immediate change but negatively related to persistence after 6 weeks. Ability to recall the position taken in the message, or its conclusion, was positively related to immediate change and unrelated to persistence, after 6 weeks. Only memory of the specific arguments used in the messages was positively related to change at both the immediate and delayed times of measurement.

In a later study (Watts, 1967), subjects who remembered both topic and side taken in messages read 6 weeks earlier again showed less persistence than their counterparts who failed to recall these aspects of the communications. (In this study, only 14% of the subjects recalled one aspect of the message without the other, so the two measures were combined into a single index.)

On the other hand, in studies in which the conclusion or side taken in a communication was reinstated after the message (Cook & Insko, 1968), or when the conclusion was overlearned by being repeated seven times in the communication, and social support for message acceptance was present (Cook & Wadsworth, 1972), persistence of induced change resulted. Similarly, although the greater immediate changes induced by high-status sources do not last, multiple presentations (Johnson & Watkins, 1971) or the reinstatement of such sources at the time of delayed opinion measurement (Kelman & Hovland, 1953) creates greater persistence. In general, however, there is little evidence that any particular features of the persuasion paradigm are consistently related to persistence. This is not to imply, however, that opinion change induced by communications is completely transitory. On the contrary, many studies found considerable persistence over time, but the dynamics of what variables lead to persistence are not well understood.

CONCLUSIONS

It appears that the most effective procedures for changing attitudes toward handicapped persons is through an active participation method (e.g., role-playing, counterattitudinal advocacy, and value confrontations). This recommendation is supported by the proven effectiveness of these methods and, more important, by the resulting changes which have been relatively permanent. If the ultimate goal is behavioral change resulting from different attitudes, it is imperative that the newly induced opinions be persisent. However, these active-participation methods typically require more time and expense because of the small number of participants who can be accommodated in any given session. Therefore, economic and other practical matters may dictate the influence procedure chosen. If it is necessary to reach large numbers of people, the use of mass media might be advisable.

It should be clear that this chapter is not meant to be a cookbook or "how to do it" manual. Such a text would not be feasible given our current state of knowledge. Rather, it is hoped that the contents have some heuristic value which will suggest possible strategies to test in particular situations. The question arises of the extent to which the findings included in the chapter, mostly from laboratory studies, can be generalized to the natural environment or "real world." Granted that carefully conducted experiments have internal validity, to what extent do they also have external validity or generalizability? In a classic article, Hovland (1959) discussed the differences between experimental and survey studies of attitude change in an attempt to reconcile the conflicting results. Many of his comments are equally appropriate to the question of generalizability of laboratory studies. Hovland pointed out that in laboratory studies the investigator has a captive audience and some degree of attention is guaranteed, thus ruling out the selective-exposure phenomenon that often occurs in naturalistic settings wherein people tend to read only communications with which they are already in agreement. Another important factor is the individual's personal involvement with the particular issue. Laboratory studies typically choose uninvolving issues to assure obtaining some degree of attitude change, whereas surveys and programs about handicapped persons deal with topics high in personal involvement. Consequently, the individual may resist opinion change.

Time of measurement is another factor differentiating laboratory studies from naturalistic settings. In laboratory studies, opinions are most often measured immediately after the influence attempt, when change would be greatest;

in reality, they may be tested weeks after the event. Thus, to the extent that the immediately induced change is ephemeral, surveys or attitude change programs may produce quite different results. A related issue is the amount of post-communication interaction that would usually be minimal in the laboratory study where, after class, students disperse; it could be considerable in attitude-change programs, however. Thus, if a hostile environment is encountered, the post-communication interaction should quickly dispel any induced change; in contrast, if the environment is supportive, induced change should be solidified. Finally, the classroom setting of many laboratory experiments may foster feelings that the school is behind the communication, thus augmenting its effect. Inasmuch as most programs designed to change attitudes toward handicapped persons probably would be conducted in school settings, there should be a less significant difference than in the case of survey research.

The extent of the congruence between these factors in the laboratory experiment and the field setting in which the findings are to be applied increases the chances of obtaining the same results. However, even when the two situations appear to be identical, it must be remembered that the naturalistic setting is far more complex and, therefore, different results may be produced. The logical conclusion is never to accept the results of studies as "truth" but, rather, as bases for making educated guesses about what program may be the most effective.

REFERENCES

Abelson, R. P., Aronson, E., McGuire, W. J., Newcomb, T. M., Rosenberg, M. J., & Tannenbaum, P. H. (Eds.). *Theories of cognitive consistency: A sourcebook.* Chicago: Rand McNally, 1968.

Amir, Y. Contact hypothesis in ethnic relations. *Psychological Bulletin*, 1969, *71*, 319-342.

Aronson, E. Dissonance theory: Progress and problems. In R. P. Abelson, E. Aronson, W. J. McGuire, T. M. Newcomb, M. J. Rosenberg, & P. H. Tannenbaum (Eds.), *Theories of cognitive consistency: A sourcebook.* Chicago: Rand McNally, 1968.

Aronson, E., & Mills, J. The effects of severity of initiation on liking for a group. *Journal of Abnormal and Social Psychology*, 1959, *59*, 177-188.

Aronson, E., Turner, J., & Carlsmith, J. M. Communication credibility and communication discrepancy as determinants of opinion change. *Journal of Abnormal and Social Psychology*, 1963, *67*, 31-36.

Baron, R. S., Baron, P. H., & Miller, N. The relation between distraction and persuasion. *Psychological Bulletin*, 1973, *80*, 310-323.

Bem, D. J. Self-perception: An alternative interpretation of cognitive dissonance phenomenon. *Psychological Review*, 1967, *74*, 183-200.

Bochner, S., & Insko, C. A. Communication discrepancy, source credibility and opinion change. *Journal of Personality and Social Psychology*, 1966, *4*, 614-621.

Brehm, J. W. *A theory of psychological reactance.* New York: Academic Press, 1966.

Brehm, J. W., & Cohen, A. R. *Exploration in cognitive dissonance.* New York: Wiley, 1962.

Brehm, J. W. & Lipsher, D. Communicator-communicatee discrepancy and perceived communicator trustworthiness. *Journal of Personality*, 1959, *27*, 352-361.

Carlson, E. R. Attitude change through modification of attitude structure. *Journal of Abnormal and Social Psychology*, 1956, *52*, 256-261.

Chapanis, N. P., & Chapanis, A. Cognitive dissonance: Five years later. *Psychological Bulletin*, 1964, *61*, 1-22.

Cialdini, R. B., Levy, A., Herman, C. P., Kozlowski, L. T., & Petty, R. E. Elastic shifts of opinion: Determinants of direction and durability. *Journal of Personality and Social Psychology*, 1976, *34*, 663-673.

Clore, G. L., & Jeffery, K. M. Emotional role playing, attitude change, and attraction toward a disabled person. *Journal of Personality and Social Psychology*, 1972, *23*, 105-111.

Cohen, A. R. An experiment on small rewards for discrepant compliance and attitude change. In J. W. Brehm & A. R. Cohen, *Explorations in cognitive dissonance*. New York: Wiley, 1962.

Cook, S. W. Motives in a conceptual analysis of attitude-related behavior (Vol. 17). *Nebraska Symposium on Motivation*, 1969, 179-231.

Cook, T. D., & Flay, B. R. The persistence of experimentally induced attitude change. In L. Berkowitz (Ed.), *Advances in experimental social psychology* (Vol. 11). New York: Academic Press, 1978, 1-57.

Cook, T. D., & Insko, C. A. Persistence of induced attitude change as a function of conclusion re-exposure: A laboratory-field experiment. *Journal of Personality and Social Psychology*, 1968, *9*, 328-377.

Cook, T. D., & Wadsworth, A. Persistence of induced attitude change as a function of overlearned conclusions and supportive attributions. *Journal of Personality*, 1972, *40*, 50-61.

Culbertson, F. M. Modification of an emotionally held attitude through role playing. *Journal of Abnormal and Social Psychology*, 1957, *54*, 230-233.

Dean, R. B., Austin, J. A., & Watts, W. A. Forewarning effects of persuasion: Field and classroom experiments. *Journal of Personality and Social Psychology*, 1971, *18*, 210-221.

Deutsch, M., & Collins, M. E. *Interracial housing*. Minneapolis: University of Minnesota Press, 1951.

Deutsch, M., Krauss, R. M., & Rosenau, N. Dissonance or defensiveness? *Journal of Personality*, 1962, *30*, 16-28.

Dillehay, R. C., Insko, C. A., & Smith, M. B. Logical consistency and attitude change. *Journal of Personality and Social Psychology*, 1966, *3*, 646-654.

Eagly, A. H. Comprehensibility of persuasive arguments as a determinant of opinion change. *Journal of Personality and Social Psychology*, June 1974, *29*, 1758-1773.

Elms, A. C. Influence of fantasy ability in attitude change through role playing. *Journal of Personality and Social Psychology*, 1966, *4*, 36-43.

Epstein, G. F. Machiavelli and the devil's advocate. *Journal of Personality and Social Psychology*, 1969, *11*, 312-320.

Festinger, L. *A theory of cognitive dissonance*. Stanford: Stanford University Press, 1957.

Festinger, L., & Carlsmith, J. M. Cognitive consequences of forced compliance. *Journal of Abnormal and Social Psychology*, 1959, *58*, 203-210.

Fishbein, M., & Ajzen, I. *Belief, attitude, intention and behavior: An introduction to theory and research*. Reading MA: Addison-Wesley, 1975.

Fisher, S., & Lubin, A. Distance as a determinant of influence in a two person social interaction situation. *Journal of Abnormal and Social Psychology*, 1958, *56*, 230-238.

Foley, L. A. Personality and situational influences on changes in prejudice: A replication of Cook's railroad game in a prison setting. *Journal of Personality and Social Psychology*, 1976, *34*, 846-856.

Freedman, J. L. Involvement, discrepancy and opinion change. *Journal of Abnormal and Social Psychology*, 1964, *69*, 290-295.

Freedman, J. L. Long term behavioral effects of cognitive dissonance. *Journal of Experimental Social Psychology*, 1965, *1*, 145-155.

Greenstein, T. Behavior change through value self-confrontation: A field experiment. *Journal of Personality and Social Psychology*, 1976, *34*, 254-262.

Greenwald, A. G. Cognitive learning, cognitive response to persuasion and attitude change. In A. G. Greenwald, T. C. Brock, & T. M. Astom (Eds.), *Psychological foundations of attitudes*. New York: Academic Press, 1969.

Grube, J. W., Greenstein, T. N., Rankin, W. L., & Kearney, K. A. Behavior change following self-confrontation: A test of the value-mediation hypothesis. *Journal of Personality and Social Psychology*, 1977, *35*, 212-216.

Haaland, G. A., & Venkatesan, M. Resistance to persuasive communications: An examination of the distraction hypotheses. *Journal of Personality and Social Psychology*, 1968, *9*, 167-170.

Hass, R. G., & Grady, K. Temporal delay, type of forewarning, and resistance to influence. *Journal of Experimental Social Psychology*, 1975, *11*, 459-469.

Heider, F. Attitudes and cognitive organization. *Journal of Psychology*, 1946, *21*, 107-112.

Henninger, M., & Wyer, R. S., Jr. The recognition and elimination of inconsistencies among syllogistically related beliefs: Some new light on the "Socratic effect." *Journal of Personality and Social Psychology*, 1976, *34*, 680.

Higbee, K. L. Fifteen years of fear arousal: Research on threat appeals: 1953-1968. *Psychological Bulletin*, 1969, *72*, 426-444.

Holt, L. E. Resistance to persuasion on explicit beliefs as a function of commitment to and desirability of logically related beliefs. *Journal of Personality and Social Psychology*, 1970, *16*(4), 583-591.

Holt, L. E., & Watts, W. A. Salience of logical relationships among beliefs as a factor in persuasion. *Journal of Personality and Social Psychology*, 1969, *11*, 193-203.

Hovland, C. I. Reconciling conflicting results derived from experimental and survey studies of attitude change. *American Psychologist*, 1959, *14*, 8-17.

Hovland, C. I., Janis, I. L., & Kelley, H. H. *Communication and persuasion.* New Haven: Yale University Press, 1953.

Hovland, C. I., Lumsdaine, A. A., & Sheffield, F. D. *Experiments on mass communication.* Princeton: Princeton University Press, 1949.

Hovland, C. I., & Mandell, W. An experimental comparison of conclusion drawing by the communicator and by the audience. *Journal of Abnormal and Social Psychology*, 1952, *47*, 581-588.

Hovland, C. I., & Pritzker, H. A. Extent of opinion change as a function of amount of change advocated. *Journal of Abnormal and Social Psychology*, 1957, *34*, 257-261.

Janis, I. L., & Feshback, S. Effects of fear-arousing communications. *Journal of Abnormal and Social Psychology*, 1953, *48*, 78-92.

Janis, I. L., & Mann, L. Effectiveness of emotional role-playing in modifying smoking habits and attitudes. *Journal of Experimental Research in Personality*, 1965, *1*, 84-90.

Johnson, H. H., & Watkins, T. A. The effects of message repetitions on immediate and delayed attitude change. *Psychonomic Science*, 1971, *22*, 101-103.

Katz, D. The functional approach to the study of attitude. *Public Opinion Quarterly*, 1960, *24*, 163-204.

Katz, D., McClintock, C., & Sarnoff, I. The measurement of ego defense as related to attitude change. *Journal of Personality*, 1957, *25*, 465-474.

Katz, D., Sarnoff, I., & McClintock, C. Ego-defense and attitude change. *Human Relations*, 1956, *9*, 27-45.

Kelman, H. C. Process of opinion change. *Public Opinion Quarterly*, 1961, *25*, 57-78.

Kelman, H. C., & Hovland, C. I. "Reinstatement" of the communicator in delayed measurement of attitude change. *Journal of Abnormal and Social Psychology*, 1953, *48*, 327-335.

King, B. T., & Janis, I. L. Comparison of the effectiveness of improvised versus non-improvised role playing in producing opinion change. *Human Relations*, 1956, *9*, 177-186.

Laswell, H. D. The structure and function of communication in society. In L. Bryson (Ed.), *Communication of ideas.* New York: Harper, 1948.

Lehman, S. Personality and compliance: A study of anxiety and self-esteem in opinion and behavior change. *Journal of Personality and Social Psychology*, 1970, *15*, 76-87.

Lerner, M. J. Evaluation of performance as a function of performer's reward and attractiveness. *Journal of Personality and Social Psychology*, 1965, *1*, 355-360.

Lerner, M. J. Justice, guilt, and veridical perception. *Journal of Personality and Social Psychology*, 1971, *20*, 127-135.

Leventhal, H. Findings and theory in the study of fear communications. In L. Berkowitz

(Ed.), *Advances in experimental social psychology* (Vol. 5). New York: Academic Press, 1970.

Leventhal, H., & Watts, J. C. Sources of resistance of fear-arousing communications on smoking and lung cancer. *Journal of Personality*, 1966, *34*, 155-175.

Mann, L. The effects of emotional role playing on smoking attitudes and behavior. *Journal of Experimental Social Psychology*, 1967, *3*, 334-348.

Mann, L., & Janis, I. L. A follow-up study of the long-term effects of emotional role playing. *Journal of Personality and Social Psychology*, 1968, *8*, 339-342.

Matefy, R. E. Attitude change induced by role playing as a function of improvisation and role taking skill. *Journal of Personality and Social Psychology*, 1972, *24*, 343-350.

McClintock, C. Personality syndromes and attitude change. *Journal of Personality*, 1958, *26*, 479.

McGuire, W. J. A syllogistic analysis of cognitive relationships. In M. J. Rosenberg, et al., *Attitude organization and change*. New Haven: Yale University Press, 1960, 65-111.

McGuire, W. J. Attitudes and opinions. *Annual Review of Psychology* (Vol. 17), 1966, 475-514.

McGuire, W. J. Personality and susceptibility to social influence. In E. F. Borgatta & W. W. Lambert (Eds.), *Handbook of personality theory and research*. Chicago: Rand McNally, 1968.

McGuire, W. J. The nature of attitudes and attitude change. In G. Lindzey & E. Aronson (Eds.), *The handbook of social psychology* (Vol. 3). Reading MA: Addison-Wesley, 1969.

McGuire, W. J. Attitude change: The information processing paradigm. In C. G. McClintock (Ed.), *Experimental social psychology*. New York: Holt, Rinehart & Winston, 1972.

McGuire, W. J., & Millman, S. Anticipatory belief lowering following forewarning of a persuasive attack. *Journal of Personality and Social Psychology*, 1965, *2*, 471-479.

McGuire, W. J., & Papageorgis, D. Effectiveness of forewarning in developing resistance to persuasion. *Public Opinion Quarterly*, 1962, *26*, 24-34.

Millman, S. Anxiety, comprehension, and susceptibility to social influence. *Journal of Personality and Social Psychology*, 1968, *9*, 251-257.

Nelson, C. E. Anchoring to accepted values as a technique for immunizing beliefs against persuasion. *Journal of Personality and Social Psychology*, 1968, *9*, 329-334.

Nisbett, R. E., Caputo, C., Legant, P., & Marecek, J. Behavior as seen by the actor and as seen by the observer. *Journal of Personality and Social Psychology*, 1973, *27*, 154-164.

Nuttin, J. M., Jr. *The illusion of attitude change: Towards a response contagion theory of persuasion*. London: Academic Press, 1975.

Oskamp, S. *Attitudes and opinions*. Englewood Cliffs NJ: Prentice-Hall, 1977.

Petty, R. E., & Cacioppo, J. T. Forewarning, cognitive responding, and resistance to persuasion. *Journal of Personality and Social Psychology*, 1977, *35*, 645-655.

Petty, R. E., Wells, G. L., & Brock, T. C. Distraction can enhance or reduce yielding propaganda: Thought disruption versus effort justification. *Journal of Personality and Social Psychology*, 1976, *34*, 874-884.

Rhine, R. J., & Severence, L. J. Ego involvement, discrepancy, source credibility, and attitude change. *Journal of Personality and Social Psychology*, 1970, *16*, 175-190.

Rogers, R. W., & Thistlethwaite, D. L. Effects of fear arousal and reassurance on attitude change. *Journal of Personality and Social Psychology*, 1970, *15*, 227-233.

Rokeach, M. J. Long range experimental modification of values, attitude and behavior. *American Psychologist*, 1971, *26*, 453-459.

Rokeach, M. *The nature of human values*. New York: Free Press, 1973.

Rosen, N. A., & Wyer, R. S. Some further evidence for the "Socratic effect" using a subjective probability model of cognitive organization. *Journal of Personality and Social Psychology*, 1972, *24*, 420-424.

Rule, B. G., & Renner, J. Involvement and group effects on opinion change. *Journal of Social Psychology*, 1968, *76*, 189-198.

Siegel, A. E., & Siegel, S. Reference groups, membership groups and attitude change. *Journal of Abnormal and Social Psychology*, 1957, *55*, 360-364.

Smith, E. E. The power of dissonance techniques to change attitudes. *Public Opinion Quarterly*, 1961, *25*, 626-639.

Smith, M. B. *Social psychology and human values*. Chicago: Aldine, 1969.

Smith, M. B., Bruner, J. S., & White, R. W. *Opinions and personality*. New York: Wiley, 1956.

Stotland, E., Katz, D., & Patchen, M. The reduction of prejudice through the arousal of self insight. *Journal of Personality*, 1959, *27*, 507-531.

Stotland, E., & Patchen, M. Identification and changes in prejudice and in authoritarianism. *Journal of Abnormal and Social Psychology*, 1961, *62*, 265-274.

Thistlethwaite, D. L., de Haan, H., & Kamenetsky, J. The effects of "directive" and "nondirective" communication procedures on attitudes. *Journal of Abnormal and Social Psychology*, 1955, *51*, 107-113.

Triandis, H. C. *Attitudes and attitude change*. New York: Wiley, 1971.

Varela, J. A. *Psychological solutions to social problems*. New York: Academic Press, 1971.

Watts, W. A. Relative persistence of opinion change induced by active compared to passive participation. *Journal of Personality and Social Psychology*, 1967, *5*, 4-15.

Watts, W. A. Intelligence and susceptibility to persuasion under conditions of active and passive participation. *Journal of Experimental Social Psychology*, 1973, *9*, 110-122.

Watts, W. A. Intelligence and opinion change through active participation as a function of requirements for improvisation and time of opinion measurement. *Social Behavior and Personality*, 1977, *5*, 171-176.

Watts, W. A. *Consistency induced persuasion as a function of salience of the relationships among beliefs and time of opinion measurement*. Paper presented at the XIX International Congress of Applied Psychology, Munich, Germany, July 30-August 5, 1978.

Watts, W. A., & Holt, L. E. Logical relationships among beliefs and timing as factors in persuasion. *Journal of Personality and Social Psychology*, 1970, *16*, 571-582.

Watts, W. A., & Holt, L. E. Persistence of opinion change induced under conditions of forewarning and distraction. *Journal of Personality and Social Psychology*, 1979, *37*, 778-789.

Watts, W. A., & McGuire, W. J. Persistence of induced opinion change and retention of the inducing message content. *Journal of Abnormal and Social Psychology*, 1964, *68*, 233-241.

Wicklund, R. A., & Brehm, J. W. *Perspectives on cognitive dissonance*. New York: Wiley, 1976.

Wyer, R. S., Jr. *Cognitive organization and change: An information processing approach*. Potomac MD: Lawrence Erlbaum, 1974.

Zellner, M. Self-esteem, reception and influenceability. *Journal of Personality and Social Psychology*, 1970, *15*, 87-94.

4

Approaches to the Measurement of Attitude

ROBYN M. DAWES

In 1928, L. L. Thurstone presented a technique for assessing the judged seriousness of crimes. The title of his article, "Attitudes Can Be Measured," clearly implied that measurement of attitude was something new, that it could not be done without using the proper techniques, and that those techniques were available.

Attitudes are complex, personal, and highly "human." When we speak about the *measurement of attitudes*, what do we mean? (a) What do we mean precisely by "measurement"? (b) What is it about attitudes that we "measure"? Because the second question is easier to answer, let's consider that first.

A frequently made statement is that a score on an attitude scale, let us say of attitude toward God, does not truly describe a person's attitude. There are so many complex factors involved in an individual's attitude on any issue that it cannot be adequately described by a simple number such as a score on some sort of test or scale. This is true, but it is equally true of all measurements.

> The measurement of any object or entity describes only one attribute of the object measured. This is the universal characteristic of all measurement. When the height of a table is measured, the whole table has not been described but only the attribute which is measured. (Thurstone, 1931, p. 19)

Note: This manuscript was prepared while the author was a James McKeen Cattell Sabbatical Fellow at the Institute for Social Research and the Psychology Department, The University of Michigan.

70

So the answer to the second question is very simple: We measure attributes (aspects, dimensions) of attitude and we design a measurement technique that will assess those aspects or dimensions. But let us turn to the first question: What is "measurement"?

In an influential article, Stevens (1951) defined *measurement* as "the assignment of numbers to objects or events according to rules" (p. 1). However, there are many ways of doing so; in fact, an infinite number of rules exist for assigning numbers to any particular set of objects or events. Consider, for example, the number of rules that can be used to assign numbers to beauty contestants or politicians (e.g., cube the distance between the candidate's chin and left forefinger when she is standing at attention and divide by the number determined from the sign of the zodiac at her birth). Few of these rules would yield meaningful predictions (e.g., who will win) if the assignment of numbers does not represent meaningful attributes.

To understand the concept at issue, let us consider physical measurement first. Weight is a simple example. It refers to an attribute of objects that is assigned according to the simplest of rules: the number of standard weights (pounds, grams, or fractions thereof) an object balances in a pan balance. Moreover, once we have determined the weight of objects, we can make meaningful predictions about them, alone, in part, or in *concatenation* (placed together). For example, one or more objects weighing a total of 6 grams will outweigh a 4-gram object. Weight is termed *representational measurement* because the weight of objects literally represents their behavior in pan balances. The behavior that can be predicted before it is observed yields a *consistency check* on our measurement system.

Not all representational measurement uses numbers. For example, the Mohs scale orders the hardness of minerals from talc to diamonds on the basis of which scratches which. The scale has a consistency check. When mineral *a* scratches mineral *b*, *a* is represented above *b* in the order; when mineral *b* scratches mineral *c*, *b* is represented above *c* in the order. It now follows that *a* must be represented above *c* in the order because orders are, by definition, *transitive*. If the representation of minerals' hardness is consistent, it follows that since *a* is ordered above *b* and *b* above *c*, then *a* must scratch *c*; it does.

At first glance, the consistency check for the Mohs scale may appear to be trivial in comparison with the consistency check for weight; nevertheless, the Mohs scale is a valid representation of one attribute (hardness) of a class of objects (minerals). Any order that represents an attribute is just as valid a representational measure as is a weight or number. In the attitude domain, the most successful type of representational measurement—Guttman scaling—consists of an order.[2]

---

[2]Guttman scaling is presented in detail in the following section.

The fact that orders can be valid representational measures seemed to have escaped some members of the British Association for the Advancement of Science in 1932. Several members of its commission who were empowered to study the problem of measurement in social science came to the conclusion that concatenation was not possible in social inquiry and, therefore, that scientific measurement was impossible; hence, social inquiry could not be a science.

Orders are not trivial. Spurious orders can be detected because they fail the consistency check. For example, one of the best known spurious orders is the pecking "order" among chickens. Close observation reveals that it is not transitive, hence fails the consistency check, hence is not an order. When chicken a pecks chicken b and chicken b pecks chicken c, it does *not* necessarily follow that chicken a will peck chicken c. Apparently, chickens are too stupid to establish the sort of pecking order (status hierarchy) found among some types of age groups; among chickens, who pecks whom is stable but depends to a large extent on the vicissitudes of the first encounter between two chicks.

Representational measurement is rare in the study of attitude; instead, questionnaires and rating scales are pervasive. Although these devices are used to try to assess important aspects or attributes of peoples' attitudes, they do not constitute representational measurement because there is no internal consistency in the subjects' responses that can be checked for correspondence to the numbers or orders derived from such responses. For example, suppose a rating scale offered subjects a range of numbers from -3 to $+3$ to indicate disagreement/agreement with the statement, "Taxes should be lowered without a simultaneous cutback in governmental services." A man chooses $+3$. What inferences can we make on the basis of this behavior? That he will probably vote for a tax reduction? That he is politically naive? That he believes in paying government workers by manufacturing money? We cannot even make a firm prediction about some other response he may make to this or another rating scale. In other words, there is no consistency check for his response; thus the rating scale is not representational measurement.

Measurement that predicts in the absence of a consistency check has been termed *index measurement* by Dawes (1972). Some theorists argue that index measurement is not measurement at all, but the important question is not the definition of measurement but whether index measurement is useful. It is, if it predicts. For example, pollsters use rating scales (index measurements) almost exclusively, and their predictions of election outcomes are usually correct; even when they are wrong it is by only slight margins, as in the Truman-Dewey election of 1948. (See Abelson, 1968, for a discussion of the remarkable accuracy of pollsters.) Of course, these predictions are statistical in nature and on occasion specific predictions can be quite wide of the mark.

Basically, two types of statistical predictability are studied to determine whether an index measure is useful: *internal predictive validity* and *external predictive validity*. *Internal predictive validity* refers to the power of responses to predict other similar responses (e.g, from one rating scale to a highly similar one); *external predictive validity* refers to the power to predict to topographically dissimilar behavior (e.g., from rating scale to responses to voting). Most good index measures can be shown to have both types of predictive validity.

Representational measurement, by definition, has predictive validity through the consistency check. Hence, the basis of all measurement is empirical prediction.

72

AN EXAMPLE OF REPRESENTATIONAL MEASUREMENT: GUTTMAN SCALING

Guttman scaling (named after Louis Guttman; he did not originate the technique but he was most influential in developing it during World War II) is a technique that represents people and stimuli in an interlocking order. It is representational in that the resulting interlocking order yields consistency checks through transitivity, just as the order of hardness represented by the Mohs scale yields such checks (although the checks in Guttman scaling are a bit more complex). It is widely used in a variety of psychological and social contexts.

The Basic Technique

Suppose that a set of arithmetic items could be ordered perfectly in terms of difficulty and that people could be ordered perfectly in terms of arithmetic ability. Then, each person who passed a given arithmetic item would pass all the easier ones, and each person who failed a given item would fail all the more difficult items. The result would be an interlocking order of people and items; people would be ordered with respect to items, and items ordered with respect to people. That is, each person could be represented between the hardest item passed and the easiest one failed; correspondingly, each item could be represented between two people (see Figure 1).

FIGURE 1
Relation of Items and People on Basic Guttman Scale

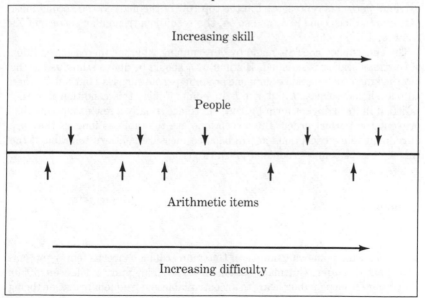

The purpose of Guttman scaling is either to construct from obtained data such interlocking scales or to test the theory that predicts the occurrence of interlocking. Usually, as in the preceding example, people are interlocked with stimuli. Abstractly, the scaling technique can be used to construct or test for interlocking orders between the elements of any two sets (Coombs, 1964). For simplicity of exposition here, however, the method is explicated in terms of stimuli and people.

The investigator wishing to construct a Guttman scale begins with the knowledge of whether each individual should be ordered above or below each stimulus (e.g., whether he or she has passed or failed an arithmetic item). A perfect Guttman scale exists given the fundamental condition that (a) if there are people who should be ordered above stimulus j but not stimulus k, then (b) there are none who should be ordered above k but not j (Ducamp & Flamange, 1969). When this fundamental condition is met, it follows that stimulus k can be unequivocally ordered above stimulus j in the resulting interlocking scale. Moreover, people can unequivocally be represented in the scale (a) below both stimuli, (b) above j but below k, or (c) above both. (If the condition is satisfied, of course, no one could be represented above k but below j.)

One simple algorithm for forming a Guttman scale is to construct a matrix in which the rows represent people and the columns stimuli. (All people with the same response pattern are treated as identical, as are all stimuli that elicit identical response patterns.) An X is put in each cell if and only if the row person surpasses the column stimulus. A perfect Guttman scale exists if and only if it is possible to rearrange the rows and columns of this matrix to obtain a triangular pattern of Xs: The person farthest out in the order should surpass all the stimuli (those surpassed by no one are irrelevant), the person next farthest should surpass all but the most extreme stimulus, the person next farthest should surpass all but the two most extreme, and so on. If the most extreme person is represented in the top row of the matrix, the second most extreme in the second row, and so on, the result is a triangular pattern of Xs (Dawes, 1972, p.46).

The consistency check is made by determining whether the basic condition of Guttman scaling is satisfied. If stimulus k should be above stimulus j in the interlocking order (because someone or some people surpass j but not k), then no one should surpass k but not j. In point of fact, this condition is rarely satisfied in its stringent form because there are usually a few exceptions that prevent the perfect order. But exceptions are tolerable as long as they are infrequent (e.g., exceptions in pan balance measurement are tolerable if the balance mechanism is crude and given to error).

Examples

The most widely known example of Guttman scaling concerns fear symptoms in combat (Stouffer, Guttman, Schuman, Lazarsfeld, Star, & Clausen, 1950); they range from pounding heart to uncontrollable and frequent urination (being

74

"scared pissless"). For example, the probability is very high that soldiers who lose control of their bowels have previously vomited; for those who do not vomit, the probability is very low that they will lose control of their bowels; and some soldiers vomit without losing control of their bowels but very few lose bowel control without having previously vomited.

Other examples of Guttman scaling have been presented by Bentler (1968), Dawes and Moore (1979), Patterson and Dawes (1975), Podel and Perkins (1957), and Spaeth (1965). Spaeth found that the voting behavior of Supreme Court Justices can be ordered on the basis of their economic liberalism and favoring of civil rights; Patterson and Dawes studied the coercive behaviors of both aggressively disturbed and normal young children and found that the behaviors can be ordered from negativism to physical humiliation; Dawes and Moore found that cheating in college conforms to a pattern whereby all who cheat on term papers also cheat on exams, but not vice versa; and sexual behavior in our society was found by Podel and Perkins and by Bentler to progress in order from touching to cunnilingus.

An Example of Guttman Scaling on Attitude Measurement

An enduring interest of social psychologists has been the study of prejudice, that is, of individuals' attitudes toward others as a function of the ethnic or national group to which those people belong. In order to evaluate prejudices, Bogardus (1925) developed a "social distance" scale; its underlying idea is that the more prejudiced individuals are against a particular group, the greater the social distance they insist on maintaining between themselves and members of that group. For example, a person who is extremely prejudiced may insist that members of a particular group not be allowed to visit his or her country; people who are only slightly prejudiced may accept those group members as neighbors but not to close kinship by marriage. Thus, an individual's prejudice is assessed by discovering the degree of social distance he or she places between himself or herself and members of the group against whom he or she is prejudiced: the greater the distance, the greater the prejudice.

Bogardus developed his social distance scale by asking whether individuals would accept specific group members as citizens, neighbors, fellow club members, and so on. He did not explicitly state the principle of the Guttman scale but the idea is implicit in his concept of social distance. An individual who would not let a group member come within a certain social distance should not let the group member come any closer (e.g., a person who refuses to grant the group member citizenship should reject that member as a neighbor); furthermore, if the individual allows the group member to come within a certain distance, he or she should allow him to come within all greater distances (e.g., people who allow the group member to become a fellow club member should allow him or her to visit the country). It should be possible, then, to construct a Guttman scale according to the principle that the ethnic group dominates a certain distance criterion if, and only if, the respondent refuses to allow a group member to come within that distance.

This example has some rather unusual features. Most often, a Guttman scale represents real people dominating or failing to dominate real stimuli. In this example, the "people" are stereotypes of a single prejudiced judge, and the "stimuli" are hypothetical situations indicative of social distance. These unique features have no bearing on the logic of Guttman scaling; the Guttman scaling procedure only requires the establishment of an interlocking order between two sets of elements; the nature of these elements is irrelevant to the procedure.

The Bogardus technique requires the construction of a separate Guttman scale for the prejudices of each individual; if the order of hypothetical situations on these scales is the same from individual to individual, then there is very strong evidence for Bogardus's concept of social distance. In general, the order is the same, but there are interesting cultural differences (Triandis & Triandis, 1965).

A Caution

How much inconsistency should be tolerated before making the decision that a set of observations cannot be represented by an interlocking order? Although there is no definite answer to this question, one word of caution is necessary: When the number of observations collected is small, it is often possible to construct something that looks like a Guttman scale—even if the response patterns are generated randomly.

Consider, for example, the sampling of 20 observations of domination of stimuli a and b in a population in which the pattern of people and stimuli do not interlock. Consider, also, that all four responses to the two stimuli are equally likely in the population; that is, 25% of the people dominate both a and b; 25% dominate a but not b; 25% dominate b but not a; and 25% dominate neither. It would not be at all unlikely to obtain a sample in which seven people dominate both a and b, two people dominate a alone, six people dominate b alone, and five people fail to dominate either. (The Pearson chi-square value for testing the hypothesis that all response patterns are equally likely is 2.80. The value needed to reject this hypothesis at the .05 level is 7.81 [df = 3].) Then 90% (18 of 20) of the response patterns conform to a Guttman scale in which a is ordered above b. Moreover, it is necessary to regard only 2 of the 40 actual responses (20 subjects times 2 responses each) to be in error in order to have a perfect Guttman scale. (The people who dominated a should have dominated b also.)

One minus the proportion of responses that must be changed in order to obtain a perfect scale is sometimes termed a coefficient of reproductibility. In this example, this coefficient is .95, which sounds impressive. However, high values of this coefficient can often be misleading. The problem is that the order of the stimuli is determined after the observations are collected; hence, "capitalization on chance" is bound to occur. It is possible, however, to specify the order a priori and see how well the response patterns fit it, in which case the coefficient does not involve such capitalization.

76

AN EXAMPLE OF INDEX MEASUREMENT: RATING SCALES

Rating scales are index measurement techniques that are used to assess individuals' attitudes by asking them to express those attitudes in terms of a categorical or numerical rating. They are widely used in social psychology, particularly in attitude assessment. Ordinarily, they consist of categories (often ordered), numbers, or lines; sometimes, they consist of combinations of categories, numbers, and lines. The individuals whose attitudes are being assessed usually are asked to select a single category, pick a single number, or place a check mark at a single point on a line; sometimes individuals are asked to do something more complicated, such as to indicate on a line a range of positions acceptable to them.

Six examples of rating scales are presented in Figure 2. In Figure 2a (Adorno, Frenekl-Brunswik, Levinson, & Sanford, 1950), subjects are presented with statements that express authoritarian attitudes and they are asked to indicate agreement with each statement by selecting a number from $+3$ to -3. Notice that they must select an integer value and that a specific verbal category is paired with each integer. Notice also that they cannot express complete indifference toward a statement; there is no 0 on the rating scale. (The first statement in Figure 2 is taken directly from the original scale on authoritarianism; the second is an adaptation of the original statement and is used more frequently.)

Figure 2b is an example of the semantic rating scales used by Osgood and his associates (Osgood, Suci, & Tannenbaum, 1957). Subjects are asked to indicate their feelings about the concept presented to the left of the scale. The extremes of this scale are defined in terms of bipolar semantic adjectives instead of agreement or disagreement; furthermore, the positions between the extremes are not paired with verbal labels, although the midposition is clearly meant to be used when a rater associates the concept with neither pole of the adjective pair.

Figure 2c is taken from a study by Sikes and Cleveland (1968) in which police and community members participated in a program of face-to-face confrontation that was meant to alleviate tensions. When the program ended, each participant was asked to rate its success by choosing one of the four evaluative labels: excellent, very good, good, poor. Notice that although these labels generally are regarded as forming a good-bad continuum, "poor" is the only possible unfavorable response.

Figure 2d is from a study (Valins, 1966) that attempted to manipulate male subjects' attitudes toward *Playboy* playmate pictures by giving the subjects false information about their heart rates while they were looking at the pictures. Here the subject is able to choose any number between 0 and 100 to indicate his feelings about attractiveness; he is not constrained to choose among only a few alternatives. Another important difference between this and previous scales is that the verbal categorizations are associated with a range of numerical values instead of with a single number.

The next example, Figure 2e, is taken from a study by Walster (reported in Festinger, 1964) in which the attitudes of inductees toward military jobs were assessed at varying times after they had chosen between two jobs. This scale, essentially, is like that presented in Figure 2d, except that the verbal labels are associated with single points on the scale and the subjects, therefore, may make a response "between" two labels.

Finally, Figure 2f is an example of a *Likert Scale*. These scales consist of declarative statements with which subjects indicate their degrees of agreement. There may be any number of categories of agreement, ranging from 2 to 9 or so (the usual is 7), and there may or may not be a neutral category. No numbers or spaces are associated with these categories. This particular example is taken from the work of Cowen, Underber, and Verillo (1958); it is discussed later, in the section "An Example Combining Direct and Indirect Assessment."

FIGURE 2
Six Examples of Rating Scales

The following statements refer to opinions regarding a number of social groups and issues, about which some people agree and others disagree. Please mark each statement in the left-hand margin according to your agreement or disagreement, as follows:

+ 1: slight support, agreement   − 1: slight opposition, disagreement
+ 2: moderate support, agreement   − 2: moderate opposition, disagreement
+ 3: strong support, agreement   − 3: strong opposition, disagreement

Sciences like chemistry, physics, and medicine have carried men very far, but there are many important things that can never possibly be understood by the human mind.

Most people don't realize the extent to which their lives are governed by secret plots hatched in hidden places.

(a)

MY FATHER active − : − : − : − : − : − : − passive
MY FATHER   soft − : − : − : − : − : − : − hard

(b)

Please rate program
by circling your choice.

Excellent
Very Good
Good
Poor

(c)

How attractive is this playmate?

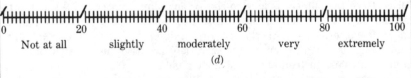

(d)

Continued on next page

78

There are many types of rating scales in addition to those presented in Figure 2; they range from simple ones that require a subject to respond only "yes" or "no" to complex ones, such as the scale presented in Figure 2e. Rating scales are found throughout social and educational psychology, especially in research concerned with attitudes. For example, almost all public opinion surveys use a rating scale, in that subjects are asked to express their attitudes directly by using a verbal category (e.g., "strongly approve," "approve," "disapprove," or "strongly disapprove"). Furthermore, a great deal of research on attitude change defines such change in terms of changes in rating scale behavior; for example, Festinger (1964) presented 10 studies of attitude change; in seven, the subjects' attitudes were assessed by rating scale methods alone.

Figure 2—*continued*

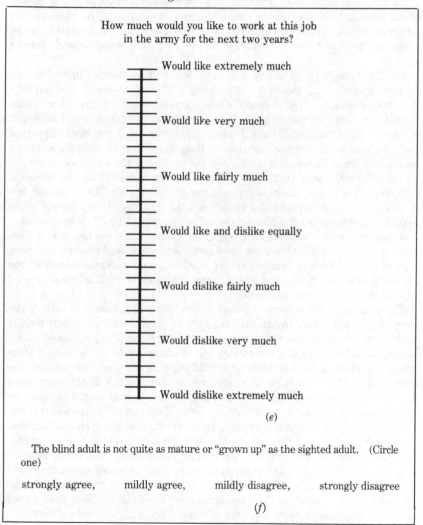

How much would you like to work at this job
in the army for the next two years?

___ Would like extremely much

___ Would like very much

___ Would like fairly much

___ Would like and dislike equally

___ Would dislike fairly much

___ Would dislike very much

___ Would dislike extremely much

(e)

The blind adult is not quite as mature or "grown up" as the sighted adult.　(Circle one)

strongly agree,　　mildly agree,　　mildly disagree,　　strongly disagree

(f)

Example of a Rating Scale: The Semantic Differential

One of the most ubiquitous of all rating scale techniques is the semantic differential (Osgood et al., 1957). Its purpose is to assess the different semantic connotations of a concept for the person doing the rating. The semantic differential consists of a word or concept (e.g., FATHER in Figure 2b) which is rated by a subject on a set of scales; each scale is anchored at both poles by adjectives that form a continuum (e.g., hard-soft). The subject places a check mark at the point on the continuum which he feels most accurately describes the concept. For example, a man rating the concept FATHER on the active-passive scale would place his mark next to the word "active" (one extreme of the scale) if he thinks of his own father as a very active person. If he thinks of his father as somewhat "passive," he would place a mark near the middle of the scale but on the passive side of the continuum; and if he thinks of his father as neither active nor passive, he would place the mark exactly in the center of the scale. This procedure is followed for each semantic scale for the concept.

The three major types of scales used to assess the semantic dimensions are (a) evaluation (i.e., good-bad), (b) potency (i.e., strong-weak), and activity (i.e., active-passive). The reason for concentrating on these three dimensions is that a number of factor analytic studies (using people from 26 different cultures around the world) have demonstrated them to be the most important factors of semantic connotation; that is, if we know how an individual rates a concept on these three dimensions, we can predict fairly well how that individual will rate it on a variety of bipolar semantic scales. Thus, the semantic differential technique has high internal predictive validity. Although the factors discovered are hypothetical variables, they correspond very closely to the actual semantic scales defined by the adjectives "good-bad," "strong-weak," and "active-passive." Because this correspondence is not perfect and the reliability of the single scales is low, additional scales are used to evaluate these three factors. Three or four scales are used to assess each; for example, the scales "good-bad," "tasty-distasteful," and "valuable-worthless" may be used to assess the evaluative dimension.

The location of the concept on each of the three dimensions is usually determined by averaging the ratings assigned to it on the three or four bipolar scales meant to evaluate that dimension; these averages are obtained by assigning values of from 1 to 7 to correspond to each position on the scales. Once these values on each dimension are obtained, it is possible to represent the concept in a three-dimensional space and to evaluate the distance between concepts in that space. Osgood and Luria (1954) believed that such distance represents "difference in meaning" (p. 580). They further proposed the feasibility of studying changes in meaning by observing changes in spatial location.

Osgood and Luria (1954) engaged in an extensive investigation of psychotherapeutic change as evidenced by change in semantic differential ratings. The concepts which they asked patients to rate and the scales which they used are present in Table 1. The coefficients at the bottom of the tables are the "factor loadings"; that is, the correlations between the scales actually used and the three hypothetical variables of evaluation, activity, and potency.

TABLE 1
Semantic Differential Concepts and Scales

Concepts		
LOVE	MENTAL SICKNESS	SELF-CONTROL
CHILD	MY MOTHER	HATRED
MY DOCTOR	PEACE OF MIND	MY FATHER
ME	MIND	CONFUSION
MY JOB	FRAUD	SEX
	MY SPOUSE	

Scales and Their Factor Loadings			
Scales	Evaluation	Activity	Potency
valuable-worthless	.79	.13	.04
clean-dirty	.82	.03	−.05
tasty-distasteful	.77	−.11	.05
fast-slow	.01	.70	.00
active-passive	.14	.59	.04
hot-cold	−.04	.46	−.06
large-small	.06	.34	.62
strong-weak	.19	.20	.62
deep-shallow	.27	.14	.46
tense-relaxed	−.55	.37	−.12

Source: C. E. Osgood & Z. Luria. A blind analysis of a case of multiple personality using the semantic differential. *Journal of Abnormal and Social Psychology*, 1954, *49*, 579–591, p. 580.

The semantic differential appears to have demonstrated external as well as internal predictive validity. It is widely used in psychological investigations of attitudes toward a variety of social objects and phenomena. It can be used to investigate attitudes toward handicapped persons held by either nonhandicapped or handicapped individuals (with the same or different handicaps). The attitudinal dimensions of evaluation, potency, and activity are particularly suited for such investigations. For example, we could compare how "active" a blind person is regarded to be by other individuals with how "active" he or she regards himself or herself to be. Further, it would be possible to trace the self-image of handicapped persons through the course of some program aimed at mastery of compensatory skills.

A word of caution in interpreting the results is in order. The semantic differential is not subtle. Any mildly intelligent people are quite aware that they are being asked to express feelings about the goodness, strength, and activeness of the concept being rated. It is possible, therefore, to fake responses in the direction deemed socially desirable. In particular, when people actually feel that crippled, blind, deaf, old, or mentally retarded persons are bad, weak, and passive, they may avoid labeling them as such during attitude assessments, especially if the investigator is actively involved in helping handicapped persons. Moreover, if one is participating in a treatment program, one may feel compelled to project through attitude assessments a more positive self-image as the program continues.

How do we "know" that a subject is not "faking"? We do not. In fact, we never can know for the simple reason that it is impossible to know directly the subjective experience of another individual. Nevertheless, we can know something *about* the experience of another, and, in contexts where self-reports of experience are highly fakable, it is wise to use direct reporting techniques in conjunction with others, such as direct behavioral observation or indirect techniques. (The latter are discussed in a later section.)

A Caution: The Literal Interpretation of Fallacy

Consider a policeman who has taken part in the Sikes and Cleveland (1968) program which was initiated to ease police-community tensions. He is asked to rate the program by choosing one of four categories—"poor," "good," "very good," or "excellent"—on an evaluative scale. If he chooses "good," does the choice mean that he regards the program as, literally, "good"?

Suppose he thought the program could best be described as "fair." In the rating scale used by Sikes and Cleveland there is no such category; our subject may, therefore, choose "good" in preference to "poor." Suppose he tends to avoid making pejorative statements about other people or their efforts. Thus, no matter how bad he may think the program is, he must say at the least that it is "good" if he is to avoid the only pejorative label, "poor." Suppose he does not have a very strong opinion of the program; it would be natural then for him to avoid using an extreme category, which leaves him with a choice of rating the program "good" or "very good."

In short, because individuals' responses on a rating scale may be determined by many factors other than attitude, their responses cannot be interpreted literally. Sikes and Cleveland were aware of the ambiguity in responses and therefore they worked out other more sophisticated techniques to evaluate police and community attitudes (Cleveland, 1970).

To interpret responses literally on a rating scale is a fallacy. The Sikes and Cleveland scale has been used to illustrate this fallacy because it clearly demonstrates the problems of the literal interpretation of responses. But all scales are subject to the same problem. For example, people may tell a pollster that they "approve" of the President's policy, not because they like the policy but because they feel that it is somehow unpatriotic to "disapprove" of the President, or that "the President deserves our support," no matter what questionable course of action he has taken, or because they do not like to say unpleasant things about people, or even because they may suspect that the pollster is compiling information about dissident citizens.

In the preceding examples, the factors other than attitude that may influence the subject's response are quite straightforward. Sometimes, however, these factors can be subtle. For example, Johnson and Foley (1969) have shown that subjects rating satisfaction with a teaching device may be manipulated by telling them that what they did was a "time-filling" instead of an educational task.

The principle that rating scale responses cannot be interpreted literally should not be surprising. Because rating scales are usually used as index measures, they must be evaluated in terms of their predictive validity. Simply presenting someone with a scale and noting his or her response to it does not demonstrate the scale's validity. The literal interpretation fallacy lies in believing that the individual's response to the scale provides a certain source of information. If it does provide any information, this fact must be demonstrated and not assumed on the basis of the scale's structure. Interpreting a response literally involves such an assumption.

Statistical Manipulation of Index Measures

This brief section is included because of the widespread misunderstanding about which statistical manipulations and tests are appropriate for index measures. Many investigators maintain that only representational numbers posessing magnitude or interval properties (e.g., weight) can be subjected to statistical analysis.[3] Others, who believe that only representational measures can be manipulated, often try to turn index measures into representational measures simply by asking subjects to take intervals or magnitudes (e.g., on rating scales) seriously. That, of course, leaves the empirical status of the numbers completely unchanged; that is, the numbers still do not consistently represent behaviors.[4] Finally, some authors maintain that *if* stable statistical results can be obtained, *then* the measure leading to these results must be representational. The following excerpt is typical:

> In brief, IQ's behave just about as much like an interval scale as do measurements of height, which we know for sure is an interval scale. Therefore, it is not unreasonable to treat the IQ as an interval scale. (Jensen, 1969, p.23)

IQs are very useful numbers, but they do not lie on an interval scale (i.e., a representational scale involving intervals) because there is no behavior that

---

[3]"You can't average rank orders." Of course, you can; we do it all the time in determining the outcome of track and swimming meets. What you cannot do is ascribe some empirical meaning to the fact that objects *a* and *b* have a higher average rank than do objects *c* and *d*, e.g., that the second- and third-best players in a tennis tournament will necessarily beat the first- and fifth-best players at doubles.

[4]I recently reviewed an article purporting to show that the results obtained when the semantic differential was converted to a "true interval" measure were the same as those obtained when it was treated as an index measure; the authors converted the scales to "true interval" ones by removing the colons between the categories!

they consistenly represent. The IQ number reflects, in a convoluted way, the number of items answered correctly on an IQ test; it has external predictive validity but it yields no firm principle for ordering people.

Two important principles must be understood about statistical manipulation: (a) Any procedure properly followed yields a correct summary that may or may not be useful. As Hays (1963) noted, "If the statistical method involves the procedures of arithmetic used on numerical scales, then the answer is formally correct" (p.74). (b) Statistical inference is based upon assumptions about the *distributions* of numbers in the population sampled, *not* upon their empirical status.

> The statistical test can hardly be cognizant of the empirical meaning of the numbers with which it deals. Consequently the validity of the statistical inference cannot depend on the type of measurement scale used. (Anderson, 1961, p.309)

Of course, cubing or taking the square root of numbers may yield a different statistical result; it is not possible to make such transformations on many representational measures because then they would no longer represent the behavior of interest (e.g., behavior in a pan balance). Thus, many statistics and statistical tests yield results that are *invariant* (Adams, Fagot, & Robinson, 1965) in the ways the numbers can be changed. It does not follow, however, that the only statistical summaries and tests that may be used are those that yield invariant results.

INDIRECT ASSESSMENT

When individuals are asked questions about attitudes toward ethnic groups or toward people with a particular type of handicap, they are well aware that their attitudes are being assessed. Their answers may be biased by this awareness. For example, it is socially unacceptable to be biased against ethnic groups or handicapped persons. Thus, responses may be determined, in part at least, by subjects' knowledge that their attitude is being assessed. Such responses have been termed *reactive* by Campbell and Stanley (1963), a term that is used widely in the research literature.

Campbell (1950) urged the development of attitude assessment techniques that will not elicit reactive responses.

> In the problem of assessing social attitudes, there is a very real need for instruments which do not destroy the natural form of the attitude in the process of describing it. There are also situations in which one would like to assess "prejudice" without making respondents self-conscious or aware of the intent of the study. (p.15)

Many psychologists have developed methods that are not reactive (Webb, Campbell, Schwartz, & Sechrest, 1966). The use of such nonreactive or indirect measures is said to have begun in American psychology with J. C. Penney;

he observed whether the people he interviewed for a job salted their soup before tasting it, a practice he interpreted as indicating the lack of an inquiring or empirical attitude. Melton (1933) assessed museum visitors' attitudes toward certain displays by noting how often the tiles in front of the displays had to be replaced (controlling for the bias of most people in our culture to turn right when entering a room). Milgram, Mann, and Harter (1965) developed the *letter drop* procedure for assessing the political attitudes of people in a given location. They hired a post office box to receive mail for various bogus political organizations. The name of each organization clearly implied a certain political philosophy (e.g., "Young Communist League"; "Citizens against Gun Control"). Stamped letters addressed to these various organizations were then "dropped" at various places in the community, and the frequency with which the letters were picked up and mailed was interpreted as an indicator of positive attitudes toward each organization.

A straightforward method of assessing attitudes through indirect measures is presented in the following section. This method has possible application for assessing attitudes toward handicapped persons.

Error Scores

The judgmental errors of people often indicate something about their underlying attitudes. For example, the person who, after reading the statistics on cigarette smoking and health, concludes that smoking lowers life expectancy by 5 years may be more favorably disposed toward smoking than the person who believes that it lowers life expectancy by 15 years (the correct answer is 10). Or the man who judges an ordinary-looking woman to be quite beautiful may be assumed to love her more than does a man who judges her to be quite ordinary looking. Whether such judgmental biases influence "pure" perceptual judgments (e.g., estimating the size of a coin) was once a matter of some debate among psychologists. In the context of assessing attitudes, however, the question is immaterial because, as has been emphasized repeatedly in this chapter, the issue of whether a particular technique is useful is empirical, and is determined by the supporting data.

It is a mistake to believe that judgmental errors are necessarily influenced by attitudes. Differing conclusions about smoking and life expectancy may, for example, result from cognitive errors and failures to process statistical information correctly. Or the man who believes that the ordinary looking woman is beautiful may judge almost all women to be beautiful (or, at least, he may offer this judgment when asked). It must be demonstrated that, in fact, a particular error *is* due to a particular aspect of an attitude. Or at least, as in the following example, a plausible case should be made.

MacNeil, Davis, and Pace (1975) investigated whether teenaged boys' errors in evaluating each others' physical skills (pitching a ball) could be used as an indirect measure of social status in the group. The boys studied were from three cliques in a male boarding school located in the southeastern United

States. Each boy's status in each clique was also evaluated by direct and indirect *scalogram* questions. The "direct" scalogram consisted of questions about whom each boy would most like to spend time with; or who decided what to do and how to do it during free time periods. The "indirect" scalogram asked whom each boy would trust and put in a position of power during a civil defense emergency. The indirect scalogram was administered approximately one month prior to the pitching evaluation; the direct scalogram, immediately afterwards.

In the pitching evaluation, each boy in turn pitched baseballs across a plate while the other boys stood behind the pitcher and scored his throws across the plate (5 for cutting corners; 3 for crossing the center of the plate; 1 for balls just outside the strike zone; and 0 for "wide" balls). At the same time, experimental assistants stood by the plate where they were able to make more "objective" evaluations of the pitches because they were aided by lines that were visible only to them. The average of each boy's pitching scores as determined by the other boys minus the average of the objective scores was the "error" score and was used to indicate his status within the group.

In two of the three cliques studied, the status rank assigned to each boy was consistent across the direct and indirect scalograms and the error scores. In the third group, however, the two scalogram rankings were in agreement but the error-score ranking differed markedly. A few hours before the evaluation, a member of this clique had downed a fifth of vodka, after being dared to do so by the group leader, and had died. (For a description of the incident and the subsequent decision to continue with the investigation, see MacNeil et al., 1975, p .294). Thus, the difference in status rank obtained from the error scores could easily be interpreted in terms of the role each boy had in the activities leading to the death; for example, the lowest status member of the group was displaced upward to the next highest rank (he had left school without permission before the drinking party), the leader moved down to fifth place, and his lieutenant, who had tried to break up the party before the "dare," was moved up to first place.

Judgmental errors in evaluating the physical (or cognitive, for that matter) skills of the handicapped may be a rich source of indirect attitude assessment. Judges—other people or the handicapped persons themselves—who expect handicapped individuals to be weak, inept, or stupid may well score performance below a more objective criterion. On the other hand, those persons who feel that it is more important to be "nice" to or "positive" with the handicapped than to give realistic feedback may, consciously or unconsciously, be biased toward scoring their performances above a more objective criterion.

It is important, however, to remember the caution that no matter how plausible a technique may sound for assessing attitude, it is necessary to demonstrate empirically that it actually works. Empirical validity for judgmental errors must be shown to be related to other phenomena, either behaviors or scores on well established tests of attitude. For example, errors—both overestimation and underestimation—in judging performances by handicapped persons may be shown to be related to scores on the Cowen scales, which are discussed in the following section.

86

AN EXAMPLE COMBINING DIRECT AND INDIRECT ASSESSMENT

The attitudes of nonhandicapped persons toward people who are blind or deaf were studied by Cowen and his associates (Cowen, Bobrove, Rockway, & Stevenson, 1967; Cowen et al., 1958). In particular, the investigators tried to develop a scale that would assess evaluative attitudes by asking respondents to agree or disagree with statements about what blind or deaf people are like and what their life expectations should be. The seemingly factual phraseology of the statements (e.g., "It is very difficult to make a blind person change his mind once he has decided on something") allows the respondent to make positive or pejorative judgments without directly stating that handicapped persons are good or bad. Nevertheless, a reasonably sophisticated respondent would understand the import of the scale. The statements are presented in the Likert format (Figure 2f); respondents are asked to circle "strongly agree," "mildly agree," "mildly disagree," or "strongly disagree," and scores of 1, 2, 3, and 4, respectively, are assigned to the possible responses.

The first step in the research was to develop an internally consistent scale of attitudes toward blind people. Judges selected 56 statements from an initial pool of 97 which, they agreed, expressed a positive or negative attitude. These items were presented to 101 adult education students. The 30 items that correlated the highest[5] with the score based on responses to all 56 statements were chosen to constitute the final "Anti-Blindness" scale. Of these 30 items, 20 had been judged to indicate a negative attitude toward blindness and 10 to reflect a positive attitude.

The second step was to show that the scale had external as well as internal predictive validity. Following Barker (1948), Cowen et al. (1958) argued that a blind person has the same status in our society as do other minority group members and, hence, "is subject to the same prejudices, fears, and negative attitudes on the part of the dominant majority group member" (p. 301). Therefore, if the Anti-Blindness scale really tapped evaluative attitudes toward blind people, the scores should have correlated with scores on scales assessing evaluative attitudes toward other minority groups. Hence, the subjects who had been used in the construction of the Anti-Blindness scale were asked to fill out an 8-item Anti-Minority scale, a 12-item Anti-Black scale, and a 21-item F ("fascism") scale. The correlations between the scores on the Anti-Blindness scale and the other three scales were .36, .45, and .33, all reliably greater than zero.

The final step in the research was to show that scores on the scale predicted actual bias in a behavioral setting. Here, Cowen et al. (1967) shifted to investigating attitudes toward the deaf. Using the same procedures as in their earlier studies, the researchers constructed an internally consistent Anti-Deaf-

---

[5]A correlation coefficient is not a law of nature. It simply assesses how well one thing can be predicted from another in a linear manner *in the population sampled.* Had the investigators used other subjects, they would have obtained different correlations and might well have chosen different items.

ness scale. They then showed that the scores on this scale also correlated with those on the Anti-Minority, Anti-Black, and F scales. (The correlation coefficients computed across 160 college students were .50, .50, and .36.)

Two and one-half months after responding to the Anti-Deafness scale, 48 male subjects who had had either "extremely high" or "extremely low" scores participated in an experiment on "personality impression." Each entered a room with two other "subjects" (actually, stooges), and the three "subjects" were told to ask each other questions for 20 minutes in order to form impressions of each other's personality. The two stooges asked a set of prearranged questions and answered all noncontroversial questions honestly; they were primed to answer controversial questions (e.g., about Vietnam) in the same manner. One stooge wore a hearing aid, the other did not. Each stooge wore the aid during a randomly selected 50% of the trials, and neither knew whether the real subject had scored extremely high or extremely low on the Anti-Deafness Scale.

At the end of 20 minutes, the subjects filled out semantic differential scales indicating their impressions of each other's personality. The main hypothesis of the study was that the responses of the high Anti-Deafness scorers on the evaluative scales would favor the stooge not wearing the hearing aid, but that the low scorers on the Anti-Deafness scale would not exhibit such a bias. The hypothesis was confirmed.

THE RELATION BETWEEN ATTITUDE AND BEHAVIOR

In the La Piere (1934) study (see discussion in Chapter 2 by Triandis, Adamopoulos, & Brinberg), the discrepancy between what was done and then said by the lodging and restaurant owners and managers directly conflicted with the then-prevalent belief that White Americans were more racially biased in their behavior than in their expressed beliefs. A Chinese couple was served at all but one establishment on a long cross-country trip, while these places, contacted by phone, indicated they would refuse to serve Chinese. The study led to a great deal of research on the relation(s) of verbally assessed attitudes and behavior. Ajzen and Fishbein (1977) found large attitude-behavior discrepancies; for instance, an attitude scale assessing favorability toward religion in general is not a strong predictor of church attendance. Wicker (1969) also found a low correspondence.

But such a general attitude scale can hardly be expected to be a strong predictor of church attendance; people may or may not attend church for a variety of reasons other than favorability toward religion. Ajzen and Fishbein (1977) recommended close correspondence between action and target components if attitude is to predict behavior; for example, in predicting church attendance, they recommended assessing attitude toward church attendance rather than toward religion in general.

However there is a *reductio ad absurdum* in such reasoning. When the action and target correspond too precisely to the behavior, the "attitude assessment" amounts to little more than asking the subject what he or she is going to do or does. Consider an attitude-behavior study in which the behavior is giving blood in a bloodmobile in front of the Illinois Student Union on the afternoon of Friday, October 6. If the subjects are asked to rate their agreement or disagreement with three items, (a) "I favor altruism," (b) "I favor giving blood," and (c) "I favor giving blood in the bloodmobile outside the Illinois Student Union on Friday afternoon October 6," it is not necessary to run a field study to conclude that the greatest attitude-behavior correspondence exists with the last item and the least with the first. Asking subjects attitude questions in which correspondence to behavior is too precise misses the point, which is to predict behavior from general attitudes, not to determine the relation between behavior and the subjects' verbal assessments of it. How much correspondence is "too much?" I do not know.

Another and more important problem in La Piere's interpretation of his findings is his conclusion: "All measurement by the questionnaire technique proceeds on the assumption that there is a mechanical and simple relation between symbolic and nonsymbolic behavior" (p.231). Not so. He postulated a 1:1 relation between verbally assessed attitude and behavior: A given attitude corresponds to a given behavior and vice versa. But the relation of attitude to behavior is many:1. Many different attitudes—including especially favorable attitudes toward complying with social norms and pressures (e.g., not turning away guests at a restaurant when they are physically present) may be associated with a particular behavior. For example, Schuman (1972) found that only 13% of Detroit area heads of households and their wives agreed to discrimination in principle, but 41% agreed if it were "necessary for the harmony of the firm," and 53% agreed if a majority of Whites in the firm favored it. Schuman wrote,

> But only to a true believer will any one of these values win out in all situations regardless of the other values with which it competes. A few people go to the stake for a single value, but history and common sense tells us that most people work out compromises depending on the exact balance of positions. (p.332)

The fact that a single behavior may be associated with many attitudes is illustrated in Figure 3b. Figure 3a illustrates a 1:1 relation.

But the relation is also 1:many. A single attitude may be associated with a multitude of behaviors; for example, a positive attitude toward a belief in a personal God may be associated with going to church, giving money to religious charities, praying, and the like. Fishbein and Ajzen (1974) illustrated this: They found a much greater correspondence between religious attitude and an aggregation of religious behaviors than between that attitude and any single behavior. (To someone conversant with classical mental test theory, this finding is hardly surprising.) One:many relations are illustrated in Figure 3c.

Because the relation is both many:1 and 1:many, it is *many:many* (Figure 3d). A single behavior is associated with many attitudes and a single attitude is associated with many behaviors. Such relations are very difficult to characterize mathematically. This structural complexity means that the attitude-behavior problem is quite ill-defined.

Finally, it should be pointed out that although most attitude-behavior researchers have treated behavior as the criterion and attitude as the predictor,

FIGURE 3
Relations Between Attitudes and Behaviors

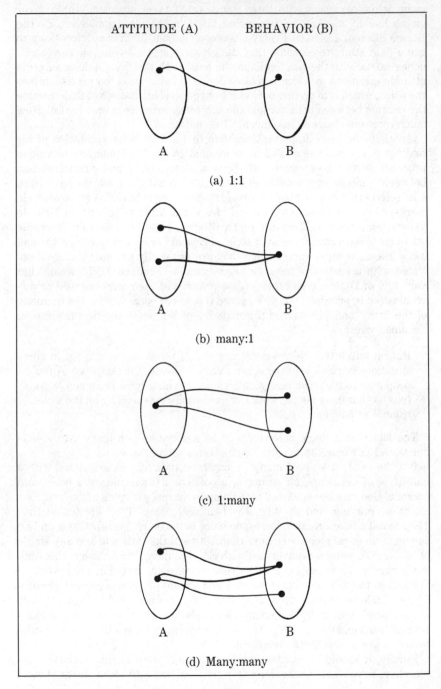

ATTITUDE (A)   BEHAVIOR (B)

A   B

(a) 1:1

A   B

(b) many:1

A   B

(c) 1:many

A   B

(d) Many:many

there is no compelling reason for doing so. Behaviors affect attitudes as well as vice versa. Nor is there any special reason to believe that behaviors are more "real" than are attitudes. Indeed, we believe the exact opposite in such contexts as course evaluations, in which we accept the anonymous questionnaire as an instrument to assess true student opinions about teaching and reject what they say to the teachers face to face (Schuman & Johnson, 1977).

CONCLUSION

In order to measure how hot it is in a room, all that is necessary is to look at a thermometer made by a reputable company. One does not need to know about the effect of heat on the expansion of mercury or about heat and molecular motion. Nor is it necessary to contemplate exactly what we *mean* by heat and to make judgments about whether the behavior of the mercury in the tube correspondes to our meaning.

Not so with attitude measurement! We must have a reasonably clear conception of the attitude we want to measure and, more specifically, know what *aspects* or attributes of the attitude we are interested in measuring. Moreover, if a representative measure is proposed, its internal consistency must be assessed; and if an index measure is developed it must be shown to have internal or external predictive validity (preferably both). Occasionally, ready-made techniques are available that seem to suit the researcher's needs, but they must never be chosen, like a thermometer, on the basis of their names. Often it is preferable to devise one's own technique and to suit it to the purposes. And that involves the most enjoyable challenge of all: to be creative and correct at the same time.

REFERENCES

Abelson, R. P. Computers, polls, and public opinion: Some puzzles and paradoxes. *Transaction*, 1968, *5*, 20-27.

Adams, E. W., Fagot, R. F., & Robinson, R. E. A theory of appropriate statistics. *Psychometrika*, 1965, *30*, 99-127.

Adorno, T. W., Frenkel-Brunswik, E., Levinson, D. J., & Sanford, R. N. *The authoritarian personality.* New York: Harper, 1950.

Ajzen, I., & Fishbein, M. Attitude-behavior relations: A theoretical analysis and review of the literature. *Psychological Bulletin*, 1977, *84*, 888-918.

Anderson, N. H. Scales and statistics: Parametric and nonparametric. *Psychological Bulletin*, 1961, *58*, 305-316.

Barker, R. G. The social psychology of physical disability. *Journal of Social Issues*, 1948, *4*, 28-34.

Bentler, P. M. Heterosexual behavior assessment. *Behavior Research and Therapy*, 1968, *6*, 21-30.

Bogardus, E. S. Measuring social distances. *Journal of Applied Sociology*, 1925, *9*, 299-308.

Campbell, D. T. The indirect assessment of social attitudes. *Psychological Bulletin*, 1950, *47*, 15-38.

Campbell, D. T., & Stanley, J. C. Experimental and quasi-experimental designs for research on teaching. In N. L. Gage (Ed.), *Handbook of research on teaching.* Chicago: Rand McNally, 1963.

Cleveland, S. E. Personal communication, July 21, 1970.

Coombs, C. H. *A theory of data.* New York: Wiley, 1964.

Cowen, E. L., Bobrove, P. H., Rockway, A. M., & Stevenson, J. Development and evaluation of an attitudes to deafness scale. *Journal of Personality and Social Psy-*

chology, 1967, *6*, 183-191.

Cowen, E. L., Underber, R. P., & Verillo, R. T. The development and testing of an attitude to blindness scale. *The Journal of Social Psychology*, 1958, *48*, 297-304.

Dawes, R. M. *Fundamentals of attitude measurement*. New York: Wiley, 1972.

Dawes, R. M., & Moore, M. Guttman scaling orthodox and randomized responses. In F. Peterman (Ed.), *Attitude measurement*, 1979, 117-133.

Ducamp, A., & Flamange, J. C. Composite measurement. *Journal of Mathematical Psychology*, 1969, *6*, 359-380.

Festinger, L. In collaboration with V. Allen, M. Braden, L. K. Cannon, J. R. Davidson, J. D. Jecker, S. B. Kiesler, & E. Walster. *Conflict, decision and dissonance*. Stanford CA: Stanford University Press, 1964.

Fishbein, M., & Ajzen, I. Attitudes toward objects as predictors of single and multiple behavioral criteria. *Psychological Review*, 1974, *81*, 59-74.

Hays, W. L. *Statistics for psychologists*. New York: Holt, Rinehart & Winston, 1963.

Jensen, A. R. How much can we boost IQ and scholastic achievement? *Harvard Educational Review*, 1969, *39*, 1-123.

Johnson, H. H., & Foley, J. M. Some effects of placebo and experiment conditions in research on methods of teaching. *Journal of Educational Psychology*, 1969, *60*, 6-10.

La Piere, R. T. Attitudes versus actions. *Social Forces*, 1934, *13*, 230-237.

MacNeil, M. K., Davis, L. E., & Pace, D. J. Group status displacement under stress: A serendipitous finding. *Sociometry*, 1975, *38*, 293-307.

Melton, A. W. Some behavior characteristics of museum visitors. *Psychological Bulletin*, 1933, *30*, 720-721.

Milgram, S., Mann, L., & Harter, S. The lost-letter technique of social research. *Public Opinion Quarterly*, 1965, *29*, 437-438.

Osgood, C. E., & Luria, Z. A blind analysis of a case of multiple personality using the semantic differential. *Journal of Abnormal and Social Psychology*, 1954, *49*, 579-591.

Osgood, C. E., Suci, G. J., & Tannenbaum, P. H. *The measurement of meaning*. Urbana: University of Illinois Press, 1957.

Patterson, G. R., & Dawes, R. M. A Guttman scale of childrens' coercive behaviors. *Journal of Consulting and Clinical Psychology*, 1975, *43*, 594.

Podell, L., & Perkins, J. A Guttman scale for sexual experience. *Journal of Abnormal and Social Psychology*, 1957, *54*, 420-422.

Schuman, H. Attitudes vs. action *versus* attitudes vs. action. *Public Opinion Quarterly*, 1972, *36*, 347-354.

Schuman, H., & Johnson, M. P. Attitudes and behaviors. *Annual Review of Sociology*, 1976, *2*, 161-207.

Sikes, M. P., & Cleveland, S. E. Human relations training for police and community. *American Psychologist*, 1968, *23*, 766-769.

Spaeth, J. H. Unidimensionality and item invariance in judicial scaling. *Behavioral Science*, 1965, *10*, 290-304.

Stevens, S. S. Mathematics, measurement, and psychophysics. In S. S. Stevens (Ed.), *Handbook of experimental psychology*. New York: Wiley, 1951.

Stouffer, S. A., Guttman, L., Schuman, E. A., Lazarsfeld, D., Star, A., & Clausen, J. A. *Measurement and prediction*. Princeton NJ: Princeton University Press, 1950.

Thurstone, L. L. Attitudes can be measured. *American Journal of Sociology*, 1928, *33*, 529-554.

Thurstone, L. L. The measurement of social attitudes. *Journal of Abnormal and Social Psychology*, 1931, *26*, 249-269.

Triandis, H. C., & Triandis, L. M. Some studies of social distance. In I. E. Steiner & M. Fishbein (Eds.), *Current studies in social psychology*. New York: Holt, Rinehart & Winston, 1965.

Valins, S. Cognitive effects of false heart-rate feedback. *Journal of Personality and Social Psychology*, 1966, *4*, 400-408.

Webb, E. J., Campbell, D. T., Schwartz, R. D., & Sechrest, L. *Unobtrusive measures: Nonreactive research in the social sciences*. Chicago: Rand McNally & Co., 1966.

Wicker, A. W. Attitudes vs. action: The relationship of verbal and overt responses to attitude objects. *Journal of Social Issues*, 1969, *25*, 41-78.

5

Sociometric Research in Special Education

DONALD L. MACMILLAN
GALE M. MORRISON

The contents of this chapter are restricted to research employing sociometric techniques in classroom settings in which handicapped children are enrolled. Before the substantive findings of these studies are reviewed, the elements of sociometrics, the kinds of information on attitudes they yield, and the limitations of the technique are examined. These discussions provide the basis for the evaluation of specific studies. The review of the substantive research leads to generalizations on the sociometric status of handicapped children in classrooms and, then, to a conceptual model that offers a more comprehensive framework to guide future thought and research on the social status of handicapped children. With this model as the framework, past and potential interventions are reviewed. The chapter concludes with an examination of the dependent variables found in the current literature and the consideration of alternative dependent variables which may provide more information on the dynamics of the social acceptance of handicapped children.

SOCIOMETRIC TECHNIQUES

The term "sociometric," as used in the special education literature, encompasses a variety of techniques which differ markedly from the orthodox techniques described by Gronlund (1959). The variations raise questions about their validity (that is, do these techniques measure the same construct which is derived from classic sociometric techniques) and about the comparability of findings where techniques vary from study to study. The principle parameters of sociometric techniques are examined first.

Note: This study was supported in part by National Institute of Child Health and Human Development Research Grants No. HD 04612 and HD 05540.

Description and Definition

The sociometric techniques originated by Moreno (1934) were used initially in classrooms to evaluate the extent to which pupils were accepted by their peers and to determine the *internal* structure of classroom groups. Lindsey and Byrne (1968) described sociometrics as a subcategory of attitude measurement in which the responses constitute the *conative* aspects of an attitude, that is, how a person would behave toward an individual or attitude object under circumstances in which that person believes that his or her choices may have consequences for himself or herself. The belief that the responses will have consequences is important, otherwise the responses tap an *affective* component of an attitude. Gottlieb (1975) and Scott (1968) developed the point further with the claim that when individuals do not believe that choices will have consequences for them, sociometric responses are "scarcely more overt than those required by the usual self-report inventories" (Scott, 1968, p. 217).

In an extended discussion of the kind of situations portrayed in the socio-metric question or criterion, Gronlund (1959) noted that certain questions fail to establish potential consequences for the choices made and, therefore, cannot be considered sociometric questions (e.g., "Whom do you like best?" "Who are your best friends?"). Moreno (1934) also insisted on basing the sociometric choices on criteria that reflect actual situations or activities in which group members have a real opportunity for participation. Hence, such choices as seating companions, partners in classroom projects, sharers of leisure time, and the like are criteria upon which a teacher can group class members and where students can see the potential consequences of their selections. Questions that ask for best friends or best looking classmates lack clearcut criteria and potential consequences and thus fail to ensure valid responses. Techniques lacking criteria and consequences have been labeled "near-sociometric" tests which run the risk of eliciting socially undesirable responses.

Sociometric techniques have been identified with peer-assessment techniques (see Kane & Lawler, 1978), yet they yield different types of information. A sociometric is designed to reveal the rater's attraction, aversion, or neutrality toward individuals; that is, the emphasis is on the rater's feelings about rather than judgment of the other individuals' characteristics. Peer assessments require the rater to evaluate the extent to which another individual exhibits or possesses a certain characteristic (e.g., attractiveness, leadership, achievement, etc.). Hence, sociometrics yield information about *internal* structure (Who would you want to _____) as opposed to information about external group structure (Who sits or plays with _____?), which can be gathered through observational procedures.

Elements and Terminology

A sociometric includes a *basis for choice* (also called the *sociometric question* or *sociometric criterion*) which the rater uses to make selections. These criteria can be either specific (e.g., select the five students with whom you prefer to eat lunch) or general (e.g., select the five students with whom you prefer to do projects). Note that the question establishes the situation-specific nature of the response and that with another basis (e.g., playing baseball) the child's nominations could change.

When the sociometric ratings are obtained, several terms are frequently used to characterize the patterns of selections among class members and their statuses.

1. **Star;** a child who receives more nominations than expected by chance (Bronfenbrenner, 1945).
2. **Isolate:** a child who receives no nominations (an extreme status).
3. **Neglectee:** a child who receives some nominations but fewer than is expected by chance.
4. **Rejectee:** a child who receives more negative choices than is expected by chance.

The first three terms are derived from the number of times a child is nominated by classmates on a positive basis of choice (e.g., name the five children you would most want to sit next to in class). The rejectee status can be established only when negative choices are sought (e.g., name the five children you would least want to sit next to in class); it indicates a rater's aversion toward a nominated child. It is important to differentiate the negative feelings reflected in nominations for negatively worded choices from the feelings reflected in the lack of nominations for positively worded choices that result in *isolate* or *neglectee* status.

Another pattern of choice which must be considered is found in the situation in which two children independently select one another; such choices are designated as *mutual or reciprocal choices*. Mutual choice must be based on the same criterion; it indicates a mutual desire to associate with one another in the activity specified.

The preceding brief descriptions of conventional sociometric terms and constructs provide a basis for evaluating research conducted in the name of sociometrics with special education populations.

Interpretation

The historical roots of sociometric techniques lie in teachers' efforts to understand the social structure of classrooms and the search for facilitators to enhance social structure. As such, the sociometric data could be displayed as a sociogram that schematically represents choice patterns (see Gronlund, 1959, for an extended discussion of sociograms) among class members. Although interpretations for one classroom must be limited to the situation in the basis for choice, sociograms can be very informative, in a descriptive sense, about the classroom's internal social structure.

Easy to develop, administer, and score, sociometrics have been increasingly used as outcome measures in evaluation projects; for example, to measure social adjustment in efficacy studies of special *vs.* regular classes (as done by Jordan reported in Thurstone, 1959), and as dependent variables in research (e.g., Johnson, 1950). The extension of sociometrics into evaluation and research created some problems in interpreting the sociometric data. For example, comparing the sociometric status of an educable mentally retarded child (EMR) in a regular fourth grade classroom to that of an EMR child in a self-contained EMR classroom is hazardous, if not downright foolhardy, because the populations making the nominations differ along a host of significant dimensions: IQ, achievement, adaptive behavior, and possibly others, such as social class and ethnicity. Even when one compares the sociometric status of handicapped to nonhandicapped children in the same classrooms, problems in interpretation arise, primarily from the desire to attribute differences to the handicap, per se.

Sociometric techniques yield descriptive data but do not tell *why* a child enjoys star status, is rejected, or is an isolate. To illustrate, let us consider a hypothetical study in which hard-of-hearing children are found to be rejected significantly more often and accepted significantly less often than are their peers with normal hearing in the same classroom. Although it is tempting to attribute such findings to the hearing loss or handicap per se, these differences also could be caused by the hard-of-hearing sample's being systematically different from the other children in terms of IQ, age, the extent to which they are socially adept, or even the amount of contact with the other children. The point is that extreme caution must be exercised in interpreting sociometric results as evidence that a disability or label causes the social status.

Gronlund (1959) also stressed that sociometrics tap the *internal structure* of a classroom as contrasted to the *external structure*, which would be tapped by an observational scheme showing which children in fact interact socially. Therefore, sociometric results must be interpreted in terms of internal preferences as opposed to actual social interactions. Independent research and interpretations must be pursued to determine the relation between the sociometric attitude and the actual social behavior. Such investigations of handicapped populations could be especially crucial to confirm or challenge the assumption that attitudes affect behavior.

One must also consider how sociometric instruments are scored and indices of social status are derived. For instance, Johnson (1950) asked for nominations under three situations: (a) Who do you best like? (b) Who would you have sit next to you? and (c) Who do you like to play with best? An "acceptance score" was derived from the total number of times a child was named across all three situations. Jones, Lavine, and Shell (1972) solicited nominations for 10 situations and analyzed the data for each situation separately. Hence, they were able to study the social status as a function of criteria, whereas Johnson interpreted his results as an indication of general social status.

The sociometric instruments in most instances specify criteria (seating, play, class projects) for selection, and these criteria must be used to interpret the data. Gronlund (1959) stated that there tends to be consistency across criteria, but this statement has not been tested with handicapped populations, for whom logic would suggest inconsistency. For example, a mildly retarded male who excels in athletics may be rejected as a coworker on an academic project because the rater perceives him as lacking the potential to contribute to it, yet he may be viewed favorably for selection on a baseball team. Until there is such research on the situation-specific versus generality of social status of handicapped populations, caution in interpreting sociometric data seems warranted.

Finally, there is a paucity of evidence on the intensity of attitudes in the sociometric research in special education which renders the results difficult to interpret. Evidence showing that EMR or learning disabled (LD) children are rejected reveals nothing about the intensity with which the raters expressed this attitude. Furthermore, without evidence on intensity, predictions of behavior that result from attitudes should be made with less confidence.

Sampling

The use of sociometric techniques in research with handicapped learners raises problems in sampling, particularly when a study entails the ratings by non-handicapped children of a handicapped child in their regular classroom. First, the integrated handicapped child is a "select" or unrepresentative case who has been selected for integration because of a favorable prognosis. Only the most promising EMR or deaf children are selected for integration. This fact makes the generalizability of findings limited; certainly one cannot generalize the findings to all children with that handicap. Differences in achievement, IQ, social behavior, and other child characteristics differentiate integrated and nonintegrated children with a particular disability.

One consideration is the "sample" of children doing the rating. The composition of a regular class varies from classroom to classroom with a host of variables that may affect the favorableness of the attitudes expressed toward handicapped children: sex, social class, age, modal achievement level, and ethnicity, for example. Clearly, there is a need to describe in some detail the characteristics of the peer group doing the ratings as well as the characteristics of the teacher and classroom.

Additionally, there is a need to describe and account for several crucial environmental variables, such as teacher variables, curriculum variations, class size, and classroom climate. Schmuck and Schmuck (1975) argued convincingly that these environmental variables can significantly affect the social acceptance patterns within and between classrooms.

Inconsistency in results across studies may be due in part to factors related to sampling; the possibility is hard to evaluate because of the insufficient descriptions which are provided in so many of the research reports and their implicit assumption that the sociometric status of handicapped learners is attributable to the handicap, per se.

Instrumentation

The inconsistency of findings across studies also may be due in part to variability in instrumentation. Three types of sociometrics are commonly used, sometimes alone and sometimes in combination:

1. **Partial rank-order.** Each child in the classroom is asked to nominate a specified number of children according to the criteria. For example, list the three children in the class with whom you would like to work on a social studies project.
2. **Guess who.** Each child is given a series of descriptive statements and is asked to name the child in the class who best fits the description. For example, who is the best in reading? or who fights a lot?
3. **Roster and rating.** Each child is given a list of every class member and is asked to rate each, usually on a continuum of like to dislike.

Gronlund (1959) contended that the results derived from these techniques yield similar results, yet the literature on EMR children suggests subtle differences which are a function of the type of sociometric or near-sociometric technique employed.

RESEARCH FINDINGS

The sociometric studies in special education usually have examined the status of a handicapped child in a regular classroom. Moreover, the majority of studies have focused on EMR children; few have focused on other kinds of handicapped learners. The basic question asked in the research is whether the handicapped learners are nominated as often as their nonhandicapped peers or, conversely, whether they are rejected more often.

Variability across studies in terms of age, IQ, instruments, sociometric criterion (when specified), and characteristics of the regular class make comparisons impossible and any generalizations very tentative. Nevertheless, a consistent trend is apparent: handicapped learners in regular classrooms enjoy lower sociometric status than do their nonhandicapped peers, but it is uncertain whether their handicaps are the reason.

For organizational purposes, we have separated the studies under review into two groups: (a) those focusing on EMR and LD children whose handicaps essentially are learning inefficiencies, and (b) those focusing on physically or sensorily handicapped children whose handicaps are more visible.

Studies of EMR and LD Children

Earlier reviews of the literature (Dentler & Mackler, 1962; Guskin, 1963) on the popularity of retarded children concluded that there is a consistent positive correlation between intelligence and social status. Since the majority of research summarized in these reviews was conducted, there has been a shift in the upper IQ limit for defining mental retardation: first to one SD below the mean (Heber, 1961) and then to two SDs below the mean (Grossman, 1973). Considering the fact that a number of the studies reviewed in this chapter were conducted between 1961 and 1973, the reader is cautioned to be careful about generalizing their results to current populations of EMR children. However, much of the work prior to 1961 was done with EMR children who were psychometrically similar to present-day EMR children (i.e., scoring below IQ 70).

Johnson's (1950) early work revealed that low-IQ children (mean IQ = 63.69) in regular grades 1–5 were accepted less often and rejected more often on sociometric measures than were typical children in the same classrooms. Johnson used a partial rank-order technique with three criteria (Who do you like best? If you were to have your seat changed, who would you like to have sit in the seat next to you? Who are the children in your class that you like to play with the best?) The same three questions were then rephrased to yield rejection nominations. Acceptance and rejection scores were derived by summing the nominations across the three criteria. It should be noted that the CAs of the retarded subjects were greater than the CAs of the typical students at every grade level. Inasmuch as the "retarded" sample was not labeled or specially programmed, the differences in acceptance and rejection were apparently due to the characteristics of the children and not to their EMR condition per se.

Baldwin (1958) studied 31 IQ-defined EMR children enrolled in grades 4–6. The median CA was almost one year older for the EMR sample than for the nonretarded sample. The IQ range for the EMR sample was 50–74. The Ohio Social Acceptance Scale (a roster and rating technique) revealed that the EMR sample was significantly lower in the degree of social acceptance. Both Johnson (1950) and Baldwin (1958) concluded that the children rating the EMRs consistently resented antisocial behavior.

Lapp (1957) used the sociometric instrument devised by Johnson (1950). In Lapp's study, the EMR subjects ranged in CA from 9 to 13 years and in IQ from 55 to 92, and were integrated into regular grades 3–6. Lapp reported that the EMR children were lower in social acceptance scores but did not differ from nonretarded subjects in terms of rejection. Although the EMR sample lacked specific abilities that would have resulted in their higher acceptance, they apparently also lacked objectionable traits that would have led to their being rejected. The fact that social acceptance scores were higher than would be expected by chance, coupled with the failure to find higher rejection scores, led Lapp to conclude that integrated EMRs were tolerated by regular classroom peers.

Integrated EMR children, 23 of whom (CA range, 11—16; IQ, 54—80) participated in junior high school academic and physical education classes, were studied by Rucker, Howe, & Snider (1969). The investigators administered the Ohio Social Acceptance Scale, which was adapted for use with older subjects, in regular and special classrooms. The EMR subjects were rated significantly lower than nonretarded subjects in both academic and nonacademic classes. Moreover, the social status of EMR subjects did not differ between academic and nonacademic settings. However, the investigators reported a more favorable rating in special classes. Although this finding is difficult to interpret, because of differences in the raters, one might speculate that the special class provided a more "accepting" environment for the EMR subjects. Confirmation of this hypothesis would entail investigation into the EMRs' perceptions of the two situations. The findings of Rucker et al (1969) do not support those of Lapp (1957), but the age differences between the two samples could account for the lack of accord.

Miller (1956) used a roster and rating technique by which each child was rated by every other child on a 1-5 scale, ranging from "wanting that person as a friend very much" to "don't want that person as a friend at all." Three other scales (1–5) also were rated on the basis of (a) that person's feelings toward you, (b) that person's popularity, and (c) learning facility. Twenty subjects were identified in each of the following IQ ranges: 60–80, 90–110, and 120–140. Comparable samples were selected at 4th- and 6th-grade levels. The superior IQ subjects were wanted most as friends, followed by the average and low-IQ samples; all differences except those between average and low-IQ children in the fourth grade were significant. No group was actually rejected, according to the ratings; in fact, even the low-IQ sample was mildly accepted.

The sociometric status of EMR children participating in an integrative resource room program was studied by Iano, Ayers, Heller, McGettigan, and Walker (1974). No specific data were provided on CA, IQ, or social class; the sample was described as elementary students in three groups: regular class pupils, former special class EMR pupils, and resource room referrals (never EMR). A partial rank-order technique modeled after Johnson's (1950) was used. Regular class children were rated highest, followed by resource room referrals, and then former EMRs; the mean scores for each group were significantly different. Former EMRs were rejected most often but their rejection scores were not reliably higher than those of resource room referrals. The distributions of acceptance scores for EMR and nonretarded subjects overlapped sufficiently so that EMR status per se was seen as an insufficient explanation for the mean difference. Some EMR children were reasonably well accepted while large numbers of nonretarded children appeared to be disliked.

Monroe and Howe (1971) used the Ohio Social Acceptance Scale to investigate the relation of length of integration time and social class to the sociometric status of EMR (IQ, 54–92) adolescents in integrated junior high schools. The 70 male subjects who were integrated were separated according to the number of years they had been integrated (1–3 years). No differences were found in the sociometric status of the EMR students as a function of the length of time they were integrated, but higher social class EMRs were less rejected than were lower social class EMRs.

The role of socioeconomic status was investigated further by Bruininks, Rynders, and Gross (1974) who added the effects of the sex of the rater. The target subjects were 65 EMR children (IQ 50–85) in elementary grades in two school districts, one urban and the other suburban. A form of roster and rating technique (the Peer Acceptance Scale) was used; raters indicated the degree to which they wanted the other children as friends. Stick figures were used to convey three alternatives—"friend," "all right," and "wouldn't like." Same-sex ratings were higher for urban EMRs than for non-EMRs of both sexes, whereas suburban EMRs received lower ratings than nonretarded children. When total ratings were analyzed, no differences were found between EMR and nonretarded samples in either urban or suburban districts. Whether the SES differences attest to differences in the social adeptness of urban EMRs or the greater tolerance of urban nonretarded children could not be ascer-

100

tained. Slightly higher IQs and lower CAs were noted by the investigators for the urban EMR sample.

Goodman, Gottlieb, and Harrison (1972) used the Peer Acceptance Scale to study the social acceptance of EMR children who were not known to peers as EMR in a nongraded elementary school. At the primary level, the names of six unidentified EMRs were included on the roster with 29 nonretarded children, a total of 35. At the intermediate level, four lists of names were randomly generated which always included four unidentified EMRs and eight segregated EMRs. Three of these lists contained 39 names each and one list contained 37 names. The results indicated that both integrated and segregated EMR children were rejected more often than the nonretarded children, that younger children and females were more accepting or tolerant of EMRs than the other children, and that males at the intermediate level were more rejecting of integrated than segregated EMRs. However, the findings may have been affected by the fact that all EMR subjects were bused to the school.

A similar design was employed by Gottlieb and Budoff (1973) to study the social position of segregated and integrated EMRs in two schools: (a) a traditional elementary school and (b) a no-interior-walls school. Eighty nonretarded children in the open school and 56 in the traditional school (spread evenly over grades 1–6) rated both integrated and segregated EMRs on the Peer Acceptance Scale. Despite the fact that the EMRs in the open school were known more often by nonretarded peers, the EMRs were not chosen as friends more often in the open school; indeed, EMRs were rejected significantly more often in the open than in the traditional school.

Gottlieb, Semmel, and Veldman (1978) explored the sociometric status of mainstreamed EMR children according to a regression model in order to ascertain the influence of certain variables. A roster and rating technique (How I Feel Toward Others) was administered as part of Project PRIME (Kaufman, Agard, & Semmel, in press). Ratings were analyzed for 324 EMR children aged 8–15 years who were integrated into grades 3–5. The independent variables included peer perceptions of cognitive and disruptive behavior, teacher perceptions of cognitive and disruptive behavior, and degree of integration. The most intriguing finding was that the acceptance and rejection scores for EMR subjects were associated with different independent variables: Acceptance was associated with perceptions of academic performance and rejection with misbehavior. Moreover, contrary to the expectations of advocates of mainstreaming, no relationship was found between the degree of integration and sociometric status.

Few studies have focused on learning disabled children. A total of six were identified: two by Bruininks (1978a, 1978b), two by Bryan (1974, 1976), and one each by Sheare (1978), and Siperstein, Bopp, and Bak (1978). Bryan (1974) administered two sociometric techniques (a partial rank-order and a "guess who") across 62 classrooms, grades 3–5, that included 84 LD children. The LD children were rejected more often and accepted less often than were the nondisabled children. When the data were analyzed by sex, race, and LD status, the investigator found that white LD boys and girls were the least popular; black LD boys and girls were next in order, followed by nondisabled black boys and girls, and white nondisabled boys and girls were the most popular.

A year later, Bryan (1976) administered her scales again in 20 classrooms in which 25 white children of the original LD sample were enrolled. She selected a matched (sex, race, and classroom) sample of nondisabled children. The results closely paralled the earlier findings: The social status of the LD sample again was significantly lower than that for the controls, even in classrooms where there was 75% or greater change in classmates from year 1 to 2.

The Bruininks (1978a, 1978b) studies focused on the social acceptance of LD students in mainstreamed settings. The LD groups consisted of students in grades 1–5 who spent the majority of their time in regular classrooms and received up to 45 minutes of instruction per day in a resource room. The control groups consisted of randomly selected same-sex peers in the same regular classroom for each LD child. Mean ratings from the Peer Acceptance Scale were compared for the LD (1978a, $N = 16$; 1978b, $N = 23$) and control groups. Both studies revealed that the social status of the LD students was significantly lower than that of their regular class peers. Additionally, the LD students were less accurate in their perceptions of their own social status. Implications were drawn regarding the effect of this lowered ability to perceive the feelings of others on social status and general social adjustments.

Siperstein et al. (1978) studied 22 LD children integrated into regular fifth and sixth grade classrooms for at least 75% of the day, resulting in a total sample of 177. A single question was asked of each child: Name the same-sex children in the class whom each liked best. In addition, each child was asked to nominate: (a) the best athlete, (b) the smartest student, and (c) the best-looking child. LD children were nominated significantly less often than nondisabled children on the sociometric question and no LD child rated a "star" position. However, LD children were not found to occupy "isolate" positions in greater proportions than were nondisabled children. All three criteria (athlete, smart, and attractiveness) were correlated with social status, attractiveness correlating the highest.

A sociometric (roster and rating) technique was one measure used by Sheare (1978) to evaluate the impact of resource interventions on 41 LD children (grades 3–5). The controls were a group of 41 nondisabled children, stratified by sex and classroom. The criterion for rating was the extent to which the child "liked the named child." A test-retest reliability after 2 months yielded a coefficient of .89. LD children received significantly lower ratings on the sociometric measure; however, pre-post differences in ratings revealed that LD children had significantly higher ratings at the end of the year than they received in November (which was also found for the nondisabled sample).

Despite wide variations in sociometric techniques and criteria for sociometric choice, the literature on mildly handicapped learners in regular grades reveals a consistent picture: These children are less well accepted and more frequently rejected than are nonhandicapped peers. Efforts designed to isolate child, peer, or situational factors that might explain why these children enjoy lower sociometric status are only beginning to appear in the literature (e.g., Bruininks et al., 1974; Gottlieb et al., 1978). The findings to date do not suggest that temporal integration per se will be successful if the criterion for success is social popularity. Thus far, the research has sought to explain findings in terms of the attributes of the handicapped child or administrative arrangements but seldom of the group doing the rating. The findings (e.g., Bruininks et al., 1974) regarding sex and SES of rater can possibly be extended to include the interaction of child X rater (age discrepancies, ethnicity, achievement differences, etc.) This type of information appears to be greatly needed for decisions on where to place mildly handicapped children in keeping with the principle of least restrictive environment.

Studies of Children with Physical/Sensory Handicaps

Far fewer sociometric studies have been conducted with sensorily impaired or severely mentally retarded children, the majority of those extant focusing on hearing-impaired children. Like the studies with EMR and LD subjects, the sociometric research with physically/sensorily handicapped children has been carried out in regular classrooms.

Force (1956) studied 361 nonhandicapped and 63 handicapped children; the latter displayed a variety of types of disabilities: cardiac, polio, cerebral palsy, congenital anomaly, visual, and hearing handicaps. The specific sociometric technique was described as . . . "A near-sociometric instrument . . . which revealed choice behavior on three criteria—friends, playmates, and workmates" (p. 104). Handicapped children were selected significantly less often than their nonhandicapped peers on all three criteria. Force attempted to ascertain the variability in terms of specific disabilities and reported that cerebral palsied children were very low in social status on all three criteria. Of the handicapped samples, children with heart problems were the most accepted as friends while hearing handicapped children were chosen the least, except for cerebral palsied children on the playmate criterion. No mention was made of age discrepancies, intellectual status, achievement, or other data on the handicapped samples which could affect social status independently of the handicap.

Elser (1959) used a partial rank-order technique whereby children nominated three children as friends, playmates, and luncheon associates, and then named the three children they would not want for each role. In addition, a "guess who" technique was used to establish a "reputation score" on the criteria of popularity, game-playing ability, and smartness. The subjects were 45 hearing-impaired children whose hearing loss was in excess of 35 dB, whose CAs ranged from 9 to 12, and who were enrolled in regular grades 3–7, and 1,248 non-handicapped children. No detailed information was provided on the latter or on the classrooms in which any of the children were enrolled. The hearing-handicapped children were not as accepted as the average nonhandicapped children; however, no differences were found between hearing-handicapped and nonhandicapped subjects on personality ratings, although the hearing handicapped were significantly lower on reputation scores. Interestingly, the children with hearing aids were more accepted than were those without hearing aids (the latter, with mild to moderate handicaps, were less "visibly handicapped").

Kennedy and Bruininks (1974) studied seven boys and eight girls with hearing handicaps who were enrolled in 13 elementary classrooms with 277 nonhandicapped peers. The sample was divided into children with moderate hearing loss (45–74 dBs, $N = 4$) and severe to profound losses (75–110 dBs, $N = 11$). All children wore hearing aids fulltime. Three sociometric tests were administered: a partial rank-order (criterion: working, playing, or sitting together), a roster and rating technique (extent to which the child is wanted as a friend), and a socioempathy scale (child indicated how classmates rated him/her). The results revealed that hearing-impaired children were rated significantly higher than nonhandicapped children on the partial rank-order scale but no significant differences were found on the roster and rating scale. The results were more favorable for the severe-profound subsample. The inconsistent findings (of Elser, 1959, and Kennedy & Bruininks, 1974) may have been due to age differences or to the presence of greater social adeptness in the severe-profound subsample who had attended preschool. Most important was the fact that the hearing-handicapped children were selected by pupils with above-average sociometric scores.

The 11 children with severe and profound hearing losses were followed over the next 2 years by Kennedy, Northcott, McCauley, and Williams (1976). Their sociometric status was evaluated by the same instruments used by Kennedy and Bruininks (1974). After 1 year, the hearing-impaired children were not different from their nonhandicapped peers, but after 2 additional years they were significantly lower in sociometric status. On the roster and rating technique, the hearing-impaired children were not significantly different from nonhandicapped peers during any of the 3 years. Efforts were made to account for the drop in popularity; observation revealed that the hearing-impaired sample interacted verbally significantly more with teachers and significantly less with peers.

Only one study used sociometrics with blind children (Jones et al., 1972). The population of concern consisted of 11 boys and 9 girls, integrated blind children (all used Braille), who were enrolled in grades 4–6. The investigators developed their own sociometric questionnaire; in the final version it consisted of 10 items for which the rater was to nominate three children. Some items were indicative of acceptance (e.g., "I would like to eat my lunch with _____"; "I would like to work on a social studies project with _____") and others tapped rejection (e.g., "I would be happy if this person were absent from school"; "During an arithmetic lesson, I would not like to sit next to _____").

In general, the blind children were found to score below the median on most of the 10 items; however, some were found to be stars who tended to be described as personally congenial and free of annoying personality and behavior problems. The investigators also analyzed the sociometric standing of the sighted children who listed a blind classmate on the sociometric items. Generally, the blind children were nominated by a cross-section of sighted classmates. That is, the blind children had been nominated by popular, isolated, and rejected children. The analysis did not consider sex or socioeconomic status of raters, but was restricted to sociometric status.

Finally, Gerber (1977) included a sociometric ("We are going to have a birthday party for you. Who will you invite? Who will you not invite?") as a measure in a study of preschool children (3-1/2 to 5 years) in a class that included three handicapped children: an orthopedically handicapped boy, an "autistic-like" boy, and a cerebral palsied girl. The names of the handicapped children appeared 5 times (31.2%) for inclusion in the party and 7 times (41.2%) for exclusion. The cerebral palsied girl was not mentioned at all on 75% of the nominations.

Research using sociometric techniques with children possessing physical or sensory impairments is so small in volume that making generalizations is hazardous. The existing studies have been conducted in classrooms where the handicapped child is integrated into regular programs. Again, acceptance and rejection appear to be related more to the personal-behavioral characteristics of the child than to the handicap per se. Additional research is needed to clarify whether the visibility of the handicap (e.g., wearing a hearing aid) facilitates greater acceptance than a handicap that is not apparent to the raters. With the exception of Jones et al. (1972), the literature lacks analyses of the characteristics of peers in relation to the degree of acceptance shown the handicapped children.

In order to clarify the factors related to the sociometric status of integrated handicapped learners, an alternative conceptual model for sociometric research is offered in the following section.

A CONCEPTUAL MODEL FOR SOCIOMETRIC RESEARCH

So far, research on the sociometric status of special education students has controlled very few independent variables in any given study. Figure 1 depicts the model controlling the majority of studies to date. The mean or medium sociometric status determined for the handicapped learners is contrasted to the median or mean value for the nonhandicapped group and some judgment

FIGURE 1
Current Model for Most Sociometric Research in Special Education

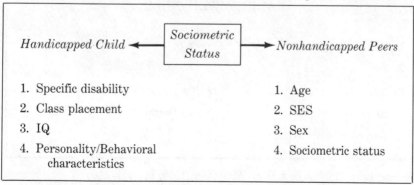

| *Handicapped Child* ← **Sociometric Status** → *Nonhandicapped Peers* |

1. Specific disability
2. Class placement
3. IQ
4. Personality/Behavioral characteristics

1. Age
2. SES
3. Sex
4. Sociometric status

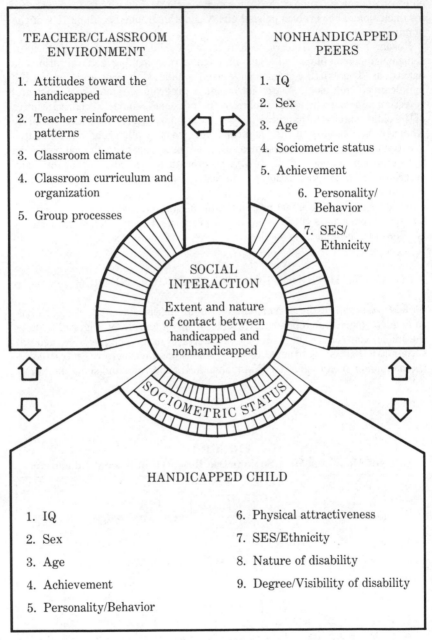

FIGURE 2
Alternative Model for Research on Sociometric Status in Speech Education

TEACHER/CLASSROOM
ENVIRONMENT

1. Attitudes toward the handicapped

2. Teacher reinforcement patterns

3. Classroom climate

4. Classroom curriculum and organization

5. Group processes

NONHANDICAPPED
PEERS

1. IQ

2. Sex

3. Age

4. Sociometric status

5. Achievement

6. Personality/ Behavior

7. SES/ Ethnicity

SOCIAL
INTERACTION

Extent and nature
of contact between
handicapped and
nonhandicapped

SOCIOMETRIC STATUS

HANDICAPPED CHILD

1. IQ

2. Sex

3. Age

4. Achievement

5. Personality/Behavior

6. Physical attractiveness

7. SES/Ethnicity

8. Nature of disability

9. Degree/Visibility of disability

Source: D.L. MacMillan & G.M. Morrison, 1979, pp. 411–450.

is made on higher, lower, or comparable sociometric status. The tendency of investigators to attribute sociometric status to the handicap per se ignores the fact that most studies in which raters have been asked *why* they accepted or rejected handicapped children have found that the attributes which are continually mentioned—personality and behavioral characteristics—are independent of the disability. The investigation by Gottlieb et al. (1978), examining variables that account for variance in sociometric status within a regression model, seems worthy of further investigation in order to identify independent variables that are related to sociometric status.

It is our contention that an alternative model for sociometric research is needed. Such a model is illustrated in Figure 2. The model has four major components—handicapped child, nonhandicapped peers, interactions of child and peers, and teacher/classroom environment—and specified independent variables for each which, somehow, should be controlled or manipulated for variations that relate to variations in social status.

One dimension not shown in the two-dimensional scheme of Figure 2 is the possible interactive nature of the four sets of independent variables. For example, although the achievement level of the handicapped child may account for some variance in social status, it might prove fruitful to determine how that child's achievement level interacts with the modal achievement level of nonhandicapped peers. A handicapped child whose achievement level is within one year of the class may enjoy higher social status than one whose achievement deviates markedly. Similarly, the interaction of age, ethnicity, SES, and other independent variables related to the handicapped child might be best studied in relation to the same variables in the nonhandicapped peers doing the rating. Moreover, there is a need to elucidate the role of teachers as they mediate the attitudes of nonhandicapped peers. For example, the social acceptance of handicapped children may be facilitated if the teacher reinforces or compliments handicapped children in the presence of nonhandicapped classmates or if the teacher reinforces nonhandicapped children who exhibit favorable social behaviors toward handicapped classmates. Indeed, the effects of teacher behavior on the acceptance of children labeled mentally retarded, who were shown in a videotaped situation, was investigated by Foley (1979). When the teacher reacted positively to the children's behavior, peer acceptance ratings were significantly higher than when the teacher reacted negatively. The data suggest that the teacher's role is critical in evaluations of mainstream situations; thus more evidence is needed.

In keeping with this model, some interventions are presented which are designed to improve the sociometric status of low-status children.

PROGRAMS TO IMPROVE SOCIAL STATUS

The literature reviewed to this point has repeatedly indicated a general lack of acceptance of handicapped children by their nonhandicapped peers. Given these discouraging findings and an educational objective of improving the social acceptance of these children, there has been a surprising lack of experimental studies attempting to manipulate social acceptance patterns. The few studies attempting to change sociometric status per se have been plagued with problems mentioned previously, such as lack of comparability of instruments and a wide variety of sampling techniques, making comparisons and/or generalizations virtually impossible.

A notable deficiency in the few reported intervention studies is the relative lack of any conceptual framework or validity base for the type of intervention implemented. Most studies have relied on intuitions or assumptions, such as the belief that increased exposure to and contact with handicapped children will increase the social acceptance of handicapped children by their nonhandicapped peers. Such assumptions are generally unfounded and even may be fallacious (Gottlieb, 1975). It should be noted here that the assumption on increased contact (the "contact hypothesis") is a philosophical cornerstone of the mainstreaming movement. The use of the word "philosophical" emphasizes that the assumption is not empirically based and the dynamics underlying the concept have not been thoroughly delineated.

The studies involving change in sociometric status are reviewed in the framework of the conceptual model (Figure 2); that is, social acceptance is viewed from the perspectives of the individual child, peers, teacher, and environmental variables, and on the effects of these components on the social interaction of a child and his peers. Because of the limited use of sociometric data as dependent variables of change, implications and directions are drawn from studies which were designed to change attitudes toward the handicapped or to change behaviors which are known to correlate with social acceptance.

Interventions with the Individual Child

Research on the dynamics of peer acceptance has focused primarily on the association of acceptance or rejection of a child with a host of personal characteristics. Found to be related to social acceptance are physical characteristics (attractiveness), age, intelligence, academic achievement, personality, and social behaviors (Gronlund, 1959). Social behaviors have been suggested as an obvious target for remediation. Oden and Asher (1977) examined the effects on the sociometric status of socially isolated children of coaching them in social skills for friendship making. The coaching consisted of instructing the children in six 5–7 minute sessions in the following concepts:

> . . . participation (e.g., getting started, paying attention); cooperation (e.g., taking turns, sharing materials); communication (e.g., talking with the other person, listening); and validation support, referred to as being friendly, fun, and nice (e.g., looking at the other person, giving a smile, offering help or encouragement). (p.499)

These sessions were followed by one in which the child was allowed to practice the skills learned in a game-playing situation with a peer. A post-play review session immediately followed. The control groups consisted of (a) socially isolated children merely paired with another child to play games and (b) socially isolated children paired with a peer to work on independent tasks. A peer nomination roster and rating sociometric technique was used to obtain ratings on the play and work situations in order to obtain a rating of friendship. Pre- and posttest measures were obtained. The results indicated that the children who received the coaching increased their play sociometric rating significantly more than either of the control groups. The coached group also showed a greater but nonsignificant increase in friendship nominations. A follow-up sociometric assessment one year later indicated that the coached children continued to increase their play sociometric ratings. This study suggests that social acceptance of socially isolated children can be improved by coaching them in social and friendship-making skills. It is not clear which aspect of the intervention (the coaching or the practice and feedback) was responsible for the change.

It should be noted, in this as well as other successful interventions, that the positive and encouraging results were obtained with socially isolated (low-acceptance ratings) children. Very different interventions may be needed for children with various handicaps. For instance, the rejection of mildly retarded children by nonretarded peers has been associated with their negative social behaviors (Baldwin, 1958; Johnson, 1950). Interventions may have to deal with these negative behaviors before instituting provisions to develop positive social behaviors.

Successful intervention in social behaviors have used modeling and behavior modification techniques, such as shaping, peer reinforcement, and self-control (Cartledge & Milburn, 1978; MacMillan & Morrison, 1979). Although potentially useful for improving social acceptance, these interventions have not been linked with actual changes in sociometric status.

Several other correlates of social acceptance which are promising for interventions are positive and negative reinforcement (Hartup, Glazer, & Charlesworth, 1967), social role-taking skills (Kitano & Chan, 1978), socioempathy (Bruininks, 1978a), and communication skills (Bryan, 1977).

The relation of academic achievement, self-concept, and peer acceptance has been emphasized by Schmuck and Schmuck (1975). The directional relations among these phenomena have not been documented but it can be postulated that improvement in academic achievement may enhance self-concept and social acceptance. Sheare (1978) investigated such a possibility. The intervention consisted of a resource program devoted primarily to the academic needs of LD students, but after the subjects attended a resource program for one year no significant changes were found in their self-concepts or acceptance by peers. However, measures were not taken to determine whether parallel changes in academic achievement were occurring because of the resource program, so the study is an inadequate test of the hypothesis that academic change causes social acceptance improvement. This line of investigation, however, is potentially interesting and fruitful.

Interventions with Peers

Interventions to improve social status also might focus on the handicapped child's peers. Research on attitudes toward the mentally retarded indicates that children who are more accepting of mentally retarded children are usually female, young, from a lower SES group, and better adjusted than those who are less accepting (Gottlieb, 1975). These demographic characteristics are not based on sociometry and do not offer guidance for possible interventions, but they represent the research on the peer component of a social acceptance model.

Guidance for intervention may be obtained from two studies that attempted to change attitudes toward handicapped people. Clore and Jeffrey (1972) explored the effects of emotional role playing on interpersonal attitudes toward disabled college students. (See Chapter 3 for detailed discussion of this study.) Wilson (1971) compared the effects of simulation of deafness and observation of a deaf person. No differences were found on an attitude scale but differences appeared on a semantic differential, the simulation group giving the deaf a lower rating (supposedly because of their experience "in the shoes of a deaf person"). Role playing and simulation experiences hold potential for application to other handicaps as well. The theory behind such techniques is that the experiences will increase empathy, understanding, and tolerance of the people with the various handicaps. This theory needs to be further validated in studies in which sociometric change is a dependent variable. One can see the promise of such techniques as role playing, simulation, discussion, and various other activities in the curricula of schools to broaden the perspective of children toward their handicapped peers.

Child-Peer Interactions

A more complex and realistic area of attitude-change study is that of interactions between handicapped children and their nondisabled peers. Group processes and other environmental variables make up the milieu in which peer acceptance patterns are developed and fostered. The majority of intervention studies attempting to change sociometric status come under the rubric of "contact." As mentioned previously, these studies assume that increased exposure to or interaction with handicapped children will increase peer acceptance of them. In addition to increased contact, some studies are based on the assumption that participation in prestigious activities with popular students will contribute to increased acceptance of an unpopular child. Chennault (1967) paired unpopular and popular students in a special class for cooperative activities that included the planning, rehearsing, and presentation of a skit. The results indicated that the experimental subjects gained significantly over control subjects on a roster and rating sociometric measure. The investigators acknowledge that the gain could have been caused by any one of numerous factors including

(1) the cooperative group experiences; (2) removal of the experimental subjects from the classroom twice weekly for five weeks; (3) attention provided by experimenter; (4) interaction with high status peers; (5) successful public performance; (6) private support and public approval by the teacher; (7) successful completion of a challenging task;

110

and (8) concrete rewards given to classes at the end of the performance. (p. 457)

Obviously, the significant factors should be determined to specify the dynamics of the very broad contact and exposure hypotheses. What mediates acceptance or rejection in the interactions between handicapped children and their peers?

McDaniel (1970) studied the effects of participation in extracurricular activities on the social acceptance of EMR students by their EMR peers. It was discovered that EMR students who participated in the activities, the experimental group, were more accepting of their peers; rejection rates were either decreased or stabilized in this group. It should be noted that the sociometric measure used by McDaniel was the acceptance of others rather than acceptance by others. The authors attributed the increased acceptance to the greater interaction with an awareness of others. However, the question of the specific nature of the interaction remains.

Lilly (1971) paired unpopular, low-achieving students with popular peers in the making of a movie to present to the class. The investigator also attempted to examine the effects of the specific variables of experimenter impact, peer impact, removal from class, and salience of participation in the movie. Although Lilly noted a gain in social acceptance due to the treatments, he was not able to differentiate the effects of the variables. Thus, again, no illumination is provided on the dynamics of the contacts or the interactions.

When Lilly looked at the social acceptance gains at a 6-week follow-up, he found that the gains did not endure. Rucker and Vincenzo (1970) also failed to find long-term effects after similar intervention. Both studies suggested that long-term endurance of social acceptance gains may be achieved only through more specific interventions that modify the behaviors which the unpopular children may be exhibiting.

Ballard, Corman, Gottlieb, and Kaufman (1978) attempted to control the behavior exhibited by mainstreamed retarded children through highly structured group activities. Groups of children that included retarded learners were provided over a period of 8 weeks with structured and ordered tasks which were designed to encourage cooperation and provide successful experiences for everyone. Pre- and post-sociometric measures indicated that the experimental group of mainstreamed retarded learners improved their sociometric status significantly more than the control groups. The investigators, noting the need to specify the component responsible for the increased acceptance, offered four possibilities: (a) the cooperative nature of the task, (b) the high degree of structure, (c) the minimal academic nature of the task, or (d) the length of the treatment period (8 weeks).

Classroom Environment

In attempting to define the nature of peer interactions and their influence on social acceptance, investigators must consider the setting or environment in which the interactions take place. Schmuck and Schmuck (1975) emphasized the influence of the classroom climate or environment created by a teacher on the social acceptance patterns in the room. Earlier, Schmuck (1966) observed two types of liking patterns in classrooms:

111

Centrally structured peer groups are characterized by a large number of pupils who agree in selecting only a small cluster of their classmates as pupils they like. Along with this narrow focus on a small number of pupils, many other pupils are neglected entirely. Diffusely structured peer groups, on the other hand, are distinguished by a more equal distribution of liking choices; by no distinct subgroups whose members receive a large proportion of preferences; and by fewer entirely neglected pupils. (p. 341)

The diffusely structured classroom patterns were associated with high levels of group cohesiveness, demonstrated by positive attitudes toward school, self, and peers. More positive behaviors consistent with the goals of the school were also seen in diffusely structured classrooms. Students were more accurate in estimating their own status in centrally structured groups; this trend was detrimental for low-status students who were made acutely aware of their social positions. Thus, the diffuse structure is considered a healthier classroom social status pattern.

Schmuck (1966) emphasized the potential influence of teachers in shaping these sociometric patterns. He found that teachers of more diffusely structured classrooms, compared to other teachers, attended to and talked with a larger variety of students per hour. Teachers of centrally structured classrooms called on fewer students for participation and seemed to ignore the slower, less involved students. Teachers in classrooms with positive liking patterns rewarded students with specific statements for helpful behaviors and controlled behavioral disturbances with general, group-oriented statements. In contrast, teachers in classrooms with less positive liking patterns tended to reward individual students less often and reprimand them publicly for breaking rules. Teachers with positive classroom climates were more aware of the mental health aspects of their students and their classroom. In general, these teacher behaviors were associated with a positive, cohesive classroom climate which, in turn, was associated with diffuse and supportive classroom liking patterns. Kaufman et al. (in press) confirmed this association in investigations of social status as a function of classroom environment; they found that the status of EMR-special class, EMR-mainstreamed, and nonretarded students was significantly related to the cohesiveness of the classroom.

Reinforcement Patterns

The importance of teacher reinforcement patterns on sociometric patterns is shown in a study by Flanders and Havumaki (1960). In one condition, the teachers were instructed to praise only the students in odd-numbered seats for participation in a group discussion; in the control condition, teachers were allowed to direct praise to the group as a whole. In the experimental condition, the students in the odd-numbered seats received significantly more sociometric choices than those in the even-numbered seats. In the control condition, there was no difference between the students of odd- and even-numbered seats. Thus, the teacher's pattern of public positive reinforcement had a significant effect on peer acceptance patterns.

Also related to teacher reinforcement patterns are the contingencies for reinforcement set by the teachers. In a study by Drabman, Spitalnik, and Spitalnik (1974) the teacher was able to change the sociometric pattern of the group by changing the contingencies in a token reinforcement program. The social status of disruptive children was improved by making group reinforcement contingent on the behavior of those disruptive children. Although the actual behavior of these children did not change significantly, improvement in their social status was attributed to the responsibility for having to behave.

Group Processes

An essentially unexplored but very important aspect of environmental influence on peer acceptance is the effect of group processes on the acceptance patterns. Schmuck and Schmuck (1975) described the contributions of group norms, expectations, communication patterns, and group cohesiveness to classroom climate and their effect on social acceptance patterns. The investigators described classroom activities which can be used to improve acceptance patterns through the broadening of norms and expectations, increasing group cohesiveness, and improving communication patterns. Research in this area should be pursued to determine the effects on these processes of the addition of handicapped children to the group, and to ascertain whether interventions designed to improve group processes affect the sociometric status of handicapped children.

Classroom Organization

Other aspects of the environment which can be considered for manipulation are the administrative arrangement (described in a preceding section), degree of structure provided, the nature of academic and social demands, and the opportunity for interaction. Hallinan (1976) studied the effect of the organizational properties of a classroom (open vs. traditional) on friendship patterns and the amount of interaction possible. It was found that the structural characteristics of schools impose constraints on the content, frequency, and duration of peer interactions. The results of the study showed a less hierarchical distribution of choices, with fewer social isolates and sociometric leaders (similar to a diffuse structure) in open classrooms as compared to traditional classes. Thus, classroom organization could be a potentially important variable to consider in studying classroom peer relations.

In summary, potential avenues for improving the social acceptance of handicapped children include treating the child or his peers as individuals, manipulating peer interactions, and attempting to change aspects of the total environment, such as reinforcement patterns, group processes, or classroom organization. Few of these possibilities have been empirically documented with handicapped children. Future investigations should focus on the use of comparable sociometric measures with various groups of handicapped children to discover subtleties that could affect interventions with each group. And, because the proof of any intervention is its robustness in the test of time, more studies should consider the longitudinal nature of sociometric change.

DEPENDENT VARIABLE: WHAT CONSTITUTES ACCEPTANCE?

It was mentioned previously that studies comparing acceptance and/or rejection of handicapped learners and nonhandicapped peers typically use mean sociometric scores. Let us assume that we are concerned only with acceptance scores which have been derived from any of the types of sociometric instruments described previously in order to illustrate how more information might be derived from these studies.

First, all nominations are given the same weight. Being nominated by the lowest status child in the class "counts" as much as being nominated by the highest status child. Jones et al. (1972) examined the nomination patterns for blind children and found that the nominators represented a cross-section of the class in terms of social status. The question raised here is whether sociometric data should be analyzed further to determine what kinds of children, in terms of age, sex, SES, achievement, and social status, are nominating the handicapped in order to discover the characteristics of children who are likely to accept handicapped classmates.

Related to the weighting issue is the apparent assumption that the more nominations an individual receives the better is his or her acceptance. Is being nominated by 10 children you cannot stand "better" than being nominated by one whose friendship you value? Somehow we must go beyond socio-empathy and ask the children who are the significant others in the class by whom they want to be nominated. In this fashion, some qualitative judgments could be made regarding the quantitative nominations a given child receives.

Another dimension of this problem relates to the desire to move from the sociometric structure of a class to the individual child's perception of acceptance and that child's feelings about his or her acceptance. It seems plausible that a child could be very happy in a class if only one other child (probably a significant other) is accepting of him or her, yet traditional scoring procedures would identify the child as an isolate. We underscore the need for some qualitative assessment to supplement quantitative assessments because we are convinced that there are individual differences in the needs of children for social acceptance which are ignored by traditional scoring procedures.

One exploration of the qualitative aspects of sociometric status was the Gronlund (1959) study of mutual choices. A child who is highly popular with one segment of the class and actively rejected by the same number of other classmates represents a different case from the child who is ignored by all segments of the class. Yet scoring procedures that subtract rejections from acceptances would obscure such differences and assume acceptance and rejection to be a single continuum. This position was challenged recently by Gottlieb et al. (1978).

Finally, in this era of mainstreaming in which sociometric techniques may be used as outcome measures in evaluations, we must caution against the uncritical interpretation of results. If one expects handicapped learners to be at or above the mean for nonhandicapped learners, it is safe to predict that mainstreaming will fail. Such a criterion for "success" strikes us as unrealistic, although we do not know what levels should be adopted as indicative of successful social acceptance. However, we propose that evaluators of such programs examine distributions and their overlap as well as mean differences, and that they consider some of the concerns expressed herein regarding exclusively quantitative analysis of the data.

REFERENCES

Ballard, M., Corman, L., Gottlieb, J., & Kaufman, J. J. Improving the social status of mainstreamed retarded children. *Journal of Educational Psychology*, 1978, *69*, 605-611.

Baldwin, W. D. The social position of the educable mentally retarded in the regular grades in the public schools. *Exceptional Children*, 1958, *25*, 106-108, 112.

Bronfenbrenner, U. The measurement of sociometric status, structure, and development. *Sociometry Monographs*, No. 6. New York: Beacon, 1945.

Bruininks, V. L. Actual and perceived peer status of learning-disabled students in mainstream programs. *The Journal of Special Education*, 1978, *12*, 51-58. (a)

Bruininks, V. L. Peer status and personality characteristics of learning- disabled and nondisabled students. *Journal of Learning Disabilities*, 1978, *11*, 29-34. (b)

Bruininks, R. H., Rynders, J. E., & Gross, J. C. Social acceptance of mildly retarded pupils in resource rooms and regular classes. *American Journal of Mental Deficiency*, 1974, *78*, 377-383.

Bryan, I. H. Peer popularity of learning-disabled children. *Journal of Learning Disabilities*, 1974, *7*, 621-625.

Bryan, T. H. Peer popularity of learning-disabled children: A replication. *Journal of Learning Disabilities*, 1976, *9*, 307-311.

Bryan, T. H. Learning-disabled children's comprehension of nonverbal communi- cation. *Journal of Learning Disabilities*, 1977, *10*, 501-506.

Cartledge, G. & Milburn, J. F. The case for teaching social skills in the classroom: A review. *Review of Educational Research*, 1978, *48*, 133-156.

Chennault, M. Improving the social acceptance of unpopular educable mentally retarded pupils in special class. *American Journal of Mental Deficiency*, 1967, *68*, 602-611.

Clore, G. L., & Jeffrey, K. M. Emotional role playing, attitude change, and attraction toward a disabled person. *Journal of Personality and Social Psychology*, 1972, *23*, 105-111.

Dentler, R. A., & Mackler, B. Ability and sociometric status among normal and retarded children: A review of the literature. *Psychological Bulletin*, 1962, *59*, 273-283.

Drabman, R., Spitalnik, R., & Spitalnik, K. Sociometric and disruptive behavior as a function of four types of token reinforcement programs. *Journal of Applied Behavior Analysis*, 1974, *7*, 93-101.

Elser, R. P. The social position of hearing handicapped children in the regular grades. *Exceptional Children*, 1959, *25*, 305-309.

Flanders, N. A., & Havumaki, S. The effect of teacher-pupil contacts involving praise on the sociometric choices of students. *Journal of Educational Psychology*, 1960, *57*, 65-68.

Foley, J. M. Effect of labeling and teacher behavior on children's attitudes. *American Journal of Mental Deficiency*, 1979, *83*, 380-384.

Force, D. G., Jr. Social status of physically handicapped children. *Exceptional Children*, 1956, *23*, 104-107, 132-133.

Gerber, P. J. Awareness of handicapping conditions and sociometric status in an integrated pre-school setting. *Mental Retardation*, 1977, *15*(3), 24-25.

Goodman, H., Gottlieb, J., & Harrison, R. H. Social acceptance of EMRs integrated into a nongraded elementary school. *American Journal of Mental Deficiency*, 1972, *76*, 412-417.

115

Gottlieb, J. Public, peer, and professional attitudes toward mentally retarded persons. In M. J. Begab & S. A. Richardson (Eds.), *The mentally retarded and society: A social science perspective*. Baltimore: University Park Press, 1975, 99-126.

Gottlieb, J., & Budoff, M. Social acceptability of retarded children in non-graded schools differing in architecture. *American Journal of Mental Deficiency*, 1973, *78*, 15-19.

Gottlieb, J., Semmel, M. I., & Veldman, D. J. Correlates of social status among mainstreamed mentally retarded children. *Journal of Educational Psychology*, 1978, *70*, 396-405.

Gronlund, N. E. *Sociometry in the classroom*. New York: Harper, 1959.

Grossman, H. J. (Ed.). *Manual on terminology and classification in mental retardation*. Washington DC: American Association of Mental Deficiency, 1973.

Guskin, S. Social psychologies of mental deficiency. In N. R. Ellis (Ed.), *Handbook of mental deficiency*. New York: McGraw-Hill, 1963, 325-352.

Hallinan, M. T. Friendship patterns in open and traditional classrooms. *Sociology of Education*, 1976, *49*, 254-265.

Hartup, W. W., Glazer, J. A., & Charlesworth, R. Peer reinforcement and sociometric status. *Child Development*, 1967, *38*, 1017-1024.

Heber, R. F. A manual on terminology and classification in mental retardation (Rev. ed.). *American Journal of Mental Deficiency Monograph*, 1961 (Supp. 64).

Iano, R. P., Ayers, D., Heller, H. B., McGettigan, J. F., & Walker, V. S. Sociometric status of retarded children in an integrative program. *Exceptional Children*, 1974, *40*, 267-271.

Johnson, G. O. A study of the social position of mentally handicapped children in the regular grades. *American Journal of Mental Deficiency*, 1950, *55*, 60-89.

Jones, R. L., Lavine, K., & Shell, J. Blind children integrated in classrooms with sighted children: A sociometric study. *The New Outlook for the Blind*, 1972, *66*(3), 75-80.

Kane, J. S., & Lawler, E. E. Methods of peer assessment. *Psychological Bulletin*, 1978, *85*, 555-586.

Kaufman, M. J., Agard, J. A., & Semmel, M. I. *Mainstreaming: Learners and their environments*. Baltimore: University Park Press, in press.

Kennedy, P., & Bruininks, R. H. Social status of hearing impaired children in regular classrooms. *Exceptional Children*, 1974, *40*, 336-342.

Kennedy, P., Northcott, W., McCauley, R., & Williams, S. M. Longitudinal sociometric and cross-sectional data on mainstreaming hearing impaired children: Implications for preschool programming. *Volta Review*, 1976, *78*, 71-81.

Kitano, M. & Chan, K. S. Taking the role of retarded children: Effects of familiarity and similarity. *American Journal of Mental Deficiency*, 1978, *83*, 37-39.

Lapp, E. R. A study of the social adjustment of slow-learning children who were assigned part-time to regular classes. *American Journal of Mental Deficiency*, 1957, *62*, 254-262.

Lilly, M. S. Improving social acceptance of low sociometric status, low achieving student. *Exceptional Children*, 1971, *37*, 341-347.

Lindsey, G., & Bryne, D. Measurement of social choice and interpersonal attractiveness. In G. Lindsey & E. Aronson (Eds.), *The handbook of social psychology* (Vol. 2). Reading: Addison-Wesley, 1968, 452-524.

MacMillan, D. L., & Morrison, G. M. Educational Programming. In H. Quay & R. Werry (Eds.), *Psychopathological disorders in childhood* (2nd Ed.). New York: Wiley, 1979.

McDaniel, C. O. Participation in extracurricular activities, social acceptance, and social rejection among educable mentally retarded students. *Education and Training of the Mentally Retarded*, 1970, *5*, 4-14.

Miller, R. V. Social status and socioempathic differences among mentally superior, mentally typical, and mentally retarded children. *Exceptional Children*, 1956, *23*, 114-119.

Monroe, J. D., & Howe, C. E. The effects of integration and social class on the acceptance of retarded adolescents. *Education and Training of the Mentally Retarded*, 1971, *6*, 20-24.

Moreno, J. L. *Who shall survive?* Washington DC: Nervous and Mental Disease Publishing Co., 1934.

116

Oden, S., & Asher, S. R. Coaching children in social skills for friendship making. *Child Development*, 1977, *48*, 495-506.

Rucker, C. N., Howe, C. E., & Snider, B. The participation of retarded children in junior high academic and nonacademic regular classes. *Exceptional Children*, 1969, *35*, 617-623.

Rucker, C. N., & Vincenzo, F. M. Maintaining social acceptance gains made by mentally retarded children. *Exceptional Children*, 1970, *36*, 679-680.

Schmuck, R. A. Some aspects of classroom social climate. *Psychology in the Schools*, 1966, *3*, 59-65.

Schmuck, R. A. & Schmuck, P. A. *Group processes in the classroom*. Dubuque IA: Wm. C. Brown Co., 1975.

Scott, W. A. Attitude measurement. In G. Lindsey & E. Aronson (Eds.), *The Handbook of Social Psychology* (Vol. 2). Reading: Addison-Wesley, 1968, 204-273.

Sheare, J. B. The impact of resource programs upon the self-concept and peer acceptance of learning disabled children. *Psychology in the Schools*, 1978, *15*, 406-412.

Siperstein, G. N., Bopp, M. J., & Bak, J. J. Social status of learning- disabled children. *Journal of Learning Disabilities*, 1978, *11*(2), 49-53.

Thurstone, T. G. *An evaluation of educating mentally handicapped children in special classes and in regular grades* (U.S. Office of Education Cooperative Research Program, Project No. OE SAE-6452), University of North Carolina, Chapel Hill, 1959.

Wilson, E. D. A comparison of the effects of deafness simulation and observation upon attitudes, anxiety, and behavior manifested toward the deaf. *Journal of Special Education*, 1971, *5*, 343-349.

6

Classroom Learning Structure And Attitudes Toward Handicapped Students In Mainstream Settings: A Theoretical Model And Research Evidence

DAVID W. JOHNSON
ROGER T. JOHNSON

David hesitates in the door of the classroom but the special education teacher escorts him firmly to the empty desk near the front of the room. He is afraid to look around. "Will the kids like me?" he wonders. "I know I'm not very smart. Will they make fun of me?" The students who recognize him shake their heads in disbelief. "Not Dumb David! What's he doing in our room?"

Similar scenes with other handicapped children are occurring in regular classrooms all over the country.[1] Often the handicapped students may be anxious and fearful and the nonhandicapped students may regard them with distaste. Students attitudes toward themselves, each other, teachers, and other school personnel may all be affected by mainstreaming. How teachers structure the interactions between handicapped and nonhandicapped students can have considerable impact on these attitudes.

This chapter presents a theoretical model and supporting evidence which establish that, as a consequence of how teachers structure student-student

---

[1]Editor's Note. The vignette describes only the child who, prior to mainstreaming, was identified as a special class student. As the mainstreaming movement gains momentum, many mildly retarded, learning disabled, and other nonvisibly handicapped children will not be known initially by their peers to be handicapped. The following discussion, however, is broad enough to encompass identified and labeled as well as identified but nonlabeled handicapped children.

interaction within the classroom, (a) attitudes of nonhandicapped toward handicapped students become more accepting or rejecting and (b) the self-attitudes
of both handicapped and nonhandicapped students become more positive or
negative.

DEFINITION OF ATTITUDE

The extensive discussion of the concept of attitude in the previous chapters
makes necessary only a brief definition here. *Attitudes* are a combination of
concepts, verbal information, and emotions that result in a predisposition to
respond favorably or unfavorably toward particular people, groups, ideas,
events, or objects (D. W. Johnson, 1979). Attitudes are useful in the sense
that they provide a simplified and practical guide to appropriate behavior.
Some attitudes, like positive self-esteem, help students to function effectively
in a variety of situations; others, like fear of failure, interfere with effective
functioning.

Appropriate attitudes are those that promote the ability to carry on trans-
actions with the environment that result in maintaining oneself, growing, and
flourishing. In terms of mainstreaming, both positive self-attitudes and positive attitudes toward handicapped peers are appropriate. *Inappropriate attitudes* are those that make for a more painful and troubled life through decreasing
one's abilities to maintain oneself, to develop in constructive and healthy ways,
and to flourish as a person. Rejection of oneself and of handicapped peers are
inappropriate attitudes in the contemporary classroom. Appropriate attitudes
promote effective behavior and feelings of satisfaction, enjoyment, and hap-
piness. Inappropriate attitudes promote self-defeating behavior and feelings
of depression, anger, anxiety, and guilt.

The content of this chapter is generally based on the Structure-Process-
Attitude theory of attitude acquisition and change proposed by Watson and
Johnson (1972). The theory posits that social structures define the process of
interpersonal interaction which, in turn, determines what interpersonal and
self-attitudes are acquired and maintained. One social structure may lead to
supportive and caring processes of interaction and, thereby, to positive interpersonal and self-attitudes; another social structure may lead to rejecting
and competitive processes of interaction and, thereby, to negative interpersonal and self-attitudes. Through the social structure maintained in learning
situations, teachers can determine whether a process of acceptance or rejection
appears in student-student interaction and, therefore, whether students develop appropriate or inappropriate interpersonal and self-attitudes.

MAKING CROSS-HANDICAPPED SOCIAL JUDGEMENTS

Mainstreaming is based on the assumption that placing handicapped students
in regular classrooms will facilitate positive cross-handicap relationships and
attitudes. Yet there is considerable disagreement as to whether there are
conditions under which physical proximity between handicapped and nonhan-

119

dicapped students will lead to constructive cross-handicap relationships. The lack of theoretical models and the apparently inconsistent research findings have left the impression that mainstreaming may not be working. Perhaps the key factor identified by the research as determining whether mainstreaming promotes positive or negative cross-handicap relationships is whether students cooperate, compete, or work independently on their academic assignments.

Physical proximity is a necessary but not sufficient condition for a reduction of negative labeling and stereotyping and for the building of positive cross-handicap relationships and attitudes. It is the actual interaction between handicapped and nonhandicapped students that determines whether initial prejudices are strengthened or replaced by acceptance and positive attitudes. The process of making social judgments about heterogeneous peers can be described as follows (see Figure 1):

1. There are preinteraction negative attitudes existing between nonhandicapped and handicapped students.
2. Depending on whether interaction takes place within a context of positive, negative, or no interdependence, a process of acceptance or rejection takes place. A cooperative, compared with a competitive or individualistic, context promotes greater interpersonal attraction among heterogeneous individuals.
3. The process of acceptance results from interaction within a context of positive interdependence, which leads to (a) promotive interaction and feelings of psychological acceptance and safety; (b) accurate perspective-taking; (c) differentiated, dynamic, realistic views of collaborators and self; (d) feelings of success; (e) positive cathexis toward collaborators and self; (f) expectations of rewarding future interaction with collaborators, regardless of their heterogeneity.
4. The process of rejection results from interaction within a context of negative or no goal interdependence. Negative goal interdependence promotes oppositional interaction and no goal interdependence results in no interaction with peers. Both lead to (a) feelings of psychological rejection; (b) inaccurate perspective-taking; (c) monopolistic, static, and stereotyped views of classmates; (d) feelings of failure; (e) negative cathexis toward classmates and self; and (f) expectations of distasteful and unpleasant future interaction with heterogeneous classmates.
5. With further interaction, the process of acceptance or rejection may be repeated.

Each aspect of making social judgments about handicapped peers is discussed in the following sections.

PREINTERACTION ATTITUDES

Preinteraction cross-handicap attitudes are based on stigmatization, impression formation, and categorizing and labeling.

FIGURE 1
Social Judgment Process

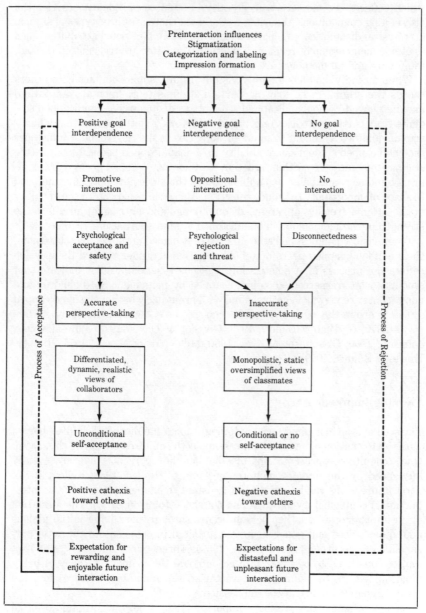

Stigmatization

Goffman (1963) defined a *stigma* as a deeply discrediting attribute of an individual. His is the only major theoretical work in the area of stigmatization.

He distinguished between an individual's "virtual social identity," which is the character imputed to the individual by society, and "actual social identity," which reflects the person's true identity. Virtual social identity carries the discrediting connotation. According to Goffman, there are three types of stigma: (a) physical disabilities, (b) character disorders, and (c) tribal attributes, such as ethnic membership or religious affiliation. The latter are transmitted through the family and all members are affected.

When an individual has a highly visible stigma, simple contact with others causes the stigma to be known. Certain stigmas (e.g., mental retardation) may be viewed by nonhandicapped students as disqualifying handicapped students from certain activities (e.g., academic work). To the extent that a handicap disqualifies a student from major activities in the classroom, it influences the handicapped student's acceptability to nonhandicapped peers. Finally, some stigmas may interfere with interaction with nonhandicapped peers (e.g., deafness, blindness, and being nonambulant) and thus are quite obtrusive and lead to a lack of opportunity to reduce rejection. These three aspects of the visibility of the stigma (readily apparent, disqualifying, and obtrusive) all affect the strength of the feelings of nonhandicapped students (Abelson, 1976).

When visibly handicapped students are first placed in the regular classroom, their nonhandicapped peers may hold negative attitudes toward them which reflect the process of stigmatization. Various research studies indicate that students who are perceived as handicapped by nonhandicapped children and adolescents are viewed negatively and with prejudice whether the handicapped students are in the same or separate classrooms (Goodman, Gottlieb, & Harrison, 1972; Gottlieb & Budoff, 1973; Gottlieb & Davis, 1973; Jaffe, 1966; G. Johnson, 1950; G. Johnson & Kirk, 1950; Miller, 1956; Novak, 1975; Rucker, Howe, & Snider, 1969).

Forming Impressions

The second step in making social judgments about handicapped children begins with the formation of an initial impression as the children enter the classroom. One's cognitive representations of what another person is like are greatly influenced by the first few minutes of contact (Heider, 1958; Kelley, 1973). First impressions can be strong and resistant to change, even with the introduction of contradictory information (Watson & Johnson, 1972). The formation of an impression of another person occurs through perceiving initial actions and appearances and generalizing these initial impressions to the total personality of the other person (Asch, 1952). Three important aspects of first impressions need to be taken into account: (a) the primary potency of being handicapped, (b) the number of characteristics included in the impression, and (c) the dynamic quality of the impression.

Some characteristics are more important than others in forming an initial impression. Asch (1952) designated some characteristics as *central* and others as *peripheral*, whereas Allport (1954) designated the characteristics that ov-

122

ershadow much observed behavior as of *primary potency*. It is important to note that even when nonhandicapped students have a great deal of information available about a handicapped peer, the characteristics "handicapped" may dominate initial impressions. Such characteristics as physical attractiveness (Berscheid & Walster, 1974) and perceived similarity to oneself (Taylor & Kowiumake, 1976) have been found to be of primary potency.

Impressions may be classified as either differentiated or monopolistic on the basis of the number of characteristics which are included in the impression and the way the impression is influenced by the requirements of a given situation. A *differentiated impression* includes many different characteristics which are weighed differently from one situation to another. When only a few characteristics are perceived and weighed the same in all situations, a *monopolistic impression* exists. According to Allport (1954), humans operate under the "principle of least effort," which states that monopolistic impressions are easier to form and maintain than are differentiated impressions.

Finally, differentiated impressions, by their very nature, stay in a dynamic state of change because of their tentativeness and the differential weighing of characteristics according to the current situation. Monopolistic impressions, by their very nature, are static due to their rigid weighing of a few characteristics of primary potency regardless of the demands of the current situation. As one forms an impression of another person, one inevitably categorizes and then labels aspects of the other's appearance and actions.

Categorizing and Labeling

Categorizing and labeling are natural functions of human learning, thought, and memory (D. Johnson, 1979). When nonhandicapped students form an impression of handicapped peers who are mainstreamed, they categorize the peers' characteristics, attach a label to each category, and form a conceptual structure that organizes the overall impression. However, the way in which the impressions of handicapped peers are categorized, labeled, and organized has important influences on mainstreaming; it may lead to a differentiated, dynamic, and realistic impression, or it may lead to errors based on rigid stereotypes.

Labels permit the consolidation of information in one easily retrievable term. Inevitably, they carry evaluative connotations as well as denotative meanings. Although labeling is inevitable, when labels are applied to handicapped peers they may have negative effects by emphasizing monopolistic categories of primary potency that carry stigma, thus encouraging treatment only in terms of the handicaps, and assigning handicapped students to a low power position.

Some labels (e.g., psychopathic, schizophrenic, and cerebral palsied) are rated more negatively than others. Teachers hold lower performance expectations for students labeled culturally deprived or juvenile delinquent (Jones, 1972). Furthermore, labels often define power relationships between the labeler and the labeled, with the latter placed in a low power position.

PHYSICAL PROXIMITY

When handicapped students enter the regular classroom, nonhandicapped students form initial impressions of them. These impressions are based on the information received earlier about the handicapped students, the visibility and primary potency of the handicaps, and the labels used to categorize the students' characteristics. Because being physically, intellectually, or psychologically handicapped carries social stigma in our society, most handicapped students are perceived somewhat negatively from the beginning. The negative perception sets up the strong possibility that nonhandicapped students will reject handicapped classmates.

Physical proximity between handicapped and nonhandicapped students—that is, placement in the same classroom—is the beginning of an opportunity but, like all opportunities, it carries a risk of making things worse as well as the possibility of making them better. Physical proximity does not mean that the stigmatizing, stereotyping, and rejecting of handicapped peers by nonhandicapped students will result automatically, or that handicapped students will be automatically included in relationships with their nonhandicapped classmates which are necessary for maximal achievement and healthy social development. Several studies indicate that placing handicapped and nonhandicapped students in close physical proximity (e.g., the same classroom) may increase nonhandicapped student prejudice toward the stereotyping and rejection of their handicapped peers (Goodman, Gottlieb, & Harrison, 1972; Gottlieb & Budoff, 1973: Gottlieb, Cohen, & Goldstein, 1974; Iano, Ayers, Heller, Mc-Gettigan, & Walker, 1974; Panda & Bartel, 1972). On the other hand, there is also evidence that placement in the same classroom may bring about more positive attitudes in nonhandicapped students toward their handicapped peers (Ballard, Corman, Gottlieb, & Kaufman, 1977; Higgs, 1975; Jaffe, 1966; Lapp, 1957; Sheare, 1975; Wechsler, Suarez, & McFadden, 1975). This contradictory evidence is consistent with previous research on ethnic integration, which indicates that although contact between stigmatized and nonstigmatized students may be a necessary condition for reducing prejudice and rejection, it is not a sufficient one (Gerard & Miller, 1975; Harding, Proshansky, Kutner, & Chein, 1969; Shaw, 1973; Watson & Johnson, 1972; Wolfe & Simon, 1975).

Furthermore, during the initial interaction between nonhandicapped and handicapped classmates, the nonhandicapped students may feel discomfort and show "interaction strain." Jones (1970), Siller and Chipman (1967), and Whiteman and Lukoff (1964) found that physically nonhandicapped persons reported discomfort and uncertainty in interacting with physically handicapped peers. Kleck and his associates found evidence indicating that nonhandicapped individuals interacting with a physically handicapped (as opposed to a physically nonhandicapped) person exhibited greater motoric inhibition (Kleck, 1968); greater physiological arousal (Kleck, 1966); less variablility in their own behavior; termination of interaction sooner; expression of opinions that were not representative of their actual beliefs; reports of discomfort in the interaction (Kleck, Ono, & Hastorf, 1966); and, in the case of a person said to have epilepsy, maintenance of greater physical distance (Kleck, Buck, Goller, London, Pfeiffer, & Vukcevic, 1968). Furthermore, Jones (1970) found that nonhandicapped college students who performed a learning task in the presence of a blind (as opposed to a sighted) confederate reported stronger beliefs that they would have performed better on the task if the blind person had not been present, even when the actual performance data indicated that the presence of a blind or sighted person had no significant effects on achievement. The discomfort many nonhandicapped students seem to feel when initially interacting with a handicapped peer may add to the risk that a monopolistic, static, and overly simplified view of handicapped peers as stigmatized may dominate relationships when handicapped students are mainstreamed into the regular classroom.

Whether mainstreaming results in constructive or destructive relationships between handicapped and nonhandicapped students is largely determined by the type of interdependence teachers structure among students' learning goals. It is this interdependence that defines the social context in which interaction between handicapped and nonhandicapped students takes place. In any learning situation, teachers can structure positive goal interdependence (i.e., cooperation), negative goal interdependence (i.e., competition), or no goal interdependence (i.e., individualistic efforts) among students (D. Johnson & Johnson, 1975).

In a *cooperative* learning situation, student goal attainments are positively correlated and students coordinate their actions to achieve their mutual goals. Students can achieve a learning goal if and only if the classmates with whom they are cooperatively linked also achieve their learning goals. In a *competitive* learning situation, student goal attainments are negatively correlated; students can obtain their goals only if the other students with whom they are competitively linked fail to obtain their learning goals. In an *individualistic* learning situation, the goal achievement of each student is unrelated to the goal attainment of others; there is no correlation among student goal attainments. Success is contingent on individual performance, irrespective of the quality of others' performances. These three types of goal interdependence create different patterns of interaction among students which, in turn, create positive attitudes toward acceptance of classmates, regardless of their handicaps, or negative attitudes toward and rejection of handicapped peers (D. Johnson & Johnson, 1975, 1978, 1983a; D. Johnson, Johnson, & Maruyama, 1983). The specific procedures teachers use in implementing the three learning situations may be found in D. Johnson and Johnson (1975) and D. Johnson, Johnson, Holubec, and Roy (1984).

PROCESS OF ACCEPTANCE

The process of acceptance begins with the placement of handicapped and nonhandicapped students in small, heterogeneous learning groups and assigning them a lesson to complete as a group, making sure that all group members master the assigned work. In other words, a positive interdependence is structured among the students' learning goals. There is a great deal of research comparing the effects of cooperative, competitive, and individualistic learning (D. Johnson & Johnson, 1975, 1978, 1983a; D. Johnson, Johnson, & Maruyama, 1983; D. Johnson, Maruyama, Johnson, Nelson, & Skon, 1981). Compared with competitive and individualistic learning situations, working cooperatively with peers

1. Will create a pattern of promotive interaction, in which there is

   a. more direct face-to-face interaction among students;
   b. an expectation that one's peers will facilitate one's learning;
   c. more peer pressure toward achievement and appropriate classroom behavior;
   d. more reciprocal communication and fewer difficulties in communicating with each other;
   e. more actual helping, tutoring, assisting, and general facilitation of each other's learning;
   f. more open-mindedness to peers and willingness to be influenced by their ideas and information;
   g. more positive feedback to and reinforcement of each other;
   h. less hostility, both verbal and physical, expressed towards peers;

2. Will create perceptions and feelings of

   a. higher trust in other students;
   b. more mutual concern and friendliness for other students, more attentiveness to peers, more feelings of obligation to and responsibility for classmates, and desire to win the respect of other students;
   c. stronger beliefs that one is liked, supported, and accepted by other students, and that other students care about how much one learns and want to help one learn;
   d. lower fear of failure and higher psychological safety;
   e. higher valuing of classmates;
   f. greater feelings of success.

Positive goal interdependence creates the preceding patterns of promotive interaction and psychological states which, in turn, create (a) differentiated, dynamic, and realistic impressions of handicapped classmates by nonhandicapped students and (b) a positive cathexis toward others and oneself.

Labeled handicaps lose their primary potency when the view of the handicapped peer as a person becomes highly differentiated, dynamic, and realistic. A differentiated, dynamic impression includes many different categories; each category is assigned a weight for its importance according to the demands of any specific situation, and the weight or salience of each category changes as the requirements of the situation change. New information on the handicapped peer is admitted into one's impression as it becomes relevant. Thus, if a peer is visually impaired, this category may be noted when the group is trying to read what the teacher has written on the blackboard, but it is forgotten when the group discusses the material they are studying. The conceptualization of the handicapped peer stays in a dynamic state of change, open to modification with new information, and takes into account situational factors.

126

When nonhandicapped students work closely with a handicapped peer, the boundaries of the handicap became more and more clear. Although handicapped students may be able to hide the extent of their disabilities when they are isolated, intensive promotive interaction under positive goal interdependence promotes a realistic as well as differentiated view of the handicapped students. If a handicapped member of a learning group cannot read or speak clearly, the other members of the learning group become highly aware of the fact. With the realistic perception, however, there also comes a decrease in the primary potency of the handicap and a decrease in the stigmatization connected to the handicapped student.

A direct consequence of cooperative experiences is a positive cathexis (Deutsch, 1949, 1962; D. Johnson & Johnson, 1975, 1978, 1983a; D. Johnson, Johnson, & Maruyama, 1983) in which

1. The positive value attached to another person's efforts to help one achieve one's goal becomes generalized to the person.
2. Students positively cathect to their own actions aimed at achieving the joint goal and they generalize that value to themselves as persons.

In other words, the acceptance of and liking for handicapped peers by nonhandicapped students increases when interaction takes place within a context of positive goal interdependence, and the self-attitudes of handicapped students become more positive. Specific research supporting these contentions is discussed in a later section.

PROCESS OF REJECTION

When handicapped students are first placed in the classroom they carry a social stigma that dominates initial impressions and leads to the formation of static monopolistic stereotypes that overshadow much observed behavior. This initial tendency toward the rejection of handicapped students is perpetuated by instructing students to work alone so that they will either outperform their peers (competition) or meet set criteria (individualistic efforts).

When interaction between handicapped and nonhandicapped students takes place within a context of negative goal interdependence, compared with cooperative learning activities (D. Johnson & Johnson, 1975, 1978)

1. There is a pattern of oppositional interaction in which students

   a. have little face-to-face interaction;
   b. expect their peers to frustrate the achievement of their learning goals;
   c. face peer pressure against achievement and appropriate classroom behavior;
   d. communicate inaccurate information and frequently misunderstand each other;
   e. are closed-minded to and unwilling to be influenced by peers;
   f. give each other negative feedback;
   g. express verbal and physical hostility toward peers;

2. There are perceptions and feelings of

   a. distrust for other students;
   b. higher fear of failure and more feelings of failure;
   c. less mutual concern and feelings of responsibility for peers;
   d. being rejected and disliked by classmates.

Negative goal interdependence creates the preceding patterns of oppositional interaction and psychological states which, in turn, create (a) monopolistic,
static, and oversimplified impressions of handicapped classmates by nonhandicapped students, and (b) a negative cathexis toward others and oneself. In
the competitive classroom, reading ability and competence in spatial reasoning
are the primary qualities that make others or oneself worthwhile; these two
qualities separate the winners from the losers.

When interaction between handicapped and nonhandicapped students takes
place within a context of no goal interdependence, students are instructed to
work on their own, not to interact with other students, to use their own
materials, and to work toward goals that are independent of the learning goals
of other students. In such a situation there is no interaction among students
and no structured interconnectedness with peers. The independence of students during learning activities creates (a) monopolistic, static, and oversimplified impressions of handicapped classmates by nonhandicapped students,
and (b) negative cathexis toward others and oneself.

Both competitive and individualistic learning activities provide little or no
information on handicapped peers, thus allowing initial stereotypes to continue.
What little information is available is likely to confirm existing stereotypes
that handicapped peers are "losers." The boundaries of the handicap are not
clarified.

A direct consequence of competitive experiences is a negative cathexis
(Deutsch, 1949, 1962; D. Johnson & Johnson, 1975, 1978, 1983a; D. Johnson,
Johnson, & Maruyama, 1983) in which

1. The negative value attached to classmates' efforts to achieve becomes generalized to them as people (if they "win," you "lose").
2. Students negatively cathect to their own actions when they lose and generalize that negative evaluation to themselves as persons (in the usual
   classroom, achievement hierarchies are relatively stable, leaving the majority of students continually to experience failure).

Generally, the research indicates that in comparison with cooperative situations, classmates in competitive situations are disliked and self-esteem is lower
for all students but the few "winners." Both self-esteem and liking for classmates are lower in individualistic than in cooperative learning situations (D.
Johnson & Johnson, 1975, 1978 1983a; D. Johnson, Johnson, & Maruyama,
1983), although the theoretical rationale for these findings is somewhat unclear.

It should be noted that the process of rejection can be replaced in the
classroom at any time by the process of acceptance by structuring cooperative
interaction between handicapped and nonhandicapped students.

COOPERATIVE INTERACTION AND MAINSTREAMING

Two of the most important aspects of the process of acceptance are the resulting cross-ethnic interpersonal attraction and positive self-esteem of the handicapped students. Recently we conducted a meta-analysis of research comparing the relative impact of cooperative, competitive, and individualistic situations on interpersonal attraction between handicapped and nonhandicapped individuals. Given the disagreement among social scientists as to whether mainstreaming can produce constructive cross-handicap relationships and the limitations of the summary-impression methodology used in previous reviews, there was a need for a comprehensive review of the existing research that examined the magnitude of any difference among the three goal structures as well as the probability of finding such differences. We reviewed 26 studies that yielded 105 relevant findings. Three types of meta-analysis were used: voting method, effect-size method, and z-score method. When cooperation was compared with interpersonal competition, the results favored cooperation with a voting method score of 14 to 0 with 9 no differences; an effect size of .86, indicating that the cross-handicap liking at the 50th percentile in the cooperative condition was comparable to the cross-handicap liking at the 81st percentile in the competitive condition; and a z-score of 7.88 ($p > .001$). When cooperative and individualistic conditions were compared, the results favored cooperation by a voting method score of 48 to 0 with 6 no differences; an effect size of .96, indicating that the average cross-handicap liking in the cooperative condition was equivalent to the cross-handicap liking at the 83rd percentile in the individualistic condition; and a z-score of 15.39 ($p > .0001$). There is, therefore, strong evidence that cooperative learning experiences promote more positive cross-handicap relationships than do competitive and individualistic ones. Our own studies, some of which have been completed since the above review, may be described as follows. (See Table 1 for summary of these studies.)

Study 1

R. Johnson, Rynders, Johnson, Schmidt, and Haider (1979) mainstreamed trainable mentally retarded students from a special station school into a junior high school bowling class with 18 nonhandicapped students from public and private schools. The study took place over 6 days. Students were randomly assigned to cooperative, individualistic, and laissez-faire conditions stratifying so that 6 nonhandicapped students and 4 trainable retarded students were in each condition. Teachers were randomly assigned to and rotated across conditions. Behavioral observations were conducted by trained observers who rotated among conditions. Average interrater reliability was 80–90%. A significantly greater number of positive cross-handicap interactions was found in the cooperative than in the other two conditions with far more encouraging and accepting cross-handicap remarks being made.

129

TABLE 1
Mainstreaming Research Summary: Characteristics of Studies

Study	Length of Study	Grade Level	Subject Area	Group Size	Type of Heterogeneity	Length of Instructional Session	Sample Size	Free Time	Comparison Conditions
1	6 days	Jr. High	Bowling	10(4)	Trainable retarded	60 min.	30(12)	None	Indiv., laissez-faire
2	9 days	2 & 3	Swimming	2(1)	Learning disabled	45 min.	12(6)	Daily: 15 min.	Individual
3	15 days	7	Science; English; geography	4(1)	Learning disabled, emotionally disturbed	180 min.	60(12)	None	Competit., individ.
4	9 days	Jr. High	Bowling	10(4)	Trainable retarded	60 min.	30(12)	None	Competit., individ.
5	17 days	5 & 6	Language Arts	4(1)	Learning disabled	90 min.	40(10)	None	Individ.
6	16 days	4	Social Studies	4(1)	Learning disabled, emotionally disturbed	45 min.	51(12)	Daily: 10 min.	Individ.
7	16 days	3	Mathematics	4(1)	Learning disabled, emotionally disturbed	25 min.	40(8)	Two; 30 min.	Individ.
8	30 days	1	Reading	3(1)	Learning disabled	30 min.	12(4)	None	Individ.

130

9	7	10 days	Mathematics	3	Learning disabled, emotionally disturbed	60 min.	11(11)	None	Individ.
10	9	17 days	Mathematics	3(1)	Learning disabled, emotionally disturbed	45 min.	16(5)	None	Individ.
11	1	9 months	All	3(1)	Emotionally disturbed	120 min.	22(5)	None	Individ.
12	4	15 days	Science, Social Studies	4(1)	Learning disabled, emotionally disturbed	45 min.	51(10)	Daily: 10 min.	Competit.
13	6	5 days	Social Studies, Science	4(1) (1)	Learning disabled, gifted	65 min.	55(7) (12)	None	Individ.
14	11	16 days	Mathematics	4(1)	E.M.R., learning disabled	55 min.	31(6)	None	Individ.
15	4	15 days	Science, Social Studies	4(1)	Learning disabled, emotionally disturbed	50 min.	59(12)	Daily: 10 min.	Competit., individ.
16	7	10 days	Science	4(1)	Mentally retarded	40 min.	48(9)	Two: 30 min.	Individ.
17	4	15 days	Social Science	4(1)	Learning disabled	55 min.	48(12)	Two: 30 min	Individ.
18	3	15 days	Mathematics	4(1)	Hearing impaired	55 min.	30(10)	None	Individ.

Continued on next page

TABLE 1 *Continued*
Bibliography

Study 1: Johnson, R., Rynders, J., Johnson, D. W., Schmidt, B., & Haider, S. (1979). Interaction between handicapped and nonhandicapped teenagers as a function of situational goal structuring: Implications for mainstreaming. *American Educational Research Journal, 16*(2), 161–167.

Study 2: Martino, L., & Johnson, D. W. (1979). Cooperative and individualistic experiences among disabled and normal children. *Journal of Social Psychology, 107*, 177–183.

Study 3: Cooper, L., Johnson, D. W., Johnson, R., & Wilderson, F. (1980). The effects of cooperative, competitive, and individualistic experiences on interpersonal attraction among heterogeneous peers. *Journal of Social Psychology, 111*, 243–252.

Study 4: Rynders, J., Johnson, R., Johnson, D. W., & Schmidt, B. (1980). Producing positive interaction among Down's Syndrome and nonhandicapped teenagers through cooperative goal structuring. *American Journal of Mental Deficiency, 85*, 268–273.

Study 5: Armstrong, B., Johnson, D. W., & Balow, B. (1981). Effects of cooperative vs. individualistic learning experiences on interpersonal attraction between learning-disabled and normal-progress elementary school students. *Contemporary Educational Psychology, 6*, 102–109.

Study 6: Johnson, D. W., & Johnson, R. (1981). The integration of the handicapped into the regular classroom: Effects of cooperative and individualistic instruction. *Contemporary Educational Psychology, 6*, 344–353.

Study 7: Johnson, R., & Johnson, D. W. (1981). Building friendships between handicapped and nonhandicapped students: Effects of cooperative and individualistic instruction. *American Educational Research Journal, 18*, 415–423.

Study 8–11: Nevin, A., Johnson, D. W, & Johnson, R. (1982). Effects of group and individual contingencies on academic performance and social relations of special needs students. *Journal of Social Psychology, 116*, 41–59.

Study 12: Johnson, R., & Johnson, D. W. (1982). Effects of cooperative and competitive learning experiences on interpersonal attraction between handicapped and nonhandicapped students. *Journal of Social Psychology, 116*, 211–219.

Study 13: Smith, K., Johnson, D. W., & Johnson, R. (1982). Effects of cooperative and individualistic instruction on the achievement of handicapped, regular, and gifted students. *Journal of Social Psychology, 116*, 277–283.

Study 14: Johnson, D. W., & Johnson, R. (1982). Effects of cooperative and individualistic instruction on handicapped and nonhandicapped students. *Journal of Social Psychology, 118*, 257–268.

Study 15: Johnson, R., & Johnson, D. W. (1983). Effects of cooperative, competitive and individualistic learning experiences on social development. *Exceptional Children, 49*, 323–329.

Study 16: Johnson, R., Johnson, D. W., DeWeerdt, N., Lyons, V., & Zaidman, B. (1983). Integrating severely adaptively handicapped seventh-grade students into constructive relationships with nonhandicapped peers in science class. *American Journal of Mental Deficiency, 6*, 611–618.

Study 17: Johnson, D. W., & Johnson, R. (in press). Building acceptance of differences between handicapped and nonhandicapped students: The effects of cooperative and individualistic problems. *Journal of Social Psychology.*

Study 18: Johnson, D. W., & Johnson, R. (1983). *Mainstreaming hearing-impaired students: The effect of effort in communicating on cooperation and interpersonal attraction.* Manuscript submitted for publication.

132

Study 2

The cooperative/individualistic design was also used by Martino and Johnson (1979) in the study of 12 2nd- and 3rd-grade boys enrolled in a summer beginning swimming program that consisted of 11 sessions. A pretest measure asking students who they would like to work with if they learned to swim in pairs found that nonhandicapped students selected a learning-disabled peer; only one learning-disabled student chose a learning-disabled peer for a partner. Six nonhandicapped and 6 learning-disabled students were then randomly assigned to each condition and, in the cooperative condition, the nonhandicapped and learning-disabled students were randomly paired. Students received 45 minutes of instruction and then were given 15 minutes of free time to swim for fun. Over the 9 days of instruction, only one friendly cross-handicap interaction was observed in the individualistic condition. In the cooperative condition there were up to 20 friendly cross-handicap interactions with an average of 10 per free-time period. An average of 3 hostile cross-handicap interactions occurred each day in the individualistic condition, while in the cooperative condition there was an average of 1 per day. The learning-disabled students in the individualistic condition spent far more time alone than did their counterparts in the cooperative condition.

Study 3

Cooper, Johnson, Johnson, and Wilderson (1980) compared the effects of cooperative, competitive, and individualistic learning situations on the cross-handicap interaction and relationship of 60 randomly selected junior high school students. Students were randomly assigned to conditions stratifying for sex and handicapped condition. Twelve of the students were either learning-disabled or emotionally disturbed. The students studied together for 3 hours a day in English, science, and geography classes for 15 instructional days. On a sociometric nominations measure, students indicated more reciprocal cross-handicap helping in the cooperative than in the other two conditions and more cross-handicap friendships in the cooperative than the individualistic condition.

Study 4

Rynders, Johnson, Johnson, and Schmidt (1980) conducted a subsequent study integrating 12 severely handicapped Down's Syndrome students into a junior high school bowling class with 18 nonhandicapped students. Students were randomly assigned to cooperative, competitive, and individualistic conditions so that 6 nonhandicapped and 4 handicapped students were included in each condition. Working in pairs, instructors were rotated across conditions. Six trained observers collected behavioral data over 9 days of 60-minute sessions, obtaining an interrater agreement of 90%. On the average, each Down's Syndrome student interacted positively with nonhandicapped peers 29 times per hour in the cooperative condition as compared with 2 positive interactions per

133

hour in the competitive condition and 4 positive interactions per hour in the individualistic condition.

Study 5

In a study by Armstrong, Balow, and Johnson (1981), 40 5th- and 6th-grade students were randomly assigned to conditions, stratifying for achievement level (learning disabled or normal progress) and sex. The students participated in either cooperative or individualistic learning experiences in language arts classes. Certified, trained teachers were randomly assigned to conditions and then rotated across treatment groups at the midpoint of the study. Effectiveness of the random assignment of students was verified through administration of the SRA achievement test prior to the study. A sociometric pretest verified the absence of friendships and acquaintances in each condition. The results indicate that greater interpersonal attraction between the learning-disabled and nonhandicapped students was evident in the cooperative condition.

Study 6

D. Johnson and Johnson (1981) studied the impact of cooperative and individualistic learning experiences on relationships between handicapped (learning disabled and emotionally disturbed) and nonhandicapped 4th-grade students. Fifty-one students, including 12 handicapped students, were assigned to conditions on a stratified random basis controlling for handicap, ability, and sex. Students participated in one instructional unit in social studies for 45 minutes a day for 16 instructional days. Teachers were trained, randomly assigned, and then rotated across conditions. Behavioral measures were taken for cross-handicap interaction within the instructional situation, during daily 10-minute free-time periods, and during a post-experimental problem-solving situation with new peers. A number of attitude measures were also given. There was more cross-handicap interaction during both instructional and free-time situations and more interpersonal attraction between handicapped and nonhandicapped students in the cooperative than in the competitive condition.

Study 7

R. Johnson and Johnson (1981) studied the effects of cooperative and individualistic learning experiences on interpersonal attraction between handicapped (learning disabled and emotionally disturbed) and nonhandicapped 3rd-grade students. Forty students (8 handicapped) were randomly assigned to conditions stratifying for sex, ability, handicap, and peer status. Students in groups of 5 participated in a math unit for 25 minutes a day for 16 instructional days. Teachers were trained, randomly assigned, and rotated across conditions. The results indicate that cooperative learning experiences, compared with individualistic ones, promote more cross-handicap interaction during instruction. The interaction was characterized by involving handicapped students in the learning activities, giving them assistance, and encouraging them to achieve. Cooperative learning experiences also resulted in more cross-handicap friendships.

Studies 8-11

Nevin, Johnson, and Johnson (1982) reported three studies conducted in three different rural Vermont school districts. The studies focused on mainstreaming low-achieving, special-needs, 1st-, 7th-, and 9th-grade students who had also been referred by several teachers and the guidance counselor because of disruptive behavior. Students were placed on an individual contingency program and then switched to a group contingency program. Variations of A-B-A designs were used in the studies. The results consistently indicated that group contingencies (compared with individual and no contingencies) promoted greater social acceptance of handicapped students by nonhandicapped peers.

Study 12

R. Johnson and Johnson (1982) compared the effects of cooperative and competitive learning experiences on interpersonal attraction between handicapped (learning disabled and emotionally disturbed) and nonhandicapped 4th-grade students. Fifty-one students were assigned to conditions on a stratified random basis controlling for handicap, ability, and sex. They participated in two instructional units for 45 minutes a day for 15 instructional days. Specially trained teachers were randomly assigned to conditions and then rotated so that each teacher taught each condition the same number of days. Cross-handicap interaction during daily free-time periods and a number of attitudes were measured. The results indicate that cooperative learning experiences, compared with competitive ones, promote more interpersonal attraction between handicapped and nonhandicapped students.

Study 13

Smith, Johnson, and Johnson (1982) compared the effects of cooperative and individualistic instruction on the relationships among learning disabled, normal progress, and gifted 6th-grade students. Fifty-five students were assigned to conditions randomly stratifying for ability and sex. They participated in one instructional unit for 65 minutes a day for 5 instructional days. Teachers were trained, randomly assigned, and rotated across conditions. The results indicate that cooperative learning experiences promoted more positive relationships among the three types of students than did individualistic learning experiences.

Study 14

D. Johnson and Johnson (1982) compared the impact of cooperative and individualistic learning experiences on interpersonal attraction between handicapped (educable mentally retarded and learning disabled) and nonhandicapped 11th-grade students. Thirty-one students were assigned to conditions randomly stratifying for handicap, ability, and sex. They participated in a math unit for 55 minutes a day for 16 instructional days. Teachers were trained, randomly assigned, and rotated across conditions. The results indicate that cooperative learning experiences promoted more cross-handicapped interaction during instruction and greater interpersonal attraction between handicapped and nonhandicapped students than did individualistic learning experiences.

Study 15

R. Johnson and Johnson (1982) compared the effects of cooperative, competitive, and individualistic learning situations on the mainstreaming of 4th-grade students with severe learning and behavioral problems. All 59 students (of whom 12 were handicapped) were randomly assigned to conditions, stratifying for ability, sex, and handicap. One regular teacher and one certified teacher trained for the study were randomly assigned to each condition and then rotated across conditions. The study lasted for 15 instructional days. Six research assistants observed the cross-handicap interaction in each condition. The results indicate that cooperative learning experiences promoted more interpersonal attraction between handicapped and nonhandicapped students than did competitive or individualistic ones.

Study 16

R. Johnson, Johnson, DeWeerdt, Lyons, and Zaidman (1983) studied the effects of cooperative and individualistic learning experiences on relationships between nonhandicapped and severely functionally handicapped students who normally spent their entire day in a self-contained special education classroom (I.Q.'s from untestable low to 80). Forty-eight 7th-grade students (9 handicapped) were randomly assigned to conditions stratifying for ability, sex, and handicap. They participated in a science unit for 40 minutes a day for 10 instructional days. Teachers were trained, randomly assigned, and rotated across conditions. In the cooperative (compared with the individualistic) condition, the mentally retarded students participated more in the learning activities, interacted more frequently with their nonhandicapped classmates, perceived greater peer support and acceptance, and were better liked and accepted by the nonhandicapped students. Nonhandicapped students in the cooperative condition indicated a greater motivation to seek out and interact with their mentally retarded classmates during free time.

D. Johnson and Johnson (in press) compared the impact of cooperative and individualistic learning on interpersonal attraction between handicapped (learning disabled and emotionally disturbed) and nonhandicapped students. Forty-eight 4th-grade students (12 of whom were handicapped) were randomly assigned to conditions stratifying for ability, sex, social class, and handicap. Teachers were trained, randomly assigned, and rotated across conditions. Students participated in a social studies unit for 55 minutes a day for 15 instructional days. The results indicate that cooperative learning experiences, compared with individualistic ones, promoted greater interpersonal attraction between handicapped and nonhandicapped students as well as more cross-handicap interaction focused on supporting and regulating efforts to learn and ensure active involvement of all students in the learning tasks.

Study 18

D. Johnson and Johnson (1983b) compared the impact of cooperative and individualistic learning experiences on relationships between nonhandicapped and hearing-impaired students. Thirty 3rd-grade students (10 of whom were hearing-impaired) were randomly assigned to conditions stratifying for ability, sex, and handicap. They participated in a math unit for 55 minutes a day for 15 instructional days. Teachers were trained and rotated across conditions. In the cooperative (compared with the individualistic) condition, there was more interaction between hearing and hearing-impaired students and the hearing students indicated more acceptance and liking for hearing-impaired classmates, greater motivation to seek out and interact with the hearing-impaired students during free time, and greater willingness to academically support and encourage their hearing-impaired peers.

SELF-ATTITUDES OF HANDICAPPED STUDENTS

Both the process of acceptance and the process of rejection affect the self-attitudes of handicapped (as well as nonhandicapped) students. In the process of acceptance, handicapped students

1. Evaluate their actions aimed at helping the group achieve its goal positively and generalize this evaluation to themselves as persons.
2. Receive positive feedback from nonhandicapped peers, including caring, personal support, academic support and help, and friendship.
3. Feel successful as a result of their own achievement and that of their groups.

These factors tend to result in the building of a differentiated view of oneself and positive self-attitudes.

In the process of rejection, handicapped students

1. Evaluate their actions negatively when they fail to achieve their learning goals and generalize this evaluation to themselves as persons.
2. Receive negative feedback from nonhandicapped peers, including rejection and being labeled in stereotypic ways as handicapped.
3. Feel like a failure due to their lack of achievement.

These factors tend to result in the building of a monopolistic view of oneself as handicapped and of negative self-attitudes.

The impact of peer expectations and labels may be especially powerful for handicapped students. Turnure and Zigler (1958) demonstrated that retarded children and children who have a history of failure are more outer-directed than are nonhandicapped children and children who have a history of success. This outer-directedness was demonstrated to increase the influence of models on the children's behavior. It may also increase the impact of peer expectations and labels on self-attitudes.

There is correlational evidence that cooperation is positively related to self-esteem in students throughout elementary and junior and senior high school in rural, urban, and suburban settings; competitiveness is generally unrelated to self-esteem; and individualistic attitudes tend to be related to feelings of worthlessness and self-rejection (Gunderson & Johnson, 1980; D. Johnson & Ahlgren, 1976; D. Johnson, Johnson, & Anderson, 1978; D. Johnson & Norem-Hebeisen, 1977; Norem-Hebeisen & Johnson, 1981). Experimental evidence indicates that cooperative as compared with competitive and individualistic learning experiences result in higher self-esteem (D. Johnson & Johnson, 1983a; D. Johnson, Johnson, & Scott, 1978; D. Johnson, Johnson, Tiffany, & Zaidman, 1983; R. Johnson, Bjorkland, & Krotee, 1983; R. Johnson & Johnson, 1981; R. Johnson, Johnson, DeWeerdt, Lyons, & Zaidman, 1983; R. Johnson, Johnson, & Rynders, 1981; Nevin, Johnson, & Johnson, 1982; Smith, Johnson, & Johnson, 1982), and promote higher self-esteem than does learning in a traditional classroom (Blaney, Stephan, Rosenfield, Aronson, & Sikes, 1977; Geffner, 1978), and that failure in competitive situations promotes increased self-derogation (Ames, Ames, & Felker, 1977).

In a series of studies with suburban junior and senior high school students, Norem-Hebeisen and Johnson (1981) examined the relation between cooperative, competitive, and individualistic attitudes and ways of conceptualizing one's worth from the information that is available about oneself. The four primary ways of deriving self-esteem are basic self-acceptance (a belief in the intrinsic accceptability of oneself), conditional self-acceptance (acceptance contingent on meeting external standards and expectations), self-evaluation (one's estimate of how one compares with one's peers), and real-ideal congruence (correspondence between what one thinks one is and what one thinks one should be). Attitudes toward cooperation were found to be related to basic self-acceptance and positive self-evaluation compared to peers, whereas attitudes toward competition were found to be related to conditional self-acceptance; individualistic attitudes were found to be related to basic self-rejection.

SUMMARY

Two sets of attitudes are basic to mainstreaming handicapped students into the regular classroom: nonhandicapped students' attitudes toward their handicapped peers and self-attitudes of handicapped students. Promoting these attitudes is not an easy task, because nonhandicapped students may have negative attitudes toward handicapped peers initially, and physical proximity can increase as well as reduce prejudice and rejection. To promote appropriate attitudes in the mainstreamed classroom, the process of making social judgments about self and others must be used. That process consists of initial impression formation, placing labels on others' and on one's own characteristics, and interaction within a context of positive, negative, or no interdependence. A context of positive goal interdependence promotes a process of acceptance that includes a differentiated, dynamic, and realistic view of others and self and a positive cathexis toward peers and self. A context of negative or no goal interdependence promotes a process of rejection that includes a monopolistic, static, and simplified view of others and a negative cathexis toward classmates and self. Each process, furthermore, promotes expectations about further interaction that affect social judgment.

REFERENCES

Abelson, A. Measuring preschool's readiness to mainstream handicapped children *Child Welfare*, 1976, *55*, 216-220.

Allport, G. *The nature of prejudice*. Cambridge MA: Addison-Wesley, 1954.

Ames, C., Ames, R., & Felker, D. Informational and dispositional determinants of children's achievement attributions. *Journal of Educational Psychology*, 1977, *68*, 63-69.

Armstrong, B., Balow, B., & Johnson, D. Cooperative goal structure as a means of integrating learning-disabled with normal-progress elementary pupils. *Contemporary Educational Psychology*, 1981, *6*, 102-109.

Asch, S. *Social Psychology*. Englewood Cliffs NJ: Prentice-Hall, 1952.

Ballard, M., Corman, L., Gottlieb, J., & Kaufman, M. Improving the social status of mainstreamed retarded children. *Journal of Educational Psychology*, 1977, *69*, 605-611.

Berscheid, E., & Walster, E. Physical attractiveness. In L. Berkowitz (Ed.), *Advances in experimental social psychology* (Vol. 7), New York: Academic Press, 1974.

Blaney, N., Stephan, C., Rosenfield, D., Aronson, E., & Sikes, J. Interdependence in the classroom: A field study. *Journal of Educational Psychology*, 1977, *69*, 139-146.

Cooper, L., Johnson, D. W., Johnson, R., & Wilderson, F. The effects of cooperation, competition, and individualization on cross-ethnic, cross-sex, and cross-ability friendships. *Journal of Social Psychology*, 1980, *111*, 243-252.

Deutsch, M. A theory of cooperation and competition. *Human Relations*, 1949, *2*, 129-152.

Deutsch, M. Cooperation and trust: Some theoretical notes. In M. R. Jones (Ed.), *Nebraska symposium on motivation*. Lincoln NE: University of Nebraska Press, 1962.

Geffner, R. *The effects of interdependent learning in self-esteem, interethnic relations, and intra-ethnic attitudes of elementary school children: A field experiment*. Unpublished doctoral dissertation, University of California at Santa Cruz, 1978.

Gerard, H., & Miller, N. *School desegregation*. New York: Plenum, 1975.

Goffman, E. *Behavior in public places: Notes on the social organization of gatherings*. New York: Free Press, 1963.

Goodman, H., Gottlieb, J., & Harrison R. Social acceptance of EMR's integrated into a nongraded elementary school. *American Journal of Mental Deficiency*, 1972, *76*, 412-417.

Gottlieb, J., & Budoff, A. Social acceptability of retarded children in nongraded schools differing in architecture. *American Journal of Mental Deficiency*, 1973, *78*, 15-19.

Gottlieb, J., Cohen, L, & Goldstein, L. Social contact and personal adjustment as variables relating to attitudes toward educable mentally retarded children. *Training School Bulletin*, 1974, *71*, 9-16.

Gottlieb, J., & Davis, J. Social acceptance of EMR's during overt behavioral interaction. *American Journal of Mental Deficiency*, 1973, *78*, 141-143.

Gunderson, B., & Johnson, D. Promoting positive attitudes toward learning a foreign language by using cooperative learning groups. *Foreign Language Annals*, 1980, *13*, 39-46.

Harding, J., Proshansky, H., Kutner, B., & Chein, I. Prejudice and ethnic relations. In G. Lindzey & E. Aronson (Eds.), *The handbook of social psychology* (Vol. 5). Reading MA: Addison Wesley, 1969.

Heider, F. *The psychology of interpersonal relations*. New York: Wiley, 1958.

Higgs, R. Attitude formation—contact or information? *Exceptional Children*, 1975, *41*, 496-497.

Iano, R. P., Ayers, D., Heller, H. B., McGettigan, J. F., & Walker, V. S. Sociometric status of retarded children in an integrative program. *Exceptional Children*, 1974, *40*, 267-271.

Jaffe, J. Attitudes of adolescents toward mentally retarded. *American Journal of Mental Deficiency*, 1966, *70*, 907-912.

Johnson, D. W. *Educational psychology*. Englewood Cliffs NJ: Prentice-Hall, 1979.

Johnson, D. W., & Ahlgren, A. Relationship between student attitudes about cooperation and competition and attitudes toward schooling. *Journal of Educational Psychology*, 1976, *68*, 92-102.

Johnson, D. W., & Johnson, R. *Learning together and alone: Cooperation, competition, and individualization*. Englewood Cliffs NJ: Prentice-Hall, 1975.

Johnson, D. W., & Johnson, R. Cooperative, competitive and individualistic learning. *Journal of Research and Development in Education*, 1978, *12*, 3-15.

Johnson, D. W., & Johnson, R. The integration of the handicapped into the regular classroom: Effects of cooperative and individualistic instruction. *Contemporary Educational Psychology*, 1981, *6*, 344-353.

Johnson, D. W., & Johnson, R. Effects of cooperative and individualistic instruction on handicapped and nonhandicapped students. *Journal of Social Psychology*, 1982, *118*, 257-268.

Johnson, D. W., & Johnson, R. The socialization and achievement crisis: Are cooperative learning experiences the solution? In L. Bickman (Ed.), *Applied social psychology annual 4*. Beverly Hills CA: Sage Publications, 1983. (a)

Johnson, D. W., & Johnson, R. The effect of effort in communicating on cooperation and interpersonal attraction: Mainstreaming hearing-impaired students. Manuscript submitted for publication, 1983. (b)

Johnson, D. W., & Johnson, R. Building acceptance of differences between handicapped and nonhandicapped students: The effects of cooperative and individualistic problems. *Journal of Social Psychology*, in press.

Johnson, D. W., Johnson, R., & Anderson, D. Relationship between student cooperative, competitive and individualistic attitudes and attitudes toward schooling. *Journal of Psychology*, 1978, *100*, 183-199.

Johnson, D. W., Johnson, R., Holubec, E., & Roy, P. *Circles of learning*. Washington DC: The Association for Supervision and Curriculum Development, 1984.

Johnson, D. W., Johnson, R., & Maruyama, G. Interdependence and interpersonal attraction among heterogeneous and homogeneous individuals: A theoretical formulation and meta-analysis of the research. *Review of Educational Research*, 1983, *53*, 5-54.

Johnson, D. W., Johnson, R., & Scott, L. The effects of cooperative and individualized instruction on student attitudes and achievement. *Journal of Social Psychology*, 1978, *104*, 207-216.

Johnson, D. W., Johnson, R., Tiffany, M., & Zaidman, B. Are low achievers disliked in a cooperative situation? A test of rival theories in a mixed-ethnic situation. *Contemporary Educational Psychology*, 1983, *8*, 189-200.

Johnson, D. W., Maruyama, G., Johnson, R., Nelson, D., & Skon, L. The effects of cooperative, competitive, and individualistic goal structures on achievement: A meta-analysis. *Psychological Bulletin*, 1981, *89*, 47-62.

Johnson, D. W., & Norem-Hebeisen, A. Attitudes toward interdependence among persons and psychological health. *Psychological Reports*, 1977, *40*, 843-850.

Johnson, G. A study of the social position of mentally handicapped children in the regular grades. *American Journal of Mental Deficiency*, 1950, *55*, 60-89.

Johnson, G. & Kirk, S. Are mentally handicapped children segregated in the regular grades? *Exceptional Children*, 1950, *55*, 60-89.

Johnson, R., Bjorkland, R., & Krotee, M. The effects of cooperative, competitive, and individualistic student interaction patterns on achievement and attitudes of the golf skill of putting. *The Research Quarterly for Exercise and Sports*, 1983, *4*.

Johnson, R., & Johnson, D. W. Building friendships between handicapped and nonhandicapped students: Effects of cooperative and individualistic instruction. *American Educational Research Journal*, 1981, *18*, 415-424.

Johnson, R., & Johnson, D. W. Effects of cooperative and competitive learning experiences on interpersonal attraction between handicapped and nonhandicapped students. *Journal of Social Psychology*, 1982, *116*, 211-219.

Johnson, R., Johnson, D. W., DeWeerdt, N., Lyons, V., & Zaidman, B. Integrating severely adaptively handicapped seventh-grade students into constructive relationships with nonhandicapped peers in science class. *American Journal of Mental Deficiency*, 1983, *87*, 611-618.

Johnson, R., Johnson, D. W., & Rynders, J. Effect of cooperative, competitive, and individualistic experiences on self-esteem of handicapped and nonhandicapped students. *Journal of Psychology*, 1981, *108*, 31-34.

Johnson, R., Rynders, J., Johnson, D. W., Schmidt, B., & Haider, S. Producing positive interaction between handicapped and nonhandicapped teenagers through cooperative goal structuring: Implications for mainstreaming. *American Educational Research Journal*, 1979, *16*, 161-168.

Jones, R. Learning and association in the presence of the blind. *New Outlook for the Blind*, 1970, 317-329.

Jones, R. Labels and stigma in special education. *Exceptional Children*, 1972, *38*, 553-564.

Kelley, H. The processes of causal attribution. *American Psychologist*, 1973, *28*, 107-128.

Kleck, R. Emotional arousal in interactions with stigmatized persons. *Psychological Reports*, 1966, *19*, 1226.

Kleck, R. Physical stigma and nonverbal cues emitted in face-to-face interaction. *Human Relations*, 1968, *21*, 19-28.

Kleck, R., Buck, P., Goller, W., London, R., Pfeiffer, J., & Vukcevic, D. Effects of stigmatizing conditions on the use of personal space. *Psychological Reports*, 1968, *23*, 111-118.

Kleck, R., Ono, H., & Hastorf, A. The effects of physical deviance upon face-to-face interaction. *Human Relations*, 1966, *19*, 425-436.

Lapp, E. A study of the social adjustment of slow learning children who were assigned part time to regular classes. *American Journal of Mental Deficiency*, 1957, *62*, 254-262.

Martino, L., & Johnson, D. W. The effects of cooperative vs. individualistic instruction on interaction between normal-progress and learning-disabled students. *Journal of Social Psychology*, 1979, *107*, 177-183.

Miller, G. A. The magical number seven, plus or minus two: Some limits on our capacity for processing information. *The Psychological Review*, 1956, *63*(2), 81-97.

Nevin, A., Johnson, D. W., & Johnson, R. Effects of group and individual contingencies on academic performance and social relations of special needs students. *Journal of Social Psychology*, 1982, *116*, 41-59.

Norem-Hebeisen, A., & Johnson, D. W. The relationship between cooperative, competitive, and individualistic attitudes and differentiated aspects of self-esteem. *Journal of Personality*, 1981, *49*, 415-425.

Novak, D. Children's responses to imaginary peers labeled as emotionally disturbed. *Psychology in the Schools*, 1975, *12*, 103-106.

Panda, K. C., & Bartel, N. R. Teacher perception of exceptional children. *Journal of Special Education*, 1972, *6*(3), 261-266.

Rucker, C., Howe, C., & Snider, B. The acceptance of retarded children in junior high academic and nonacademic regular classes. *Exceptional Children*, 1969, *35*, 617-623.

Rynders, J., Johnson, R., Johnson, D. W., & Schmidt, B. Effects of cooperative goal structuring in producing positive interaction between Down's Syndrome and nonhandicapped teenagers: Implications for mainstreaming. *American Journal of Mental Deficiency*, 1980, *85*, 268-273.

Shaw, M. Changes in sociometric choices following forced integration of an elementary school. *Journal of Social Issues*, 1973, *29*, 143-157.

Sheare, J. The relationship between peer acceptance and self-concept of children in grades 3 through 6. *Dissertation Abstracts International*, 1975. (University Microfilms No. 76-10, 783.)

Siller, J., & Chipman, A. *Attitudes of the nondisabled toward the physically disabled.* New York: New York University, 1967.

Smith, K., Johnson, D. W., & Johnson, R. Effects of cooperative and individualistic instruction on the achievement of handicapped, regular, and gifted students. *Journal of Social Psychology*, 1982, *116*, 277-283.

Taylor, S., & Kowiumake, J. The perception of self and others: Acquaintanceship, affect, and actor-observer differences. *Journal of Personality and Social Psychology*, 1976, *33*, 403-408.

Turnure, J., & Zigler, E. Outer-directedness in the problem solving of normal and retarded students. *Journal of Abnormal and Social Psychology*, 1958, *57*, 379-388.

Watson, G., & Johnson, D. W. *Social psychology: Issues and insights.* Philadelphia: Lippincott, 1972.

Wechsler, H., Suarez, A., & McFadden, M. Teachers' attitudes toward the education of physically handicapped children: Implications for implementation of Massachusetts Chapter 766. *Journal of Education*, 1975, *157*, 17-24.

Whiteman, M., & Lukoff, I. A factorial study of sighted people's attitudes toward blindness. *Journal of Social Psychology*, 1964, *64*, 339-353.

Wolfe, R. L, & Simon, R. J. Does busing improve the racial interactions of children? *Educational Researcher*, 1975, *4*, 5-10.

7

Attitudes Toward Mentally Retarded Children

JAY GOTTLIEB
LOUISE CORMAN
RICHARD CURCI

Attitudes can be defined as a set of predispositions, with responses to a specified class of objects or people, possibly taking different forms as elements of the set vary. These forms are expressions of the cognitive, affective, and conative components of an attitude. The cognitive component is described sometimes as perceptual, informational, or stereotypic; the affective component as feelings of liking and/or disliking, and the conative component as behavioral intentions or behavior per se.

Attitudes do not appear full-blown in the child; they are learned gradually through experience. To our knowledge, no research has been published specifically on the cognitive-social developmental processes that underlie the formation of attitudes toward retarded people; however, Proshansky (1966) discussed a related subject—the development of intergroup attitudes as it evolves through three overlapping phases: awareness, orientation, and attitudes.

According to Proshansky (1966), attitudes begin to take shape at 3 to 4 years of age as the child starts to develop a sense of self and learns to distinguish self from others. For example, by the age of 4 years and 3 months, 85% of both Black and White children are aware of physical characteristics that distinguish the two races (Goodman, 1952). In addition to being aware of intergroup differences, the child from 4 to 7 develops rudimentary attitudes with some of the words, concepts, and phrases for describing members of other groups. Support for this assertion is available from a field study of preschool children (Corsaro, 1981) in which the word "retard" was used by one 4-year-old to describe the inappropriate behavior of another 4-year-old. By the early grade school years, attitudes become fully developed with the addition and organization of new details as the child learns to differentiate increasingly more subtle cues from the environment and to internalize them in the cognitive system. The child can then begin to differentiate his or her affect, cognitions, and behavioral tendencies toward a particular attitude referent. Thus, by the age of approximately 8 years, or third grade, relatively detailed portraits of others and accompanying attitudes toward them emerge.

Five factors are considered important contributors to the formation of attitudes: (a) heredity, (b) physiology, (c) total institutions (e.g., parental influences during child rearing), (d) direct experiences (e.g., repeated contacts or a single traumatic experience), and (e) social communication (e.g., information dissemination) (McGuire, 1969). In this chapter, direct and indirect experiences, of which social communication is a primary example, are highlighted because these two factors are most readily influenced by schools. Both direct and indirect experiences are elaborated on inasmuch as they affect attitudes in general and attitudes toward mentally retarded individuals in particular.

Direct and indirect experiences that affect attitude formation may be considered as the *input* phase of the attitude equation. That is, the attitude holder takes in information from the environment and uses it to form an attitude or to change it. Any discussion of attitudes, however, must be concerned with two additional phases of the attitude equation: *process* and *output*. The process phase is concerned with the internal cognitive restructuring that serves a number of functions, including rendering the stimulus material compatible with the person's pre-existing conceptions, feelings, and past experiences. The output phase deals with the actual attitudinal response, expressed either verbally, as in an opinion, or behaviorally, as in a motor response.

Although this chapter is concerned with attitude formation as distinct from attitude change, it should be borne in mind that the formation of an attitude is integral to change in the attitude. Attitudes undergo continual change as people acquire new experiences and information about the object in question. Therefore, attitudes are not completely static but are constantly changing.

The first and third phase of attitude formation, input and output, are discussed in the following sections. For discussion of the process phase, see Triandis, Adamopoulos, and Brinberg (Chapter 2).

INPUT PHASE

Inputs that affect attitude formation (and attitude change) include the person who presents information designed to affect the attitude in question, the nature of the information presented, and the medium through which the information is communicated. In the social psychological literature, these factors are labeled the *source*, the *message*, and the *channel*, respectively. Inasmuch as the majority of research in mental retardation has focused on channel variables (i.e., direct and indirect experiences), only these variables are discussed here.

Direct Experiences

In the course of direct experience shared by two persons, each forms an impression of the other by considering the information provided for forming a judgment, the frequency of interactions, and the intensity of the relationship. These initial impressions are important because they can have an enduring effect on later attitudes (Kleck, Richardson, & Ronald, 1974).

In addition to actual information, the frequency of one person's interaction with another influences his or her attitude toward the other. Several studies have found that opportunity for frequent contact is related to positive attitude. For example, Festinger, Schacter, and Back (1950) reported that occupants of an apartment house for married students, after having had considerably more experience interacting with each other in a tenant's organization, were more apt to choose each other as friends than were students who did not choose to participate actively in the organization.

Duration of interaction does not have a linear relation to liking. Brief contact has been found to strengthen initial attitudes; that is, a person whose initial attitude is hostile is likely to become more hostile after brief contact with the attitude referent, whereas an initially favorable attitude is likely to become more favorable (Myers & Lamm, 1976). Long-term interactions, on the other hand, produce a general trend toward positive attitudes (McGuire, 1969), although this phenomenon has not been observed when mentally retarded people are the attitude referent.

The intensity of relation between a person and the attitude referent also influences attitudes (Secord & Backman, 1964). For example, parents of retarded children have been shown to have more favorable attitudes than a randomly selected sample of parents toward educational services for the retarded (Meyers, Sitkei, & Watts, 1966); and siblings of retarded children have different attitudes toward retarded children than do nonsiblings, although the direction of this difference is not always positive (Grossman, 1972).

Although contact with a retarded person is probably the preeminent influence on attitudes, in an educational setting it is certainly not the only way that attitudes toward mentally retarded persons are formed. Indirect experiences—the absence of the mentally retarded person during the formation of a person's attitude—is also an important contributor.

Indirect Experiences

In the literature on attitudes in general, indirect experiences with an attitude referent are usually discussed as a means of changing attitudes. However, since indirect experiences (e.g., spot announcements on television) are often employed to inform people about mental retardation and, hence, to influence the formation of their attitudes, this means of influencing attitudes is briefly mentioned.

The major approach to attitude influence in the indirect experience category may be referred to as passive participation. The person whose attitude is to be influenced receives information about the attitude referent either through reasoning or, for example, from listening to a lecture by a teacher, group leader, or television announcer.

Relatively little research has been conducted on the effectiveness of indirect experiences on attitudes toward mentally retarded children. The reason is that it is commonly thought that the retarded children must be physically present for enduring change to occur. This assumption is tenuous, however. It should be kept in mind that, to date, investigators have been singularly unsuccessful in securing durable attitude improvement toward mentally retarded children regardless of the technique employed (e.g., Ballard, Corman, Gottlieb, & Kaufman, 1978), and even when the mentally retarded child was physically present.

OUTPUT PHASE

Theories of attitudes and attitude change are elaborations of a basic input-process-output model. The inputs that act on them have been discussed in the preceding sections. Here the outputs that result when an individual processes inputs are briefly discussed. The outputs are the three components of normal subjects' attitudes toward retarded children—affect, cognition, and behavior.

A Review of the Literature

The framework presented for studying attitudes is useful for reconceptualizing the literature on attitudes toward mentally retarded people; the view that attitudes are composed of cognitive, affective, and behavioral components which are influenced by direct and indirect experiences can be applied to the existing body of literature on attitudes toward mentally retarded persons. In doing so, it may be possible to provide some structure to an existing body of research which, traditionally, has been composed of a series of atheoretical studies that have yielded a confusing and contradictory body of findings (Gottlieb, 1975a).

Direct Experiences

One of the principal arguments advanced to support the movement to integrate retarded people into the mainstream of society is that contact between retarded and nonhandicapped people will produce beneficial consequences, such as reducing strangeness. This "contact" hypothesis was strongly advocated as a reason for mainstreaming retarded children who had been placed in self-contained special classes (e.g., Christoplos & Renz, 1969). The argument was advanced that if retarded children were enrolled in regular classes, nonhandicapped children would become more familiar with them and, consequently, would like them better.

In 1972, a series of studies was initiated to test this hypothesis. In the first study (Goodman, Gottlieb, & Harrison, 1972), the sociometric status of 10 educable mentally retarded (EMR) children who attended regular classes in a nongraded elementary school was compared with that of 8 EMR children who remained in a special class in the same school. It was hypothesized that non-EMR children would rate the mainstreamed EMR children more favorably than the segregated children. A sociometric scale was administered to 40 non-

146

EMR children who rated the integrated and segregated EMR children and a randomly selected sample of other non-EMR children. The raters were asked whether they liked, tolerated, didn't like, or didn't know each child whose name appeared on a list of their schoolmates. The data revealed that (a) nonretarded children occupied a more favored social status in the peer hierarchy than either integrated or segregated retarded children, and (b) male raters rejected integrated EMR children significantly more frequently than segregated EMR children. These results failed to support the contact hypothesis that mainstreamed placement promotes the social acceptance of retarded children by providing greater opportunity for contact between retarded and nonretarded peers.

Based upon the findings of Goodman et al. (1972), Gottlieb and Budoff (1973), in the second study, speculated that the greater exposure of retarded to nonretarded children actually may be accompanied by the lowered social status of the first group. The same sociometric measure used in the previous study was administered to 136 nonretarded elementary school pupils. The raters provided sociometric ratings of a randomly selected group of nonretarded peers, 12 partially integrated EMR children, and 12 segregated EMR children who attended the same schools as the raters. Both the integrated and segregated EMR children were enrolled in one of two schools; (a) a traditional school that contained classrooms accommodating approximately 25 to 30 children in each; and (b) a school that had no interior walls so all children, including the retarded, were visible to each other.

Two specific hypotheses were advanced: (a) regardless of placement, EMR children in the no-interior-walls school would have lower social status than EMR children in the traditional school, and (b) partially integrated EMR pupils would receive less favorable ratings than segregated EMR pupils. The results supported both hypotheses. Furthermore, integrated pupils had lower social status than segregated pupils, regardless of the school in which they were enrolled. This study also confirmed the finding by Goodman et al. (1972) that non-EMR children in general enjoy more favorable social status than either partially integrated or segregated EMR children.

Because the results of the first two studies not only failed to support the contact hypothesis that mainstreaming would result in improved acceptance of retarded children but actually failed to contradict the hypothesis, we decided to conduct additional studies using different measuring tools. Our thinking was that, possibly, the sociometric scales we employed were providing inappropriate data to test the contact hypothesis. Therefore, different measures of social acceptance were used in two additional studies to replicate the previous sociometric investigations.

Gottlieb, Cohen, and Goldstein (1974) assessed the attitudes of 399 nonretarded elementary school children toward integrated retarded children. This study consisted of two independent replications employing subjects at different socioeconomic levels. In the first, 284 lower-middle-class children in three elementary schools were given an adjective-rating scale that measured attitudes toward retarded children. Eighty-eight children attended a no-interior-walls school (the same one that figured in Gottlieb & Budoff, 1973) where visibility of the behaviors of the 19 EMR children in the school was maximized, and 84 pupils attended a traditional school in which 7 EMR children were integrated into regular classes and 12 others were segregated. A third school in the same town enrolled 112 pupils but did not contain special education children. Because of Gottlieb and Budoff's (1973) findings, Gottlieb et al. (1974) predicted that attitudes toward EMR children would be most favorable in the school with no EMR pupils and least favorable when the non-EMR children had the greatest opportunity to witness EMR children's behavior, that is, in the no-interior-walls school. The results indicated that attitudes were most favorable in the school with no EMR children. Although students in the traditional school displayed somewhat more favorable attitudes toward retarded children than students in the no-interior-walls school, the difference between the two schools was not statistically significant. The second replication by Gottlieb et al. (1974) was conducted in an affluent community; almost identical results were obtained.

In yet another replication of the sociometric studies, Gottlieb and Davis (1973) conducted a behaviorally based social choice experiment in which non-retarded children in the intermediate grades were asked to select either a nonretarded child or an EMR pupil as a partner for a ring toss game. Three treatment conditions were established with 14 subjects randomly assigned to each treatment. Depending on the treatment condition, the non-EMR subject selected (a) a non-EMR or an integrated EMR child, (b) a non-EMR or a segregated EMR child, or (c) an integrated or a segregated EMR child. The results showed that non-EMR children almost invariably selected another non-EMR child when given the choice between an EMR and a non-EMR child; that is, in the first two treatment conditions a nonretarded child was selected as the preferred partner 27 of 28 possible times. In the third treatment condition, when the non-EMR subject was asked to choose either a segregated or an integrated EMR child, there was no statistically significant difference in the choice distribution; integrated EMR children were selected by 8 of 14 non-EMR subjects. Thus, neither this study nor the previous sociometric investigations supported the notion that integrated EMR children are better liked than segregated children. In these studies, too, the data suggest that mainstreamed retarded children were less well liked than EMR children who remained in self-contained classes.

Aloia, Beaver, and Pettus (1978) investigated the effect of competence attributions on the selection frequency of EMR students by their nonretarded peers in a social choice paradigm. A partner for a simple bean bag game was chosen by each of 304 intermediate school students from two pairs of students under three treatment conditions. Prior to selection, each subject was provided information about the competency level of each pair member. The data showed that attributing competence to an EMR student does influence statements of intended choice of an EMR student as a partner or opponent in a game. Analysis of the selection frequencies of EMR students showed greater selection of nonretarded pair members as partners and EMR pair members as opponents. The results support the finding by Gottlieb and Davis (1973) that non-retarded peers are the preferred partners of nonretarded participants in a game-playing situation.

The findings of this series of studies, taken as a whole, suggest rather

148

convincingly that greater contact between retarded and nonretarded children is not automatically accompanied by an increase in the social acceptance of retarded children.

Whereas the preceding studies with elementary school children indicated that placement of retarded children in regular classes failed to result in more favorable attitudes toward them, different results were obtained in Sheare's (1974) study of adolescents. In this study, 400 nonretarded adolescents at three junior high schools were given a questionnaire to assess their attitudes toward special class pupils; 200 subjects were then randomly assigned to classes with no EMR pupils and the remaining 200 were assigned to classrooms with 1 to 3 EMR pupils who were partially integrated into at least two regular classes. Analysis of the retest data provided by Sheare's attitude scales indicated that non-EMR adolescents who had been given the opportunity to interact with EMR students expressed significantly more favorable attitudes toward special class pupils than did the non-EMR pupils who had not interacted with EMR pupils in their classes.

Stager and Young (1981) conducted a study similar to Sheare's (1974). A six-item sociometric questionnaire was administered verbally at the beginning and end of a high school academic semester to 382 nonretarded adolescents who were classmates of 26 mainstreamed EMR students. The retest data failed to replicate the results of Sheare's study. The physical presence of EMR and nonretarded students in the same classrooms did not promote more favorable attitudes toward the EMR students.

With the exception of the Sheare study, research has failed to support the proposition that integration into regular classrooms, with its resulting interaction between retarded and nonretarded children, improves the social status of EMR children. Although effects of integrated placement may reflect factors other than contact (e.g., teacher behaviors), integrated placement provides greater opportunities for non-EMR children to observe the behaviors of retarded children. This factor of increased exposure is also present in studies that examined the effects of a school with no interior walls on acceptance of retarded pupils (e.g., Gottlieb & Budoff, 1973; Gottlieb et al., 1974). When viewed in this way, the results of studies of integration and architecture are remarkably consistent: Retarded children whose behavior is more visible to their nonretarded peers occupy a social position either similar to or lower than their less visible retarded peers.

In a related line of research, Johnson, Rynders, Johnson, Schmidt, and Haider (1979) examined the effects of cooperative, individualistic and laissez-faire goal structures on the interpersonal attractions of nonhandicapped students and severely retarded peers in a junior high school. Six nonhandicapped and four retarded students were randomly assigned to three treatment conditions; cooperative, individualistic and laissez-faire. Depending upon the treatment condition, the frequency of positive, neutral, and negative interactions between retarded and nonhandicapped team members was recorded by outside raters. Analysis of the results revealed that nonhandicapped students positively reinforced MR teammates considerably more often under the cooperative than under the other two conditions. These data support the use of a cooperative goal structure as a means of soliciting positive responses from

149

nonhandicapped students toward retarded peers.

The amount of time that retarded children actually are exposed to nonretarded children during the school day was not directly examined in any of the preceding studies because none operationally defined mainstreaming in terms of the extent to which retarded children attend regular classes. Given the findings of the studies on placement and architecture, and the earlier findings that retarded children are rejected because they are perceived to misbehave (Baldwin, 1958; Johnson, 1950), one could speculate that the more time retarded children are visible to their nonhandicapped peers, the more they are likely to occupy an unfavorable social position.

This hypothesis was tested by Gottlieb, Semmel, and Veldman (1978), who assessed the relative contribution of perceptions of behavior and ability, as well as the linear and quadratic components of time integrated, to the acceptance and rejection of retarded children. The subjects were 300 elementary school EMR children who were integrated with nonhandicapped peers for different amounts of time during the school day. Sociometric status was measured by a forced-choice instrument in which non-EMR raters were asked to indicate whether they liked, tolerated, did not like, or did not know each child in their classes. Rejection and acceptance were the dependent variables in two commonality analyses in which the predictors were teacher and peer perceptions of EMR pupils' academic ability and aggressive behavior and the linear and quadratic components of the number of hours of academic integration per week. Results indicated that teacher and peer perceptions of EMR children's misbehavior were significantly related to social rejection scores. Teacher and peer perceptions of EMR children's academic competence, although not related to rejection, significantly correlated with social acceptance scores. Neither the linear nor quadratic component of time contributed a significant percentage of unique variance in social acceptance or rejection scores. This study revealed that the amount of time for which a retarded child is integrated has little if any effect on social status. These results support the findings of previous research that indicated that mere contact between normal and retarded children does not improve attitudes toward the latter. Rather, this study suggests that the behavior which the retarded child is perceived to display has a greater influence than amount of exposure does on others' attitudes toward him or her.

MacMillan and Morrison (1980) replicated and extended the study by Gottlieb et al. (1978). They explored the perceptions of teachers and peers toward EMR and educationally handicapped children in self-contained classes on two dimensions—academic competence and misbehavior. Results differed from those of Gottlieb et al. (1978) in that teacher perceptions of both academic competence and misbehavior were found to correlate significantly with the social acceptance and rejection scores of EMR children. The ratings of EMR children by their retarded peers failed to correlate significantly with their social acceptance or rejection scores.

The implication of research employing direct experience, then, is that contact between retarded and normal children will not produce positive attitude change unless the retarded children can be taught to exhibit behavior that conforms to the standards expected by their nonretarded peers. In other words, the placement of retarded children with nonretarded children must follow or coincide with efforts to modify the retarded children's inappropriate behavior patterns, assuming that a retarded child is more apt to be accepted by nonretarded peers when his or her behavior meets an acceptable standard of appropriateness and/or competence. This speculation has received empirical support in a controlled laboratory study by Strichart and Gottlieb (1975) who examined the extent to which normal children will imitate a retarded child as a function of the latter's competence on a rigged task. As predicted, the more competent the retarded child, the more often he or she was imitated. Furthermore, the more competent the retarded child, the more frequently he or she was selected as a play companion on a future game task. This study demonstrates that the more competent the behavior displayed by the retarded child, the more social acceptance by nonretarded peers is likely to improve.

Indirect Experiences

To our knowledge, only two studies have used the indirect experience, active participation design. In the first, Siperstein, Bak, and Gottlieb (1977) found that after group discussion attitudes became more negative. Several limitations to that study, however, were (a) the fact that the participants were forced to reach consensus, which usually does not happen in naturally occurring situations; (b) subjects' initial attitudes were not controlled, thus the negative attitude change could have been the result of a pretest by treatment interaction; and (c) no attempt was made to study the nature of the ongoing discussion to determine whether the information generated during the discussion could explain the negative attitude change.

A later refinement of the Siperstein et al. (1977) investigation systematically manipulated the attitude favorability of group members who discussed mental retardation (Gottlieb, 1980). Four treatment conditions were established:

1. Three nonhandicapped subjects with positive pretest attitudes were paired with one nonhandicapped, low-sociometric status child exhibiting negative pretest attitudes toward mentally retarded people.
2. Three nonhandicapped children with positive pretest attitudes were paired with one nonhandicapped, high-sociometric status child exhibiting negative pretest attitudes.
3. Three nonhandicapped subjects having neutral pretest attitudes were paired with a nonhandicapped, low-sociometric status child holding negative pretest attitudes toward the retarded.
4. The control condition, in which three nonhandicapped positive pretest attitude children were paired with one nonhandicapped, low-sociometric status child with negative pretest attitudes to discuss a topic unrelated to mental retardation.

Results indicated that the three experimental treatments produced significantly more positive attitude change than did the control condition. Thus, the indirect experience, active participation paradigm can result in positive attitude change toward mentally retarded people if the majority of the group members have, initially at least, neutral attitudes toward retarded people.

The effect on attitudes of videotaped displays of a retarded child has been examined in studies using the indirect experience, passive participation design. For example, Gottlieb (1974) reported that an actor who displayed incompetent behavior was liked less by nonretarded peers than was the identical actor who displayed competent behavior, regardless of whether the actor was labeled mentally retarded. On the other hand, Gottlieb (1975b) employed a similar paradigm to examine the effect of aggressive behavior and found that an actor who displayed aggressive behavior was liked significantly less by nonretarded peers when he was labeled retarded than when he was not so labeled. Further, in a relatively similar paradigm, Yoshida and Meyers (1975) found that teachers formed impressions of retarded children on the basis of behavior they observed rather than the label. Freeman and Algozzine (1980) also found no differences in social-acceptance ratings by peers as a function of the assigned label.

A recent study by Siperstein, Budoff, and Bak (1980) employed audiotaped vignettes and photographs to examine the effect of the clinical label "mentally retarded" and the idiomatic label "retarded" on social acceptability. Their results found that children responded more negatively to the idiomatic than to the clinical label.

PROCESS PHASE

Very few studies have investigated the nature of consistency among the components of attitudes toward mentally retarded people. The most detailed study of attitude consistency was conducted by Begab (1968) who reported that the cognitive, affective, and conative components of attitudes of social work students toward mentally retarded persons were not highly correlated when the factor of subjects' prior experience with retarded people was not taken into account. Higher correlations were obtained for students who had had direct experiences with retarded persons.

Somewhat similar results were reported by Siperstein and Gottlieb (1977) and Gottlieb and Gottlieb (1977). In both investigations, no significant relationship was found between the cognitive and conative components of an attitude when no attempt was made to structure situations in which the likelihood of the relation could be maximized. Conceivably, providing the subjects with more information about the retarded referent toward whom they were asked to express their attitude might have resulted in greater consistency between the two attitude components.

OUTPUT PHASE

As could be expected from the preceding section, few studies have measured specific components of attitudes toward mentally retarded persons. Typically, a general attitude has been assessed. However, measures used to assess general attitudes in certain studies can actually be considered to assess specific attitudinal components. For example, Clark (1964) assessed nonretarded children's cognitions of EMR children by asking each nonretarded child to describe the retarded child he knew best. After classifying the children's responses into four categories—identification, description, evaluation, and association—he reported that responses were based on the stimulus value of the particular retarded child being described rather than on a general characteristic attributed to EMR children, such as intellectual deficiency or special class placement. Nonretarded children's affect toward retarded children was assessed by sociometric questionnaires in many of the studies reviewed previously; these instruments indicate the extent to which retarded children are liked or disliked by their classmates (Gottlieb, 1975a). Finally, the conative component of attitudes toward retarded children was assessed in several studies (Aloia et al., 1978; Gottlieb, 1972; Gottlieb & Davis, 1973; Strichart & Gottlieb, 1975) by asking nonretarded subjects to choose a retarded child as a partner with whom to play a game.

Attitude Referent

An additional topic critical to the study of attitudes toward mentally retarded people is the precise nature of the attitude referent. It has been indicated elsewhere (Gottlieb, 1975a) that the attitude referent in studies of mental retardation sometimes has differed in ways that are known to affect attitudes (e.g., severity of retardation). Research has shown that attitudes toward the mildly retarded are significantly more favorable than toward the severely retarded (Gottlieb & Siperstein, 1976; Warren & Turner, 1966).

The attitude referent may differ not only in the particular characteristics the subject attributes to a mentally retarded person, but also in the manner in which the investigator presents the concepts of retardation to the subject. Some researchers have required subjects to evaluate "retardation" in its most abstract form; that is, the label "mentally retarded person" is provided without any additional information (Gottlieb et al., 1974; Hollinger & Jones, 1979; Jaffe, 1966; Strauch, 1970). On the other hand, Meyers et al. (1966), accompanied the label "slow learner" or "retarded" with a statement indicating that retarded persons will never be able to read better than about the fourth-grade level, and will always be like a 9-year-old child. Other researchers have asked subjects to indicate their feelings about a particular mentally retarded person (Bruininks, Rynders, & Gross, 1974; Goodman et al., 1972; Gottlieb & Budoff, 1973; Johnson, 1950). Still others have supplied a sketch of a hypothetical mentally retarded person and asked their subjects to rate the person in the sketch (Gottlieb & Miller, 1974; Guskin, 1963a; Jaffe, 1966; Smith & Greenberg, 1974). Finally, some experimenters have presented videotapes of mentally retarded persons (Freeman & Algozzine, 1980; Gottlieb, 1974; Guskin, 1963b) or provided live encounter situations (Gottlieb & Davis, 1973; Strichart & Gottlieb, 1975).

153

Method of Presentation

The question arises whether different methods of presenting the concept of mental retardation contribute to differences in subject attitudes. Most probably they do. Jaffe (1966), for example, found that the mentally retarded label was evaluated less favorably and with greater variability than a sketch of a retarded person. If an abstract label and a sketch of a retarded person are evaluated differently, it is likely that a label and/or sketch may also be evaluated differently from a videotaped presentation of a mentally retarded person. The difference may occur because the subject is able to witness a greater variety of behavior on the videotaped display than in a static sketch of a person. Similarly, it is likely that a videotaped presentation elicits attitudes that differ from those expressed in a live encounter with a retarded person. One important difference between the two situations is that in the live encounter subjects may be more likely to believe that their actions lead to real consequences which can affect them (Kiesler, Collins, & Miller, 1969).

CONCLUSIONS

The literature on peer attitudes toward retarded children does not indicate a favorable picture. Contrary to initial expectations, mainstreaming retarded children in regular classes does not appear to promote more positive attitudes. In fact, the preponderance of evidence suggests that the opposite is true.

One of the most glaring deficiencies in the attitude literature relating to mental retardation or any handicapping condition, for that matter, is the almost complete absence of any attempt to tie research to existing theories of social psychology. Although there is an extensive literature on theories of attitude formation and change, the theories have not been employed to advance research in retardation. Clearly, the research suffers for this lack. Little unified knowledge has emerged from 30 years of research. When Johnson (1950) first observed that mentally retarded children in regular classes were sociometrically rejected far more frequently than were nonretarded children, a long-term body of research should have been aimed at determining how to reverse the rejection. Such research was not begun. To date, the systematic research needed to improve the plight of the retarded school child is still not being conducted.

REFERENCES

Aloia, G. F., Beaver, R. J., & Pettus, W. F. Increasing initial interactions among integrated EMR students and their nonretarded peers in a game-playing situation. *American Journal of Mental Deficiency*, 1978, *82*(6), 573-579.

Baldwin, W. K. The social position of the educable mentally retarded child in the regular grades in the public schools. *Exceptional Children*, 1958, *25*, 106-108, 112.

Ballard, M., Corman, L., Gottlieb, J., & Kaufman, M. J. Improving the social status of mainstreamed retarded children. *Journal of Educational Psychology*, 1978, *69*, 605-611.

Begab, M. J. *The effect of differences and experiences on social work student attitudes and knowledge about mental retardation.* Bethesda MD: U.S. Department of Health, Education, and Welfare, Public Health Service, National Institute of Health, 1968.

Bruininks, R. H., Rynders, J. E., & Gross, J. C. Social acceptance of mildly retarded pupils in resource rooms and regular classes. *American Journal of Mental Deficiency*, 1974, *78*, 377-383.

Christoplos, F., & Renz, P. A critical examination of special education programs. *Journal of Special Education*, 1969, *3*, 371-380.

Clark, E. T. Children's perceptions of educable mentally retarded children. *American Journal of Mental Deficiency*, 1964, *68*, 602-611.

Corsaro, W. A. Friendship in the nursery school: Social organization in a peer environment. In S. A. Asher & J. Gottman (Eds.), *The development of friendship*. Cambridge, England: Cambridge University Press, 1981.

Festinger, L., Schacter, S., & Back, K. *Social pressures in informal groups*. New York: Harper, 1950.

Freeman, S., & Algozzine, B. Social acceptability as a function of labels and assigned attributes. *American Journal of Mental Deficiency*, 1980, *84*(6), 589-595.

Goodman, M. E. *Race awareness in young children.* Cambridge MA: Addison-Wesley, 1952.

Goodman, H., Gottlieb, J., & Harrison, R. H. Social acceptance of EMRs integrated into a nongraded elementary school. *American Journal of Mental Deficiency*, 1972, *76*, 412-417.

Gottlieb, J. Attitudes toward retarded children; Effects of labeling and academic performance. *American Journal of Mental Deficiency*, 1974, *79*, 268-273.

Gottlieb, J. Public, peer, and professional attitudes toward mentally retarded persons. In M. J. Begab & S. A. Richardson (Eds.), *The mentally retarded and society: A social science perspective*. Baltimore: University Park Press, 1975. (a)

Gottlieb, J. Attitudes toward retarded children: Effects of labeling and behavioral aggressiveness. *Journal of Educational Psychology*, 1975, *67*, 581-585. (b)

Gottlieb, J. Improving attitudes toward retarded children by using group discussion. *Exceptional Children*, 1980, *47*(2), 106-111.

Gottlieb, J., & Budoff, M. Social acceptability of retarded children in non-graded schools differing in architecture. *American Journal of Mental Deficiency*, 1973, *78*, 15-19.

Gottlieb, J., Cohen, L., & Goldstein, L. Social contact and personal adjustment as variables relating toward EMR children. *Training School Bulletin*, 1974, *71*, 9-16.

Gottlieb, J., & Davis, J. E. Social acceptance of EMRs during overt behavioral interaction. *American Journal of Mental Deficiency*, 1973, *78*, 141-143.

Gottlieb, J., & Gottlieb, B. W. Stereotypic attitudes and behavioral intentions toward handicapped peers. *American Journal of Mental Deficiency*, 1977, *82*, 65-71.

Gottlieb, J., & Miller, M. *Effects of labeling on behavioral expectations.* Unpublished manuscript, 1974.

Gottlieb, J., Semmel, M. I., & Veldman, D. J. Correlates of social status among mainstreamed mentally retarded children. *Journal of Educational Psychology*, 1978, *70*, 396-405.

Gottlieb, J., & Siperstein, G. N. Attitudes toward mentally retarded persons: Effects of attitude referent specificity. *American Journal of Mental Deficiency*, 1976, *80*, 376-381.

Grossman, F. K. *Brothers and sisters of retarded children.* Syracuse: Syracuse University Press, 1972.

Guskin, S. L. Dimensions of judged similarity among deviant types. *American Journal of Mental Deficiency*, 1963, *68*, 218-224. (a)

Guskin, S. L. Social psychologies of mental deficiency. In N. R. Ellis (Ed.), *Handbook of mental deficiency*. New York: McGraw-Hill, 1963. (b)

Hollinger, C. S., & Jones, R. L. Community attitudes toward slow learners and mental retardates: What's in a name? *Mental Retardation*, 1979, *8*, 19-23.

Jaffe, J. Attitudes of adolescents toward the mentally retarded. *American Journal of Mental Deficiency*, 1966, *70*, 907-912.

Johnson, G. O. A study of the social position of mentally handicapped children in the regular grades. *American Journal of Mental Deficiency*, 1950, *55*, 60-89.

Johnson, R., Rynders, J., Johnson, D. W., Schmidt, B., & Haider, S. Interaction between handicapped and nonhandicapped teenagers as a function of situational goal structuring: Implications for mainstreaming. *American Educational Research Journal*, 1979, *16*(2), 161-167.

Kiesler, C. A., Collins, B. E., & Miller, N. *Attitude change*. New York: Wiley, 1969.

Kleck, R., Richardson, S., & Ronald, L. Physical appearances, cues and interpersonal attraction in children. *Child Development*, 1974, *45*, 305-310.

MacMillan, D. L., & Morrison, G. M. Correlates of social status among mildly handicapped learners in self-contained special classes. *Journal of Educational Psychology*, 1980, *72*(4), 437-444.

McGuire, W. J. The nature of attitudes and attitude change. In G. Lindzey & E. Aronson (Eds.), *Handbook of social psychology* (Vol. 3). Reading MA: Addison-Wesley, 1969.

Meyers, C. E., Sitkei, E. G., & Watts, C. A. Attitudes toward special education and the handicapped in two community groups. *American Journal of Mental Deficiency*, 1966, *71*, 78-84.

Myers, D. G., & Lamm, H. The group polarization phenomenon. *Psychological Bulletin*, 1976, *83*, 602-627.

Proshansky, H. M. The development of intergroup attitudes. In L. W. Hoffman & M. L. Hoffman (Eds.), *Review of child development research* (Vol. 2). New York: Russell Sage Foundation, 1966.

Secord, P. F., & Backman, C. W. *Social psychology*. New York: McGraw-Hill, 1964.

Sheare, J. B. Social acceptance of EMR adolescents in integrated programs. *American Journal of Mental Deficiency*, 1974, *78*, 678-682.

Siperstein, G. N., Bak, J. J., & Gottlieb, J. Effects of group discussion on children's attitudes toward handicapped peers. *Journal of Educational Research*, 1977, *70*, 131-134.

Siperstein, G. N., Budoff, M., & Bak, J. J. Effects of the labels "mentally retarded" and "retarded" on the social acceptability of mentally retarded children. *American Journal of Mental Deficiency*, 1980, *84*(6), 596-601.

Siperstein, G. N., & Gottlieb, J. Physical stigma and academic performance as factors affecting first impressions of handicapped children. *American Journal of Mental Deficiency*, 1977, *81*, 455-462.

Smith, I. L., & Greenberg, S. *Test of assumptions underlying the six hour retardate.* Unpublished manuscript, Yeshiva University, 1974.

Stager, S. F., & Young, R. D. Intergroup contact and social outcomes for mainstreamed EMR adolescents. *American Journal of Mental Deficiency*, 1981, *85*(5), 497-503.

Strauch, J. D. Social contact as variable in the expressed attitudes of normal adolescents toward EMR pupils. *Exceptional Children*, 1970, *36*, 485-494.

Strichart, S. S., & Gottlieb, J. Imitation of retarded children by their non-retarded peers. *American Journal of Mental Deficiency*, 1975, *79*(5), 506-512.

Warren, S. A., & Turner, D. R. Attitudes of professionals and students toward exceptional children, *Training School Bulletin*, 1966, *62*, 136-144.

Yoshida, R. K., & Meyers, C. E. Effects of labeling as educable mentally retarded on teachers' expectancies for change in student's performance. *Journal of Educational Psychology*, 1975, *67*, 521-527.

8

Attitudes Toward the Learning Disabled in School and Home

BARBARA WENTZ REID

The research literature suggests that if children are generally met with positive attitudes by their teachers, peers, and parents, they are likely to thrive both academically and socially (Bradley & Newhouse, 1975; Coopersmith, 1967; Gronlund, 1959). In contrast, a barrage of negative attitudes, hostility, and rejection may be devastating and cause children to discredit or reject themselves. Coffman (1963) observed that handicapped adults often view themselves as tainted or less than whole as a consequence of negative attitudes. A physically handicapped adult indicated the depth of self-derogation as follows:

> I didn't want anyone . . . to know how I felt when I saw myself for the first time. But there was no noise, no outcry; I didn't scream with rage when I saw myself. I just felt numb. That person in the mirror couldn't be me. I felt inside like a healthy ordinary, lucky person—oh, not like the one in the mirror! Yet when I turned my face to the mirror there were my own eyes looking back, hot with shame . . . when I did not cry or make any sound, it became impossible that I should speak of it to anyone, and the confusion and the panic of discovery were locked inside me then and there, to be faced alone, for a very long time to come. (pp.7-8)

The possibility that learning disabled (LD) children may also suffer so poignantly as a consequence of negative attitudes suggests the need to change attitudes toward these children and to teach them how to protect themselves.

Traditionally, research has focused on the etiology, diagnosis, and remediation of learning disabilities rather than on the social factors which influence these children. Bryan and Bryan (1978) suggested that one reason for the historic absence of social research may have been professional politics. In a perhaps overzealous attempt to differentiate the LD from the emotionally

157

disturbed child, some professionals insisted that LD children had no significant social or adjustment problems, and, hence, there was no need to investigate this area. Another reason may be the view that the term "learning disability" is one label that has not generated the stigma of labels such as "retardation" or "brain injury" (Hallahan & Cruickshank, 1973). Although current research indicates that LD may be preferred to other labels, the findings do not rule out the possibility that it, too, may convey a negative stereotype (Abrams & Kodera, 1979). A final reason may be the lack of a consensual definition of a learning disability and the identification of population parameters. The research results cannot be generalized. This is a major problem, which confronts researchers working in any area of learning disabilities.

During the last few years, however, a social research renaissance has begun to emerge in this field. Because of their rapid development, variety of sources, and different foci, the studies are by no means systematic or comprehensive. However, when taken as a group, they provide important information on the general trends of the attitudes of teachers, nonexceptional peers, and parents toward LD children.

The diverse nature of this research requires that the review of the literature be undertaken with two specific limiting factors in mind. First, there is a question of consistency across learning disability populations. One study, for example, referred to the disabled population in terms other than "learning disabled"; it is included because the difference in labels was regional and did not seem to imply a difference in child characteristics (Keogh, Tchir, & Windeguth-Behn, 1974). The other studies referred to their child populations as "learning disabled," but even with this consistently used label, it is difficult to make comparisons across studies because given the many variations in and conflicts over the characteristics of LD children, each population of children may differ in subtle ways.

Second, few of the studies reviewed here addressed the question of "attitudes" directly; many focused on issues identified by terms such as "expectations" and "interactions." These studies have been included because their content falls into the broad definition of attitudes used in this book.

Chapters 2 and 3 of this volume provide detailed descriptions of current theories of attitude components and attitude change. In order to structure this chapter, the reviews of research have been arranged according to attitude components: cognitive, conative, and affective. The groupings here are somewhat fluid and arbitrary because insufficient methodological information was presented in some of the reports.

TEACHER ATTITUDES

It is difficult to overestimate the potential importance of the child's teacher on his or her development. The teacher is likely to be the first adult outside the immediate family to play a major role in the child's life and to continue to have a significant influence throughout the school years (Mussen, Conger, & Kagan, 1974).

During the 1970's, the mainstream movement and Public Law 94-142 focused attention on the development of new program designs to allow the placement of handicapped children in least restrictive environments. One population of children whom mainstream programs have been designed to serve is the learning disabled (Lilly, 1970). As a result of the humanitarian wish to avoid the segregation of any major group of children, many LD children are now in direct contact with regular classroom teachers for most of the school day. Therefore, the attitudes of regular classroom as well as special education teachers profoundly influence the LD child's growth and development.

The attitudes of regular education teachers toward LD children have been extensively researched, possibly because they are critical to successful mainstreaming. While investigators have addressed each of the three attitude components, the cognitive component has received the most attention.

Cognitive Component Studies

In four of the seven investigations discussed here, children who were labeled "LD" for experimental purposes were perceived more negatively than when they were labeled "normal." Educationally handicapped children were also perceived negatively during an interview situation (Keogh, Tchir & Windeguth-Behn, 1974). Only Shotel, Iano, and McGettigan (1972) studied teachers' attitudes before and after exposure to LD children under mainstream and other administrative arrangements, and their feelings were positive. Sutherland and Algozzine (1979), unlike the other investigators, attempted to determine the subtle effects of the "LD" label on children's performances under laboratory conditions.

To measure the expectancy created in teachers by the term "learning disability," Foster, Schmidt, and Sabatino (1976) asked two groups of elementary grade teachers to participate in the study of a "newly developed teacher referral instrument." Both groups were shown the same videotape of a child engaged in various activities and were asked to rate him on the form. The "normal expectancy group" was told that a clinical team had classified the child as learning disabled.

The analysis of the ratings indicated that the low-expectancy group had rated the child more negatively than the normal expectancy group. The investigators suggested, in conclusion, that the "LD" label attached to the child had generated a negative bias in the low-expectancy group which was sufficient to alter the participants' observations of the actual child behavior.

A number of other investigators (Foster & Salvia, 1977; Jacobs, 1978; Ysseldyke & Foster, 1978) have measured the expectancy created in teachers by the term "learning disability." They used elaborations on the experimental technique described by Foster, Schmidt, and Sabatino (1976). Foster and Salvia used the same general approach but included a demand condition, an oral request to be as objective as possible versus no such request, as well as a label condition. The results indicated a significant label-instruction interaction. During the objective conditions, the presence of the LD label did not significantly influence teacher ratings of the hypothetical videotaped child. In the nonobjective conditions, the LD label influenced teacher observations and ratings and the labeled children received significantly lower ratings. It appears to be important, then, to develop ways of teaching teachers to give themselves "objective instructions."

Jacobs (1978) assessed the effect of the "LD" label on classroom teacher observations of a child's performance after expectations for the behavior had been created. The investigator developed a Personality Questionnaire and Behavior Checklist which were completed by the teachers; they were divided into control and experimental groups before and after viewing the same videotape of a child engaged in various activities. In the pre-viewing condition, the two groups were asked to complete the measures for a hypothetical child—normal, for the control group; LD, for the experimental group. The child in the videotape sequence was then identified as normal for the control group and LD for the experimental group, and the measures were completed again after the film was viewed. Analysis of the responses revealed that the experimental group rated both the hypothetical "LD" child and the videotaped subject significantly more negatively than the control group rated the hypothetical "normal" and videotaped child.

Ysseldyke and Foster (1978) also used similar procedures to study the effects of two disability labels, "emotionally disturbed" and "learning disabled," on initial teacher bias and on the ability of teachers to disregard stereotypes when evaluating behavior that is inconsistent with the stereotypes. In this study, elementary school teachers were divided into three groups: a control group; an experimental group for the label "learning disability"; and an experimental group for the label "emotionally disturbed." The teachers rated a videotaped fourth-grade boy more negatively when he was labeled either learning disabled or emotionally disturbed, even when his behavior was inconsistent with a label's stereotype. The investigators concluded that the labels "emotionally disturbed" and "learning disabled" generated negative stereotypes that remained consistent during the observations of the child's actual behavior.

Teacher perceptions of the behavior characteristics of "educable mentally retarded" children and "educationally handicapped" children were studied by Keogh, Tchir, and Windeguth-Behn (1974). ("Educationally handicapped" is the term used in California to describe the LD population.) The participants were randomly selected and interviewed. Analysis of the similarities and differences between teacher perceptions of the EH and EMR label indicated that the EH group was perceived much more negatively and as having disruptive personality and behavior problems. The terms "hyperactivity" and "aggressive" were consistently applied to these children. The problems of EMR pupils, on the other hand, were seen as more academic in nature, and EMR personalities were seen as gentler and more positive.

Many teachers in this study indicated that they had not had direct experience with EMR children; others indicated that they felt unqualified to judge such children. Keogh et al. (1974) suggested that this variable may have influenced the results and contributed to the comparable negative characteristics attributed to the EH child.

Shotel, Iano, and McGettigan (1972) studied teacher attitudes toward various handicapped children, including those with learning disabilities. Their subjects were regular classroom teachers in six elementary schools in three school districts: Three elementary schools that were participating in an integrated resource room program constituted the experimental group; the control group consisted of the other three schools which had been matched on size, nature of the student body, and presence of two self-contained special classes.

A paper-and-pencil questionnaire was administered at the beginning and end of the school year to assess the teachers' attitudes. All participants expressed generally positive attitudes toward LD children at the beginning and end of the school year in regard to integration into regular classes, academic and social adjustment potential, teachers' competency to teach these children, and the need for special methods and materials.

The only significant difference in attitude between the two testing periods was in expressions about teacher competence. Initially, both the experimental teacher group (91.4%) and the control group (85.2%) agreed they could be competent with help. On the posttest, 89.7% of the experimental teachers still agreed with this statement, but in the control group the proportion of agreement dropped to 74.1%, a significant change. The researchers hypothesized that, as the school year progressed, the control group teachers had received little support with difficult pupils and thus had experienced discouragement, whereas the resource room program provided enough support to help the experimental teachers maintain their initial optimism.

Although the results of this study appear to reflect positive teacher attitudes toward LD children, the results, unfortunately, are somewhat confounded by a definitional issue. In Pennsylvania, where the study was conducted, the term "brain injury" rather than "learning disability" was used at that time for purposes of special class placement and diagnosis. When, as part of the study, many teachers were asked how many children in their classrooms were learning disabled, the estimates ranged from 10 to as many as 30 pupils. The authors reported that quite a few teachers seemed to consider the term "learning disabled" to be synonomous with "culturally disadvantaged," so the attitudes may have been directed toward children other than those intended by the investigator. However, the population in this study was so opportune—a large group of teachers who were faced with the prospect of actually teaching LD children—that the inclusion of the study in this review seems justified.

All the preceding studies, excepting Shotel et al. (1972), indicate that the stereotype—the cognitive component of teacher attitudes—of LD children includes negative characteristics. Teachers "know" that LD children are hyperactive, aggressive, and disruptive (Keogh et al., 1974) and that the more negative descriptors on a rating form apply to a child (even though normal) who is labeled as learning disabled (Foster & Salvia, 1977; Foster et al., 1976; Jacobs, 1978; Ysseldyke & Foster, 1978).

The argument can be made that the majority of LD-labeled children possess the traits which are attributed to them by teachers, such as hyperactivity, aggressiveness, and disruptive behavior, and therefore the teachers in these studies accurately described LD children. However, investigators who have reviewed the incidence of such characteristics in the LD population have found that they are not so widespread in fact as they are assumed to be by the stereotypical picture (Bryan, 1974a; 1976).

Although only a small percentage of LD children may display these char-

161

acteristics, they have become well known and almost interchangeable with the label. Therefore, what many teachers may "know" to be true about the LD child may be only an inaccurate, artifically induced stereotypical picture. Unfortunately, the studies discussed so far in this section demonstrate that such inaccurate knowledge can affect teacher ability to observe, assess, and teach the LD child in the classroom.

Teachers in training who were enrolled in advanced undergraduate special education courses were the first-order subjects of Sutherland and Algozzine (1979). The investigators studied the effects of the LD label during tests of children's visual-motor integration. The children were normal, but each had been randomly labeled "normal" or "learning disabled." Each student teacher tested and trained eight children on the machine that was used and gave each a subjective score; at the same time, the machine, which was fitted with an event recorder, provided an objective score for each child. The purpose of the study was to determine if the bias of the "LD" label, which was known to the student teachers but not to the children, could, through a complex process, affect the children's performances. Girls who were labeled "LD" differed significantly in performance from girls who were not so labeled. No significant difference was found between the subjective and objective scores.

Connotative Component Studies

Three studies were found in which the investigators had attempted to measure the connotative or behavioral component of teacher attitudes toward LD children in the classroom.

Bryan and Wheeler (1972) conducted a small observational study of the behaviors of LD and average learners in naturalistic classroom environments. Each of five teachers identified two LD and two average learners who were grouped for comparison. The interactions of the four children in each group were observed and coded, using an interaction process analysis. The findings failed to indicate any differences in the amount of time each group spent interacting with the teachers; the failure may have resulted from the fact that the time spent on the observation of this variable was only 2% of the total observation time spent on each child.

In order to verify the findings and to increase the scope of the investigation, Bryan (1974b) conducted another observational study to systematize, record, quantify, and analyze the ongoing behavior of both LD and average achieving third-grade boys. The behaviors of five teachers were observed concomitantly.

The results of the study show that the interaction patterns of the teachers and the LD children differed from those of teachers and average achievers. Teachers were three times as likely to respond to the verbal initiations of the comparison children as to those of the LD children. In addition, half the teachers' time was directed to school work with the LD children, whereas only one-quarter of their time was given to school work with average achievers.

Chapman, Larsen, and Parker (1979) also conducted an observational study to determine if the interaction patterns of teachers and LD children differed from those of teachers and normally achieving children. The subjects were

162

110 first graders who were divided among four classrooms located in public schools in middle class, suburban neighborhoods.

The study had two stages. The first took place during the first 13 weeks of the children's first year in school (kindergarten), when the verbal interaction patterns of the teachers and each child were recorded. The second stage was conducted during the end of the children's second year in school (first grade). It consisted of interviews with the teachers who were anticipating having the students in the second grade. Data were collected on kindergarten and first grade teachers' ratings of the children's academic abilities, grades distributed, achievement test scores (CAT), and referrals to special education. Based on these data, the students were assigned by the investigators to one of four groups: learning disordered, low achievement, medium achievement, and high achievement.

The results of this study present a complex pattern. The type of teacher-child interaction appears to relate to the type of activity observed: Results of interactions during work periods contrasted with those of classroom procedures. When work was the focus of the period, LD children received more criticism, praise, and feedback when teachers initiated the interactions than did the comparison peers. The latter group received more praise and criticism when they initiated the work-related interactions. In contrast, LD children were the recipients of significantly more criticism during procedural activities, and they received more criticism and warnings regarding classroom behavior.

The pattern suggests that teachers may use specific and varied strategies during the more structured periods of direct educational instruction but may not be flexible or competent during periods of unstructured activities. At the same time, LD children may be more responsive to praise and feedback during structured work periods. The unstructured nature of procedural transitions may be difficult for the LD children and thus may lead to inappropriate behaviors which frustrate or irritate teachers.

Affective Component Studies

Only one study addressed the issue of teachers' feelings of liking or disliking LD children. Garrett and Crump (1980) used a modified Q-sort technique to measure regular classroom teacher preferences for LD and matched control children in grades 4, 5, and 6. Fifty-eight teachers were asked to sort the names of all their students on a 9-column form resembling a normal curve. Each column received a number value of from 1 to 9 indicating a preference range from "most preferred" to "least preferred." The results indicate that LD children were significantly less preferred than their nonexceptional peers.

Analysis of Teacher-Attitude Studies

The pattern that emerges in the investigations of teacher attitudes toward LD children is that the attitudes are negative because the stereotypes generated by the label "learning disability" or "educationally handicapped" are

163

negative. Learning disabled children are perceived as having many more academic and personality problems than normally achieving children, and this stereotype persists even when the behavioral evidence is to the contrary. Teachers behave differently toward LD children than toward their nondisabled peers, a difference that tends to be negative (Bryan & Bryan, 1978). Teachers spend less free time with LD children and respond less frequently to their verbal initiations. These results raise questions about the regular classroom teacher's competence to assess accurately and to teach LD children, and to interact socially with them in a positive manner.

Because of methodological problems the results of the studies reviewed are far from conclusive. It is difficult to generalize from the populations because the definition of "learning disability" is often absent or vague; children may be identified as "labeled by the school district as learning disabled" (e.g., Bryan & Wheeler, 1972).

Precise definitions of LD children are necessary. Mercer, Forgone, and Wolking (1976) surveyed the definitions of LD children used in different states and found nine components, but each state combined selected elements to form a unique definition. Thus, when teachers' attitudes are studied, it is difficult to determine whether negativism is directed toward a particular criterion (e.g., "neurological involvement" or "discrepancy") or toward the children. Shotel et al. (1972) also found this type of definitional problem.

In investigations using original assessment tools (Bryan, 1974b; Bryan & Wheeler, 1972; Foster & Salvia, 1977; Foster, Schmidt & Sabatino, 1976; Jacobs, 1978; Ysseldyke & Foster, 1978), instrument development information, or, in some cases, reliability data were not reported. Without this information it is not possible to gauge accurately the internal consistency of the studies.

The conative research contained many sampling problems, such as bias built into the selection method. Teachers volunteered themselves or their students for participation and the effects were not balanced by large samples of detailed subject descriptions. Too few teachers or LD children were used to warrant generalization of the conclusions.

Finally, there is little indication that the methodology of the conative studies was controlled for response bias. One type of response bias mentioned in the literature is the tendency to "fake good" (Scott, 1968). The researchers did not indicate specific attempts to disguise observations or to visit the sites prior to observation, to reduce the tendency. Interestingly, Bryan and Wheeler (1972) hypothesized the occurrence of response bias; during their initial observation study, when they found that teacher interactions with both the LD and normal children represented only 2% of the total interactions, they concluded that the teachers did not interact with the research subjects because of the presence of observers.

Many areas, such as the affective attitude component, were not addressed adequately. Because of the complex nature of an attitude and the uncertain relation among attitude components, teachers may have negative stereotypes of but still "like" LD children. Further, attitude components have not been studied simultaneously. For example, studies using an interaction process analysis might have broadened their results by combining this method with an additional instrument which was designed to measure the cognitive component. Few studies were found to have been designed specifically to determine attitudes, and none reflected a clear perspective on the multidimensional nature of attitudes, which may account for the lack of attention to more than one attitude component at a time.

The studies found were limited to teacher and child populations at the elementary school level. Teacher attitudes may vary according to the age of a child because the prominence of certain characteristics may increase or decrease with age. Further, children may be influenced by the attitudes of a number of different teachers. On the whole, the current literature is addressed primarily to attitudes of regular classroom teachers (except for Sutherland & Algozzine, 1979). It seems important to determine the attitudes toward LD children of other kinds of teachers, for example, learning disability specialists, resource teachers, and teachers with special subject credentials.

There is a need to determine whether particular child characteristics play an essential role in determining teacher attitudes toward learning disabilities and to identify them. Solomon Asch's "formation of impressions" theory suggests that some traits are perceived as central and determining while others are peripheral (Deutsch & Krauss, 1965). Hypothetically, then, a teacher may form a total impression of a child who is identified as learning disabled on the basis of a central trait associated with the label. Determining this trait could provide a basis for the development of teacher attitude change programs and programs geared to helping children develop behaviors necessary for successful mainstreaming experiences.

Finally, we have no comparative data on the attitudes of teachers who have and have not been identified as effective teachers of LD children. Possibly the attitudes of these two groups of teachers are the same; if not, the differences should be studied from a multidimensional perspective to determine differences in attitude components.

NONEXCEPTIONAL PEER ATTITUDES

The academic and social adjustment of LD children in classrooms is influenced not only by the attitudes of teachers but also by those of their nonhandicapped peers. Peer influence increases markedly during the school years and gradually becomes more important than the influence of teachers. Because gaining acceptance through the making of friends is one of the strongest needs during adolescence, LD children approaching their teens may be especially affected by negative peer attitudes.

Research on the attitudes of nonhandicapped peers toward LD children has been focused mainly on the conotative and affective components. Two observational studies that were previously discussed (Bryan, 1974b; Bryan & Wheeler, 1972) also yield information on the conotative component of nonexceptional peer attitudes. In both studies, the investigators attempted to determine whether peer interactions could discriminate between small samples of LD and nonexceptional children. The findings indicated that the amount of time spent in any type of peer interaction was approximately equal for both the LD and comparison children. However, patterns of interactions differed: The

LD child who initiated interactions was significantly ignored by his peers. Unfortunately, the sample of children was too small to generalize the finding to other populations.

A number of sociometric studies which have explored the affective component of nonexceptional peer attitudes toward LD children have already been discussed in Chapter 5 (Bryan, 1974c, 1976; Bruininks, 1978b; Siperstein, Bopp, & Bak, 1978).

The study by Garrett and Crump (1980), mentioned briefly in regard to teacher attitudes, also compared peer status of LD children with the status of their nonexceptional peers. All fourth-, fifth-, and sixth-grade students, including 100 LD students, in 58 classrooms participated in a sociometric investigation in their regular classrooms. Students were given booklets with the names of all their classmates. The participants were asked to select three students who would be chosen and three students who would not be chosen for a free-time play period. The results indicated that LD children had significantly lower social status. Additionally, each child completed a modification of the Peer Acceptance Scale. No absolute differences were found between the LD and control groups on social status and self-appraisal, but the LD group tended to overestimate their status whereas the nonexceptional group tended to underestimate theirs. Bruinink's (1978a; 1978b) findings that LD children consistently rate themselves higher than their actual standing is consistent with this result.

The research on nonexceptional peer attitudes toward LD children overwhelmingly indicates that LD children have been perceived negatively. However, the studies are unidimensional in that the majority are concerned with only one attitude component—the affective—which somewhat limits generalizable conclusions. The populations of the studies that dealt with the conative component are insufficient in size to allow the data to be generalized. There is no information on the cognitive component. Therefore, although the results confirm that LD children are not liked by their peers, further study is needed of (a) the stereotype that nonexceptional peers associate with LD children and (b) their behavioral intentions or actions.

The findings that, however low in peer status LD children may be, they consistently rate themselves much higher, holds possibilities for hypotheses on how LD children cope with their low-status positions (Bruininks 1978a, b; Garrett & Crump, 1980). One way in which many disabled adults cope with the psychologically threatening consequences of disability is denial (Chaiklin & Warfield, 1973; Edgerton, 1976; Wright, 1960). It is possible that LD children use this same defense mechanism to deny their low status among peers in a psychologically protective fashion.

PARENTAL ATTITUDES TOWARD THE LD CHILD

Little research has been done in the area of LD child-parent interaction and parental attitudes toward LD children. The results of the two studies reviewed here suggest that parents are hostile toward their LD children. Strag (1972) used a questionnaire concerned with neurological dysfunction and behavioral and emotional disturbances to compare parental ratings of LD, mentally retarded, and normal children. The results suggested that parents of normal children and parents of LD children rate them differently on several variables. The LD child was described as one who clung more than the normal child, had less ability to receive affection, showed less consideration for other people, and was more jealous. However, LD children were seen as less stubborn than mentally retarded children.

Wetter (1972) compared the attitudes of parents whose children had been diagnosed as learning disabled with the attitudes of parents whose children did not present learning disorders. All the children of the 70 sets of parents were registered at a pediatric outpatient clinic. Each parent was given the Child Behavior Rating Scale; the mothers were also given the Mother-Child Relationship Evaluation.

Wetter hypothesized that the attitudes of mothers of LD children would display more overprotection, overindulgence, and rejection than the attitudes of mothers of nonexceptional children. Part of this hypothesis was validated: A significant difference was found between experimental and control groups on overindulgence and rejection, which confirmed the author's hypothesis. No differences were observed on overprotection.

The attitudes of the fathers of the LD children did not differ significantly from those of the mothers. However, the statistical analysis indicated that parents of children with a learning disorder displayed greater disagreement in assessing a child's overall adjustment than do parents of normal children.

Much more research on parental attitudes is necessary before the negative results of the two studies discussed here can be generalized.

CONCLUSIONS AND DIMENSIONS FOR FUTURE RESEARCH

The literature on attitudes toward LD children can be faulted for a number of methodological weaknesses and in some instances for unsystematic approaches which have left many unevenly explored or totally unexplored areas. Although the results of a specific study may not stand up to criticism, still certain general trends of the research in toto appear to hold significance and cannot be discounted:

- Regular classroom teachers associate the label "learning disability" with a negative stereotype.
- LD children have significantly lower social status than their nonexceptional peers.
- Regular classroom teachers and nonexceptional peers behave more negatively toward LD children than toward their normal classmates.
- Parents appear to describe their LD children in comparatively negative terms.

LD children are now placed in environments that appear to be decidedly hostile and unsupportive. The awareness of these circumstances requires professionals to respond with a three-pronged program:

First, research efforts must concentrate on determining the sources of hostility and rejection. Certain hypotheses emerge from the literature to explain why attitudes toward LD children are negative and to help to interrelate the results of the various studies. One hypothesis puts the source of negative attributes in some discrediting characteristic or stigma, for example, low academic achievement, which causes other persons to categorize the LD child as "less than whole" or "tainted" (Coffman, 1963). Research findings support the notion that children who are low academic achievers but have not been identified as learning disabled also are recipients of negative attitudes and rejection (Brophy & Good, 1974; Larsen & Ehly, 1978). Teachers appear to like bright, high-achieving students. If this is the case, attitude-change programs should be cognizant of this information.

Another hypothesis that recently emerged from the literature focuses on the manifestations of the learning disability as the source of the rejection. Bryan and Perlmutter (1979) found that female undergraduates judged unlabeled videotapes of female LD children in social interactions in a laboratory setting as more negative than comparison non-LD children, even though the undergraduates were not privy to the children's personal histories, current academic status, or current social status. Salient characteristics of LD children may interfere with successful social interaction. One characteristic that may impede social interaction is nonverbal behavior. Differences have been found in the nonverbal behaviors of LD children in comparison with non-LD controls (Bryan & Sherman, 1980; Bryan, Sherman, & Fisher, 1980). LD children spent less time looking at the interviewer and smiling, behavior that may affect adults' judgments. Other suggested characteristics that may interfere with successful social interaction include deficits in social perception, lack of schematic and organizational judgment, and affective processing (Bryan & Bryan, 1975; Bryan, Wheeler, Felcan & Henek, 1976; Kronick, 1978). "In terms of total life-functioning, social ineptitude tends to be far more disabling than academic dysfunction" (Kronick, 1978, p.87).

Second, programs need to be developed to assist LD children to cope with the threat of negative attitudes. When Jones (1972), for example, summarized studies on the stigma attached to educable retarded children, his major conclusion was startling: Although stigma was shown to be a real problem for noninstitutionalized educable mentally retarded students, there is little reason to believe that teachers have developed adequate programs to help the children to cope with it. "Most striking in all their [teachers'] responses, however, is the uncertainty with which teachers approach this area and the paucity of validated techniques for dealing with the problem" (p. 562). When children are faced with name calling or other such negative behavior, the most sophisticated teacher response at this time seems to be the brief "ignore it."

In addition, the concept of mainstream classrooms as a fertile place for the growing together of differences must be re-examined. Although the economic and psychological investments in this movement are extensive, we have a responsibility to do our best to provide LD children with a setting in which they can survive. Mainstream classooms may not be the setting.

REFERENCES

Abrams, K., & Kodera, T. Acceptance hierarchy of handicaps: Validation of Kirk's statement, "Special education often begins where medicine stops." *Journal of Learning Disabilities*, 1979, *12*, 24-29.

Bradley, E., & Newhouse, R. Sociometric choice and self-perceptions of upper elementary school children. *Psychology in the Schools*, 1975, *12* 217-222.

Brophy, J. E., & Good, T.L. *Teacher-student relationships*. New York: Holt, Rinehart & Winston, 1974.

Bruininks, V. L. Actual and perceived peer status of learning disabled students in mainstream programs. *Journal of Special Education*, 1978, *12*, 51-58. (a)

Bruininks, V. L. Actual and perceived peer status of learning disabled and nondisabled students. *Journal of Learning Disabilities*, 1978, *11*, 29-34.

Bryan, J. H., & Perlmutter, B. Immediate impressions of LD children by female adults. *Learning Disability Quarterly*, 1979, *2*, 80-88.

Bryan, J. H., & Sherman, R. Immediate impressions of nonverbal ingratiation attempts by learning disabled boys. *Learning Disability Quarterly*, 1980, *3*, 19-28.

Bryan, J. H., Sherman, R., & Fisher, A. Learning disabled boys' nonverbal behaviors within a dyadic interview. *Learning Disability Quarterly*, 1980, *3*, 65-72.

Bryan, T. H. Learning disabilities: A new stereotype. *Journal of Learning Disabilities*, 1974, *1*, 621-622. (a)

Bryan, T. H. An observational analysis of classroom behaviors of children with learning disabilities. *Journal of Learning Disabilities*, 1974, *7*, 26-34. (b)

Bryan, T. H. Peer popularity of learning disabled children. *Journal of Learning Disabilities*, 1974, *7*, 621-625. (c)

Bryan, T. H. Peer popularity of learning disabled children: A replication. *Journal of Learning Disabilities*, 1976, *9*, 49-53.

Bryan, T. H., & Bryan, J. H. *Understanding learning disabilities*. Port Washington NY: Alfred, 1975.

Bryan, T. H., & Bryan, J. H. Social interactions of learning disabled children. *Learning Disability Quarterly*, 1978, *1*, 33-38.

Bryan, T. H. & Wheeler, R. Perception of learning disabled children: The eye of the observer. *Journal of Learning Disabilities*, 1972, *5*, 484-488.

Bryan, T. H., Wheeler, J., Felcan, J., & Henek, T. Come on dummy: An observational study of children's communications. *Journal of Learning Disabilities*, 1976, *9*, 611-669.

Chaiklin, H., & Warfield, M. Stigma management and amputee rehabilitation. *Rehabilitation Literature*, 1973, *34*, 162-166.

Chapman, R. B., Larsen, S. C., & Parker, R. M. Interactions of first grade teachers with learning disordered children. *Journal of Learning Disabilities*, 1979, *12*, 225-230.

Coffman, E. *Stigma*. Englewood Cliffs NJ: Prentice-Hall, 1963. Coopersmith, S. *The antecedents of self-esteem*. San Francisco: Freeman, 1967.

Deutsch, M., & Krauss, R. *Theories in social psychology*. New York: Basic Books, 1965.

Edgerton, R. *The cloak of competence*. Berkeley CA: University of California Press, 1976.

Fishbein, M., & Ajzen, I. *Belief, attitude, intention and behavior*. Reading MA: Addison-Wesley, 1975.

Foster, G. G., & Salvia, J. Teacher response to label of learning disabled as a function of demand characteristics. *Exceptional Children*, 1977, *43*, 533-534.

Foster, G. G., Schmidt, C. R., & Sabatino, D. Teacher expectancies and the label "learning disabilities." *Journal of Learning Disabilities*, 1976, *43*, 464-465.

Garrett, M. K., & Crump, W. D. Peer acceptance, teacher preference, and self-appraisal of social status among learning disabled students. *Learning Disability Quarterly*, 1980, *3*, 42-47.

Gronlund, N. E. *Sociometry in the classroom*. New York: Harper & Row, 1959.

Hallahan, D. W., & Cruickshank, W. M. *Psychoeducational foundations of learning disabilities.* Englewood Cliffs NJ: Prentice-Hall, 1973.

Jacobs, W. The effect of the learning disability label on classroom teachers' ability objectively to observe and interpret child behaviors. *Learning Disability Quarterly,* 1978, *1,* 50-55.

Jones, R. Labels and stigma in special education. *Exceptional Children,* 1972, *38,* 553-564.

Keogh, B., Tchir, C., & Windeguth-Behn, A. Teachers' perceptions of educationally high risk children. *Journal of Learning Disabilities,* 1974; *7,* 43-50.

Kronick, D. An examination of psychosocial aspects of learning disabled adolescents. *Learning Disability Quarterly,* 1978, *1,* 86-93.

Larsen, S., Ehly, S. Teacher-student interactions: A factor in handicapping conditions. *Academic Therapy,* 1978, *13,* 267-276.

Lilly, M. S. Special Education: A teapot in a tempest. *Exceptional Children,* 1970, *37,* 43-49.

McGuire, W. The nature of attitudes and attitude change. In G. Lindzey & E. Aronson (Eds.), *Handbook of social psychology* (Vol. 3). Reading MA: Addison-Wesley, 1969.

Mercer, C., Forgone, C., & Wolking, W. Definitions of learning disabilities used in the United States. *Journal of Learning Disabilities,* 1976, *9,* 47-56.

Mussen, P., Conger, J., & Kagen, J. *Child development and personality.* New York: Harper & Row, 1974.

Schuman, H., & Johnson, M. Attitudes and behavior. In A. Inkeles (Ed.), *Annual Review of Sociology.* Palo Alto: Annual Reviews, 1976.

Scott, W. Attitude measurement. In G. Lindzey & E. Aronson (Eds), *Handbook of social psychology* (Vol. 2). Menlo Park CA: Addison-Wesley, 1968.

Shotel, J., Iano, R., & McGettigan, J. Teachers' attitudes associated with the integration of handicapped children. *Exceptional Children,* 1972, *38,* 677-683.

Siperstein, G., Bopp, M., & Bak, J. Peers rate LD children on who is the smartest, best looking, and most athletic. *Journal of Learning Disabilities,* 1978, *11,* 98-102.

Siperstein, G., & Gottlieb, J. Physical appearance and academic performance as factors affecting children's attitudes toward handicapped peers. *American Journal of Mental Deficiency,* 1977, *5,* 456-462.

Strag, G. A. Comparative behavioral rating of parents with severe mentally retarded, special learning disability, and normal children. *Journal of Learning Disabilities,* 1972, *5,* 631-635.

Sutherland, J., & Algozzine, B. Bias resulting from being labeled LD. *Journal of Learning Disabilities,* 1979, *12,* 17-23.

Wetter, J. Parent attitudes toward learning disabilities. *Exceptional Children,* 1972, *38,* 490-491.

Wright, B. *Physical disability: A psychological approach.* New York: Harper & Row, 1960.

Ysseldyke, J., & Foster, G. Bias in teacher's observations of emotionally disturbed and learning disabled children. *Exceptional Children,* 1978, *44,* 613-614.

9

Children's Attitudes Toward Emotionally Disturbed Peers

CONSTANCE CHIBA

Research in the area of emotional disturbance has traditionally focused on questions of etiology, identification, and remediation. Very little comparative research has been conducted on attitudes of children toward their emotionally disturbed peers. The literature available on this topic is reviewed in this chapter.

Investigations of emotional disturbance have carried a variety of generic labels that usually reflect the investigators' underlying assumptions of the cause of the disturbance. For the purpose of this review, the category of emotional disturbance is taken to include children who have been classified as emotionally disturbed, behaviorally disordered, socially maladjusted, and educationally handicapped; the latter is a catch-all term that is used in California and includes children with emotional disturbances. This review is not concerned with the issue of internal versus environmental causes of the behavior of the subjects under investigation, and the discussion is restricted to the literature pertaining to the attitudes of children. For a review of the literature on adult attitudes toward mental illness, see Rabkin (1972, 1974, 1979).

Following McGuire (1969), attitudes are considered as having affective, cognitive, and conative components.

In a study of children who had been placed in classes for the emotionally disturbed, Quay, Morse, and Cutter (1966) distinguished three dimensions of behavior: unsocialized aggression or conduct problems, symptoms of personality problems or neuroses, and immaturity-inadequacy problems. Implicit in each dimension are problems with relationships. In fact, a major reason for the referral of children to special education classes for the emotionally disturbed has been the inability to get along with classmates (Rubin, Simson, & Betwee, 1966). In a study of 172 elementary-school-aged children placed in classes for the emotionally disturbed, Woody (1969) found that the central reason was poor social relations for 47% of the boys and 46% of the girls.

Despite the importance of interpersonal behavior in the identification and diagnosis of emotional disturbance, very little systematic research has explored the attitudes of nonhandicapped children toward their emotionally disturbed peers. The few investigations of the topic can be classified as (a) studies of peer perception of emotional disturbance, (b) studies of peer acceptance of emotionally disturbed children, and (c) studies of the correlates of peer acceptance and peer rejection.

PEER PERCEPTION OF EMOTIONAL DISTURBANCE

Research on peer perception of emotional disturbance has largely focused on two topics: (a) developmental changes in children's perceptions of emotional disturbance and (b) children's attitudes toward emotional disturbance in relation to their attitudes toward other disabilities. Research on developmental changes in peer perception of emotional disturbance reflects the larger body of research concerned with the development of social cognition. Investigations of the latter have shown, in general, a developmental trend in children from concrete to abstract modes of person perception. Young children perceive others in terms of external or surface attributes, such as specific acts and external possessions. With increasing age, their perceptions come to include awareness that their peers have internal dispositions and stable attributes (Livesley & Bromley, 1973).

In general, research findings on peer perception of emotional disturbance agree with the findings in the field of social cognition. Children's reports of the disturbed behaviors of their peers reveal that their concepts of deviant behaviors progress from concrete descriptions of self-evident acts to attempts to explain the behaviors in terms of underlying psychological dimensions.

One method used to study developmental changes in the perception of emotional disturbance is to present children with descriptions of imaginary deviant peers whose characteristics are like those which adults attribute to mental disorder. In addition, in a number of studies, children have been asked to describe known peers whom they consider to behave in a deviant manner. Consequently, the attitude-component focus of investigations has been the cognitive and affective components.

In a two-part study, Coie and Pennington (1976) investigated the point at which children become aware of behavior that, to adults, indicates emotional disturbance. The subjects were 10 girls and 10 boys at each of four grade levels (1st, 4th, 7th, and 11th). In the first part of the study the children were asked to describe peers whom they considered to be markedly different from the rest of their classmates. These deviance attributions were classified according to seven categories of behavior: aggression, social norm violations, adult rule violations, social withdrawal, interest, appearance, and self-reference. In the second part of the study, the children were presented with two story descriptions. In "The Distorted Perception Story" the stimulus figure was that of a child with a seriously distorted social perspective. In "The Loss of Control Story," the stimulus character was that of a child who behaved in an aggressive manner and was frequently unable to control himself.

172

The results of the second part—the story descriptions—indicated significant age trends in the responses to the stimuli. The first-grade subjects reconstructed and normalized the events and characters of the stories into forms which they could understand. For example, in "The Loss of Control Story" the first-grade children explained the character's aggressive behavior as the result of actual provocation by someone. In contrast, the older subjects recognized the irrational qualities of the story character and tried to explain and understand the described behavior. Similarly, the response for "The Distorted Perception Story" showed that with age more children were aware that the story figure had a deviant perception of social reality. In turn, the older subjects assigned an increasingly deviant status to the stimulus figure.

The results of the open-ended interviews on the kind of children whom the subjects regarded as deviant indicated that aggression and social-norm violations accounted for over half the nominations for deviance. Subjects across all grade levels described aggressive children as deviant. No significant differences were found across grade levels for aggression attributions. However, a significant age-group effect was found for social-norm violations; they were mentioned infrequently by first graders as indications of deviance. Furthermore, only the 11th-grade subjects made deviance attributions on the basis of the language and phenomenon of psychological disorder; for example, only 11th-grade subjects identified peers as deviant with such comments as "crazy," "needs to see a psychiatrist," and "has mental problems."

Middle-grade-level subjects are not only able to make deviance attributions but, also, to judge severity of emotional disturbance in the same manner as adults. Mardsen and Kalter (1976) investigated whether fourth- through sixth-grade children could discriminate degrees of severity of emotional disturbance in descriptions of imaginary peers. The subjects were eight boys and seven girls in the fourth grade and nine boys and seven girls in the sixth grade. Five vignettes were read in random order to the subjects. The central figures in the vignettes were depicted as manifesting normal behavior, incipient school phobia, passive-aggressive behavior, antisocial behavior, and borderline psychotic behavior (the order represents the investigators' ratings of severity of disturbance). In addition, the central figure always was described as male and in the same grade as the subject interviewed. Clinical labels were not used.

The children's responses to the central figure in each vignette were coded on a 5-point scale indicating judgments of severity of emotional disturbance. The scale points were as follows:

1. Subject explicity states or implicitly suggests normality with no hint of emotional disorder.
2. Subject suggests possible presence of emotional problems in the central figure but the suggestion is so implicit it cannot be assigned a higher scale point.
3. Subject indicates that the central figure has emotional problems which are minor in degree.
4. Subject indicates central figure has moderate emotional problems.
5. Subject explicitly states that the central figure has serious emotional problems.

173

The results revealed that 68% of the children's responses to the normal central figure were scored as "1" on the scale, a rating of normal; and 55% of the responses to the borderline psychotic central figure were scored as "5" on the scale, the most severe judgment of behavior disorder. The central figure seen as the second most disturbed character was the antisocial figure. Mardsen and Kalter (1976) concluded that fourth- and sixth-grade children recognize emotional disturbance and judge its severity in a manner that corresponds to the views of mental health professionals.

Like or dislike for a person has been shown to be related to the kind of deviance attributed to him or her. Using the same techniques as Mardsen and Kalter (1976) as well as two 4-point scales measuring degrees of liking and disliking for the stimulus figures, Mardsen, Kalter, Plunkett, and Barr-Grossman (1977) were able to relate liking/disliking to type of deviance attribution.

The results showed that the normal vignette character was liked more than the passive-aggressive or borderline psychotic figures and was disliked significantly less than the aggressive and passive-aggressive characters. The aggressive and passive-aggressive imaginary figures were disliked most.

These findings on the relation of aggression attributions and dislike for the imaginary stimulus figure were substantiated by Novak (1974). Novak presented fourth- through sixth-grade subjects (N = 326) with descriptions of six imaginary peers who exemplified depressed, phobic, immature, aggressive, schizoid, and normal behavior. Each subject was asked to evaluate each stimulus figure on three dependent measures: attractiveness (10 bipolar adjectives), a social distance scale, and a scale of perceived similarity to self.

The analysis of the responses showed that the normal stimulus figure was rated more positively on all three dependent measures than were the other imaginary characters. On the attractiveness dependent variables, the aggressive figure was rated significantly less attractive than the others. The greatest social distance was assigned to the figures described respectively as phobic, immature, and aggressive. On the scale of perceived similarity to self, the figure described as schizoid was rated the most dissimilar.

The responses of the subjects to the aggressive deviant stimulus suggest that they were reacting in part to the possible impact of the disturbed behavior on themselves. Aggressive and immature behaviors (both highest on the social distance measures) cause pain to other children (Novak, 1974).

In the aforementioned studies, target children were not labeled emotionally disturbed. Consequently, the subjects' responses reflect attitudes toward behaviors rather than toward the concept of emotional disturbance.

Novak (1975) hypothesized that children may tolerate a wide range of deviant behavior but may be less tolerant of the same behavior when it is associated with some type of mental illness label. He also hypothesized that the sex of a stimulus subject may influence children's ratings of deviance. Next, using the same task and dependent measures but with two additional conditions, Novak (1975) investigated the responses of 625 fourth- through sixth-grade students. In the additional conditions, the participants received labeled and unlabeled descriptions of the stimulus figures in the six vignettes. All the figures in the first condition were labeled "emotionally disturbed"; in the second condition, no labels were attached to the figures.

The responses to the description of the normal stimulus figure provide the clearest effects of the label "emotional disturbance." When the imaginary normal peer was of the same sex as the subject, the label had no effect on the subject's evaluation, but when the imaginary normal peer was of the opposite sex, the label elicited ratings that were negative on attractiveness, social distance, and perceived similarity. In general, labeling had no effect on the deviant behavior descriptions. Novak concluded that the lack of a labeling effect on the responses to the deviant behavior descriptions may have been due to the concrete bases for making judgments. In interpreting the labeling effect on responses to the opposite sex imaginary normal peer, the investigator suggested that, in the absence of abnormal behavior upon which to make judgments, the subjects responded mainly to the mental illness label and that the sex of the stimulus figures evoked the subjects' responses.

The behavior of a child has also been shown to be more salient than the label "emotional disturbance" in research by Freeman and Algozzine (1980). In this study, 96 fourth grade children were randomly assigned to one of eight conditions. In each condition the children were shown a videotape of a non-handicapped fourth-grade boy engaging in various "normal" behaviors. Depending on the experimental condition, the participants were told that the target child was emotionally disturbed, learning disabled, retarded, or non-handicapped.

After viewing the first part of the videotape, the subjects were asked to rate the target child. Then, before they were shown the second part of the videotape, the subjects in each condition were given either positive or neutral information about the target child. The results of the study indicate no difference in the subjects' social acceptability ratings of the target child as a function of the disability label. The investigators concluded that children are more responsive to the behaviors of their peers than to labels. In addition, the results showed that the assignment of positive attributes to the target child favorably influenced social acceptability ratings in all labeled conditions.

Children's beliefs about what causes a peer to behave in a deviant manner were the subject of only one study. Maas, Maracek, and Travers (1978) investigated children's beliefs about internal versus external causation of disordered behavior. The subjects were 60 children, 10 males and 10 females in each of grades two, four, and six. Three vignettes, each describing a character who exhibited antisocial, withdrawn, or self-punitive behaviors, were read to the children. They were then asked to respond to forced-choice and open-ended questions on the reasons for each character's behaviors, desires, intentions, and ability to change. A list of traits was also presented to the children and they were asked which traits they would ascribe to each story character.

A response to the questionnaire was categorized as "internal causation" if a child said that the stimulus figure was born that way, that the behavior resulted from disease or injury, or that the child did not know the cause of the behavior. A response was categorized as "environmental or external causation" if a child said that the behavior resulted from treatment which the character had received from friends, family, or teachers.

The results indicate that as children grow older they explain the causes of behavior disorder more in terms of external causation. Similarly, with increasing age, children are more likely to believe that undesirable behavior can be changed by altering the external environment. In contrast, the responses of the younger children attributed disordered behavior to internal causation.

The traits attributed to the three different stimulus figures agreed with those of the studies reviewed previously. Across all age levels, the most negative traits were ascribed to the antisocial character.

Children's attitudes toward the concept of emotional disturbance in relation to their attitudes toward other exceptionalities have been assessed by a variety of attitude-scale measures. The results of these studies, based on different methodologies, indicate that in general children perceive the concept of emotional disturbance more negatively than other disability concepts.

Research based on the semantic differential technique indicated that third- and sixth-grade students rated mental illness more negatively than orthopedic handicaps or mental retardation. Wilkins and Velicer (1980) had third- and sixth-grade subjects ($N = 40$) rate the concepts of "person," "crippled," "retarded," and "crazy" on a 5-point semantic differential scale. The bipolar adjectives in the scale measured evaluation of potency, activity, and understandability. The findings revealed that the subjects evaluated the concept of "crazy" more negatively than the concepts of "normal," "crippled," or "retarded." Moreover, "mentally ill" was evaluated as less understandable than the concepts "normal," "crippled," or "retarded." However, mentally ill persons were perceived as active and potent, like average persons. The investigators postulated that the reasons children rate mental illness more negatively than other disabilities may be that mentally ill persons are thought to be bad and are also perceived to have the ability to act out the motivations attributed to them.

A hierarchical rating of disabilities in which emotional disturbance was rated the lowest was also obtained in the research of Parish, Ohlsen, and Parish (1978). Female and male students in fifth, sixth, and seventh grades were given an attitude inventory consisting of 24 positive and 24 negative adjectives. All students were asked to select the 15 adjectives that best described emotionally disturbed, physically handicapped, learning disabled, and normal children. The score for each disability was determined by the number of negative adjectives selected as characteristic of a given target group. The emotionally disturbed group was rated least favorable of all the groups.

Greater social distance was ascribed by high school students to the concept of emotional disturbance than to the majority of other disabilities. The study by Jones, Gottfried, and Owens (1966) measured how much social distance was assigned by high school students ($N = 186$) to 11 exceptionalities and a normal condition. The exceptionalities were *deaf, blind, hard of hearing, partially seeing, delinquent, chronically ill, emotionally disturbed, speech handicapped, mildly mentally retarded, severely mentally retarded, gifted,* and *crippled.* Students were asked to rank pairs of exceptionalities on a 10-point social distance scale. Using the paired comparison technique, the 11 exceptionalities were ordered from most to least acceptable for each of the 10 social distance statements.

The results indicate, in general, that the average and gifted conditions were anchored at the high end of the continuum, while the severely retarded were grouped at the low end. The social distance ratings assigned to emotional disturbance were in the lowest quartile (i.e., one of the four lowest rated groups on the following social distance statements: "I would accept this person as a neighbor." "I would exclude this person from my country." "I would accept this person as a co-worker." "I would accept a child of this type for a playmate of my own child.") This study suggests that high school students hold negative attitudes toward the category or label of emotional disturbance.

Certain methodological limitations are apparent in the research reviewed thus far. Most studies are limited to middle-grade populations. When attitude scales were used, the reliability and validity of the assessment instruments were not discussed. However, the major deficiency is that no study was concerned with the relation between children's perceptions of emotional disturbance and social interactions with emotionally disturbed peers. Given the implicit assumption of investigators that children's conceptions of emotional disturbance are related to their social behavior, it is unfortunate that none of the studies actually investigated this relation. Future research should focus on the impact of the cognitive and affective attitudinal dimensions of children upon subsequent behavior toward disturbed peers.

PEER ACCEPTANCE OF EMOTIONALLY DISTURBED CHILDREN

Very little research has directly addressed the attitudes of nonhandicapped children toward their emotionally disturbed peers. The scant findings that exist are based on peer-assessment techniques in which the affective and cognitive components of the subject's attitudes are measured. The conclusions have a familiar ring, however; emotionally disturbed children as a group are less accepted than are their counterparts who are not disturbed.

Bower (1969) used a peer-assessment index, "A Class Play," which he developed, to study 200 fourth- through sixth-grade classes. The measure contains hypothetical descriptions of 20 roles in a play, some positive, some negative, and some neutral. Each subject is instructed to choose a classmate who would be most suitable for each role. By counting the number of times a pupil is picked for each role, a percentage is obtained that indicates the positive or negative perceptions of each pupil by his or her classmates.

In Bower's findings, educationally handicapped children most often were chosen for the negative roles; hostile children, in particular, were selected for roles consistent with their behaviors; and educationally handicapped children were seldom seen as able to play positive or neutral roles.

A variation of the "Class Play" was used by Vac (1968) to ascertain the comparative social positions of emotionally disturbed and nondisturbed children in regular classrooms. The subjects were 16 classes, ranging from grades one through six. The criterion for selection was that the class contain one pupil identified as emotionally disturbed. Thus the sample included 17 emotionally disturbed children and 368 students not so classified.

An acceptance score of 1 was given each time a child was named by a classmate in response to a positive question, and the mean acceptance and rejection scores of the emotionally disturbed and normal groups were compared. The investigator found that the emotionally disturbed children were not as acceptable as their peers who were not emotionally disturbed. The differences between the mean acceptance and rejection scores for the two groups were statistically significant. The percentage of "stars," that is, sociometrically high subjects, was greatest in the nonemotionally disturbed group, and the percentages of rejectees and isolates were greatest in the emotionally disturbed group. In general, the social positions of the emotionally disturbed children were relatively stable throughout the school year. The percentage of rejected emotionally disturbed children remained consistent from fall to spring, but the percentage of rejected chilren in the normal group decreased slightly.

The impact of social interaction on the attitudes of nonhandicapped children toward autistic children was investigated by McHale and Simeonsson (1980). The attitudes of second- and third-grade nonhandicapped subjects ($N = 28$) toward children with childhood autism confounded by mental retardation were measured before and after the subjects participated in a week of daily half-hour play sessions with six autistic children in a special education classroom. The nonhandicapped subjects were told that they were to teach the autistic children how to play. The attitude questionnaire was composed of adjective ratings and sociometric and open-ended questions.

Analysis of the pre- and posttest attitude questionnaire indicated that at both periods the subjects were positive regarding interaction with the autistic children. The subjects' understanding of autism increased as a result of the interactions.

The disparate findings of this study and the preceding research may be attributed to the differences in both the characteristics of the handicapped children and the nature of the interventions. McHale and Simeonsson suggested that the short duration of the nonhandicapped children's interactions with the autistic children may have been an important variable and influenced the results. Moreover, the authors explained that the nonhandicapped subjects probably did not expect the autistic children to behave "normally," given the nature of the instructions, the severity of the autistic children's handicap, and the special education setting of the interaction.

Reger (1963) found peer rankings and degree of emotional disturbance to be significantly negatively correlated. The subjects were 25 males ages 9 to 14 in a residential treatment unit. Admission to the unit was based on the presence in each boy of emotional disturbance or academic or social retardation. As a measure of peer acceptance, the children were asked to rank every child, including themselves, according to popularity. Two occupational therapists and two special education teachers ranked each child in the group on degree of emotional disturbance. The results indicated that the children judged to be the least emotionally disturbed were more popular than the children who were more disturbed.

However, caution is warranted in generalizing the results of studies based on emotionally disturbed children in residential treatment units to children in regular classroom settings who are categorized as emotionally disturbed. The subjects being rated as well as the subjects doing the rating in the two settings most likely vary in many dimensions.

The relation of sociometric status and the behaviors of institutionalized behaviorally deviant preadolescents was investigated by Kaplan and Kaufman (1978). The children (N = 20) ranged in age from 6.5 to 11 years with the 10- to 11-year olds accounting for two-thirds of the population. A sociometric test was given to the subjects monthly, a total of 11 for the year. Each child was asked to name the three peers he or she liked best and the three he or she liked least. A like-dislike score (the number of positive choices minus the number of negative choices) was then computed for each child.

In addition, staff members rated the subjects' behaviors each day on a checklist that contained 82 daily behaviors. A correlational analysis and an ANOVA were done on the sociometric data and checklists. The analysis indicated that like-dislike status correlated with a number of negative behavioral items. Physical and verbal aggression toward staff members and peers were significantly negatively correlated with social status. On the other hand, correlations were low between like-dislike status and socially valued qualities. Consensus was higher among peers for the most disliked than for the most liked child. The investigators hypothesized that because socially valued behaviors do not have the visibility or impact of overtly aggressive acts, children show more agreement on the negative characteristics of their peers. Here again, the applicability of these findings to regular classroom settings is questionable.

The scattered findings on peer acceptance of emotionally disturbed children indicate that as a group the latter are more rejected than are their peers who are not disturbed. A methodological limitation of the few studies carried out in regular classroom settings is that all used the same peer-assessment techniques. Research based on other methods of assessment is essential. Future research on the topic should use various sociometric and observational methodologies. Studies of mainstreamed emotionally disturbed children in regular classrooms which use both sociometric and observational analyses, such as the procedures followed by Kaplan and Kaufman (1977), are needed. Their methods enable an investigator to specify the behaviors exhibited by accepted and rejected students from which suggestions can be drawn for remediation.

CORRELATES OF PEER ACCEPTANCE

Recall that in the study by Quay et al. (1966) of children placed in classes for the emotionally disturbed, the presenting behaviors were characterized as unsocialized aggression, personality problems, and immaturity-inadequacy problems. Inferences can be made about the peer status of emotionally disturbed children to the extent that the three syndromes have been found to be associated with peer acceptance or rejection.

Aggressive behavior, according to a fairly large body of literature, correlates with peer rejection across all age levels. Moore (1967) found that preschool children who respond aggressively in situations of interpersonal conflict are more disliked by their peers than are children who manage interpersonal conflicts more effectively.

Millman, Baker, Davis, Schaefer, and Zavel (1975) studied the relation between sociometric status and personal social behavior in 38 popular and 38 unpopular boys, all with serious learning and behavioral problems, who resided in a residential treatment unit. To determine sociometric status, each child was given a composite score on the basis of peer responses to the following two questions: "If you were going on an off-campus trip, which boy in the cottage would you most like to sit next to on the bus?" "If you were going on an off-campus trip, which boy in the cottage would you not like to sit next to on the bus, if any?" The Devereaux Elementary School Behavior (DESB) Rating Scale was used to measure each child's behavioral adjustment.

The results indicated that unpopular boys had more problem behavior on the DESB factors that measure movement against others (e.g., classroom defiance, disrespect-defiance, and external blame) than did popular boys. In addition, the unpopular subjects had more problem behavior on the DESB factors measuring movement away from as well as toward others.

Peretti (1975) attempted to determine which characteristics were related to student acceptance or rejection in sixth-grade subjects. The 30 students were given a sociometric questionnaire in which they were asked to name three classmates they would like to sit by, and three classmates with whom they would not want to sit. A forced choice questionnaire was also given. The children were asked to check the personality characteristics that best fit their accepted and rejected choices.

The personality descriptions attributed to the accepted students tended to be centered on qualities such as pleasantness, sharing, and other similar behaviors. Conversely, the personality impressions ascribed to the rejected classmates were aggressiveness and rudeness. Peretti concluded that a child's perception of the personality of the other is the most important factor in making choices about whom one would like to sit with. The second most important factor is participation in extracurricular activities, for boys, and physique of friend, for girls.

Goertzen (1959) asked 1,773 seventh-grade students to rate 32 behaviors on a social distance scale. The items were obtained from a pilot study in which seventh-grade children were asked to write descriptions of people or things people did that made the students dislike them or not select them as friends. These "objectionable" behaviors included such items as "Some seventh graders hit, push, and pick fights. They try to beat up on people"; and "Some seventh graders always do what is right. They don't get into trouble."

On the basis of the pilot responses, each of the 32 negative behavioral items was ranked from least to most acceptable. The lowest ranked items (indicating a majority of subjects responding to the social distance scale with "dislike" or "hate") included the behavioral items of "hitting, pushing, fighting," "bossing," "taking things which are not one's own." The highest ranked negative items (indicating a majority of subjects responding to the social distance scale with "Have as a friend," or "okay") were the items of "not paying attention," "being shy," "poor in sports or dance."

The results of these studies indicate that peer rejection of emotionally disturbed children can be expected to the extent that emotional disturbance is manifested in aggressive behavior. There is much less evidence, however, regarding the acceptance or rejection of children classified as emotionally disturbed on the basis of the other two behavioral syndromes identified by Quay et al. (1966)—immaturity-inadequacy problems and withdrawn-neurotic behaviors.

A tentative case can be made that peer rejection of emotionally disturbed children with withdrawn or immature behaviors may occur to the extent that these behaviors are associated with the incapacity to give positive and neutral reinforcement to others. A number of studies have shown that giving positive reinforcement to another child or to the group is associated with peer acceptance. For example, Hartup, Glazer, and Charlesworth (1967) showed that, in nursery school children, the number of responses a child made to peers was positively correlated with peer acceptance. In an observational study, Bonney and Powell (1953), found that the most accepted first-grade students were those who were best able to function effectively in a group situation. The popular children conformed more to the group, smiled more, and made more voluntary contributions to the group than did the unpopular children. Similarly in 1977, Ladd and Oden (cited in Asher, 1978) found that children who are helpful have more best friends.

An observational study by Masters and Furman (1981), showed that popularity is correlated with the overall rates of emitting and receiving neutral as well as positive acts. The study found that conversation, associative play, and other neutral behaviors are also correlates of popularity.

Much of the evidence for the association of peer rejection with aggressive behavior and of peer acceptance with positive and neutral social behavior has been based on correlational analysis. However, causal direction cannot be inferred from correlational data. Peer rejection may lead to aggressive social behavior, and acceptance by one's peers may lead to positive social behavior, but the reverse also may be true. Most likely, the relation of social behavior and acceptance-rejection is a reciprocal rather than a one-way process. Research on the correlates of peer acceptance and rejection underscores the need for observational analyses of the social interaction of children who are and are not disturbed.

SUMMARY

Most of the research has focused on the cognitive and affective components of children's attitudes; almost none has directly examined the behavioral tendencies of nondisturbed children toward their emotionally disturbed peers.

The major findings may be summarized as follows:

Developmental changes occur in the cognitive component of children's attitudes toward emotional disturbance. Young children generally attribute deviance to their peers on the basis of aggressive behavior. Fourth- through seventh-grade subjects are able to discern both emotional disturbance and its severity in story characters. Behaviors that violate social norms and aggressive behaviors are the basis for middle-grade pupils' deviance attributions to imaginary characters as well as deviant peers. Seventeen-year-old students' perceptions of emotional disturbance parallel adult conceptualizations of the phenomenon.

181

The studies which have been reviewed illustrate that the cognitive and affective components of children's attitudes toward their emotionally disturbed peers are related. Story characters to whom deviance attributions are made are disliked more than the characters not so described. Similarly, peer acceptance studies of emotionally disturbed peers indicate that in general emotionally disturbed children are perceived in a negative fashion and liked less than their nondisturbed counterparts.

A consistent finding is the significance of aggressive behavior as a determinant of both deviance attribution and peer rejection. Regardless of the age group under investigation or the particular methodological technique used, negative attitudes are held toward a child who behaves in an aggressive manner.

A major deficiency of the research was the lack of studies on the behavioral component of children's attitudes. Future research should be directed to the general question of children's behavioral tendencies toward their emotionally disturbed peers. Both sociometric and observational studies are needed.

Most important, research is needed to provide a data base for social intervention. With the growing awareness of the importance of relationships in the development of social competencies, it seems likely that in the future remediation of emotional disturbance will include more emphasis on understanding and modifying the interactions between disturbed and nondisturbed children. According to Hartup (1978),

> Peer relations contribute substantially to the development of social competencies in children. Capacities to create and maintain mutually regulated relations with others, to achieve effective modes of emotional expression, and to engage in accurate social reality testing derive from interaction with other children as well as from adult child interaction. (p.91)

Research is needed which is directed to assessing how the attitudes of children toward their disturbed peers affect the perceptions of the emotionally disturbed children and the subsequent social interaction between the two. This information could provide a basis for programs of social intervention.

REFERENCES

Asher, S. R. Children's peer relations. In M. E. Lamb (Ed.), *Sociopersonality development*. New York: Holt, Rinehart & Winston, 1978.

Bonney, M. E., & Powell, J. Differences in social behavior between sociometrically high and sociometrically low children. *Journal of Educational Research*, 1953, *46*, 481-495.

Bower, E. M. *Early identification of emotionally handicapped children in school* (2nd ed.). Springfield IL: Charles C Thomas, 1969.

Coie, J. D., & Pennington, B. F. Children's perceptions of deviance and disorder. *Child Development*, 1976, *47*, 407-413.

Freeman, S., & Algozzine, B. Social acceptability as a function of labels and assigned attributes. *American Journal of Mental Deficiency*, 1980, *84*, 589-595.

Goertzen, S. Factors relating to opinions of seventh grade children regarding acceptability of behaviors in their peer group. *Genetic Psychology*, 1959, *94*, 29-34.

Hartup, W. W. Children and their friends. In H. McGurk (Ed.), *Child social develop-*

ment. London: Methuen, 1978.

Hartup, W. W., Glazer, J., & Charlesworth, W. Peer reinforcement and sociomet status. *Child Development*, 1967, *38*, 1017-1024.

Jones, R. L., Gottfried, N. W., & Owens, A. The social distance of the exceptional: A study at the high school level. *Exceptional Children*, 1966, *32*, 551-556.

Kaplan, H., & Kaufman, J. Consensus and stability of peer acceptance-rejection status in emotionally disturbed children. *Social Behavior and Personality*, 1977, *5*, 345-350.

Kaplan, H., & Kaufman, I. Sociometric status and behaviors of emotionally disturbed children. *Psychology in the Schools*, 1978, *15*, 8-15.

Livesley, W. J., & Bromley, D. B. *Person percepting in childhood and adolescence*. New York: Wiley, 1973.

Maas, E., Marecek, J., & Travers, J. Children's conceptions of disordered behavior. *Child Development*, 1978, *49*, 146-154.

Mardsen, G., & Kalter, N. Children's understanding of their emotionally disturbed peers. *Psychiatry*, 1976, *39*, 227-238.

Mardsen, G., Kalter, N., Plunkett, J., & Barr-Grossman, T. Children's social judgments concerning emotionally disturbed peers. *Journal of Consulting and Clinical Psychology*, 1977, *45*, 948.

Masters, J. C., & Furman, W. Popularity, individual friendship selection, and specific peer interaction among children. *Developmental Psychology*, 1981, *17*, 344-350.

McGuire, W. The nature of attitudes and attitude change. In G. Lindzey & E. Aronson (Eds.), *Handbook of social psychology* (Vol. 3). Reading MA: Addison-Wesley, 1969.

McHale, S. M., & Simeonsson, R. J. Effects of interaction on nonhandicapped children's attitudes toward autistic children. *American Journal of Mental Deficiency*, 1980, *85*, 18-24.

Millman, H. L., Baker, E. A., Davis, J. K., Schaefer, C. E., & Zavel, D. The relationship between sociometric status and personal social behavior in emotionally disturbed boys. *Journal Supplement Abstract Service of the American Psychological Association*, MS. No. *936*, 1975, *5*, 238.

Moore, S. G. Correlates of peer acceptance in nursery school children. In W. W. Hartup & N. Smothergil (Eds.), *The young child* (Vol. 1). Washington DC: National Association for the Education of Young Children, 1967.

Novak, D. Children's reactions to emotional disturbance in imaginary peers. *Journal of Consulting and Clinical Psychology*, 1974, *42*, 462.

Novak, D. Children's responses to imaginary peers labeled as emotionally disturbed. *Psychology in the Schools*, 1975, *12*, 103-106.

Parish, T. S., Ohlsen, R. L., & Parish, J. G. A look at mainstreaming in light of children's attitudes toward the handicapped. *Perceptual and Motor Skills*, 1978, *46*, 1019-1021.

Peretti, P. Perceived personality impression in student acceptance and rejection interaction patterns in the classroom. *Research Quarterly*, 1975, *46*, 457-462.

Quay, H., Morse, W., & Cutter, H. Personality patterns of pupils in special classes for the emotionally disturbed. *Exceptional Child*, 1966, *32*, 297-301.

Rabkin, J. G. Opinions about mental illness: A review of the literature. *Psychological Bulletin*, 1972, *77*, 153-171.

Rabkin, J. G. Public attitudes toward mental illness: A review of the literature. *Schizophrenia Bulletin*, 1974, *10*, 9-33.

Rabkin, J. G. Who is called mentally ill: Public and professional views. *Journal of Community Psychology*, 1979, *7*, 253-258.

Reger, R. Eye hand coordination, peer acceptance, and emotional disturbance. *American Journal of Mental Deficiency*, 1963, *67*, 589-591.

Rubin, D., Simson, C., & Betwee, M. C. *Emotionally handicapped children and the elementary school*. Detroit: Wayne State University Press, 1966.

Vac, N. A study of emotionally disturbed children in regular and special classes. *Exceptional Children*, 1968, *38*, 197-204.

Wilkins, J. E., & Velicer, W. F. A semantic differential investigation of children's attitudes toward three stigmatized groups. *Psychology in the Schools*, 1980, *17*, 364-371.

Woody, R. A. *Behavioral problem children in the schools*. New York: Appleton-Century-Crofts, 1969.

Attitudes Toward the Physically Disabled

JEROME SILLER

Although attitudes toward physically disabled persons have been investigated from a variety of viewpoints, systematic studies using developed instrumentation, defined samples and substantial populations are relatively infrequent. This chapter will describe general trends in the overall research, review selected systematic studies, and discuss some of the methodological problems that arise.

There is ample evidence that the term "physically disabled," although adequate for certain purposes, may not be a sufficiently clear referent for many other purposes. As used in this review, "physically disabled" focuses primarily on the sensory conditions, such as deafness and blindness, and on the skeletal and motor conditions, such as amputation, poliomyelitis, and body deformations. However, skin disorders, burns, obesity, and other physical conditions that arouse strong social responses clearly fall within its purview. Other conditions, such as cancer, heart disease, epilepsy, muscular dystrophy, and the like, also are considered here because there is a clear continuity of attitude orientation toward them. One other definitional note must be added. The presence of neurological involvement affecting a person's cognitive coping potential—for example, cerebral palsy with cognitive dysfunction—substantially changes the stimulus picture for nondisabled respondents. The frame of reference here assumes that any central nervous system problem involves motoric behavior without higher intellectual dysfunction, unless otherwise noted.

The specific topic areas covered are measurement considerations, the structure of attitudes, ways in which the disabled are different, developmental aspects of disability, the social position of the disabled, attitudes of rehabilitation workers, and variables affecting the interactions of disabled and nondisabled persons.

By now, there is abundant literature on attitudes toward disabled persons.

Adding to the problems of coverage is the wide dispersement of relevant articles and books through many journals and other publications directed to many different professional groups. The basis for organizing our material, and even for determining what material to include, is the principle that no adequate total review of this literature is available and that it would be of value, within the space limits of this volume, to provide a representative sample of the research-based literature on attitudes toward the disabled. Many studies that could and would have been included, if space were not a constraint, can be found in some of the general texts and reviews (e.g., Barker, Wright, Myerson, & Gonick, 1953; Cruickshank, 1980; Kutner, 1971; McDaniel, 1976; Safilios-Rothschild, 1970; Siller, 1976a, 1976b, 1984, in press; Siller, Chipman, Ferguson, & Vann, 1967; Siller, Ferguson, Vann, & Holland, 1967; Wright, 1960; Yuker, Block, & Younng, 1966). Since most of the work which has been done with adults has import for children, data from all age groups are considered.

The absence of a separate section on parental attitudes stems not from the subject's lack of importance but from the almost complete lack of significant research on this vital topic.

MEASUREMENT CONSIDERATIONS

Inasmuch as virtually all techniques generally employed in the measurement of attitudes have been used in relation to disability, evaluation of individual studies becomes difficult because of the absence of adequate technical information to assess the measuring instruments and the limits to the generalization of results. Most instruments have been used only once, with no follow-up studies. Other major deficiencies in attitude research have been the lack of a theoretical framework to guide scale development and insufficiently sensitive measures of children's attitudes. However, several systematic and programmatic approaches have been undertaken.

A basic conceptual division of the attitude measurement domain is whether attitudes toward the disabled are best represented along a single positive-negative dimension (e.g., the Attitude Toward Disabled Persons Scale, ATDP, of Yuker et al., 1966) or as multidimensional in character (Siller, 1970a; Siller, Chipman et al., 1967; Siller, Ferguson et al., 1967).

Unidimensional approaches to attitude measurement derive a single score, such as degree of acceptability, positiveness, or willingness to associate with. Even when multiple scores are obtained, as on a sociometric scale, a single underlying dimension is assumed. In practice, despite the name offered by the scales developed and the different areas of content tapped, such scales usually intercorrelate fairly highly. Most single-score measures probably tap a mixture of dimensions on an affective (feeling) level (Siller, Ferguson et al., 1967).

Cowen and his associates have provided unidimensional scales on blindness (Cowen, Underberg, & Verillo, 1958; Cowen, Underberg, Verillo, & Benham, 1961) and deafness (Cowen, Bobrove, Rockway, & Stevenson, 1967) which have received more than the usual peripheral development and usage. Also widely used are the semantic differential (Osgood, Suci, & Tannenbaum, 1957) and a set of stimulus pictures depicting children in which all features of appearance are held constant except the presence or absence of a visible physical handicap and the type of handicap (see the 10 references to Richardson, alone and with his associates). The picture stimuli have been widely used with children.

A variety of social-distance measures have also been reported and are discussed throughout this chapter. The results of such studies are mostly uninteresting in that the ratings are highly influenced by the other conditions which were rated concurrently and that the empirical findings are virtually never tied to a priori theories. Psychometric sophistication is usually lacking and assumptions of dimensionality are sometimes inappropriately made (Siller, Chipman et al., 1967). The precise dimension upon which the social-distance indices are taken (e.g., preference, seriousness for oneself) often differ from study to study, making comparison difficult.

A strong relation between a measure of disability attitude and nondisability indices is yet to be demonstrated (Siller, Chipman et al., 1967; Siller, Ferguson et al., 1967). Does this mean that such relations are absent or that extant instruments are too insensitive? The latter possibility is the more likely. The relation of methodological problems of measuring disability attitudes to two theoretical issues was suggested by Siller (1966). The first methodological difficulty, mentioned earlier, is the vague referent for the general term "disability." This procedural problem reflects the theoretical issue of the extent to which the public's attitudes generalize across disabilities and the extent to which they are specific to a disability. The second theoretical issue pertains to the dimensionality of attitude structure. By employing only a single summative score, both the Cowen scales and the ATDP treat this domain as unidimensional. Other work supports the contention of multidimensionality.

An important implication of the multidimensional approach is that one's definition, conceptualization, and measurement of the attitudinal domain become more differentiated and flexible. Major theoretical and empirical issues of this attitude domain were investigated in a series of studies under the writer's direction (Ferguson, 1970; Siller, 1970a, 1970b; Siller, Chipman et al., 1967; Siller, Ferguson, Vann, & Holland, 1968; Siller, Ferguson et al., 1967; Vann, 1970). The purpose of these studies was to describe and measure salient dimensions of attitudes of nondisabled persons toward the physically disabled. The latter measurement aspect is discussed here; the theoretical aspect of dimensionality and the empirical findings based on it are discussed in the section on structure of attitudes.

Siller and his associates developed a series of factor analytically based scales, collectively called the Disability Factor Scales (DFS), which clearly demonstrate multidimensionality in this domain. Eschewing the general term "disability," separate questionnaires (Likert-type) have been developed on the conditions of amputation, blindness, cosmetic condition (Siller, Ferguson et al., 1968; Siller, Ferguson et al., 1967), deafness (Ferguson, 1970), obesity (Vann, 1970), cancer (Siller & Braden, 1976), and a general scale (Siller, 1970). The set of questionnaires provides wide flexibility in assessing attitudes toward specific disabilities or toward disability in general. Each questionnaire is scored for a number of dimensions, usually seven. The scales are self-reported, objectively scored, economically administered in terms of time, and comprehensible to adolescents. Reliabilities, with few exceptions, range from the high .70's to the .90's. Validity and cross-validation studies have proven to be very supportive. The DFS has been widely used and has often been discriminating when other instruments have not been (e.g., Marinelli & Kelz, 1973). The DFS has been used to assess the attitudes of a number of disability groups and a rewritten version for the deaf has been tested (Zuckerman, 1980).

Whiteman & Lukoff (1964, 1965) also have applied a components approach to the study of attitudes toward the disabled. Unlike the Siller approach, in which a similar-item format was deliberately used to minimize instrument variance, Whiteman and Lukoff used a diversified-item format to minimize response set and to lend support to clusters or factors cutting across indices that refer to common content but differ in modes of presentation. Essentially, the particular factorial dimensions obtained in their studies can be subsumed within the set obtained in the Siller work, thus lending credence to both orientations and to the meaningfulness of the dimensions obtained.

An interesting different multidimensional approach to attitude measurement in disability was followed by Jordan in a series of studies extending over a number of years (Jordan, 1971). A priori attitude behavior scales (ABS) were developed by Jordan, using Guttman facet theory,[1] and using the following ordered levels: societal stereotype, societal norm, personal moral evaluation, personal hypothetical action, personal feeling, and personal action. The conditions studied by Jordan were deafness, mental illness, Black-White relations, and mental retardation. The reports of certain reliability and validity data support the approach. An interesting feature of the ABS has been Jordan's extensive use of cross-cultural samples.

Although the ATDP has been used in studies with the DFS and the ABS, sample sizes have not been sufficiently large or representative to draw firm conclusions regarding their interrelations. However, the contention indicated previously, that the ATDP is basically a measure of general affect, receives empirical support from the fact that when the DFS and the ATDP were used together, what were identified as general affect scales on the DFS correlated most highly with the ATDP (Siller, Ferguson et al., 1967). This last finding has been repeated in a number of unpublished studies by the writer since the earlier report.

One final note: Considerable dissatisfaction has been raised in many quarters regarding the omission of situational factors in the assessment of personality and attitudinal effects. Sloat and Frankel (1972) examined the contributions of subjects, disabilities, situations, sex of target persons, and items to the variations of attitudes toward persons with disabilities, and their results strongly suggest the need for including the situational aspect within a multidimensional analytic framework, and for considering the interaction of these variables.

STRUCTURE OF ATTITUDES

Conceptualization of the dimensionality of attitudes in relation to structure obviously has considerable practical and theoretical implication. The most direct and extensive research bearing on this concept was conducted by Siller and associates (Ferguson, 1970; Siller, 1970a; Siller, Chipman et al., 1967; Siller, Ferguson et al., 1967; Vann, 1970; and unpublished work). The investigations have been cross validated on a variety of populations and substantial numbers of persons and have been confirmed by the work of others. In short, seven fairly comprehensive dimensions of attitude, along with scales to measure these dimensions, have been found for a range of conditions. Although, for certain conditions (cancer and obesity), the basic seven have not been completely obtained, in general the findings on attitudinal components can be described as follows:

1. *Interaction Strain:* uneasiness in the presence of disabled persons and uncertainty about how to deal with them.
2. *Rejection of Intimacy:* rejection of close, particularly familial, relationships with the disabled.
3. *Generalized Rejection:* a pervasive negative and derogatory approach to disabled persons with consequent advocacy of segregation.
4. *Authoritarian Virtuousness:* ostensibly a "pro-disabled" orientation, this factor is really rooted in an authoritarian context that manifests itself in a call for special treatment which is less benevolent and more harmful than it seems.
5. *Inferred Emotional Consequences:* intense hostile references to the character and emotions of the disabled person.
6. *Distressed Identification:* personalized hypersensitivity to disabled persons who serve as activators of anxiety about one's own vulnerability to disability.
7. *Imputed Functional Limitations:* devaluation of the capacities of a disabled person to cope with the environment.

The study of these components has led to a number of strong conclusions, some of which are noted here. The seven dimensions represent an initial taxonomy of the attitudinal domain in disability and undoubtedly have implications for other deviant conditions. Attitude components are highly general across disabilities. Components of attitudes within a disability tend to be positively correlated, and a person favorable or unfavorable toward one disability likely will have similar feelings toward others. The greatest consistencies in attitudes across disabilities ordinarily will be on the same component (e.g., Inferred Emotional Consequences on amputations with Inferred Emotional Consequences on any other condition). The structure of attitudes for physical disability is organized more strongly around attitude component than by specific disability condition.

Whereas attention to a specific attitudinal component may be justified for a particular purpose, careful thought should be given to what one is really interested in and to pursuing the flexible and differentiated attitudinal path rather than an unnecessarily less differentiated path.

With more work on the structure of attitudes, it is almost certain that there will emerge various disability-specific dimensions like those found for cancer (Siller & Braden, 1976) and obesity (Vann, 1970). It is less likely that a major general dimension will emerge using the same factor analytic approach, although it is not impossible.

ARE THE PHYSICALLY DISABLED REALLY DIFFERENT?

Do the physically disabled, in fact, so present themselves as to promote differential treatment by others? Writers in the area of blindness, for example, have found such points of difference as "unevenness in level of functioning from one cognitive area to another" (Witkin, Birnbaum, Lomonaco, Lehr, & Herman, 1968, p. 767), developmental delays (Fraiberg, 1968), differential ego delays (Sandler, 1963), and lost interplay with the mother due to inability to look and smile at each other (Burlingham, 1964). The frequent mannerisms ("blindisms") and stare of the blind have decided social impact.

The possibility of actual systematic differences in social perception of the disabled has been raised (Schiff & Thayer, 1974). Richardson, Hastorf, and Dornbusch (1964) studied 9- to 11-year olds and concluded that restricted access to direct experience in social interaction leads to the impoverishment of perceptual categorization. Kleck demonstrated experimentally in a series of studies how the behavior of a nonhandicapped person is modified in the presence of a handicapped person—for example, shorter responses to questions and more distortion of opinion (Kleck, 1969; Kleck, Ono, & Hastorf, 1966). Comer and Piliavin (1972) demonstrated that disabled persons experience considerable discomfort in encounters with physically normal persons. As Schiff and Thayer (1974) observed, there is a pattern of mutual difficulty in disabled/nondisabled interactions. Schoggen (1963) pointed out that behavior settings were more of a behavior determinant than a child's physical characteristics, a position that is at variance with the usual tendency to identify the determinant of problem interaction within the individual.

Such behaviors of nondisabled, unthinking, and unempathic persons as staring, rude questions or actions, and devaluative and subordinating actions precipitate resentment and anger in reaction. The attitudinal dimension of "Inferred Emotional Consequences" (described previously) may be derived in part from the insistence that disability distorts one's character and, in part, from the angry reactions of a person who "has had it."

To deal with the pressures upon them, disabled persons, like the nondisabled, use various defensive and coping techniques (Lipp, Kolstoe, James, & Randall, 1968; Siller, 1976a). Denial of the implications of the disability is a particularly important defensive mechanism whose operation varies greatly among persons. A consequence for measurement is that self-reports by disabled persons may be based upon real feelings, what they wish were so, or beliefs of greater negativity than may actually exist (Dixon, 1977; Friend 1971; Weinberg-Asher, 1976).

Disturbances in nondisabled-disabled person interactions are attributed to an assumed "impairment in empathic ability" due to the supposed different developmental tracks imposed by disability. Black (1964), using a projective-type test involving disabled participants in helping roles, reported that the physically normal people found it difficult to think of a disabled person as a helper. Two more studies found quite opposite results: nondisabled and un-dergraduates who responded to hypothetical counseling situations preferred disabled over nondisabled counselors (Brabham & Thoreson, 1973; Mitchell & Fredrickson, 1975).

One might infer that, as soon as one departs from the direct fact of disability, evidence can be provided to demonstrate either the presence or absence of psychological differences among the disabled. The obvious physical difference cannot define resulting reactions. As Wright (1964) has shown, a "spread" may occur where improper generalizations are made from one characteristic of a person (e.g., the physical) to other characteristics (e.g., the intellectual or emotional). Much of the data suggest that if the disabled present themselves as "different" the behavior is often a secondary consequence of the social climate rather than of the inherent disability-specific phenomenon. Moriarty (1974) pointed out, "Only when minority group members are stigmatized do they feel and act like social deviants" (p. 849). The somatopsychological ap-proach, which is based upon the dynamic interaction of disabled and nondis-abled persons, seems to be the most suitable for understanding this complex situation because there can be no static "right" answer to the question of the degree to which an undefined person with an ambiguously perceived disability is "different": Different to whom and for what purpose?

DEVELOPMENTAL ASPECTS

Physical disability confronts parents, peers, and other significant others (as well as oneself) with something of great import (Richardson, 1969). Our knowl-edge of familial attitudes consists mostly of anecdotal and clinical-type reports. The more research-based studies generally are weak because of, for example, small numbers, limited nonrandom samples, poor instrumentation and meth-odologies, and inadequate or crude statistical handling (Jordan, 1962).

Only a few studies report on the emerging perception of disability in pre-school age children (Fine, 1978; Jones & Sisk, 1970; Popp & Fu, 1981; Wein-berg, 1978). Weinberg (1978) examined 3- to 5-year-old children's awareness of physical impairment. The participants were shown pictures of a same-sex, abled-bodied child sitting in either a regular chair or wheelchair and were asked a series of yes/no questions to assess their attitudes toward the pictured child. Weinberg found a shift of understanding between ages 3 and 4. The younger children did not appear to relate to the disability, whereas the 4-year-olds responded that what was different was that the child was in a wheelchair. It would seem that by age 4, children have learned something about physical disability and attending to it as a distant but important element. Further, Weinberg reported that knowledge about disability does not have a significant effect on liking, willingness to share, or perception of the disabled child's desire to play.

Jones and Sisk (1970) studied 230 nondisabled children, ages 2 to 6, who responded to drawings of a same-sex child wearing a leg brace and without the brace. Standard questions were asked regarding interpersonal acceptance

190

and limitations imposed by orthopedic disability. At age 4, children began to consistently perceive the limitations imposed by orthopedic disability. Responses to the two drawings were not significantly different (aside from the 5-year-olds greater rejection of the orthopedically disabled child in response to the question, "Would you play with him?"). The disabled child was perceived as less likely to have fun by 4- to 5-year olds; 5- to 6-year olds, in general, qualified their responses by indicating conditions under which they believed the disabled child would have fun or be acceptable.

Popp and Fu (1981) investigated by means of slides and a tape recording whether preschool children ($N = 121$) had a realistic understanding of the limitations imposed by various orthopedic disabilities. They found that preschoolers were aware that such conditions might impose physical limitations and tended to perceive the able-bodied children as more capable in performing various tasks. Affective measures were not obtained, so the implications of the findings for the interpersonal consequences for the orthopedically disabled were not established.

Fine (1978), using 125 pre-schoolers (ages 3½ to 6 years, 5 months) found that 50% or more of an age group did not correctly identify the deviant picture (missing left arm) as "different" from the two others that were identical except for the presence of the left arm until the interval of 5–6 to 5–8. Children at all age intervals studied were able to discriminate the perceptually different picture; however, as a group, the majority did not do so until almost time for regular school entrance. It was found that the base rate for the entire population in applying negatively toned adjectives (ugly, bad, mean) to the disabled picture was so high that it virtually precluded differentiation between early and non-early perceivers (i.e., those who could correctly identify the "difference" before their age peers). This result suggests that awareness was present although it did not meet a rigorously set criterion for correct perception of the difference.

Hypotheses regarding the relations of castration anxiety and self-concept to age of onset of perceptual discrimination were tested by comparing 20 early perceivers to 20 matched (age, sex, IQ) controls on the Children's Thematic Apperception Test (CTAT) and the Children's Self-Social Constructs Test (CSSC) for the variables in question. The results supported both hypotheses regarding castration anxiety: There were higher castration anxiety scores for early perceivers, and those with higher castration anxiety scores were more negative. The hypothesis on the greater negative self-image of early perceivers received support, but no relation was found between attitudinal evaluations of physical deviation and self-concept.

The findings of Weinberg (1978) and Fine (1978) extend downward the previous findings of Richardson (1970) regarding the negative attitudes toward the disabled held by first graders. That attitudes of elementary school and older children continue to be negative has been documented in many other studies. Adolescence in particular poses threats and increases negativity (Siller, Chipman et al., 1967). The key position of the preschool years for subsequent attitude formation certainly deserves considerably more attention than it has received.

Important sustained research on the developmental aspects of disability has been conducted by Richardson and his associates (see references to aspects of their work in various sections of this chapter). Richardson's basic measurement device has been a picture-preference ranking method (see Chapter 4). Some of the essential findings of his research suggest (a) widespread preference for nonhandicapped over handicapped children, with preference for certain disabilities; (b) a remarkably consistent ordering of disability conditions by groups of children from very different geographical settings and social backgrounds; (c) a period of close interaction does not change preferences; and (d) neither interaction nor being disabled oneself change the order of preferences (Richardson, 1969, 1970, 1971; Richardson & Royce, 1968; Richardson, Goodman, Hastorf, & Dornbusch, 1961; Richardson, Ronald, & Kleck, 1974).

Richardson (1970) maintained that positive or negative preferences for specific disabilities reflect widely held social attitudes toward the handicapped and that as children become more socialized through aging, their order of preference becomes similar to that of adults.

Interestingly, the use of the picture-preference technique has failed to support certain possible preconceptions, to wit, (a) an intense interaction in a relatively short period of time can overcome initial barriers (Kleck, 1969; Richardson, 1963); (b) greater contact facilitates personal knowledge of one's peers and thus affords greater opportunity to make judgments based on more than physical appearance alone (Richardson et al., 1974); (c) high sociometric status would lead one to express more normative values toward the handicapped while low sociometric status would lead to less-often expressed normative values (Richardson & Friedman, 1973); and (d) functional impairments are least liked (Richardson et al., 1961).

The conclusions reached by Richardson and his associates using the Picture Ranking Task have not gone unchallenged. Yuker (1983), in a highly critical article, challenges the conclusion that a stable order of preference for handicaps has been established and cautions that "the interpretations obtained through the use of the Picture Ranking Task are, at best, applicable only to data obtained using this task, and should not be generalized" (p. 92). A full response to Yuker's criticisms subsequently was made by Richardson (1983) and study of both articles is highly recommended both for their substantive implications and for insight into the conceptual and methodological issues involved.

THE SOCIAL POSITION OF THE PHYSICALLY DISABLED AND PREFERENCE RANKINGS FOR TYPES OF DISABILITIES

Probably the most widely quoted summary of attitudes toward physically disabled persons is that of Barker et al. (1953): "Public, verbalized attitudes toward disabled persons are on the average mildly favorable; an appreciable minority openly express negative attitudes...Indirect evidence suggests that deeper unverbalized attitudes are more frequently hostile" (p. 84). Twenty years of work in this domain and close review of the literature convince me of the continued truth of Barker's summary statement. Physical disability, in most instances, is a stigmatized condition with distinct social problems for the disabled person.

Sociometry has been a major tool in examining the social status of handicapped children. In one early study (Force, 1956) it was found that physically handicapped children were not accepted by normal children in integrated classes and that few had enough positive assets to offset completely the negative effect of being labeled handicapped by their classmates. Around the same time, Freeman and Sonnega's (1956) results provided no basis for assuming that speech handicapped children were socially rejected merely because of speech. Soldwedel and Terrill (1957) found the sociometric status of disabled children to be similar to that of their normal classroom peers, while Elser (1956) found the sociometric status of hearing-handicapped children to be lower on the average than that of their classmates; the least accepted children were the mildly handicapped and those without hearing aids. The findings by Raskin (1962) paralleled these results; he noted that blind children tended to be liked but not well respected. A general pattern of conclusions from the early studies suggests that despite the practice of placing exceptional children in regular classes to enable them to maintain normal relations with their peers, segregation from their peers was not prevented (Gronlund, 1959).

Studies carried out in the 1960's continue to support the earlier findings of impaired social status for disabled children: Centers and Centers (1963), for elementary school-age amputee children; Bansavage (1968), for orthopedically impaired adolescents; and Gallagher (1969) and Marge (1966) for speech-defective children. In the latter studies, however, acceptability of speech-disabled children was not found to be a factor in playground activities for first- and third-grade peers; teachers' attitudes toward speech deficiencies were thought to be highly influential on the other children (Gallagher, 1969), although there was a trend for teachers to prefer normally speaking children (Marge, 1966). Mothers of normally speaking children did not differ greatly from mothers of speech-handicapped children in attitude toward speech disorders. Richardson's work, already cited, also supports the differentiated situation of disabled children. Thus, although some differentiation is found to be related to specific activities and may be a factor in the interactions of disabled and nondisabled children, a general picture of status devaluation repeatedly emerges.

Inasmuch as the pressures for mainstreaming have increased during and since the 1970's, one would expect the influx of disabled children into the regular school system to impact on peers and teachers far more than in the past. Definitive studies are yet to be forthcoming. The complexity of the issues and methodological problems are such that one would not expect isolated studies based on small, unrepresentative samples of students, teachers, administrators, and communities to be a suitable mode for the exploration of these problems.

Two studies are representative of significant research. McCauley, Bruininks, and Kennedy (1976) used an observation schedule of interactive behavior to compare the behavior of hearing-impaired and nondisabled children in a classroom setting. They reported no significant differences; however, disabled children relied more heavily on teachers as a source of rewarding social interactions whereas the nondisabled children relied more on their peer groups. Reich, Hambleton, and Houldin (1977) conducted a study of 195 hearing-impaired students in four programs that varied in degree of integration. After controlling for relevant variables, Reich and his associates concluded that the results indicate that integration is beneficial to academic development but may stimulate personal and social difficulties; regardless of the type of program, students who are integrated must have highly developed oral skills, at least average intelligence, and supportive parents.

Implications from such studies suggest a need to create a milieu that will maximize successful interactions because (leaving aside criticisms regarding specific studies or parts of studies) children demonstrate pronounced early attitudes toward disability which tend to be negative. Children maintain and build upon these attitudes during the course of their development, tend to isolate or at least to treat children with disabilities differentially, and are highly influenced by parental and teacher attitudes. Actual performances of disabled children may or may not influence interaction outcomes positively, but they can rather easily affect such interactions negatively. Careful attention to setting the stage for constructive interactions is necessary because contact alone may have negative rather than positive aspects.

Studies with adults are spread over many areas, such as professional-client attitudes, teacher attitudes, and employment; some of these are discussed elsewhere in this or other chapters.

In research with adults, attention has not been directed so much toward the sociometric status of disabled persons as toward establishing the general population's perceptions of different disabilities. Social-distance-type studies have established consistent and stable relative rankings among adults for a variety of physical and other conditions (e.g., Jones, 1974; Shears & Jensema, 1969; Siller, Chipman et al., 1967; Tringo, 1970). Typical results find cerebral palsy, body deformations, and obesity to be among the most rejected disabilities, whereas amputation and blindness are more favorably ranked, and many other conditions fall at various points along a continuum. A consistent finding has been that a relatively high degree of social acceptance is noted up to the point of marriage. A sharp decrease in percentages of subjects who would accept disabled persons occurs between the points on the scale labeled "Would Have as a Friend" and "Would Marry." Thus, in one representative study, the percentages for amputees drop from approximately 80 to 18; for persons in wheelchair, from 79 to 7; for the blind, 77 to 16; harelip, 69 to 8; stutterer, 65 to 7; deaf mute, 53 to 10; and cerebral palsied, 38 to 1 (Shears & Jensema, 1969). A general order of preference is, usually, physically disabled first, sensory disabled second, and brain injured third. "Social" conditions, such as mental illness, alcoholism, and delinquency are invariably rejected.

Shears and Jensema (1969) suggested that six dimensions probably combine and interact in the formation of stereotypes of anomalous persons: visibility, communication, social stigma, reversibility, degree of incapacity, and difficulty in daily living. Barker (1964) described an "organic" and "functional" dichotomy. Siller (unpublished) identified a set of primary variables that mediate between real aspects of a disability and the ultimate form in which the components of attitude are structured toward that disability (transient-permanent, organic-functional, etiology, terminal-nonterminal, and personal responsibility). Each individual condition also has the possibility

194

for connoting certain psychological qualities, e.g., paralysis-dependency, cerebral palsy-uncontrolled, skin conditions-dirtiness (Siller, Chipman et al., 1967).

Previously, in discussing the multidimensional nature of attitudes and Siller's components approach, it was mentioned that attitudes can be specific to a condition (e.g., fear of castration) or more general, encompassing many conditions (e.g., interaction strain). The question of which components are salient to a particular disability or set of disabilities is an empirical question to which data already have provided some answers (Ferguson, 1970; Siller, 1970a; Siller & Braden, 1976; Siller, Chipman et al., 1967; Siller, Ferguson et al., 1967; Vann, 1970). The findings of Siller (1970a) and Siller and Braden (1976) are unequivocal in regard to the presence of attitude components across disabilities which were operationalized in the DFS-General measure. Jones (1974), following up implications of the generality of attitudes toward exceptional children, used hierarchical factor analysis to analyze responses to a social-distance questionnaire (6 interpersonal situations and 13 categories of exceptionality-nonexceptionality). The results revealed a general factor concerning attitudes toward the disabled which cut across type of disability and interpersonal situation. The general factor was differentiated into attitudes toward the physically disabled, psychologically disabled, and mildly mentally retarded-nonexceptional. Attitudes toward the gifted emerged as a separate factor. Tringo (1970) also found a generally higher correlation of each disability variable on his social-distance scale with the overall score than with other disability variables, suggesting the usefulness of generalized measures, such as the ATDP or the combining of DFS scores. However, Siller (1970a) specifically demonstrated that the organization of attitudes toward physical disabilities is much more strongly based upon the specific attitude component than toward the disability type. One might infer that the most useful approach to understanding the attitudes of the general population is a sensitive appreciation of whether one is interested in disability in general or in a specific disability, and whether one needs to approach the problem through an overall score or through measures of specific components. Conceptualization and instrumentation for proceeding in all necessary ways are now available.

ATTITUDES OF PROFESSIONALS AND REHABILITATION WORKERS

An important aspect of the milieu of disabled persons is the interaction with various professional personnel in rehabilitation and educational efforts. (For the review of studies of educators' attitudes toward handicapped pupils, see Chapter 11). Here, only some aspects of the attitudes of rehabilitation personnel toward the disabled are discussed.

Certain kinds of conditions traditionally have lesser "appeal" than do others to professional workers. Thus aging, mental retardation, dying, and chronic disability all seem to have relatively restricted interest for professionals in general. Professionals, like most people, prefer working with the "beautiful people"—those who are most like themselves intellectually and socially, and those who can benefit from assistance.

Thus, in one typical study, the major reasons given by rehabilitation counselors for the preference not to rehabilitate persons with particular kinds of disability were lack of speed and ease of success in achieving vocational rehabilitation and unpredictability of client behavior (Goldin, 1966).

Eight major physical disabilities were ranked on how disturbing they would be as personal afflictions by 7 rehabilitation professors, 32 future rehabilitation counselors, and 50 Mensa members (Wilson, Sakata, & Frumkin, 1968). The latter two groups were significantly different from the seven experts (professors), whose attitudes were judged to represent a more objective view. Wilson and his associates noted that ". . . one may not take for granted that either highly intelligent or highly interested but relatively uninformed persons will view handicaps with the same objectivity as experts" (p. 1304).

Warren and Turner (1966) provided data showing consistent relative rankings of a variety of conditions of exceptionality by several groups of professionals. The subjects included 24 teachers of the mentally retarded, 22 social workers, 63 student nurses, 17 medical students, 27 graduate students in school administration, and 219 psychology and education students. The preferences for the total group were, in order: academically talented, antisocial, sight handicapped, mildly retarded, hearing handicapped, brain injured, and severely retarded. Rankings were also obtained on the educational emphasis that respondents felt disabilities were given in current training in their fields of specialization and on their familiarity with disabled persons. The results of these rankings were almost identical with the ranking of preference. The absence of much differentiation among the three categories suggests that a common attitudinal element underlies all.

Several studies have demonstrated that the expectations of significant others ("Pygmalion" effect) affect the performance of institutionalized blind adolescents in response to their houseparents (Mayadas, 1975) and the "blind role" assumed by blind persons (Mayadas & Duehn, 1976). Mayadas pointed out how important it is for significant personnel to be carefully selected and to receive continued training. These findings are probably as highly generalizeable to all disability conditions and all rehabilitation professions as they are to most basic relationships between persons of discrepant statuses.

For the characterizations of specific conditions, the research on attitudes toward deafness and cancer is a "sampler" (studies on blindness are reviewed in Monbeck, 1973). The attitudes held by professionals toward deafness seem to be "mildly positive" (Ferguson, 1970; Schroedel, 1972). Educators familiar with the difficulty imposed upon communication are less positive. Research-based studies on the attitudes of professionals toward cancer are only now emerging. Generally, the clinical findings of professionals' strong reactions and negative differential treatment have been supported (Pinkerton & McAleer, 1976; Tichenor & Rundall, 1977). The factorial structure of attitudes toward cancer held by health-related professionals and students only partially reflects the structure of attitudes repeatedly found for other disability conditions (Siller & Braden, 1976). It is obvious that the condition of cancer projects a unique quality which must be taken into consideration in the training of professionals in terms of impact both on patients and social perceptions, including perceptions of the professionals.

The crucial nature of the personal element injected by the rehabilitation worker is observed in the frequency with which direct-care personnel contribute to their own difficulties in dealing with children and adults around rehabilitation issues. Workers who attempt to "reassure away" depressed feelings may unwittingly reinforce denial and obscure dependency needs and, in acute cases, appropriate mourning reactions. Frustration and anger toward persons who do not improve or conform are also evident. One also can observe anger and rejection on the part of staff and teachers toward individuals who manifest hostility or passive-aggressive behavior.

It is crucial that clients with chronic conditions be self-sufficient and active in their own behalf. This imperative can come into conflict with some professionals' orientation toward client passivity. Wright (1969) found that emphasis on negative aspects of disability was needed by professionals who "needed to reassure themselves of the importance of their services and thereby of themselves" (p. 94).

Olshanksy (1974) wrote of feelings of "mutual resentment" between counselors and their clients and described a number of causes of the supposed resentment. This investigator concluded that by increasing the counselor's self-esteem through status and financial rewards, as well as allowing him or her the freedom to express feelings in an atmosphere of mutual support provided by members of the same profession, the counselor's own resentment would diminish, thus leaving him or her able to help the client deal with his or her resentment. Olshansky pointed out that one aspect of client resentment is that in counselor-client relationships the latter is always in an "inferior" position.

The status-differential between professional and client and between teacher and student was the topic of a set of papers by Frankel (1970), Kerr (1970), and Siller (1970b). It was evident that power elements enter into the status differential and that the professional can symbolize domination, degradation, and inferiority or safety, security, and confidence. Siller attributed the primary significance of destructive status differential situations to "transference distortions" and countertransference.

Much of the attitudinal and behavioral literature becomes more meaningful if it is viewed from the position of transference-counter-transference. The psychoanalytic literature on transference (the tendency for an individual to distort the realities of the present interpersonal relationship in accordance with impulses and wishes derived from past experiences) and countertransference (similar actions by the professional upon the client) is substantial. Although the action of transference-countertransference is basic in the clinical literature, particularly of psychodynamically oriented writers, there has been almost no effort to deal with this topic in rehabilitation.

A noteworthy exception to the absence of attention to transfer phenomena is Blank's (1954) description of certain prevalent attitudes based on transference and countertransference in counselors who work with the blind. He pointed out that workers with serious countertransference problems are usually regarded as having "blind spots," being inept, hostile, too disturbed to work with clients, or lacking initiative (being anxious and inhibited). Blank indicated that many countertransferences are not deep seated and, per se, are not pathognomonic or personality disorders. The author offered the hypothesis that a great part of a worker's "growth" which is attributed to "experience" actually represents the gradual and progressive resolution of countertransference problems, principally on a preconscious level, in interactions with clients (and co-workers) so that he or she continually becomes better able to see the client's problem and the indicated line of help.

Some examples of frequent countertransference problems may help to make this concept clearer. One may unconsciously overidentify with the client as "crippled-defective-castrated," which, in turn, can lead to rejecting or subordinating behaviors. One may also respond to the client's transference expectation for the counselor to be the "good" parent who will make things well by trying to be an omniscient benevolent savior. Failure to fulfill this role can then evoke anger in the client and resentment and/or guilt in the professional (Siller, 1969).

A few investigators have written in some depth on attitudes of professionals toward disabled clients (e.g., Leviton, 1971, 1973; Sussman, 1965; Wright, 1960) and the general importance of the topic is universally recognized, but there has been a conspicuous absence of extended programmatic work in pursuit of in-depth analyses and concomitant variables. The total number of available studies and the quality of research dealing specifically with attitudinal aspects fail to reflect the topic's importance. In general, the level of research sophistication is relatively low; most studies have used small samples of nonrandomly selected professional populations and weak instruments for assessment.

Systematic research of both a quantitative and qualitative nature should be undertaken in this area. The available data are quite adequate for most "nose counting" purposes. What is needed now is more work of an explanatory nature which could be used to direct attitude-change programs.

VARIABLES AFFECTING INTERACTION OF THE DISABLED-NONDISABLED

A variety of factors have been identified as important in the interaction process of disabled with nondisabled persons. Age, sex, and other demographic variables are important mainly in the manner in which attitudes toward the disabled are expressed rather than formed. Thus, women may have attitudes similar to men's but will be more likely to express them in ways which are influenced by their sex role. Adolescents of both sexes tend to be more rejecting than are younger or older persons, and persons better educated to be most accepting. Ethnicity (Richardson et al., 1961) and cultural bias (Dow, 1965; Jaques, Linkowski, & Sierka, 1970; Jordan, 1968) also may be implicated in reactions to the disabled. Hard generalizations on the influence of these various demographic factors are difficult because their operations are complex and unlikely to be described directly and simply.

The personality of the nondisabled person has been studied in relation to the person's attitudes toward the disabled. In general, significant but weak relations have been found for a variety of personality dimensions, with "favorable" variables such as ego strength, body image, boundaries, nurturance, good adjustment, and social interaction measures correlating with acceptance, and more "negative" variables such as anxiety, hostility, alienation, and authoritarianism correlating with rejection (Cloerkes, 1981; Noonan, Barry, & Davis, 1970; Siller, 1984, in press; Siller, Chipman et al., 1967; Yuker et al., 1966). Particular ego defensive structures of nondisabled persons have been shown to be related to negativity (Gladstone, 1977). The pattern of results from numerous studies suggests that ego strength and the ability to attain stable relations with others underlie positive reactions toward the disabled. Ethnocentricism is clearly related to negative attitudes and is highly general in nature. People who express ethnocentrism toward other outgroups tend to express negative attitudes toward the physically disabled.

Studies using the physical status (disabled or nondisabled) of the person as a variable are beginning to be reported, but so far no trends are evident. Increasing attention is being paid to the attitudes of disabled persons themselves, but results are as yet indefinite. Speculation upon the realism of disabled persons' perceptions of their social position and of the attitudes of nondisabled people toward them would profit from systematic research efforts.

The context in which interactions take place is usually undefined or limited in the typical research study, yet there is evidence that context is an important element (e.g., Shurka & Katz, 1976; Sloat & Frankel, 1972). One might certainly expect that the question of whether the disability will affect outcomes (as in a competitive situation involving limitations assumed to involve the disability) would be a factor in interactions.

A start is being made on specifying concrete operations that can enhance or retard disabled-nondisabled interactions. Thus, Bazakas (1977), in an experimental study of a person in a wheelchair interacting with a nondisabled person, found that the former received the most favorable response only when he or she presented him or herself as both coping and openly acknowledging the condition. Either coping or acknowledgement alone was insufficient to promote positive responses. Shurka, Siller, and Dvonch (1982) experimentally manipulated the variables of coping or succumbing orientations toward one's disability and being responsible or not responsible for becoming disabled to determine their effects upon evaluation by the nondisabled of someone with a disability. Nondisabled subjects viewing videotapes of an interview of a person in a wheelchair rated the disabled person on a number of indices. Being portrayed as coping and not responsible resulted in the most favorable evaluations, with coping being more potent than responsibility. The order of favorability is coping-not responsible, coping-responsible, succumbing-not responsible, succumbing-responsible. Achievement level of the disabled person and the type of school service received also have been shown to influence acceptance (Havill, 1970). The search for more such variables that directly affect attitudes and consequent social interactions is clearly indicated.

FINAL REMARKS

Attitude-change studies in physical disability have not been numerous. (For a theoretical discussion of attitude change, see Chapter 3; for a review of attitude-change studies, see Chapter 12.) Positive findings have been reported, but the total impact of any approach or study is not encouraging for broad programs of change. Some useful themes that have emerged are that social coping skills in the disabled (Bazakas, 1977; Shurka et al., 1982) and emotional role playing in the nondisabled (Clore & Jeffrey, 1972) should be encouraged; that contact and informational techniques should be used jointly and not alone (Anthony, 1972); and that the attractiveness of disabled persons will increase if they are seen as attitudinally similar (Asher, 1973). Contact with the disabled is an important variable determining interactions, but the consequences of the contact can be either favorable or unfavorable, depending upon other contingencies (e.g., Amir, 1969). It appears that attitude change toward the disabled will be most successful when it is directed toward the affective state of the nondisabled person. Discovering the sources of negative attitudes will provide cues for effective change procedures. Pinpointing attitudinal components will suggest differential change procedures and promote appropriate assessment of the effects of interventions.

Although the contents of this publication are concerned mostly with children, some correlation between the educational efforts for children and their subsequent behavior as workers must be considered.

Employment, transportation problems, architectural barriers, and attitudinal states are the most frequently mentioned major impediments to successful rehabilitation. A compilation of the research literature on attitudes in the work situations of disabled persons was assembled by Schroedel and Jacobson (1978). The review of the reported studies reveals that for the most part researchers have used nonstandardized instruments upon nonrandomized populations. Actual practice studies are rare, and most information is based upon stated beliefs, opinions, and perceptions of the respondents. Basic terms of the disability conditions often are vague. Employment practices regarding the disabled are highly idiosyncratic, and while employer acceptance of handicapped workers is increasing (Hartlage, 1974), most employers, regardless of the size of the business, anticipate increased expenses despite their recognition of such benefits as lower absenteeism, less tardiness, and decreased turnover costs (Williams, 1972). Employer misconceptions regarding the capability of disabled persons abound; the work of Siller, Ferguson et al. (1967) on the attitudinal dimension of "Imputed Functional Limitations" suggests an assocation between judgments of functional capability of and unfavorable attitudes toward disabled persons. In effect, although pessimistic expectations for the performance of the disabled may reflect actual conditions for some, many persons may be using supposedly "valid" functional reasons to rationalize their own disturbed feeling states. The Disability Factor Scales (DFS) can be useful to help differentiate between legitimate assessments and disturbed affective reactions. Legal, moral, economic, and other pressures clearly are indicated as tools to support the verbalized favorable attitudes of employers and to overcome the resistance of others.

Any inclination to consider disability outside the larger social context and as residing only in the person is destructively erroneous. It is hoped that the citations and analyses provided in this chapter have conveyed the complexity and dynamic nature of attitudes toward the physically disabled. Continuities exist between the physically disabled and other exceptional individuals but, for that matter, even stronger continuities exist between physically disabled and all other persons.

In opting for wide coverage in this chapter, the critical assessment of individual research has been sacrificed and most reports have been taken at face value. There is justification for strong criticism of much of the past research literature on a variety of grounds, some of which have been expressed. It is of considerable satisfaction to note that studies are becoming increasingly sophisticated and more appropriate to the complexity of the subject. It appears that we now have sufficiently "tooled up" conceptually and methodologically to look forward to a new wave of significant research that will be of direct use to people who work with disabled individuals. It is to be hoped that systematic programs of research directed toward specific problems of need will be accomplished by attention to basic theoretical and measurement concerns.

REFERENCES

Amir, Y. Contact hypothesis in ethnic relations. *Psychological Bulletin*, 1969, *71*, 319-342.

Anthony, W. A. Societal rehabilitation: Changing society's attitudes toward the physically and mentally disabled. *Rehabilitation Psychology*, 1972, *19*, 117-126.

Asher, N. W. Manipulating attraction toward the disabled: An application of the similarity-attraction model. *Rehabilitation Psychology*, 1973, *20*, 155-164.

Bansavage, J. C. Social acceptance in a group of orthopedically impaired adolescents. *Proceedings of the 81st Annual Convention of the American Psychological Association*, 1968, *3*, 647-648.

Barker, D. Concepts of disabilities. *Personnel and Guidance Journal*, 1964, *43*, 371-374.

Barker, R. G., Wright, B. A., Meyerson, L., & Gonick, M. R. *Adjustment to physical handicap and illness: A survey of the social psychology of physique and disability* (2nd ed.). New York: Social Science Research Council, 1953.

Bazakas, R. *The interpersonal impact of coping, dependency, and denial self-presentations by the disabled.* Unpublished doctoral dissertation, New York University, 1977.

Black, K. V. *Attitudes toward the disabled acting in the helper role.* Unpublished M.A. thesis, University of Colorado, 1964.

Blank, H. R. Countertransference problems in the professional worker. *The New Outlook for the Blind*, 1954, *48*, 185-188.

Brabham, R. E., & Thoreson, R. W. Relationship of client preferences and counselor's physical disability. *Journal of Counseling Psychology*, 1973, *20*, 10-15.

Burlingham, D. T. Hearing and its role in the development of the blind. *Psychoanalytic Study of the Child*, 1964, *19*, 95-112.

Centers, L., & Centers, R. Peer group attitudes toward the amputee child. *Journal of School Psychology*, 1963, *61*, 127-132.

Cloerkes, G. Are prejudices against disabled persons determined by personality characteristics? *International Review of Rehabilitation Research*, 1981, *4*, 35-46.

Clore, G. L., & Jeffrey, K. M. Emotional role playing, attitude change, and attraction toward a disabled person. *Journal of Personality and Social Psychology*, 1972, *23*, 105-111.

Comer, R. J., & Piliavin, J. A. The effects of physical deviance upon face-to-face interaction: The other side. *Journal of Personality and Social Psychology*, 1972, *23*, 33-39.

Cowen, E. L., Bobrove, P. H., Rockway, A. M., & Stevenson, J. Development and evaluation of an attitudes to deafness scale. *Journal of Personality and Social Psychology*, 1967, *6*, 183-191.

Cowen, E. L., Underberg, R. P., & Verillo, R. T. The development and testing of an attitudes to blindness scale. *Journal of Social Psychology*, 1958, *48*, 297-304.

Cowen, E. L., Underberg, R. P., Verillo, R. T., & Benham, F. G. *Adjustment to visual disability in adolescence*. New York: American Foundation for the Blind, 1961.

Cruickshank, W. M. *Psychology of exceptional children and youth* (4th ed.). Englewood Cliffs NJ: Prentice Hall, 1980.

Dixon, J. K. Coping with prejudice: Attitudes of handicapped persons toward the handicapped. *Journal of Chronic Disease*, 1977, *30*, 307-322.

Dow, T. E., Jr. Social class and reaction to physical disability. *Psychological Reports*, 1965, *17*, 39-62.

Elser, R. P. Social status of physically handicapped children. *Exceptional Children*, 1956, *23*, 305-309.

Ferguson, L. T. Components of attitudes toward the deaf. *Proceedings of the 78th Annual Convention of the American Psychological Association*, 1970, *5*, 693-694.

Fine, J. A. *Castration anxiety and self-concept of physically normal children as related to perceptual awareness of and attitudes toward physical deviance*. Unpublished doctoral dissertation, New York University, 1978.

Force, D. G. Social status of physically handicapped children. *Journal of Exceptional Children*, 1956, *23*, 104-107.

Fraiberg, S. Parallel and divergent patterns in blind and sighted infants. *Psychoanalytic Study of the Child*, 1968, *23*, 264-300.

Frankel, A. Uses and abuses of status in teacher-student relationships. *Rehabilitation Counseling Bulletin*, 1970, *14*. 95-101.

Freeman, G. G., & Sonnega, J. A. Peer evaluation of children in speech correction class. *Journal of Speech and Hearing Disorders*, 1956, *21*, 178-182.

Friend, E. *Social interaction of amputees and nonamputees as related to their attitudes toward amputation*. Unpublished doctoral dissertation, New York University, 1971.

Gallagher, B. Teachers' attitudes and the acceptability of children with speech defects. *The Elementary School Journal*, 1967, *9*, 277-281.

Gladstone, L. R. A study of the relationship between ego defense style preference and experimental pain tolerance and attitudes toward physical disability (Doctoral dissertation, New York University, 1977). *Dissertation Abstracts International*, 1977, *37*, 77-5306.

Goldin, G. J. Some rehabilitation counselor attitudes toward their professional roles. *Rehabilitation Literature*, 1966, *27*, 360-364, 369.

Gronlund, N. E. *Sociometry in the classroom*. New York: Harper & Brothers, 1959.

Hartlage, L. C. Ten-year changes in attitudes toward different types of handicaps. *Interamerican Journal of Psychology*, 1974, *8*, 25-28.

Havill, S. J. The sociometric status of visually handicapped students in public school classes. *Research Bulletin*, 1970, *20*, 57-90.

Jaques, M. E., Linkowski, D. C., & Sierka, F. L. Cultural attitudes toward disability: Denmark, Greece, and the United States. *International Journal of Social Psychiatry*, 1970, *16*, 54-62.

Jones, R. L. The hierarchical structure of attitudes toward the exceptional. *Exceptional Children*, 1974, *40*, 430-435.

Jones, R. L., & Sisk, D. Early perceptions of orthopedic disability. *Rehabilitation Literature*, 1970, *31*, 34-38.

Jordan, J. E. Research on the handicapped child and the family. *Merrill-Palmer Quarterly*, 1962, *8*, 243-260.

Jordan, J. E. *Attitudes toward education and physically disabled persons in eleven nations*. Latin American Studies Center, Michigan State University, 1968.

Jordan, J. E. Attitude-behavior on physical-mental-social disabilities and racial-ethnic differences. *Psychological Aspects of Disability*, 1971, *18*, 5-26.

Kerr, N. Staff expectations for disabled persons: Helpful or harmful. *Rehabilitation Counseling Bulletin*, 1970, *14*, 85-94.

202

Kleck, R. E. Physical stigma and task oriented interaction. *Human Relations*, 1969, *22*, 53-60.

Kleck, R. E., Ono, H., & Hastorf, A. H. The effects of physical deviance upon face-to-face interaction. *Human Relations*, 1966, *19*, 425-436.

Kutner, B. The social psychology of disability. In W. S. Neff (Ed.), *Rehabilitation Psychology*. Washington DC: American Psychological Association, 1971.

Leviton, G. L. Professional-client relations in a rehabilitation hospital setting. In W. S. Neff (Ed.), *Rehabilitation Psychology*. Washington DC: American Psychological Association, 1971.

Leviton, G. L. Professional and client viewpoints on rehabilitation issues. *Rehabilitation Psychology*, 1973, *20*, 1-80.

Lipp, L., Kolstoe, R., James, W., & Randall, W. Denial of disability and internal control of reinforcement: A study using a perceptual defense paradigm. *Journal of Consulting and Clinical Psychology*, 1968, *32*, 72-75.

Marge, D. K. The social status of speech-handicapped children. *Journal of Speech and Hearing Research*, 1966, *9*, 165-177.

Marinelli, R. P., & Kelz, J. W. Anxiety and attitudes toward visibly disabled persons. *Rehabilitation Counseling Bulletin*, 1973, *17*. 198-205.

Mayadas, N. S. Houseparents' expectations: A crucial variable in the performance of blind institutionalized children. *New Outlook for the Blind*, 1975, *69*, 77-85.

Mayadas, N. S., & Duehn, W. D. The impact of significant adults' expectations on the life style of visually impaired children. *New Outlook for the Blind*, 1976, *70*, 286-290.

McCauley, R. W., Bruininks, R. H., & Kennedy, P. Behavioral interaction of hearing impaired children in regular classrooms. *Journal of Special Education*, 1976, *10*, 277-284.

McDaniel, J. W. *Physical disability and human behavior* (2nd ed.). New York: Pergamon, 1976.

Mitchell, D. C., & Fredrickson, W. A. Preferences for physically disabled counselors in hypothetical counseling situations. *Journal of Counseling Psychology*, 1975, *22*, 477-482.

Monbeck, T. E. *The meaning of blindness*. Bloomington: Indiana University Press, 1973.

Moriarty, T. Role of stigma in the experience of deviance. *Journal of Personality and Social Psychology*, 1974, *29*, 849-855.

Noonan, J. R., Barry, J. R., & Davis, H. C. Personality determinants in attitudes toward visible disability. *Journal of Personality*, 1970, *38*, 1-15.

Olshansky, S. Mutual resentment: An obstruction in the counselor-client relationship. *Rehabilitation Counseling*, 1974, *35*, 36-43.

Osgood, C. E., Suci, G. J., & Tannenbaum, P. H. *The measurement of meaning*. Urbana IL: University of Illinois Press, 1957.

Pinkerton, S., & McAleer, C. A. Influence of client diagnosis-cancer-on counselor decisions. *Journal of Counseling Psychology*, 1976, *23*, 575-578.

Popp, R. A., & Fu, V. R. Preschool children's understanding of children with orthopedic disabilities and their expectations. *Journal of Psychology*, 1981, *107*, 77-85.

Raskin, N. J. Visual disability. In J. F. Garret & E. S. Levine (Eds.), *Psychological practices with the physically disabled*. New York: Columbia University Press, 1962.

Reich, C., Hambleton, D., & Houldin, B. K. The integration of hearing impaired children in regular classrooms. *American Annals of the Deaf*, 1977, *122*, 534-543.

Richardson, S. A. Some social psychological consequences of handicapping. *Pediatrics*, 1963, 291-297.

Richardson, S. A. The effect of physical disability on the socialization of a child. In D. A. Goslin (Ed.), *Handbook of socialization theory and research*. Chicago: Rand McNally, 1969.

Richardson, S. A. Age and sex differences in values toward physical handicaps. *Journal of Health and Social Behavior*, 1970, *11*. 207-214.

Richardson, S. A. Children's values and friendships: A study of physical disability. *Journal of Health and Social Behavior*, 1971, *12*, 253-258.

Richardson, S. A. Children's values in regard to disabilities: A reply to Yuker. *Reha-*

bilitation Psychology, 1983, *28*, 14-23.

Richardson, S. A., & Friedman, M. J. Social factors related to children's accuracy in learning peer group values toward handicaps. *Human Relations*, 1973, *26*, 77-87.

Richardson, S. A., Goodman, N., Hastorf, A. H., & Dornbusch, S. M. Cultural uniformity in reaction to physical disabilities. *American Sociological Review*, 1961, *26*, 241-247.

Richardson, S. A., Hastorf, A. H., & Dornbusch, S. M. Effects of physical disability on a child's description of himself. *Child Development*, 1964, *35*, 893-907.

Richardson, S. A., Ronald, L., & Kleck, R. E. The social status of handicapped and nonhandicapped boys in a camp setting. *Journal of Special Education*, 1974, *8*, 143-152.

Richardson, S. A., & Royce, J. Race and physical handicap in children's preference for other children. *Child Development*, 1968, *39*, 467-480.

Safilios-Rothschild, C. *The sociology and social psychology of disability and rehabilitation*. New York: Random House, 1970.

Sandler, A. M. Aspects of passivity and ego development in the blind infant. *Psychoanalytic Study of the Child*, 1963, *18*, 343-360.

Schiff, W., & Thayer, S. An eye for an ear? Social perception, nonverbal communication, and deafness. *Rehabilitation Psychology*, 1974, *21*, 50-70.

Schoggen, Phil. *Environmental forces in the lives of children with and without physical disability*. Paper presented at the meeting of the American Psychological Association Convention, 1963.

Schroedel, J. G. *A study of behavioral validation of attitudes to deafness scales*. New York University Deafness Research and Training Center, 1972.

Schroedel, J. G., & Jacobsen, R. J. *Employment attitudes toward hiring workers with disabilities*. Albertson NY: Human Resources Center, 1978.

Shears, L. M., & Jensema, C. J. Social acceptability of anomalous persons. *Exceptional Children*, 1969, *35*, 91-96.

Shurka, E., & Katz, S. Evaluations of persons with a disability: The influence of disability context and personal responsibility for the disability. *Rehabilitation Psychology*, 1976, *23*, 65-71.

Shurka, E., Siller, J., & Dvonch, P. Coping behavior and personal responsibility as factors in the perception of disabled persons by the nondisabled. *Rehabilitation Psychology*, 1983, *28*, 225-233.

Siller, J. *Conceptual and methodological issues in the study of attitudes toward disability*. Paper presented at the annual convention of the American Personnel and Guidance Association, April 1966.

Siller, J. Psychological situation of the disabled with spinal cord injuries. *Rehabilitation Literature*, 1969, *30*, 290-296.

Siller, J. The generality of attitudes toward the disabled. *Proceedings of the 78th Annual Convention of the American Psychological Association*, 1970, *5*, 697-698. (a)

Siller, J. The psychopathology of status. *Rehabilitation Counseling Bulletin*, 1970, *14*, 102-107. (b)

Siller, J. *An outline of the development from discrimination of a person with a physical disability to behavior of that individual*. Unpublished manuscript, New York University.

Siller, J. Psychosocial aspects of disability. In J. Meislin (Ed.), *Rehabilitation medicine and psychiatry*. Springfield IL: C. C Thomas, 1976. (a)

Siller, J. Attitudes toward disability. In H. Rusalem & D. Malikin (Eds.), *Contemporary vocational rehabilitation*. New York: New York University Press, 1976. (b)

Siller, J. The role of personality in attitudes toward those with physical disabilities. In C. J. Golden (Ed.), *Current topics in rehabilitation psychology*. San Diego: Grune & Stratton, in press, 1984.

Siller, J., & Braden, B. *A factor analytically derived scale to measure attitudes toward cancer*. Unpublished manuscript, New York University, 1976.

Siller, J., & Chipman, A. Factorial structure and correlates of the Attitudes Toward Disabled Persons Scale. *Educational and Psychological Measurement*, 1964, *24*, 831-840.

Siller, J., Chipman, A., Ferguson, L., & Vann, D. H. *Attitudes of the nondisabled toward the physically disabled.* New York: New York University, School of Education, 1967.

Siller, J., Ferguson, L. T., Vann, D. H., & Holland, B. Structure of attitudes toward the physically disabled: The Disability Factor Scales—amputation, blindness, cosmetic conditions. *Proceedings of the 76th Annual Convention of the American Psychological Association,* 1968, *3,* 651-652.

Siller, J., Ferguson, L. T., Vann, D. H., & Holland, B. *Structure of attitudes toward the physically disabled.* New York: New York University, School of Education, 1967.

Sloat, W. L., & Frankel, A. The contributions of subjects, disabilities, situations, sex of target person, and items to the variation of attitudes toward persons with a disability. *Rehabilitation Psychology,* 1972, *19,* 3-17.

Soldwedel, B., & Terrill, I. Sociometric aspects of physically handicapped and nonhandicapped children in the same elementary school. *Exceptional Children,* 1957, *23.* 371-372, 381-383.

Sussman, M. B. (Ed.) *Sociology and rehabilitation.* American Sociological Association, 1965.

Tichenor, C. C., & Rundall, T. G. Attitudes of physical therapists toward cancer: A pilot study. *Physical Therapy,* 1977, *57,* 160-165.

Tringo, J. L. The hierarchy of preferences toward disability groups. *Journal of Special Education,* 1970, *4,* 295-306.

Vann, D. H. Components of attitudes toward the obese including presumed responsibility for the condition. *Proceedings of the 78th Annual Convention of the American Psychological Association,* 1970, *5,* 695-696.

Warren, S. A., & Turner, D. R. Attitudes of professionals and students toward exceptional children. *The Training School Bulletin,* 1966, *62,* 136-144.

Weinberg, N. Examination of pre-school attitudes toward the physically handicapped. *Rehabilitation Counseling Bulletin,* 1978, *22,* 183-188.

Weinberg-Asher, N. The effect of physical disability on self-perception. *Rehabilitation Counseling Bulletin,* 1976, *20,* 15-20.

Whiteman, M., & Lukoff, I. P. A factorial study of sighted people's attitudes toward blindness. *Journal of Social Psychology,* 1964, *64,* 339-353.

Whiteman, M., & Lukoff, I. P. Attitudes toward blindness and other physical handicaps. *Journal of Social Psychology,* 1965, *66,* 135-145.

Williams, C. Is hiring the handicapped good business? *Journal of Rehabilitation,* 1972, *38,* 30-34.

Wilson, M. E., Jr., Sakata, R., & Frumkin, R. M. Attitudes of some gifted adults, future rehabilitation counselors, and rehabilitation professors toward disabilities. *Psychological Reports,* 1968, *22,* 1303-1304.

Witkin, A., Birnbaum, J., Lomonaco, S., Lehr, S., & Herman, J. L. Cognitive patterning in congenitally totally blind children. *Child Development,* 1968, *39,* 767-786.

Wright, B. A. *Physical disability—A psychological approach.* New York: Harper & Row, 1960.

Wright, B. A. Spread in adjustment to disability. *Bulletin of the Menninger Clinic,* 1964, *28,* 198-208.

Wright, B. A. Some psychosocial aspects of disability. In D. Malikin & H. Rusalem (Eds.), *Vocational rehabilitation of the disabled.* New York: New York University Press, 1969.

Yuker, H. E. The lack of a stable order of preference for disabilities: A response to Richardson and Ronald. *Rehabilitation Psychology,* 1983, *28,* 93-103.

Yuker, H. E., Block, J. R., & Younng, J. H. *The Measurement of Attitudes Toward Disabled Persons.* Albertson NY: Human Resources Center, 1966.

Zuckerman, W. *Deaf, blind, and nonhandicapped adults' attitudes toward each other as related to authoritarianism, alienation and ego strength.* Unpublished doctoral dissertation, New York University, 1980.

11

Attitudes of Educators toward the Handicapped

JANET D. JAMIESON

If the concept of mainstreaming is to be translated into practice, it will depend in large part on the readiness of general education administrators to make appropriate decisions (e.g., establish policies, determine informative guidelines, and provide adequate resources) and of classroom teachers to maximize the educational experiences of handicapped children. Although several special educators (e.g., McGinty & Keogh, 1975) have expressed concern about the ability of regular educators to accomplish these tasks successfully, the motivation for accomplishment may prove to be more important. The concern for educators' attitudes toward handicapped students is reflected in the literature. Prior to the passage of Public Law 94-142, investigations of educators' attitudes tended to focus on regular classroom teachers; since then the focus has shifted somewhat to include administrators and other types of educators.

ATTITUDES OF ADMINISTRATORS

The administrations of public school systems are complicated managerial structures in which school building principals are usually at the lowest rung and program (e.g., special education) administrators are just below the top; thus, principals are accountable to a hierarchy of middle management administrators, whereas program administrators are accountable only to superintendents of schools. Nevertheless, the administrators at all levels play key roles in instituting changes in public education. The degree to which administrators support new concepts often is determined by the enthusiasm evinced for the concepts in the attitudes and behaviors of administrators higher up in the management hierarchy. Hallard (1977), for example, found a moderate correlation between the attitudes of administrators of special education programs and the attitudes of superintendents, as perceived by the "administrators,"

206

toward the serving of severely handicapped students in the public schools.

There are also indications that school administrators' attitudes and behaviors toward handicapped students may have some effect on the quality of the educational programs provided for handicapped students as well as on the attitudes of school-level staff toward these students. McGuire and Throop (no date), for example, found that the attitudes of chief school officers and principals are significantly related to the quality of educational programs provided for EMR students. In a study by O'Rourke (1980), the results indicated a significant relation between the attitudes of building principals and those of their teaching staffs toward handicapped students.

It was possible to find 19 studies (many of them doctoral dissertations) providing information on the attitudes of public school administrators toward handicapped students and the concept of mainstreaming. One study (Restad, 1972) was found in which the attitudes of administrators toward the hiring of a handicapped teacher were addressed. From the responses to a two-part questionnaire consisting of both descriptive and attitude items, Restad ascertained that his sample of elementary and secondary school administrators generally held positive attitudes toward the employment of a blind teacher; however, the responses varied according to the administrators' level of education and the degree of their previous experience with blind teachers.

The primary purpose of the 19 identified studies was to ascertain administrator attitudes toward handicapped pupils through measures of "willingness to serve" and "program placement decisions."

Overall, questionnaires were the most frequent method of collecting data (16 studies); the Rucker-Gable Educational Programming Scale (RGEPS) was used in five investigations. Interviews, conducted either in person or by telephone, were employed in four studies. Although several studies used more than one questionnaire, only one investigation (Guerin & Szatlocky, 1974) included multiple measurement techniques in its design. In three of the studies using questionnaires (DeLeo, 1976; Hallard, 1977; Savage, 1971) the return rates were reported to be fairly high. All in all, the research on administrator attitudes cannot be described as rigorous; nevertheless, the results indicate important attitudinal tendencies.

Although some studies included more than one focus, they are presented here according to four major foci: (a) the relation of attitudes to placement decisions for different categories of handicapped pupils; (b) the relation of attitudes to environmental characteristics, such as geographical area of assignment and community size; (c) the relation of attitudes to personal characteristics, such as sex, and knowledge of and experience with handicapped children, including that acquired in inservice training, and (d) the comparison of administrator attitudes with the attitudes of educational personnel in other roles.

Administrator Attitudes and Type of Handicap

In studies examining the relation of administrator attitudes toward serving handicapped children in regular education settings with the severity and category of handicapping conditions, the attitudes of principals and other administrators generally disagreed with the trend to mainstreaming severely handicapped students. In general, administrator attitudes appear to differ with the type and severity of the handicap identified. Through a post hoc analysis of principals' RGEPS scores, Pupke (1977) found a significant relation between the types and degrees of severity of handicapping conditions and attitudes toward the placement of handicapped pupils. In Payne and Murray's (1974) investigation, the attitudes of principals toward the concept of integrating handicapped students into regular education settings were positive for students who were categorized as visually handicapped, hearing impaired, physically handicapped, and learning disabled. In contrast, principals and superintendents were less accepting of students who were labeled educable mentally retarded, trainable retarded, and emotionally disturbed (Payne & Murray, 1974; Savage, 1971) although some secondary school principals perceived learning disabled students to be more like their normal than their educable retarded peers (Smith, Flexer, & Sigelman, 1980).

Both state directors of special education and administrators of local districts seemed to perceive emotionally disturbed children as the most difficult to program (Nazzaro, 1973), and principals viewed mentally retarded pupils as having the poorest prognosis for successful mainstreaming (Davis, 1980). Another investigator (Leonetti, 1977) who compared attitudes of principals toward the placement of moderately handicapped and mentally retarded children with those of special education "experts" found the principals to be far less restrictive. In a cross-cultural study, Morris and McCauley (1977) compared the attitudes of Canadian "regular school administrative personnel" with those of special education experts from the United States and also found that the school administrators selected placement options that were closer to the regular classroom than did the special education "experts."

Administrator Attitudes and Environmental Characteristics

Several studies examined the relation of administrator attitudes toward handicapped children and selected aspects of the school setting. Generally, the information derived from these studies is inconclusive and somewhat confusing. Payne and Murray (1974) found that urban school principals were more reluctant to integrate handicapped children into regular school programs than were their suburban counterparts, but Peterson (1977) found that urban principals and superintendents did not differ from their rural counterparts in attitudes toward the integration of handicapped children. Overline (1977) found more positive attitudes toward mainstreaming among rural teachers and principals than among either suburban or urban principals. There are some indications that community and school size also affect attitudes. Educators, including directors of special education and principals, in small or medium-sized communities were found to hold somewhat more favorable attitudes toward the concept of mainstreaming than did their colleagues in larger communities (DeLeo, 1976). Directors of special education and principals in small high schools were found to be more positive toward the mainstreaming of learning disabled and mentally retarded students into extracurricular activities than were their counterparts in medium sized and large high schools (Collins, 1979).

Inasmuch as small communities and smaller schools usually are associated with rural areas, it may be that the more personalized the educational setting the more positive are the attitudes toward including handicapped students in regular education settings. However, it is difficult to draw conclusions from these investigations because of reported variations in the level of resources available, the prevalence of different handicapping conditions, or other general characteristics of the community (e.g., socioeconomic status of the residents and their attitudes toward handicapped persons).

Administrator Attitudes and Personal Characteristics

The personal characteristics of administrators, such as sex, level of responsibility, level of education, knowledge, and experience with the handicapped, also have been examined in relation to attitudes held toward the concept of mainstreaming. Sex does not appear to be a significant factor in administrator acceptance of handicapped pupils (Lazar, 1974; Peterson, 1977).

The results of several studies indicated that administrators' experience with handicapped students may be related to their knowledge and attitudes, as measured by the appropriate placement of the children. Overline (1977) found that principals who had one or more years of mainstreaming experience tended to hold more positive attitudes toward the integration of handicapped children in regular classes than did those with less experience. However, Peterson (1977) found that the general level of experience (e.g., number of years in an administrative position) did not appear to contribute significantly to the superintendents' and principals' knowledge or attitudes toward handicapped children.

According to Smith (1978), the number of interactions with mentally retarded students was the variable most predictive of principals' attitudes toward mentally retarded and learning disabled students. Nevertheless, when Pupke (1977) examined the effects of relative experience (e.g., an inservice training session) and grade level on the attitudes and knowledge of public school principals involved with mainstreaming, the two variables proved not to be significant. Specific experience with the skills required to mainstream may affect attitudes; for example, in a school district evaluation of the mainstreaming concept (Marshall Independent School District Study, 1973) where principals and teachers had previously volunteered to individualize their instructional programs, attitudes toward the mainstreaming concept were positive.

Education and inservice training have also been suggested as variables that may affect administrator perceptions of realistic placement for handicapped children. The results of Leonetti's (1977) study differed somewhat from those of Pupke's (1977) in that Leonetti found that principals who attended many inservice sessions on special education, expended a great deal of time reading literature on special education, and had M.A. degrees plus 30 units exhibited closer agreement with experts in special education on measures of knowledge and placement of handicapped children. Comer (1977) attempted to evaluate

209

the effects of a specific training experience on district-level regular education administrator attitudes toward and knowledge of appropriate placement. He found that the experience variable (scores on the workshop content instrument and amount of administrative experience) was significantly related to the knowledge scores on the RGEPS but not to the attitude scores.

Although specific experiences with exceptional students and mainstreaming, along with professional training, appear to be somewhat related to administrator knowledge of and attitudes toward handicapped pupils, administrators generally do not appear to be very knowledgeable about handicapped children. As noted previously, two investigations found administrators to differ significantly from the experts on the program placements they select for handicapped children (Leonetti, 1977; Morris & McCauley, 1977), which led Leonetti to suggest that inasmuch as principals are less knowledgeable about appropriate placement than the experts in all areas of exceptionality, their preference for nonrestrictive placements is a function of currently accepted practice and not sound knowledge. He also found that the number of workshops attended by administrators contributed most to the prediction of knowledge of placement; as the number of workshops increased, the administrators' "knowledge" came closer to agreeing with the experts.

Inservice education appears to be an important variable in relation to knowledge of appropriate placement, but administrators do not seem to be so prepared and informed. In 1970, a survey of academic requirements for school principals reported that none of the 50 states required any course in special education for certification. As of July 1, 1975, Colorado and Missouri included special education course work among the requirements. Not only was course work not required earlier, but 65% of the principals surveyed in 1970 had elected to take no course work in special education, and an additional 33% had taken only one course (Newman, 1970). The picture has changed with the requirements of Public Law 94-142, but given their lack of knowledge and experience with handicapped children, it is doubtful that the positive attitudes of administrators toward mainstreaming mildly handicapped pupils reflect realistic assessments. The fact that they tend to choose program options closer to the regular classroom than experts do may indicate a positive attitude, but such an attitude, unfortunately, is based upon a lack of knowledge regarding realistic placement.

Administrator Attitudes Versus the Attitudes of Other School Personnel

Several studies have compared the attitudes of administrators with those of other educators, such as regular classroom teachers, special education teachers, and nonteaching personnel (e.g., school psychologists). Overline (1977) found that principals show significantly more positive attitudes toward mainstreaming handicapped pupils than do either regular or special education teachers. Barngrover (1971) examined the attitudes of teachers, administrators, and school psychologists who had daily contact with handicapped children and found that teachers more often favored the retention of special classes whereas nonteaching educators tended to prefer regular classroom placement. Savage (1971) found that the attitudes of administrators and superintendents toward exceptional students were more positive than were those of the special education personnel, and Peterson (1977) found that superintendents' attitudes were more favorable toward the concept of mainstreaming than were those of principals.

Guerin and Szatlocky (1974) interviewed central office administrators directly responsible for special education, school administrators, and teachers to learn their attitudes toward programs of integration for the handicapped. With one exception, the attitudes of both groups of administrators were positive, and the majority of the teachers also expressed positive attitudes. DeLeo (1976) examined attitudes toward the concept of mainstreaming expressed by educators in several different educational roles; according to his results, the most favorable attitudes were held by the directors of special education, followed in order by special education teachers, principals, and regular classroom teachers; the attitudes of the latter were the least favorable.

Essentially, all these studies show that school district staff members who are the most distant from students (e.g., superintendents and central office administrators) express the most positive attitudes toward mainstreaming handicapped students, whereas personnel who are closest to the regular classroom (teachers) present the greatest incidence of negative attitudes.

In general, superintendents have indicated the most positive attitudes toward mainstreaming, followed by school principals and psychologists. School principals appear to hold more positive attitudes than do special education teachers, and regular teachers appear to be the most apprehensive about the concept of mainstreaming.

TEACHER ATTITUDES TOWARD HANDICAPPED STUDENTS

Classroom teacher understanding of and attitudes toward handicapped children were perceived to be influential in determining the intellectual, social, and emotional adjustment of handicapped children many years before the passage of Public Law 94-142. As early as 1956, Haring suggested that teachers who have an "adequate understanding of the nature of exceptionality and a knowledge of the special instructional techniques and methods are potentially more capable in their teaching realtionships with exceptional children," and that "teacher acceptance" may lead to an "atmosphere of acceptance" in the classroom.

Attitudes of regular classroom teachers toward the concept of teaching handicapped children in regular classrooms have been determined from several different approaches, including both formal measurement studies and "attitude indicators." The latter include information abstracted from other than formal attitude studies. For example, Birch (1974) described and analyzed the mainstreaming programs for educable mentally retarded children in six school districts, of various sizes and pupil composition, in five different states. He found that teachers were generally willing to try mainstreaming, even if they had not had direct experience with it, and after experience the majority of the teachers volunteered to continue. He also found that regular teachers without mainstreaming experience were apprehensive about having exceptional children in their classrooms, a finding which could indicate negative attitudes. Birch suggested that what is needed to ensure that handicapped children are not greeted with initial rejection is inservice education to build up teacher confidence and competence in working with these children.

Teacher contracts and contract negotiations also have given indications of teacher attitudes toward the inclusion of handicapped students in regular classrooms. In an examination of the provisions directly or indirectly related to special education in 70 teacher-negotiated contracts, Sosnowsky and Coleman (1971) concluded that to some degree teachers feel a need for contractual protection in dealing with the concept of mainstreaming. The majority of identified contract items that reflected teacher concern were related to emotionally disturbed or behavior-problem children. In some states, teacher organizations have proposed the use of "weighting formulae" to assign handicapped students to regular classrooms (California Teachers' Association, *Memo*, 1977). Weighting formulae are usually viewed as a way to reduce overall class size in mainstream situations, but they can also be interpreted as reflecting teachers' concerns about and attitudes toward handicapped children. Generally, these indirect assessments of teacher attitudes show that teachers are not enthusiastic about working with handicapped learners and that they have many concerns about the practicality of mainstreaming.

Forty-four studies were located which provide information on teacher attitudes toward handicapped children through formal studies or (a) evaluations of inservice treatment effects; (b) measuring specific program effects and administrative arrangements (e.g., resource room programs); (c) examining the relation between teacher characteristics of experience, sex, level of education, and knowledge of handicapped children with their attitudes toward program placement; and (d) measuring teacher attitudes toward specific disability groups. Other studies have compared teacher attitudes toward handicapped pupils with attitudes of nonteaching populations, with teacher attitudes toward nonhandicapped students, and with the effects of labels.

Teacher Attitudes and Inservice Training

In a large number of studies, investigators have attempted to measure cognitive and affective changes in teachers in order to evaluate inservice treatment effects, but these studies generally show only an increased amount of special education information acquired by the teachers. The effects of inservice training on teachers' attitudes and their ability to make realistic assessments in terms of placement for handicapped children are less clear (Becker, 1980; Kauffman, 1977; Nielsen, 1979).

Brooks and Bransford (1971) found notable attitude shifts in regular teachers toward the concept of special education after a summer inservice program; they concluded that it is the lack of knowledge concerning the role and function of special educators that causes many regular educators to be unwilling to accept special needs children.

Glass and Meckler (1972) tried to evaluate the effects of an inservice program on teacher attitudes and found that by pairing information about special education with experience with handicapped students, teachers perceived themselves as being more competent to teach these children in their classrooms. Finn (1980) also found that pairing exposure with inservice training produced significant changes in teacher attitudes toward mainstreaming.

Yates (1973), too, used a laboratory/experiential teacher inservice model to prepare regular classroom teachers for mainstreaming. His results indicated that the inservice experience not only increased the amount of information teachers had about special education but, to some extent, also increased their perceptions of the possibility that handicapped students could be successfully integrated into regular classrooms. Similar results were found by Singleton (1978) when the investigator paired inservice with a direct assistance program. Teachers not only had daily experiences with handicapped students, but were also able to use the services of a resource teacher. This inservice approach appeared to create both positive attitudes toward mainstreaming and more positive teacher expectations.

These eight studies suggest a relation between the amount of knowledge teachers have about special education and handicapped children and their acceptance of handicapped children in regular classrooms. In each of the studies, teacher attitudes were ascertained by measures of willingness to accept handicapped children in regular classrooms. Although inservice workshops may increase teacher knowledge and acceptance of handicapped children, there are indications that it may not lead to their becoming more realistic about placements for handicapped children.

Nearly all the studies addressed only the cognitive component of attitudes. They do not reflect thorough understanding of the complexity of attitudes and attitude measurement. Paper-and-pencil measures prevailed in the methodologies and few attempts were made to include the use of observations, teacher interviews, or other unobtrusive measures to validate the measurements taken. The generalizability of the information from this group of studies is questionable, primarily because most of them addressed elementary level teachers only and included only teachers who had volunteered to participate in inservice training or those who were already involved in mainstreaming projects. Characteristics of the samples selected for the studies, such as sex, previous experience, or level of knowledge before inservice, are seldom described. In some studies measures of teacher attitudes were confounded with those of administrators (Brooks & Bransford, 1971; Haring, 1956). Furthermore, no study addressed in its methodological approach the problem of teachers giving socially acceptable responses.

Teacher Attitudes and Program Evaluation

A group of studies (Barngrover, 1971; Bradfield, Brown, Kaplan, Richert, & Stannard, 1973; Guerin & Szatlocky, 1974; Johnston, 1972; Shotel, Iano, & McGettigan, 1972) measured teacher attitudes as part of an attempt to evaluate the effects of specific programs, resources, or administrative arrangements for handicapped students. For the most part, these studies also are problematic; they tend to have the same limitations as the studies on inservice treatment effects and therefore may not contribute much to our knowledge of teacher attitudes toward handicapped pupils.

One important teacher-attitude study was conducted as part of a comprehensive evaluation of a mainstreaming project. Harasymiw and Horne (1976) formed an experimental and a control group from a large, randomized sample of teachers in schools where handicapped children were being mainstreamed and comparable schools where the integration of handicapped children had not been instituted. The selected schools were similar in terms of the family socioeconomic status of the students, type of facility, and services available. This is one of the few attitude studies in which instrument validity was assessed. The results supported previous findings on the positive effect of inservice preparation on teachers' opinions and attitudes toward integration issues. However, although teachers became more liberal in opinions and assessments of their ability to manage handicapped students in regular classrooms, their basic attitudes toward disability were not changed. Other interesting findings include the fact that teacher estimates of the manageability of emotionally disturbed and blind pupils did not seem to be altered by the project experience of inservice and mainstreaming, nor did the experience modify their basic social distance attitudes. Yet teachers came out of the project with significantly more favorable feelings toward mainstreaming. They did not significantly differ in their acceptance scores on such variables as age, education (number of special education courses taken and degrees achieved), or sex.

Two studies examined the effects of class size and class composition on teachers' attitudes toward mainstreaming. Mandell and Strain (1978) found that when class size ranged from 25 to 27 students, teachers were more favorable toward mainstreaming. Buttery (1978) examined student teachers' attitudes toward exceptional children and found that they perceived mainstreaming to be more acceptable when only one handicapped pupil needed to be integrated into the class.

Several other studies examined the effects of the type of integration program used on teacher attitudes toward mainstreaming. Shotel et al. (1972) found that providing a resource room has a slight to moderate effect on teachers' attitudes toward mainstreaming EMR students. However, Guerin and Szatlocky (1974), in examining the effects of different program models, found that the type of integration program used had no effect on either teacher or administrator attitudes. There are indications that the degree to which a particular integration program provides support for and exposure to handicapped children has some effect on teacher knowledge of and attitudes toward handicapped students. In a study that examined the effect of special education support services on teacher attitudes, Perry (1980) found that the availability and numbers of such support services had a significant effect on their attitudes toward the mainstreaming of mildly handicapped students. It can be concluded from the studies reviewed on program evaluation and teacher attitudes that the existence of an integration program may not adversely affect attitudes when the teachers perceive the integration program as supporting their mainstreaming efforts, the class size is reasonable, and the number of mainstreamed students is minimal. The teachers then are apt to be more positive toward the presence of mildly handicapped children in their regular classrooms.

Teacher Attitudes and Teacher Status Characteristics

In several studies of teacher attitudes toward handicapped children and the concept of mainstreaming, the variable of teacher characteristics was also included. Teacher attitudes toward the inclusion of mentally retarded children in the public schools were not differentiated by the teachers' sex, levels of formal education (e.g., baccalaureate vs. master's), or years of teaching experience, although significant attitudinal differences were found between regular and special education teachers toward providing regular classroom instruction for the children (Greene, 1976). Harasymiw and Horne (1976) also found that sex did not differentiate teacher attitudes toward handicapped children on several variables.

There is some evidence that teachers may vary in their attitudes toward students in general as a function of the level of teaching assignment. Wandt (1952) examined teachers' attitudes toward the general population of school children and found that elementary teachers were more favorable toward all students than were secondary teachers, and that secondary teachers and teachers with more years of experience were more homogeneous in their attitudes toward students. However, no significant differences in attitudes toward handicapped students were found between primary and intermediate teachers by Kinnison (1972) or between elementary and secondary teachers in the California Teachers' Association (CTA) study of 1977.

Some indications are present that although teacher attitudes toward handicapped students may not vary significantly by grade level, their receptivity toward handicapped students in their classrooms may so vary. Mark (1980) examined the attitudes of regular teachers toward the mainstreaming of EMR students and found that elementary teachers are more positive than are intermediate teachers. Lake (1979) found middle-school educators generally to be open to serving handicapped students but lacking the necessary knowledge of disabilities and related programs and services to do so. Hence they did not perceive mainstreaming to be successful. Even at elementary grade levels there appears to be some variance in teacher attitudes toward mainstreaming. For example, in a study of the effects of support services on teacher attitudes toward mainstreaming, Perry (1980) found that teachers in grades 1-3 are more supportive of mainstreaming and more confident of their abilities to teach mainstreamed students than are teachers in grades 4-6. The reason may be that the formal training of elementary teachers better prepares them to work with children who differ in developmental progress. Also, teachers at the intermediate level have been described as more curriculum- and less child-oriented. Another explanation may be that the academic structure of intermediate schools is less supportive of the mainstreaming concept than is the structure of elementary schools.

Type and amount of teaching experience and age have been examined in relation to teacher attitudes toward handicapped students, although with somewhat contradictory results. For example, Peters (1977) found no significant differences in teacher acceptance of handicapped children which related to type and amount of teaching experience, whereas significant attitudinal differences were related to the amount of the teachers' academic course credits; the resource room teachers, who had more academic course work in special education than did regular teachers, were significantly more knowledgeable about exceptionalities than were regular teachers and significantly more realistic in their attitude toward the educational placement of exceptional children.

Two studies seem to indicate that prior experience teaching handicapped students produces more positive attitudes toward mentally retarded students and the possibility of mainstreaming them. Kennon and Sandoval (1978) measured the effects of specialized experience by comparing the attitudes of regular teachers toward mentally retarded students with the attitudes of special class teachers. They found that regular teachers who had some prior experience with such students expressed more positive attitudes toward them. Mark (1980) also found that previous teaching experience with mentally retarded students produces more positive attitudes toward mainstreaming these students. However, in contrast to these findings, LeVine (1976) found that experience teaching handicapped students did not differentiate teacher attitudes toward specific disability groups, and Lake (1979) found that specific teaching experience is not related to teacher attitudes toward mainstreaming mildly handicapped students.

A decade earlier Proctor (1967) had found that amount of experience helped teachers to achieve more realistic attitudes toward the educational placement of exceptional children, although the type of experience did not appear to relate to the attitudes. Like Peters (1977) and Stephens and Braun (1980) 10 years later, Proctor found that the amount of previous course work pertaining to the exceptionalities of children was significantly related to the teachers' attitudes toward mainstreaming; nevertheless, Panda and Bartel (1972) suggested that course work may not affect more general teacher attitudes toward specific handicapped groups. Harasymiw and Horne (1976) indicated that younger teachers have more positive attitudes toward mainstreaming than do older teachers, and Perry (1980) found that elementary teachers with 2 or fewer years of general teaching experience were more receptive to mainstreaming than were those with 2 or more years.

There are some indications that teacher knowledge of appropriate teaching methods and materials for working with handicapped students also affected their level of acceptance (Lovitt, 1974) by increasing their confidence and self-perceptions of competence to teach such children. Several studies found that the amount of resources and support, in the form of materials, services, and resource teachers, available for working with a handicapped child may also affect a teacher's willingness to accept the child in the classroom (CTA, 1977; Mandell & Strain, 1978; Perry, 1980).

Specific characteristics of a handicapped child may be a factor related to acceptance by the mainstreaming teacher. It has been shown that teachers who report fewer discipline problems or interruptions in integrated settings express more positive attitudes toward the concept of mainstreaming (CTA,

1977). Student personality characteristics and the use of certain handicap labels also have been found to influence teachers' attitudes of acceptance or rejection (Helton & Helton, 1977).

Teacher Attitudes Toward Specific Disability Groups

Studies of teacher attitudes toward specific disability groups often yield conflicting information and thus are difficult to interpret.

Shotel et al. (1972) examined teacher attitudes toward different categories of handicapped children in relation to integrating the children into regular programs and perceiving their potential for academic and social adjustment, the teachers' competencies for teaching the children, and the need for special methods and materials to teach the children. The results indicated that teachers who participated in a mainstreaming program became more negative in their perceptions of educable mentally retarded children as suitable for mainstream placements and able to make good social adjustments. Emotionally disturbed children also were seen as lacking the potential for good social adjustment in mainstreaming situations. The teachers in this study, like those in several others (Gillung & Rucker, 1977; Guerin, 1979), were consistently more positive and optimistic in their responses to learning disabled children and were least positive toward educable retarded children.

Categorical labels appear to influence the attitudes of future educators, although somewhat inconsistently. For example, in a study of the attitudes of students who were enrolled in a teacher-education program for mentally retarded children, Warren, Turner, and Brody (1964) found that the children who were labeled educable mentally retarded were more acceptable than those who were labeled brain damaged. In Combs and Harper's study (1967) of the attitudes of college students, a mentally retarded child was seen more negatively when the description was unlabeled than when it was labeled, but the descriptions of children labeled psychopathic, schizophrenic, and cerebral palsied were rated more negatively than the descriptions of the same children that contained no labels. The investigators concluded that although labeling affects perceptions of exceptional children, the effects are not consistent across labels and, furthermore, that experience does not appear to affect teacher perceptions of the children.

Moderately physically handicapped children may experience greater acceptance by regular education classroom teachers. When Pell (1973) examined the behaviors of classroom teachers after physically handicapped pupils had been transferred from special to regular classes, a high degree of acceptance was evidenced by the regular classroom teachers. The studies that examined the effects of exposure to and contact with specific disability groups on teachers' attitudes also presented some confusing results. For example, Keilbaugh (1977) found that teachers having prior contact with and exposure to visually handicapped students were slightly more positive toward mainstreaming such students, and Kennon and Sandoval (1978) found that previous exposure to EMR students resulted in more positive teacher attitudes toward mental retardation. However, Kuhn (1971) found that exposure to blind students through a resource room located in the school did not affect the attitudes of regular teachers toward the blind. Stephens and Braun (1980) identified having a special education child in the family as the only variable that generates positive teacher attitudes toward handicapped pupils.

CONCLUSIONS

Several tentative conclusions can be drawn about the variables that affect teacher attitudes toward handicapped children. Specific experience with mainstreaming handicapped children seems to have a greater effect than inservice workshops alone (Haring, 1956); thus several researchers recommended pairing inservice courses with actual experience. However, there are indications that although actual experience with mainstreaming increases teacher knowledge of appropriate placements for handicapped children (Proctor, 1967), it may lead to more negative teacher attitudes toward the placement of these children in the classroom (Fanning, 1970; Kinnison, 1972; Overline, 1971). These studies also suggest that sex, age, and teaching experience alone are not directly related to teacher attitudes toward the concept of mainstreaming and handicapped children.

On the other hand, amount of course work or education appears to be significantly related to teacher acceptance of and knowledge about handicapped children (Harasymiw & Horne, 1976; Haring, 1956; Peters, 1977; Proctor, 1967). Less rather than more formal education appears to lead to more positive teacher attitudes, and greater amounts of specific special education course work tends to result in more realistic teacher attitudes toward the placement of handicapped children, although not necessarily in more positive attitudes toward mainstreaming. In the studies reviewed here and in the preceding sections, special education teachers (defined as those having extensive amounts of course work and knowledge of and experience with handicapped students) were consistently found to be more realistic in their attitudes toward the placement of such students than either administrators or regular classroom teachers.

Generally, no one variable can be identified as a strong predictor of educator attitudes. Increased special education inservice and formal course work may lead to more realistic placement decisions but greater experience also may lead to more negative attitudes. These more negative attitudes often are reflected in teachers being less willing to mainstream handicapped children after having had mainstreaming experience. Whether this negative attitude occurs as a result of acquiring more realistic perceptions of what is possible or because of a lack of materials, resources, and support is not known. Educators generally appear to be more rejecting of behaviorally or emotionally disturbed and mentally retarded pupils than of other categories of exceptional children.

Educator attitudes may not be the best indicators of success for any particular mainstreaming effort. Literature on the relation of attitudes and behavior is inconclusive, especially when paper-and pencil tests have been the sole measures of attitudes. It may be that teachers' classroom behaviors toward mildly handicapped children do not differ from those toward average children (Reilly, 1974). A great deal of intra- and intervariability in educators' attitudes toward handicapped children is apparent.

If accurate predictors of success or failure in mainstreaming efforts are desired, then we may want to look to measures of educators' ability to make realistic placement assessments, rather than to attitude measures. Measures of educator attitudes may reflect many considerations other than behavior, such as a realistic assessment of the amount of resources and services available, the lack of knowledge and experience, "false confidence," the degree of freedom teachers perceive themselves to have in decision making, or characteristics of a particular handicapped child being integrated. Attitude measures may not indicate how teachers will behave or the outcomes for integrated students. Attitudes may be situationally specific as a result of the interaction of all the different variables.

In sum, therefore, the use of an ecological approach to prediction is suggested—much like that used by Foley (1979) in which teacher characteristics, the nature of the student's disabilities, and the supportive services available, were all examined. This type of approach includes an assessment model that gives educators the knowledge to make more accurate assessments of the learning needs of a particular handicapped child, the resources available to work with the child, the limitations of the classroom environment, and the knowledge and skills for teaching the child in a particular setting. This model could provide a conceptual framework for designing measures that will better predict the outcomes for handicapped children in integrated settings.

REFERENCES

Barngrover, E. D. A study of educators' preferences in special education programs. *Exceptional Children*, 1971, *37*, 754-755.

Becker, S. G. The effectiveness of inservice training using simulation videotape and participatory lecture in changing attitudes and increasing diagnostic abilities of elementary teachers involved in mainstreaming. *Dissertation Abstracts International*, 1980, *40*, 11A.

Birch, J. W. *Mainstreaming: Educable mentally retarded children in regular classes.* Reston VA: Council for Exceptional Children, 1974.

Bradfield, H. R., Brown, J., Kaplan, R., Richert, E., & Stannard, R. The special child in the regular classroom. *Exceptional Children*, 1973, *39*, 384-390.

Brooks, B. L., & Bransford, L. A. Modification of teachers' attitudes toward exceptional children. *Exceptional Children*, 1971, *38*, 259-60.

Buttery, T. J. Affective response to exceptional children by students preparing to be teachers. *Perceptual and Motor Skills*, 1978, *46*(1), 288-290.

California Teachers' Association. *Memo to legislative analyst*, 1977.

California Teachers' Association/IPD. *Mainstreaming, some effects of the special education program in California classes.* September 1977.

Collins, D. L. *Perceptions of Texas high school principals and special education directors in regard to the participation of mentally retarded and learning disabled students in extracurricular activities.* North Texas State University, 1979, EC 123840.

Combs, R. H., & Harper, J. L. Effects of labels on attitudes of educators toward handicapped children. *Exceptional Children*, 1967, *33*, 399-403.

Comer, M. S. *An evaluation of the effects of an administrators' training institute on attitudes toward and knowledge of appropriate programming for the handicapped.* Unpublished doctoral dissertation, University of Mississippi, 1977.

219

Davis, W. E. Public school principals' attitudes toward mainstreaming retarded pupils. *Education and Training of the Mentally Retarded*, 1980, *15*(3), 174-178.

DeLeo, A. V. *The attitudes of public school administrators and teachers toward the integration of children with special needs into regular education programs.* Unpublished doctoral dissertation, Boston University, 1976.

Fanning, P. S. Attitudes of educators toward the educable mentally retarded and their integration into regular education classes. Unpublished doctoral dissertation, University of Arizona, 1974.

Finn, T. E. Teacher inservice education to ease the mainstreaming process and enhance student development. *Dissertation Abstracts International*, 1980, *40*(3A), 4524.

Foley, J. D. Teacher attitudes toward the handicapped and placement preferences for exceptional students. *Dissertation Abstracts International*, 1978, *39*(2A), 773.

Gillung, T. B., & Rucker, C. N. Labels and teacher expectations. *Exceptional Children*, 1977, *43*(7), 464-465.

Glass, R. M., & Meckler, R. S. Preparing elementary teachers to instruct mildly handicapped children in regular classrooms: A summer workshop. *Exceptional Children*, 1972, *39*, 152-156.

Greene, W. R. *Teacher attitudes in Nevada toward inclusion of mentally retarded children in public schools.* Unpublished doctoral dissertation, Illinois State University, 1976.

Guerin, G. R. Regular teacher concerns with mainstreamed learning handicapped children. *Psychology in the Schools*, 1979, *16*(4), 543-545.

Guerin, G. R., & Szatlocky, R. Integration programs for the mildly retarded. *Exceptional Children*, 1974, *41*, 173-179.

Hallard, R. E. *Relationships among Texas special education directors' personnel and program variables and their attitudes toward serving the severely handicapped.* Unpublished doctoral dissertation, University of Texas at Austin, 1977.

Harasymiw, S. J., & Horne, M. D. Teachers' attitudes toward handicapped children and regular class integration. *The Journal of Special Education*, 1976, *10*, 393-400.

Haring, N. G. A study of classroom teachers' attitudes toward exceptional children. *Dissertation Abstracts*, 1956, *17*, 103-104.

Helton, G. B., & Helton, T. D. Oakland teachers attitudinal responses to differing characteristics of elementary school students. *Journal of Educational Psychology*, 1977, *69*(3), 261-265.

Johnston, W. A study to determine teacher attitudes toward teaching special children with regular children. In *Mainstreaming—Resource Room/Attitudes*, Exceptional Child Bibliography Series No. 663, 1972.

Kauffman, D. J. Effects of contact and instruction on regular classroom teachers' attitudes toward the mentally retarded. *Dissertation Abstracts International*, 1977, *38*(2A), 729.

Keilbaugh, W. S. Attitudes of classroom teachers toward their visually handicapped students. *Journal of Visual Impairment and Blindness*, 1977, *71*(10), 430-434.

Kennon, A. F., & Sandoval, J. Teacher attitudes toward the educable mentally retarded. *Education and Training of the Mentally Retarded*, 1978, *13*(2), 139-145.

Kinnison, L. R. *An investigation of elementary classroom teachers' attitudes toward the mentally retarded.* Unpublished doctoral dissertation, University of Kansas, 1972.

Kuhn, J. A comparison of teachers' attitudes toward blindness and exposure to blind children. *New Outlook for the Blind.* 1971, *64*(10), 337-340.

Lake, M. E. Attitudes toward and knowledge of mildly handicapped students held by middle school general educators. *Dissertation Abstracts International*, 1978, *39*(2A), 814-815.

Lazar, A. L. *Attitudes of future administrators toward the handicapped.* Paper presented at the annual international conference (52nd) of The Council for Exceptional Children, April 1974, New York.

Leonetti, P. A. *The compatibility of selected California elementary principals' attitudes toward and knowledge of appropriate placement of exceptional children with the master plan mainstreaming philosophy.* Unpublished doctoral dissertation, University of Southern California, 1977.

220

LeVine, B. G. *Attitudes of head start teachers and aides toward handicapped children.* Temple University, 1976, EC 091697.

Lovitt, E. T. *Teacher acceptance of classroom integration of children with learning disabilities.* Unpublished doctoral dissertation, Arizona State University, 1974.

Mandell, C. J., & Strain, P. S. An analysis of factors related to the attitudes of regular classroom teachers toward mainstreaming mildly handicapped children. *Contemporary Educational Psychology,* 1978, *3*(2), 154-162.

Mark, F. D. *The attitudes of elementary teachers toward the mainstreaming of educable mentally retarded students in northwestern Ohio school districts.* Bowling Green State University, 1980, EC 131150.

Marshall Independent School District, Texas. *The impact of resource room instruction on principal and teachers' attitudes,* 1973. (ERIC 07 8610)

McGinty, A. M., & Keogh, B. K. *Needs assessment for inservice training: A first step for mainstreaming exceptional children into regular education.* Technical Report, University of California, Los Angeles, 1975.

McGuire, D. E., & Throop, R. K. *Educators' attitudes toward exceptional children.* North Country School Study Council, State University College (Potsdam NY), no date. (EC 071693)

Morris, P. S., & McCauley, R. W. *Placement of handicapped children by Canadian mainstream administrators and teachers: A Rucker-Gable survey.* Paper presented at the annual international convention (55th) of The Council for Exceptional Children, Atlanta, Georgia, April 1977.

Nazzaro, J. *Second dimension: Special education administrators view the field.* Reston VA: Council for Exceptional Children, Information Center on Exceptional Children, January 1973.

Newman, K. S. Administrative tasks in special education. *Exceptional Children,* 1970, *36*, 521-524.

Nielsen, L. An in-service program for secondary learning disabilities teachers. *Journal of Learning Disabilities,* 1979, *12*(6), 423-427.

O'Rourke, A. P. A comparison of principal and teacher attitudes toward handicapped students and the relationship between those attitudes and school morale of handicapped students. *Dissertation Abstracts International,* 1980, *40*(7-A), 3954.

Overline, H. M. *Mainstreaming—making it happen.* A research report prepared for the California State Department of Education, 1977.

Panda, K. C., & Bartel, N. R. Teacher perception of exceptional children. *Journal of Special Education,* 1972, *6*(3), 261-266.

Payne, R., & Murray, C. Principals' attitudes toward integration of the handicapped. *Exceptional Children,* 1974, *41*, 123-125.

Pell, D. M. *Teacher acceptance and perception of behavior of physically handicapped pupils transferred from special to regular classes.* Unpublished doctoral dissertation, Brigham Young University, 1973.

Perry, H. L. The effect of special education supportive services on teacher attitudes toward regular class integration of mildly handicapped children. *Dissertation Abstracts International,* 1980, *40*(9A), 5003-5004.

Peters, R. S. *A study of the attitudes of elementary teachers toward exceptional children in the mainstream.* Unpublished doctoral dissertation, University of Maryland, Baltimore, Maryland, 1977.

Peterson, E. L. A study of Mississippi public school superintendents and selected principals' attitudes toward and knowledge of educating exceptional children in the "Least Restrictive Environment." *Dissertation Abstracts International,* 1977, *38*(10), 6059-A.

Proctor, D. I. An investigation of the relationships between knowledge of exceptional children, kind and amount of experience, and attitudes toward their classroom integration. *Dissertation Abstracts,* 1967, *28*, 1721-A.

Pupke, W. R. The effects of school principals' experience on attitude toward and knowledge of handicapped students. *Dissertation Abstracts,* 1977, *38*(08), 4737-A.

Reilly, T. E. *Differences in programming and placement decisions for mildly handicapped children made by special and regular education teachers.* Unpublished doc-

221

toral dissertation, University of Southern California, 1974.

Restad, R. D. *A survey of attitudes held by school administrators toward blind teacher applicants*. M.S. thesis, Moorhead State College, 1972. (ERIC 07 7877)

Savage, M. J. *An investigation of the differences in attitudes between and among school administrators and special education personnel toward exceptional children*. Unpublished doctoral disseration, Boston College, 1971.

Shotel, J. R., Iano, R. P., & McGettigan, J. R. Teacher attitudes associated with the integration of handicapped children. *Exceptional Children*, 1972, *38*, 677-683.

Singleton, K. W. Creating positive attitudes and expectancies of regular classroom teachers toward mainstreaming educationally handicapped children: A comparison of two inservice methods. *Dissertation Abstracts International*, 1977, *38*(1A), 186-187.

Smith, T. E. *High school principals' attitudes toward the handicapped and the work study program*. Paper presented at the annual international convention, The Council for Exceptional Children, Kansas City, Missouri, May 1978.

Smith, T. E., Flexer, R. W., & Sigelman, C. K. Attitudes of secondary principals toward the learning disabled, the mentally retarded, and work-study programs. *Journal of Learning Disabilities*, 1980, *13*(2), 62-64.

Sosnowsky, W. P., & Coleman, T. M. Special education in the collective bargaining process. *Phi Delta Kappan*, 1971, *52*, 610-613.

Stephens, T. M., & Braun, B. L. Measures of regular classroom teachers' attitudes toward handicapped children. *Exceptional Children*, 1980, *46*(4), 292-294.

Wandt, E. The measurement of teacher attitudes toward groups contacted in the school. *Journal of Educational Research*, 1952, *46*, 113-122.

Warren, S. A., Turner, D. R., & Brody, D. S. Can education students' attitudes toward the retarded be changed? *Mental Retardation*, 1964, *2*, 235-242.

Yates, J. R. A model for preparing regular classroom teachers for "Mainstreaming." *Exceptional Children*, 1973, *40*, 471-472.

12

Modifying Attitudes Toward the Handicapped: A Review of the Literature and Methodology

ARTHURLENE GARTRELL TOWNER

The high interest in modifying the attitudes of nondisabled toward disabled populations appears to be fairly recent and, in fact, to parallel the growing concern with mainstreaming. Most of the 47 studies discussed in this chapter were published during the 1970's, the period of greatest change in the legal and social status of handicapped persons. Investigators used a number of approaches to try to modify the attitudes of different populations of nondisabled persons toward persons with different disabilities, but statistically significant results were reported in somewhat less than half the studies and long-term effects were seldom demonstrated. Even when the same approaches were used by different investigators, the results tended to be inconsistent.

In order to determine, if possible, some of the reasons for the variability in results, this review was undertaken to try to relate what we know about attitude change to how the studies were conducted. Therefore, in addition to examining methodology, each study was examined for the presence or absence of seven factors which have been hypothesized to be necessary to programs attempting the effective modification of attitudes. The factors were extrapolated from theories of and research in attitude change.[1]

---

[1]A similar analytic review of research on the modification of attitudes toward disabled persons was completed by Donaldson (1980). She analyzed 24 studies in an attempt to delineate factors common to successful interventions and offered several theoretical constructs as explanations. Although some of our basic theoretical notions and interpretations of results show similarities, there are sufficient differences in format and focus to provide information from somewhat different perspectives. The combination of this chapter and Donaldson's 1980 review offers a comprehensive analysis of the literature on modifying attitudes toward disabled persons.

OVERVIEW

To assess attitudes in the reported studies, investigators used various measures—generally paper and pencil techniques—sometimes singly (22 studies), in pairs (10 studies), or more numerously (3 measures in each of 8 studies; 4 or more in the remaining 7). The preferred measures were the Attitudes Toward Disabled Persons Scale (ATDP), developed by Yuker and Young; questionnaires constructed by the investigators themselves, the Rucker-Gable Educational Programming Scale (RGEP), an instrument designed for use with teacher populations; and behavioral observation, interviews, and measures of a formal nature (e.g., Minnesota Teacher Attitudes Inventory). However, behavioral observation was employed in only five studies (Ballard, Corman, Gottlieb, & Kaufman, 1977; Guskin, 1973; Rusalem, 1967; Skrtic, 1977; Wilson, 1971); interviews and follow-up assessments were found in only four studies (Clore & Jeffrey, 1972; Forader, 1970; Guskin, 1973; Rusalem, 1967); and follow-up assessments alone in two studies (Ballard et al., 1977; Westervelt & McKinney, 1980).

The instruments devised by investigators included questionnaires of informational and attitudinal items (Alese, 1973; Baran, 1977; Carlson & Potter, 1972; Dahl, Horsman, & Arkell, 1978; Euse, 1976; Friedman & Marsh, 1972; Guskin, 1973; Hersh, Carlson, & Lessino, 1977; Koch, 1975; Scheffers, 1977; Shotel, Iano, & McGettigan, 1974); written descriptions of reactions to experiences (Clore & Jeffrey, 1972; Wilson & Alcorn, 1969); an attitude scale and disguised attitudinal telephone assessment (Clore & Jeffrey, 1972); picture, sentence completion, and drawing completion tests (Granofsky, 1956); adapted achievement tests and attitude scales (Orlansky, 1977); self-report inventories, unstructured interviews, and self-evaluations (Chafin & Peipher, 1979; Glass & Meckler, 1972; Handlers & Austin, 1980; Naor & Milgram, 1980); structured, multiple choice, sentence completion, attitude questionnaires (Rusalem, 1967); sociometric and social distance questionnaires (Ballard et al., 1977; Dahl et al., 1978; Westervelt & McKinney, 1980); and adjective and descriptive traits checklists (Gottlieb, 1980); Hastorf, Wildfogel, & Cassman, 1979; Jones, Sowell, Jones, & Butler, 1981; Siperstein, Bak, & Gottlieb, 1977; Siperstein, & Bak, 1980; Weinberg, 1978).

Few attempts were made to address the complexity of attitude measurement. For the most part, investigators addressed the cognitive or affective components, not the multidimensional aspects of attitude.

The reports of the majority of studies did not indicate theoretical bases for the approach to attitude change. In some of the studies which did apply attitude-change principles, it was not possible to determine whether their application was intentional or coincidental because the authors did not provide such information. Several investigators used theoretical constructs for post hoc explanations of outcomes; however, it was not apparent that the constructs were used to design the studies.

Only nine studies were found in which the theoretical bases were explicit in the designs: (a) theories of cooperation and competition (Ballard et al., 1977); (b) source credibility and status in persuasive communication (Baran, 1977); (c) cognitive dissonance and its production of empathy through role playing

224

(Clore & Jeffrey, 1972); (d) Lewin's change theory regarding reduction in the restraining of forces to reduce interaction strain (Evans, 1976); (e) group polarization and its informational influences (Gottlieb, 1980); (f) deviance disavowal (Hastorf et al., 1979); (g) person perception through playing the role of a so-called helpless individual (Koch, 1975); (h) perceived similarity and attraction (Weinberg, 1978); and (i) Siller's multidimensional theory of attitudes coupled with Katz's functional theory of attitude change (Yerxa, 1978).

The attitude-change techniques used in the studies lent themselves to 10 groupings, as follows:

1. Repetition, frequent contact with a credible source, and continuous feedback.
2. Selective information (designed with specific attitudinal goals).
3. Role playing of a disabling condition.
4. Personal and social contact.
5. Direct contact with the attitude object (in an educational setting).
6. Face-to-face contact through media (film, video- and audiotape).
7. Group discussion and active participation (usually in a lecture-discussion format).
8. Overt and covert positive reinforcement.
9. Vicarious role playing or observation.
10. Especially prepared persuasive communications.

The most widely followed, alone or in combination, were the fifth (direct contact with the attitude object in an educational setting); the seventh (group discussion and active participation); and the third (role playing of a disabling condition). Essentially, all the techniques fall under three of the influential factors of attitude change identified by Hovland, Janis, and Kelley (1953) in the Yale Approach to Attitude Change: (a) the source, (b) the channel, and (c) the destination. With the exception of Baran (1977) and Forader (1970), no investigator mentioned the importance of the type and style of the message or the particular audience who was to be the receiver, and all attended only minimally to the source and destination. The channel was the major area in which principles were identifiable.

In Table 1, the studies reviewed in this chapter are summarized by the population with which some attitude change was attempted, the disabled population toward whom the attitudes were directed, the measures used to assess attitudes and changes therein, and the theory and/or change techniques which could be identified in each. Not surprisingly, the populations whose attitudes were studied the most were regular classroom teachers, sometimes including administrators (12 studies) and college students (15 studies). With the first population, attitudes toward children with learning and behavior problems were the major focus of change attempts; with the second, the major focus was on changing attitudes toward persons with physical disabilities. In the remaining 20 studies under review, attitude change toward disabled persons, mostly those with physical disabilities, were attempted with 4 populations of lay persons (3 "community groups," 1 "general public") and with 10 of elementary students, 4 of high school students, and 2 of related professionals.

TABLE 1

Studies Attempting to Modify Attitudes Toward Disabled Persons: Summary

Study	Disabled Population of Concern	Subjects	Assessment Measures Utilized	Attitude Theory and/or Attitude Change Techniques Specified or Applied
1. Alese (1973)	Mentally retarded	Community groups N = 964	Investigator's questionnaire (informational and attitudinal)	2. Selective information 6. Face-to-face contact through media
2. Ballard et al. (1977)	Mentally retarded	Elementary students N = 37 EMR students currently enrolled in 37 regular classrooms	Behavioral Observation Forced choice sociometric questionnaire Follow-up measure	5. Direct contact in educational setting 7. Group discussion plus active participation
3. Baran (1977)	Mentally retarded	General public N = 80	Telephone attitude survey	6. Face-to-face contact through media 10. Especially prepared persuasive communication
4. Brooks & Bransford (1971)	Learning & behavior problems	Regular classroom teachers & administrators N = 30	Semantic differential scale	2. Selective information 5. Direct contact in educational setting
5. Carlson & Potter (1972)	Learning & behavior problems	Regular classroom teachers N = 10	Investigator's questionnaire (open-ended)	1. Repetition, feedback, credible source
6. Chafin & Peipher (1979)	Hearing impaired	Childcare workers with regular teaching backgrounds N = 3	Informal self-reports through unstructured interview	3. Role playing disabling condition 5. Direct contact in educational setting

7. Clore & Jeffrey (1972)	Physically disabled	College students N=76	Semantic differential scale; Written reactions to experiences; Attitude scale & disguised telephone assessment; Interview & follow-up assessment; Evaluation form	Cognitive dissonance theory; 3. Role playing disabling condition; 9. Vicarious role playing/observation
8. Dahl et al. (1978)	Physically disabled	Elementary students N=63	Social distance checklist; Attitudes Toward Disabled Persons Scale (Vinish); Abilities of Handicapped Persons Scale; Attitudes Toward Handicapped Scale	3. Role playing disabling condition
9. Daniels (1976)	Physically disabled; Emotionally disturbed	College students N=153	Attitudes Toward Disabled Persons Scale; Opinion about Mental Illness Scale	8. Covert reinforcement
10. Donaldson & Martinson (1977)	Physically disabled	College students N=96	Attitudes Toward Disabled Persons Scale	6. Face-to-face contact through media; 8. Covert reinforcement
11. Euse (1976)	Physically disabled	College students N=20	Investigator's questions on attitudes and amount of looking time	8. Covert reinforcement
12. Evans (1976)	Blind	College students N=60	Amount of Contact Scale; Attitudes Toward Disabled Persons Scale—Form B; Semantic differential scale (type of contact)	Lewin's Change Theory; 4. Personal & social contact
13. Felton (1975)	General disabilities; Multiply handicapped	Paraprofessional trainees N=7	Attitude Toward Disabled Persons Scale	4. Personal & social contact

Continued on next page

TABLE 1 Continued

Study	Disabled Population of Concern	Subjects	Assessment Measures Utilized	Attitude Theory and/or Attitude Change Technique Specified or Applied
14. Fenton (1975)	Learning & behavior problems	Regular classroom teachers $N = 546$	Rucker-Gable Educational Programming Scale	7. Group discussion
15. Forader (1970)	Physically disabled	High school students $N = 142$	Attitudes Toward Disabled Persons Scale Interviews & follow-up assessments	6. Face-to-face contact through media 10. Persuasive communications
16. Friedman & Marsh (1972)	Blind	High school students $N = 215$	Attitude to Blindness Scale	2. Selective information 3. Role playing disabling condition 7. Group discussion plus active participation
17. Glass & Meckler (1972)	Learning & behavior problems	Regular classroom teachers & administrators $N = 18$	Self-report inventory of workshop effectiveness Minnesota Teacher Attitude Inventory	5. Direct contact in educational setting
18. Gottlieb (1980)	Educable mentally retarded	Elementary school students $N = 208$	Adjective Checklist	7. Group discussion
19. Granofsky (1956)	Physically disabled	Community groups $N = 205$	Picture tests; sentence completion; drawing completion Interest Values Inventory Minnesota Inventories of Social Attitudes	4. Personal & social contact

228

			Preferred Student Experience Blank	
20. Guskin (1973)	Learning & behavior problems	College students N = not provided	Investigator's questionnaire (standard game evaluation form) Behavioral Observation Interviews & follow-up assessments	7. Group discussion 9. Vicarious role playing and simulated experiences
21. Handlers & Austin (1980)	General disabilities	High school students N = 20	Self-evaluation questionnaire	3. Role playing disabling condition 4. Personal contact 6. Face-to-face contact through media 7. Group discussion plus active participation
22. Haring et al. (1958)	General disabilities	Regular classroom teachers & administrators N = 141	General Information Inventory Classroom Integration Inventory Activities Index Picture Judgment Test Critical Incidence Test	5. Direct contact in educational setting 6. Face-to-face contact through media 7. Group discussion plus active participation
23. Hastorf et al. (1979)	Physically disabled	College students N = 53	Impression Scale	6. Face-to-face contact through media
24. Hersh et al. (1977)	Mentally retarded	College students N = 20	Client Preference/Rank Ordering Semantic differential scale	5. Direct contact in family setting 7. Group discussion plus active participation

Continued on next page

229

TABLE 1 *Continued*

Study	Disabled Population of Concern	Subjects	Assessment Measures Utilized	Attitude Theory and/or Attitude Change Techniques Specified or Applied
25. Jones et al. (1981)	Mental and physical handicaps	Elementary students N=74	Descriptive Characteristics Scale	3. Role playing disabling condition 4. Direct contact in educational setting 6. Face-to-face contact through media 7. Group discussion plus active participation
26. Koch (1975)	Blind	Community groups N=not provided	Investigator's likert-type questionnaire	Person Perception Theory 3. Role playing disabling condition 7. Group discussion plus active participation
27. Lazar et al. (1971)	General disabilities	Elementary school gifted students N=44	Attitudes Toward Disabled Persons Scale—Form O	5. Direct contact in educational setting 7. Group discussion plus active participation
28. Lazar et al. (1976)	General disabilities	College students N=20	Attitudes Toward Disabled Persons Scale Preferred Student Characteristic Scale	7. Group discussion plus active participation 8. Positive reinforcement plus
29. Naor & Milgram (1980)	Mentally retarded, emotionally disturbed, learning disabled, physically or sensorily handicapped	College students (training teachers) N=80	Knowledge & Attitude Scale Behavioral Intention Questionnaire Course Evaluation	5. Direct contact with educational setting 7. Group discussion plus active participation

Study	Disability	Population	Instrument	Intervention
30. Orlansky (1977)	General disabilities	College students N = 50	Attitude scales Adapted achievement tests	3. Role playing disabling conditions 7. Group discussion plus active participation
31. Rapier et al. (1972)	Physically disabled	Elementary school students N = 152	Semantic differential scale	5. Direct contact in educational setting
32. Rusalem (1967)	Deaf-blind	High school students N = 28	Structured multiple choice completion sentence attitude questionnaire Behavioral observation Interview & follow-up assessment	5. Direct contact in educational setting 7. Group discussion plus active participation
33. Sadlick & Penta (1975)	Physically disabled	Nurses N = 84	Semantic differential scale	6. Face-to-face contact through media
34. Scheffers, W. (1977)	Blind	Elementary school students N = 27	Knowledge and Attitude Questionnaire	3. Role playing disabling condition 7. Group discussion plus active participation
35. Schorn (1977)	Learning & behavior problems	Regular classroom teachers N = 49	Rucker-Gable Educational Programming Scale	2. Selective information 5. Direct contact in educational setting
36. Shaw & Gillung (1975)	Learning & behavior problems	Regular classroom teachers N = 35	Rucker-Gable Educational Programming Scale	2. Selective information
37. Shotel et al. (1974)	Learning & behavior problems	Regular classroom teachers N = 116	Investigators' questionnaire (yes/no)	5. Direct contact in educational setting

Continued on next page

TABLE 1 *Continued*

Study	Disabled Population of Concern	Subjects	Assessment Measures Utilized	Attitude Theory and/or Attitude Change Techniques Specified or Applied
38. Siperstein et al. (1977)	Mentally retarded	Elementary school students N = 86	Adjective Checklist	6. Contact through media (audiotaped) 7. Group discussion plus active participation
39. Siperstein and Bak (1980)	Blind	Elementary school students N = 109	Adjective Checklist Activity Preference Scale	2. Selective information 3. Role playing disabling condition 6. Face-to-face contact through media (video- and audio-tape) 7. Group discussion and active participation
40. Skrtic (1977)	Learning & behavior problems	Regular classroom teachers N = 31 Learning disabled students N = 62	Modifications of Attitudes toward Handicapped Individuals Scale Teacher Approval-Disapproval Scale Behavior observation	2. Selective information
41. Soloway (1976)	Learning & behavior problems	Regular classroom teachers N = 74	Rucker-Gable Educational Programming Scale EMR-EH Placement Survey	5. Direct contact in educational setting 7. Group discussion plus active participation
42. Weinberg, N. (1978)	Physically disabled	Elementary school students and College students N = 265	Rapier et al. scale plus six additional items Descriptive trait attitude scale Person-description Questionnaire Contact with Disabled Scale	4. Personal and social contact

43. Westervelt & McKinney (1980)	Physically disabled	Elementary school students $N = 46$	Social distance questionnaire Activity Preference Scale Follow-up measure	6. Face-to-face through media (film)
44. Wilson (1971)	Deaf	College students $N = 60$	Semantic Differential Scale Attitudes Toward Deaf Persons Scale Situational Anxiety Scale—Form A Behavioral observation	3. Role playing disabling condition 9. Vicarious role playing/Observation
45. Wilson & Alcorn (1969)	General disabilities	College students $N = 80$	Attitudes Toward Disabled Persons Scale Written reactions to experiences	3. Role playing disabling condition
46. Yates (1973)	General disabilities	Regular classroom teachers and administrators $N = 40$	Dogmatism Scale, Form E Critical Thinking Appraisal Adjective Self-Description Classroom Integration Inventory Special Education Information Questionnaire	7. Group discussion plus active participation
47. Yerxa (1978)	Physically disabled	College students $N = 154$	Attitudes toward Disabled Persons Scale Disability Factor Scales McCloskey & Schaars Anomy Scale	Siller's Multidimensional Theory of Attitudes Krathwohl's Affective Domain Sequence Katz's Functional Theory of Attitude Change 7. Group discussion plus shared active participation 9. Vicarious role playing

233

ANALYSIS

This review was directed to (a) the discussions of the samples, instrumentation, and procedures; (b) the outcomes of the programs; and (c) the presence of a series of factors which have been suggested by theories of and research in attitude change to be useful elements (Halloran, 1967; McGuire, 1968; Triandis, 1971; Zimbardo & Ebbeson, 1970). These elements are as follows:

1. Defining the term "attitude" in the context in which it is used.
2. Specifying the component(s) of the attitude(s) of concern.
3. Employing instruments that appropriately measure the component(s) of concern.
4. Identifying or suggesting the function(s) of the attitude(s).
5. Attending to the influence of the subjects' personalities.
6. Specifying or suggesting a theory of attitude change.
7. Specifying and/or applying attitude-change principles.

These factors are referred to by number in the following analyses.

Regular Classroom Teachers and Administrators

Regular classroom teachers, inexperienced and experienced, and a few administrators comprised one of the larger populations exposed to programs designed to produce changes in attitudes toward disabled children. The investigators attempted to explore teacher attitudes toward instructing and/or working with exceptional children in a variety of educational situations, with and without supportive services.

Table 2 lists 12 relevant studies, separated into populations involved and not involved with disabled children. In the programs, attempts were made to assess the effectiveness of different modes of instruction with various formats (e.g., workshops, courses, inservice training, and continuing education) to produce increases in teacher knowledge about and attitudinal changes toward the integration of exceptional children in regular classrooms. Most investigators sought to determine the effectiveness of their programs in increasing the participants' knowledge about exceptional children with concomitant improvement in attitudes toward the children.

In most studies, but not that by Chafin and Peipher (1979), the samples were adequate in size. Only Haring, Stern, and Cruickshank (1958) used random sampling to assign subjects to treatments. Carlson and Potter (1972) and Chafin and Peipher (1979) provided sketchy but fairly adequate descriptions of their subjects; in the rest of the reports, the subjects were not well enough described. Adequate descriptions of instrumentation were given by Carlson and Potter (1972), Haring et al. (1958), Schorn (1977), Shaw and Gillung (1975), and Shotel et al. (1974). The interview conducted by Chafin and Peipher (1979) was not described sufficiently to determine its appropriateness. Only Shaw and Gillung (1975) provided reliability data; no investigator reported validity data.

TABLE 2
Studies with Regular Classroom Teachers and Administrators:
Purposes, Attitude-Change Procedures, and Reported Successes

Study	Purpose(s) of Study[a]	Technique Employed[b]	Success Reported[c]
Populations Involved with Disabled Children			
Brooks & Bransford (1971)	A	II	X
Carlson & Potter (1972)	A	II	X
Chafin & Peipher (1979)	A	III	
Fenton (1975)	B	I	
Glass & Meckler (1972)	A	II	X
Schorn (1977)	C	III	
Shotel et al. (1972)	C, D	III	
Skrtic (1977)	A	III	X
Populations Not Involved with Disabled Children			
Haring et al. (1958)	A	I	X
Shaw & Gillung (1975)	A	I	
Soloway (1976)	A	I	
Yates (1973)	A	I	X

[a]Purposes of Study:
  A. Determine effectiveness of program to increase knowledge about exceptional children and to produce concomitant change in attitudes toward them.
  B. Determine relation of experience and sex as predictor of degree of shift in attitude change.
  C. Identify differential responses toward various disability groups.
  D. Establish consensus of teacher desire for special methods and materials to meet needs of disabled children.

[b]Techniques Employed:
  I. Lecture/Discussion with or without observation of disabled children.
  II. Practicum placement with formal instruction.
  III. Practicum placement with observation.

[c]Success = statistically significant results.

For the most part, treatments were clearly reported but the descriptions of the procedures followed were insufficient to permit effective replication. Adequate illustrations of treatments or techniques were lacking in Fenton (1975), Soloway (1976), and Yates (1973). Except for Carlson and Potter (1972) and Chafin and Peipher (1979), investigators used pretreatment measures to establish the initial attitudes of the participants. Only Shaw and Gillung (1974) and Skrtic (1977) made pre-, post-, and follow-up assessments, and they were the only investigators to examine the long-term effects of their treatments.

Brooks and Bransford (1971), Glass and Meckler (1972), Haring et al. (1958), Skrtic (1977), and Yates (1973) presented evidence of the participants' increased knowledge and acceptance of exceptional children after several treatments. Although little evidence was found of increased knowledge of the realistic placement of disabled children or of subsequent changes in teacher behavior toward the children in instructional settings, changes in instructional techniques were noted subsequently by Carlson and Potter (1972) and Haring et al. (1958).

In the comparisons of the subjects, Shaw and Gillung (1975) found no difference between the participants and the teachers who elected not to participate in the programs, and Soloway (1976) found that more favorable attitudes toward disabled children were demonstrated by teachers without integration experience and by those who had had more than two college courses in special education. Sex and years of experience were of little or no value as predictors of attitudes (Fenton, 1975).

Negative changes in attitude toward and optimism concerning the integration of exceptional learners were found by Fenton (1975) and Shotel et al. (1974). Schorn (1977) was able to differentiate the effects of the identical treatment-practicum placement-within various school districts.

Except for Carlson and Potter (1972) and Haring et al. (1958), investigators did not report concomitant changes in teacher behavior within instructional settings, perhaps because no technique was used to a sufficient degree to produce the desired interaction of attitude and behavior change. Even these investigators could make only general statements about the subsequent changes in instructional techniques learned through the treatment.

Elements of attitude-change theory included the following:

1. The use of the term "attitude(s)" in their studies was specifically defined by Haring et al. (1958) and Schorn (1977).
2. All reports specified or suggested the attitude component(s) of concern: the cognitive for the majority of the investigators; the affective for Chafin and Peipher (1979), Schorn (1977), and Shaw and Gillung (1975); both cognitive and affective for Haring et al. (1958), Soloway (1976), and Yates (1973); and all three components—cognitive, affective, and behavioral—for Skrtic (1977).
3. In all studies except Chafin and Peipher (1979), the measures employed were appropriate for the components of concern.
4. The issue of the functions of attitudes was not addressed in any study.
5. The influence of subjects' personalities was ignored.
6. Only Skrtic (1977) specified the application of attitude theory in the development of his program. The assessment of this element was not possible for the Fenton (1975), Soloway (1976), and Yates (1973) studies because the descriptions of the program content were insufficient.
7. Except for Shaw and Gillung (1975), there was evidence in all studies of the application of certain principles of attitude change, but they were not identified as such. For these and the other studies in this review, when the principles were not identified as such, it was impossible to determine whether their application was coincidental or intentional.

236

When studies reporting more success are compared to those reporting less success in attitude change on the application of the elements of change theory (Table 3), little if any difference in the patterns of application is evident.

College Students

Although 15 studies were identified in which the populations consisted of college students, only 14 are discussed in this section. (The report by Daniels, 1976, did not include sufficient information to permit analysis.) The subjects were mostly undergraduates. Guskin (1973) recruited a mixture of graduate and undergraduate students from special education courses and Lazar, Orpet, and Demos (1976) used only special education graduate students in their investigation. Among the undergraduates, the most popular source of subjects was introductory psychology courses.

Table 4 presents the classified studies by purpose, technique employed, and reported success. Several examples of methodological deficiencies were noted.

TABLE 3
Application of Elements of Theory to Attitude Change Studies by Significance of Results

Study	Elements of Theory[a]						
Studies Reporting Statistically Significant Results	1	2	3	4	5	6	7[c]
Brooks & Bransford (1971)		X	X				X[c]
Carlson & Potter (1972)		X	X				X[c]
Glass & Meckler (1972)		X	X				X[c]
Haring et al. (1958)	X	X	X				X[c]
Skrtic (1977)		X	X			X	X[c]
Yates (1973)		X	X			X[b]	X[c]
Studies Not Reporting Statistically Significant Results							
Chafin & Peipher (1979)		X					X[c]
Fenton (1975)		X	X			X[b]	X[c]
Schorn (1977)	X	X	X				X[c]
Shotel et al. (1974)		X	X				X[c]
Shaw & Gillung (1975)		X	X				
Soloway (1976)		X	X			X[b]	X[c]

Note: Regular classroom teachers and administrators were the subjects of the studies.
[a]1. Attitude(s) defined.
  2. Component(s) defined.
  3. Appropriate instruments used.
  4. Function of attitudes identified.
  5. Personality factors considered.
  6. Theory of attitude change specified or suggested.
  7. Principles of attitude change applied or suggested.
[b]Could not be determined. [c]Were not identified, but applied.

TABLE 4
Studies with Undergraduate and Graduate College Students:
Purposes, Attitude-Change Procedures, and Reported Successes

Study	Purpose of Study[a]	Technique(s) Employed[b]	Success Reported[c]
UNDERGRADUATES			
Psychology Courses			
Clore & Jeffrey (1972)	A	II	X
Donaldson & Martinson (1977)	B	III	
Evans (1976)	C	III	X
Hastorf et al. (1979)	B	III	X
Wilson (1971)	E	II	
Special Education Courses			
Naor & Milgram (1980)	M	IV, V	X
Orlansky (1977)	F	IV	
Wilson & Alcorn (1969)	J	II	
In Dormitory Settings			
Weinberg (1978)	M	III	X
Physical & Occupational Therapy Courses			
Yerxa (1978)	G	VI	X
Vocational Rehabilitation Services			
Euse (1976)	D	III	
GRADUATES			
Special Education Courses			
Guskin (Included undergraduates) (1973)	H	I	X
Hersh et al. (1977)	L	V	
Lazar et al. (1976)	I	IV	
Job Sites			
Chafin & Peipher (1979)	J	II	

[a]Purpose of Study: To explore
  A. Effectiveness of emotional role playing.
  B. Mode variation in a panel presentation by individuals with visible physical disabilities.
  C. Reduction of interaction strain through active or passive participation by the disabled person.
  D. Application of covert positive reinforcement to induce change.
  E. Disability simulation versus observation.
  F. Lecture versus active learning approaches.
  G. Programmed instruction.
  H. Simulation games in the modification of attitudes.
  I. Effectiveness of lecture/discussion techniques.
  J. Disability simulation.
  K. Effectiveness of the tactic of acknowledging the handicap in interactions between handicapped and nonhandicapped individuals.
  L. Effectiveness of a course including direct contact in family setting, role playing, and group discussion.

Continued on next page

238

Table 4 *Continued*

M. The differences in effectiveness of a traditional lecture-discussion strategy with an experimental strategy that combined lecture discussions with direct contact through field experiences.
N. Effectiveness of optimal conditions for contact between disabled and able-bodied persons.
[b]Techniques Employed:
  I. Role playing and simulated experiences.
  II. Disability simulation through actual experiences and/or observation.
  III. Face-to-face contact with disabled persons.
  IV. Lecture/discussion.
  V. Lecture/discussion without participation in field.
  VI. Shared active participation.
[c]Success = statistically significant results.

With the exception of Chafin and Peipher (1979), the samples used in the studies were of adequate size. The descriptions of the subjects were sufficient in the reports by Donaldson and Martinson (1977); Hastorf et al. (1979); Hersh et al. (1977); Naor and Milgram (1980); Weinberg (1978); Wilson (1971); and Yerxa (1978). In most studies, subjects were randomly assigned to treatments; however, no indication of randomization was provided by Guskin (1973); Lazar et al. (1976); and Orlansky (1977). In all except Yerxa's (1978) study, a major weakness was the absence of reliability and validity data for the instrumentation. Inadequate descriptions of the content and/or development of the instrumentation were evident in the majority of the studies, but this deficiency could be due to the need to abbreviate reports for journal publication. Yerxa's (1978) study was reported in a dissertation and was the only one to describe basic procedures sufficiently to permit replication. Clore and Jeffrey (1972), Donaldson and Martinson (1977), and Wilson (1971) included pretreatment measures in their studies, but other investigators did not. Follow-up measures to assess the longterm effects of treatment were found only in Clore and Jeffrey (1972), Euse (1976), and Evans (1976).

Enthusiasm for the activities and for the creation of realistic perspectives on mainstreaming resulted from role playing and simulated experiences. However, contradictory responses varying from improved acceptance to increased skepticism could be noted (Guskin, 1973). Lecture-discussion course-type experiences yielded nonsignificant results and showed variability in the scores of female and male subjects (Lazar et al., 1976; Orlansky, 1977). The combination of lecture/discussions and direct contact with different kinds of exceptional children was found to have an advantage over training limited to lecture-discussions (Naor & Milgram, 1980). Both live and videotaped panel presentations by individuals with visible physical disabilities were of equal effectiveness, with no significant differences between male and female respondents

239

(Donaldson & Martinson, 1977). Contact alone was not found to affect attitudes significantly, but structured social interactions with disabled persons led to the formation of positive attitudes by the nondisabled participants (Evans, 1976; Hastorf et al., 1979). Only contact in an intensive situation was shown to result in major changes in subjects' perceptions of disabled persons (Weinberg, 1978). Attitude scale scores and amount of time spent looking at pictures of physically disabled persons were increased significantly through the application of covert positive reinforcement (Euse, 1976).

Similar effects resulted whether subjects actually participated in the role playing or observed another person playing the role of a disabled person. Both techniques had immediate and longterm effects on interpersonal attitudes toward disabled students (Clore & Jeffrey, 1972). There was wide variation in the insight and frustration experienced depending upon the type of disability simulated, but these differences were not found to be related to age, sex, or educational background (Wilson & Alcorn, 1969). Significant differences were found in anxiety level either before or after interaction with the disabled persons, and the active or passive role of the disabled persons during the interactions appeared to affect post-interaction scores. Behavioral differences were nonsignificant (Wilson, 1971).

For health and non-health students, participation in a dyadic self-instruction program was equally effective; however, the health students demonstrated more pretreatment comfort at the thought of interaction with disabled persons. It was much more difficult to change attitudes related to an individual's feeling of vulnerability than to change those related to authoritarian condescension toward the disabled (Yerxa, 1978).

Elements of attitude-change theory included the following:

1. Only Yerxa (1978) defined the use of the term "attitude(s)."
2. All investigators suggested or specified the attitude component(s) of concern: Naor and Milgram (1980) and Wilson (1971) tackled all three components--cognitive, affective, and behavioral; Clore and Jeffrey (1972) also explored the behavioral component. The majority of studies addressed primarily the cognitive component, although a few included the affective component. The affective component appeared to be the primary concern in the studies by Hastorf et al. (1979) and Weinberg (1978).
3. All measures were appropriate for the component(s) of concern. Euse (1976) provided no information on his choice of instrumentation, and Chafin and Peipher (1979) did not describe theirs sufficiently for identification.
4. Yerxa (1971) used the functional theory of attitude change in the development of her program; other studies did not identify or suggest the functions of attitudes.
5. Yerxa (1978) alone considered the personality factors of subjects by using Siller's multidimensional theory of attitudes toward the physically disabled.
6. Attitude theory was applied to the development of attitude modification techniques by Clore and Jeffrey (1972), Evans (1976), Hastorf et al. (1979), and Yerxa (1978).
7. All studies applied some principles of attitude change in their techniques but only Donaldson and Martinson (1977), Euse (1976), Evans (1976), Guskin

240

TABLE 5
Application of Elements to Attitude-Change Studies by
Significance of Results

Study	Elements of Theory[a]						
Studies Reporting Statistically Significant Results	1	2	3	4	5	6	7
Clore & Jeffrey (1972)		X	X			X	X[c]
Evans (1976)		X	X			X	X
Guskin (1973)		X	X				X
Hastorf et al. (1979)		X	X			X	X
Lazar et al. (1976)		X	X				X
Naor & Milgram (1980)		X	X				X[c]
Weinberg (1978)		X	X			X	X
Yerxa (1978)	X	X	X	X	X	X	X
Studies Not Reporting Statistically Significant Results							
Chafin & Peipher (1979)		X					X[c]
Donaldson & Martinson (1977)		X	X				X
Euse (1976)		X	b				X
Hersh et al. (1977)		X	X				X[c]
Orlansky (1977)		X	X				X[c]
Wilson (1971)		X	X				X[c]
Wilson & Alcorn (1969)		X	X				X[c]

Note: College students were the subjects of the studies.
[a] See Table 3.
[b] Could not be determined.
[c] Were not identified, but applied.

(1973), Hastorf et al. (1979), Weinberg (1978), and Yerxa (1978) specified the intended application of the principles.

The pattern of the application of the elements of attitude-change theory for the studies reporting statistically significant or nonsignificant results (Table 5) is very much like that for the studies of regular classroom teachers, with the exception of Yerxa: She was the only investigator to use all seven elements in her research.

Community Groups

Members of social and civic groups and the general public were the participants in the four studies discussed in this section. The purposes, change techniques, and reported successes for each are provided in Table 6.

241

TABLE 6

Studies with Community Groups, Elementary and High School Students, and Related Professionals: Purposes, Attitude-Change Procedures, and Reported Successes

Study	Purpose of Study	Technique(s) Employed	Success Reported[a]
Community Groups			
Alese (1975)	To enhance acceptance and understanding of retarded individuals and to dispel damaging misconceptions about them.	Film depicting retarded individuals in productive activity, in contrast to stereotyped images.	
Baran (1977)	To determine the effectiveness of a series of television programs on changing public attitudes toward mentally retarded people.	Four 1½-hour television dramas employing mentally retarded people as talented, and depicting them in everyday situations.	X
Granofsky (1956)	To determine influence of social contact as a technique for modifying attitudes toward visibly disabled persons and the relation of psychological and situational variables.	Social interaction for 8 hours.	
Koch (1975)	To correct misinformation about blind persons and to change view of blind as inferior, helpless, and dependent.	Role playing and group discussion.	X
Elementary School Students			
Ballard et al. (1977)	To improve the social status of mainstreamed educable mentally retarded children among nonretarded classmates.	Direct contact, group discussion, and shared active participation.	X
Dahl et al. (1978)	To determine the effectiveness of experiences with simulation in changing elementary school students' attitudes toward their handicapped peers.	Disability simulation.	X

Gottlieb (1980)	To develop interventions that can improve the attitudes of nonhandicapped children through the use of group discussion.	Group discussion.	X
Jones et al. (1981)	To study the possible effects of a concentrated program on young children's perceptions of people who have mental or physical handicaps.	Disability simulation, personal contact in interviews, film, and group discussion.	X
Lazar et al. (1971)	To determine if greater understanding and acceptance of disabled would result from special instructional program.	Lecture, group discussion, and direct contact.	X
Rapier et al. (1972)	To determine effects of school-site integration of orthopedically handicapped children.	Direct contact.	X
Scheffers (1977)	To determine the effectiveness of a 20-lesson unit of study as a technique for improvement of children's knowledge of and attitudes toward blindness.	Role playing disabling conditions, group discussion plus active participation.	
Siperstein et al. (1977)	To examine group discussions as a factor affecting children's attitudes toward competent, normal-appearing children and incompetent, abnormal-appearing children.	Group discussion.	X
Siperstein & Bak (1980)	To improve the social acceptability of a blind child by teaching sighted children about blindness and accentuating a potential "redeeming virtue" of a blind child's academic competence.	Role playing, disability simulation, group discussion, and video- and audio-tapes.	X
Westervelt & McKinney (1980)	To evaluate the effects of a brief film designed to point out how the aspirations and interests of a handicapped child are similar to those of his or her nonhandicapped classmates.	Film showing handicapped children in wheelchairs participating in physical education and classroom activities with nonhandicapped children.	X

Continued on next page

243

Table 6 *Continued*

Study	Purpose of Study	Technique(s) employed	Success Reported[a]
High School Students			
Forader (1970)	To differentiate effectiveness of various modes of instruction.	Persuasive messages via TV, audio-tape, and live presentations.	
Friedman & Marsh (1972)	To promote the integration of the blind students into the social and educational life of the school by eliminating the mystery surrounding blindness and the resource program.	Five instructional periods taught in coeducational freshman health education, including group discussion, disability simulation, and active participation with a braille writer.	
Handlers & Austin (1980)	To foster an awareness of the problems of handicaps and handicapped people and to foster a more positive and accepting attitude toward handicapped people.	Group discussion, research reports, film, disability simulations, face-to-face contact by personal interview with a blind person.	
Rusalem (1967)	To ascertain effects of various attitude-change procedures on feelings toward deaf-blind persons.	Group discussions, active participation, and direct contact during 6 1-hour sessions.	
Related Professionals			
Felton (1975)	To determine effects of personal and social interactions with disabled persons.	Information and professional training courses.	
Sadlick & Penta (1975)	To promote attitude change toward quadriplegic persons.	Face-to-face interactions with physically disabled persons via a video-tape and group discussion.	X

[a]Success = statistically significant results

Methodologically, the studies had some limitations. Alese (1973), Baran (1977), and Granofsky (1956) reported adequate size samples, but Koch (1975) provided no comparable data. In all four studies, sampling procedures were nonrandomized and nonrepresentative.

Although the descriptions of procedures were fairly clear, they were not sufficiently detailed for replication, except for Koch (1975), who spelled out her procedures. Alese (1973) alone provided reliability data for his instrumentation; none provided validity data. More important, in all four reports the content and development of the measures were inadequately described. Nevertheless, three of the four studies displayed one major strength: the use of more than one instrument to assess attitude change (Alese, 1973; Granofsky, 1956; Koch, 1975). Koch also assessed the longterm effects of the treatment used.

The results of the film presentation in Alese's study and of social contact in Granofsky's investigation revealed no significant changes in attitude; neither was any relation established between various personality and background factors and attitudes. In the Koch study the tendency to view blind persons as helpless, inferior, and dependent was significantly reduced by role playing and group discussion, but not to the the the extent expected. Baran (1977) found the respondents who viewed four 1 1/2-hour dramas about mentally retarded people to be significantly more positive in their attitudes toward mental retardation than respondents in the nonviewing conditions.

Elements of attitude-change theory included the following:

1. The term "attitudes(s)" was not defined.
2. The components of attitude were specified or suggested in all four investigations; they were primarily cognitive and/or affective.
3. Appropriate measurements were employed for the component(s) in all four studies.
4. The function(s) of the attitude(s) were not identified.
5. Only Granofsky (1956) considered personality factors.
6. Only Koch (1975) provided a theoretical basis for her approach to the attitude-change process.
7. Baran (1977) specifically stated his principles but Koch did not identify hers as such.

Elementary School Students

In the 10 studies in this classification, the populations were students in grades 3-6 from predominantly white middle-class backgrounds. The purposes, attitude-change procedures, and reported successes are provided in Table 6. Several methodological problems were evident. The sample sizes were adequate in all studies but that of Lazar, Gensley, and Orpet (1971). Samples were poorly described and nonrandomized in the studies reported by Dahl et al. (1978), Lazar et al. (1971), Rapier, Adelson, Carey, and Croke (1972), and Scheffers (1977). The rest of the studies were adequately described and subjects were randomly selected or randomly assigned to treatments. Pretreatment measures were used by Gottlieb (1980), Jones et al. (1981), Scheffers (1977), and Westervelt and McKinney (1980). Longterm effects were measured by Ballard et al. (1977) and Westervelt and McKinney (1980). Because the majority of the samples were white, middle-class students, they cannot be accepted as representative.

The descriptions of the attitude modification techniques or treatments applied were fairly clear, but not sufficiently so for replication. Reliability and validity data were not provided for the instruments in any study, even for the Attitude Toward Disabled Persons Scale (ATDP), which is widely used. The majority of the investigators developed their own instruments. Their content was described but not the development and evaluation procedures. The generalizability of the results and conclusions of these studies, therefore, should be viewed with caution.

Although Lazar et al. (1971) used lecture, group discussion, and direct contact, and Rapier et al. (1972) used only direct contact, both studies yielded significant increases in positive attitudes. Interestingly, the ATDP was found to be sufficient to detect shifts in the attitudes of the gifted group in the Lazar et al. study. Some sexual differences were noted in the population used by Rapier et al.; that is, the definite attitude differences between boys and girls found prior to integration diminished afterwards. Age and maturity appeared to be influential in that older children expressed more realistic attitudes than did the younger ones.

Participation in cooperative activities with educable mentally retarded children resulted in increased social acceptance by nonhandicapped peers who did or did not directly participate in the treatment (Ballard et al., 1977). Disability simulation was more effective in changing attitudes toward physically disabled persons than toward persons with other handicapping conditions (Dahl et al., 1978). The information influence of group discussion on attitude change was supported in the study by Gottlieb (1980). Significant positive changes in children's perceptions of handicapped people resulted from the combined use of disability simulation, interviews, films, and discussions (Jones et al., 1981).

Competent, normal-appearing children were found to be more attractive than incompetent, abnormal-appearing children (Siperstein et al., 1977). However, when a similar technique was used to portray a blind child on video- and audiotapes and in group discussions as competent and incompetent, the participants developed better feelings for blind children but were less inclined to engage in activities with them than were the students not given the instruction. It was suggested that participation may have increased individual awareness of the limitations of blindness.

Although no evidence was found of widespread rejection of physically handicapped children, participants tended to be attracted to wheelchair-bound children more than to children on crutches and braces (Jones et al., 1981).

Elements of attitude-change theory included the following:

1. The term "attitude(s)" was not defined.
2. The components of attitudes of concern were cognitive and/or affective.
3. The measurements were appropriate to the components.
4. The functions of attitude were not indicated.

246

5. No consideration was given to the personality factors of the subjects except for Ballard et al. (1977).
6. Indications of the application of attitude theory to the development of the treatment were found in four studies (Ballard et al., 1977; Gottlieb, 1980; Siperstein & Bak, 1980; Siperstein et al., 1977).
7. Attitude-change principles were applied but not identified as such in most of the studies except for Ballard et al. (1977), Gottlieb (1980), Siperstein and Bak (1980), and Siperstein et al. (1977).

The pattern of the application of the elements of attitude-change theory is shown in Table 7.

High School Students

Forader (1970) and Rusalem (1967) respectively investigated attitude change procedures involving physically disabled and deaf-blind persons with high school students. Friedman and Marsh (1972) attempted to improve attitudes toward blind students. Handlers and Austin (1980) were concerned with general disabilities. The purposes of the four studies and the attitude-change procedures used are shown in Table 6.

In each study the sample sizes were adequate but the subjects were not well described in the reports. Forader used stratified random sampling to assign his subjects to treatments, whereas Rusalem used pretesting to identify high- and low-scoring groups. The treatments were fairly well described by Rusalem, inadequately by Forader. The samples in Friedman and Marsh (1972) and Handlers and Austin (1980) were nonrandomized and did not include control groups.

Rusalem employed three types of data collection: (a) observation of the students during sessions, (b) changes in scores on attitude measures, and (c) follow-up and self-reports, which greatly increased the strength of his investigation. Unfortunately, no reliability or validity data were provided for the instrumentation in the studies, and Rusalem did not describe his test development. Forader used formal measures: the Attitude Toward Disabled Persons Scale and the Marlowe-Crowne Social Desirability Scale. The Attitude Toward Blindness Scale was used by Friedman and Marsh (1972). Handlers and Austin (1980) used teacher-made questions for students to self-evaluate their attitude changes.

Regardless of the mode of instruction, no difference in attitudes was found in the subjects of Forader's study who were exposed to persuasive communication, and no difference was evident 2 weeks after the exposure. In the Rusalem study, the attitudes of the students who, prior to treatment, had been assigned to the low-scoring group changed significantly after the six 1-hour sessions, but the identified high-scoring group changed only slightly in attitude. This result suggests that the ceiling of the instrumentation may have been too low to detect changes in the high-scoring group. Both Friedman and Marsh (1972) and Handlers and Austin (1980) reported positive reactions to their instructional programs. However, deficits in their research design ne-

247

cessitate limited acceptance of their conclusions.

Elements of attitude-change theory included the following:

1. The term "attitude(s)" was not defined.
2. The components of attitude were identified as cognitive and/or affective.
3. The measurements employed in three of the studies were appropriate to the components; that in the fourth (Handlers & Austin, 1980) could not be determined.
4. The function(s) of "attitude(s)" were not specified.
5. Some consideration for the personality factors of the subjects was shown by Rusalem.
6. No theory of attitude change was suggested.
7. Attitude-change principles were applied by all investigators but were not identified as such.

The pattern of the application of the elements of attitude-change theory is shown in Table 7.

Related Professionals

Two studies were found which involved persons in this category (Table 6). Felton's (1975) sample of health care workers was very small, nonrandomized, nonrepresentative, and not fully described in the report. The treatment used was described so inadequately that replication would be impossible.

Sadlick and Penta's (1975) sample was adequate in size and the subjects were randomly selected. The inadequate description of the sample, however, raises questions about the representativeness of the study sample. The development of the instrumentation was described, but neither the Felton nor the Sadlick and Penta study provided reliability or validity data for its instrumentation.

According to Sadlick and Penta, their results indicate an increase in positive attitudes toward physically disabled persons after direct contact and viewing a videotape of a successfully rehabilitated quadriplegic patient. The senior nurses' interactions with quadriplegic patients for a 10-week period appeared to greatly increase the longterm effects of the positive attitude change. The generalizability of both studies must be viewed with reservation.

Elements of attitude-change theory included the following:

1. Sadlick and Penta (1975) were among the few investigators to define their use of the term "attitude(s)."
2. The use of attitude components of concern was specified by both Felton (1975) and Sadlick and Penta.
3. Measures appropriate to the components were employed in both studies.
4. The function of "attitude(s)" was not addressed.
5. No consideration was given to the personality factors of the subjects.
6. The use of attitude-change theory was specified by Sadlick and Penta.
7. In both studies, attitude-change principles were intentionally applied.

The pattern of the application of the elements of attitude-change theory is shown in Table 7.

TABLE 7
Application of Elements of Theory to Attitude Change Studies by Significance of Results

Study	1	2	3	4	5	6	7
Studies Reporting Statistically Significant Results							
Ballard et al. (1977)		X	X		X	X	X
Baran (1977)		X	X				X
Dahl et al. (1978)		X	X				X[c]
Gottlieb (1980)		X	X			X	X
Jones et al. (1981)		X	X				
Koch (1975)		X	X			X	X[c]
Lazar et al. (1971)		X	X				X[c]
Rapier et al. (1972)		X	X				X[c]
Sadlick & Penta (1975)		X	X			X	X
Siperstein & Bak (1980)		X	X			X	X
Siperstein et al. (1977)		X	X			X	X
Westervelt & McKinney (1980)		X	X				X[c]
Studies Not Reporting Statistically Significant Results							
Alese (1973)		X	X				[b]
Felton (1975)		X	X				
Forader (1970)		X	X			[b]	[b]
Friedman & Marsh (1972)		X	[b]				
Granofsky (1956)		X	X		X		
Handlers & Austin (1980)		[b]	[b]				
Rusalem (1967)		X	X		X		X
Scheffers (1977)		X	X				X[c]

Note: Community groups, elementary and high school students, and related professionals were the subjects of these studies.
[a]See Table 3.
[b]Could not be determined.
[c]Were not identified, but applied.

SUMMARY ANALYSIS

The various approaches to the modification of attitudes of nondisabled toward disabled persons have been used with different populations with apparently equal effectiveness. When similar techniques were applied to the different disability groups, the applications yielded discouraging and contradictory findings. Both positive and negative attitudinal changes, in addition to numerous reports of nonsignificant changes, resulted from interactions with disabled persons as well as from the provision of educational and general information.

Several studies reported nonsignificant differences in attitudes between subjects who received treatments and those who did not. The mode of presentation—live, videotaped, audiotaped, simulated, role-played, or observed experiences with disabled persons or disabling conditions—did not produce any significant differences in the amount of attitude change. Furthermore, numerous methodological deficiencies in most studies reduced their generalizability.

Although significant increases in positive attitudes were minimal in most studies and rarely included longterm effects, a few investigators reported more success than others. These successes are worthy of examination for clues to the reason(s) for the variability in effectiveness. Analysis of the studies reporting success suggests a possible relation to one or more of the following factors: (a) the extent of the use of the seven elements extrapolated from attitude-change theory and/or research, (b) the attitude-change technique(s) employed, (c) the type of assessment used to detect the shifts in attitude, and (d) the presence of general methodological requirements. It may also be helpful to determine whether successes with some subject populations were more frequent than with others, or whether successes may be related to the disability population of concern.

Twenty-five of the 47 attitude-change studies reviewed reported statistically significant increases in positive attitudes following treatment (Ballard et al., 1977; Baran, 1977; Brooks & Bransford, 1971; Carlson & Potter, 1972; Clore & Jeffrey, 1972; Dahl et al., 1978; Evans, 1976; Glass & Meckler, 1972; Gottlieb, 1980; Guskin, 1973; Haring et al., 1958; Hastorf et al., 1979; Jones et al., 1981; Koch, 1975; Lazar et al., 1971; Naor & Milgram, 1980; Rapier et al., 1972; Sadlick & Penta, 1975; Siperstein & Bak, 1980; Siperstein et al., 1977; Skrtic, 1977; Weinberg, 1978; Westervelt & McKinney, 1980; Yates, 1973; Yerxa, 1978). (The report by Daniels [1976] was not analyzed because it did not contain sufficient information.) Most of these investigators sought attitude change through the cognitive component; thus they based their approaches upon the notion that increasing knowledge about disabled persons would bring about change in the affective component and would result in the desired attitudinal changes. In some cases, the investigators expected the attitudinal changes to be reflected in overt behaviors.

The extent of the application of the seven elements extrapolated from attitude-change theory and/or research varied across the studies from two to seven, although three or more elements were identified in most of them (Table 8). It was possible to determine the component(s) of attitudes of concern (element 2) in all studies, either through inference or specific reference, and the appropriateness of the instrumentation (element 3) to measure the component(s) of concern in 42 studies. In the reports of 40 studies it was possible to identify attitude-change principles (element 7) in the treatments applied; unfortunately, few of the investigators clearly specified their intent to apply the principles so their application may have been coincidental.

Because teachers and administrators, college students, and elementary and secondary students were the populations investigated in 41 of the 47 studies that were analyzed, most of the change techniques used by the investigators were related to educational situations. The most frequently employed techniques were direct contact in educational settings and group discussion via

250

TABLE 8
Applications of Combination of Elements of Theory to Attitude Change Studies by Significance of Results

Combination of Elements[a]	Studies Reporting Statistically Significant Results	Studies Not Reporting Statistically Significant Results
1, 2, 3, 4, 5, 6, 7	1	
1, 2, 3, 6, 7	1	
1, 2, 3, 7	1	1
2, 3, 5, 6, 7	1	
2, 3, 6, 7	9	
2, 3, 5, 7		1
2, 3, 5		1
2, 3, 7	12	14
2, 3		3
2, 7		2

Note: In most studies, the application of factor 7 was not identified, hence it cannot be determined whether the applications were intentional or coincidental.
[a]See Table 3.

lecture-discussion formats followed by role-playing and face-to-face contact through media.

The instrumentation did not seem to have any major effect in the detection of shifts in attitudes; several types were used singly or in combination to an equal degree across studies. Those used more frequently were investigator-developed questionnaires and attitude scales, semantic differential scales, and the Attitude Toward Disabled Persons Scale; those used to a somewhat lesser degree were interviews, behavior observations, and the Minnesota Teacher Attitude Inventory.

There is no indication that the successes reported in the 25 studies were related to the populations studied: Seven of the more successful studies used populations of regular classroom teachers; six used college students, nine used children, one used a community group, and one used nurses. All the subjects appeared to be comparable in their responses to the various treatments. No evidence was found that the amount of attitude change was related to a specific disability group.

The reports revealed numerous methodological deficiencies: insufficient descriptions of procedures for adequate replication; absence of reliability and validity data for the instrumentation; poor sampling procedures; poorly described subjects; and inadequately described content and development of instrumentation. Because the strength of the research design is critical to the degree to which the results can be accepted, the findings can only be characterized as contaminated. Unfortunately, this contamination makes it impossible to identify or even suggest with any degree of certainty that success is related to the application of the change elements identified. Any hypothesis of the reason for the variability in the successes reported by the investigators would be inappropriate and presumptuous.

Nevertheless, it is possible to identify those investigators whose methodology was somewhat stronger and to specify the presence of certain change elements. These studies can be viewed with less caution and with a greater degree of confidence. Some of the better designed studies were those by Clore and Jeffrey (1972), Gottlieb (1980), Haring et al., (1958), Hastorf et al. (1980), and Yerxa (1978). In each of these studies random sampling, descriptions of the development and content of the instrumentation, and fairly adequate descriptions of the procedures are present. Clore and Jeffrey also included follow-up measures to assess the longterm effects of the treatment.

The methodological and theoretical change elements are juxtaposed in Table 9. The studies in which four or more change elements could be identified display fewer methodological deficiencies than those in which only three elements were identified. In the three studies with the fewest methodological problems, four change elements were identified for Clore and Jeffrey, Gottlieb, Haring et al., Hastorf et al., Siperstein, and Bak, Siperstein et al., and Weinberg (1978), and seven were identified for Yerxa. Yet only Clore and Jeffrey satisfied all four methodological criteria. The change techniques employed in these eight studies included disability simulation, vicarious role playing, lecture/discussion, shared active participation with discussion, face-to-face contact through media, and direct contact in educational settings. Clore and Jeffrey, Hastorf et al., Naor and Milgran, Weinberg, and Yerxa studied attitude change in college student populations; Haring et al. in regular classroom teachers; and the remaining seven investigators focused on elementary school students (Ballard et al., Dahl et al., Gottlieb; Jones et al., Siperstein & Bak, Siperstein et al., and Westervelt & McKinney). Weinberg investigated the influences of optimal contact conditions in two separate experiments: one with elementary school students and the other with college students. Successful results were obtained only with the college students.

It is not possible to attribute unsuccessful results to any single factor. Whether the failure to achieve satisfactory results is the fault of poor methodology, failure to use elements of attitude-change theory, or some unknown factor cannot be substantiated; too many other variables are involved. The combination of the confusion created by poorly described studies, suspect methodology, and lack of specific indication of intent to apply principles of attitude change does not permit conclusions about the influence of the elements on the outcome. It is possible that studies entailing more elements tend to have better methodology.

Although we cannot be confident of the general findings of most of the research, and there is a critical need for improvements in the methodology of most studies, the elements found in the better designed studies do provide some information that may suggest which factors should be present in order to develop more effective attitude-change programs. Nevertheless, only after more well-designed research is completed can we be reasonably certain of the elements that contribute to the variability in effectiveness. At the very least, we should consider and apply what can be gleaned from theories of attitude

TABLE 9
Comparison of Elements of Theory and Methodology In Studies Reporting Success

Investigator(s)	Elements of Theory Included	Randomized Sample and/or Assignment to Treatment	Description of Treatment Sufficient for Replication	Information on Reliability and Validity	Follow-up Measure
Ballard et al (1977)	2,3,5,6,7	x			x
Baran (1977)	2,3,7				
Brooks and Bransford (1971)	2,3,7[a]				
Carlson and Potter (1972)	2,3,7[a]				
Clore and Jeffrey (1972)	2,3,6,7[a]	x	x	x	x
Dahl et al. (1978)	2,3,7[a]	[b]		x	
Evans (1976)	2,3,6,7	x			x
Glass and Meckler (1972)	2,3,7[a]				
Gottlieb (1980)	2,3,6,7	x	x	x	
Guskin (1973) (an evaluation report vs. research report)	2,3,7				
Haring et al. (1958)	1,2,3,7[a]	x	x	x	
Hastorf et al. (1979)	2,3,6,7	x	x	x	
Jones et al. (1981)	2,3,7	x	x		
Koch (1975)	2,3,6,7[a]		x		x
Lazar et al. (1976)	2,3,7[a]				
Naor & Milgram (1980)	2,3,7[a]	x			
Rapier et al. (1972)	2,3,7[a]				
Sadlick and Penta (1975)	1,2,3,6,7	x			x
Siperstein & Bak (1980)	2,3,6,7	x	x	x	
Siperstein et al. (1977)	2,3,6,7	x			
Skrtic (1977) (dissertation abstract)	2,3,6,7[a]				x
Weinberg (1978)	2,3,6,7	x	x		
Westervelt & McKinney (1980)	2,3,7[a]	x			x
Yates (1973)	2,3,7[a]				
Yerxa (1978)	1,2,3,4,5,6,7	x	x	x	

Note: Evaluations are made solely upon availability of methodological information in *this* report of the study.

[a]Principles of attitude change applied, but not identified.

[b]Unable to determine.

253

change and/or attitude research in our future attempts to modify attitudes toward disabled individuals.

RETROSPECT AND PROSPECT

The examination of the literature on techniques of modifying attitudes toward disabled persons revealed numerous deficiencies in methodology and, in most cases, the lack of a systematic application of attitude theory and principles of attitude change to the development of the treatments. Nevertheless, with appreciation of the limitations of the current work, and with appreciation of the magnitude of the task of developing and validating strategies of attitude change for diverse objectives and populations, it is appropriate—indeed necessary—to draw from extant work.

Despite the discouraging outcomes of the analysis of the studies reviewed, it is possible to extract some information that could be helpful in the development of future research in this area. Although it is impossible to disregard the methodological deficiencies in the studies, several recurring factors were apparent. It has been established that there were no significant differences in the amount of attitude change based upon the technique employed; however, examination of the presence or absence of these factors tentatively suggests criteria for future research. Of course, we must recognize that the basis for the suggestions will be refined and strengthened in some instances and refuted in others.

The effectiveness of future research could no doubt be greatly improved if researchers would employ the following guidelines—some obvious and others less so—in the development and implementation of studies designed to modify attitudes toward disabled individuals. Persons researching and writing in this area, therefore, should attend to the following:

1. Clearly define the disability group of concern.
2. Provide an operational definition of the term "attitudes" for the context in which it is to be used.
3. Develop the treatment using principles and theories of attitude change which seem to be the most appropriate to objectives, and describe the principles and theories thoroughly.
4. Select instrumentation that will measure the specific component(s) of attitudes being examined.
5. Provide reliability and validity data for all instrumentation, and describe the development and content of investigator-developed instruments.
6. Use multidimensional measures to assess attitude change, including behavioral and (where possible) physiological as well as verbal measures.
7. Use posttreatment as well as pretreatment measures and include procedures to determine longterm effects of the treatment. (Pretreatment measures may be eliminated with a randomized and representative sample.)
8. Use samples that are randomized and representative, and clearly describe the subjects.
9. Examine situational variables which may provide information on the possible function of the attitudes and personality characteristics that may

influence the persuasibility of the subjects, and use this information when selecting strategies for attitude change.

10. Determine whether a relation between verbal expression of attitudes and overt behaviors resulted from the treatment.

11. Validate the treatment in the complex reality of the public schools, rather than only in laboratory settings.

Despite limitations, extant literature on attitude theory and research has much to commend it with respect to conceptualizing the nature of attitudes, the techniques for modifying them, and their measurement. It can facilitate our understanding of how attitudes in special education context develop and the functions they serve, and it can suggest strategies for attitude change.

The necessity for testing principles and theories in special education contexts as a prelude to decisions about their value for our special education purposes must be recognized. Inasmuch as there appears to be no comprehensive theory which can be used for such purposes, we can draw from existing literature that which seems most appropriate and immediately useful.

REFERENCES

Alese, J. A. Operation awareness. *Mental Retardation*, 1973, *11*(5), 38-39.

Ballard, M., Corman, L., Gottlieb, J., & Kaufman, M. Improving the social status of mainstreamed retarded children. *Journal of Educational Psychology*, 1977, *69*, 605-611.

Baran, S. J. T.V. programming and attitudes toward mental retardation. *Journalism Quarterly*, 1977, *54*, 140-142.

Brooks, B., & Bransford, L. Modification of teacher attitudes toward exceptional children. *Exceptional Children*, 1971, *38*, 259-261.

Carlson, L. B., & Potter, R. E. Training classroom teachers to provide in-class educational services for exceptional children in rural areas. *Journal of School Psychology*, 1972, *10*(2), 147-150.

Chafin, P., & Peipher, R. A. Simulated hearing loss: An aid to inservice education. *American Annals of the Deaf*, 1979, *124*, 468-471.

Clore, G. L., & Jeffrey, K. M. Emotional role-playing, attitude change and attraction toward a disabled person. *Journal of Personality and Social Psychology*, 1972, *23*, 105-111.

Dahl, H. G., Horsman, K. R., & Arkell, R. N. Simulation of exceptionalities for elementary school students. *Psychological Reports*, 1978, *42*, 573-574.

Daniels, L. K. Covert reinforcement and hypnosis in modification of attitudes toward physically disabled persons and generalization to the emotionally disturbed. *Psychological Reports*, 1976, *38*(2), 554.

Donaldson, J. Changing attitudes toward handicapped persons: A review and analysis of research. *Exceptional Children*, 1980, *46*, 504-514.

Donaldson, J., & Martinson, C. Modifying attitudes toward physically disabled persons. *Exceptional Children*, 1977, *43*, 337-341.

Euse, F. J. An application of covert positive reinforcement for the modification of attitudes toward physically disabled persons. *Dissertation Abstracts International*, 1976, *36*(11-B), 5787-5788.

Evans, J. H. Changing attitudes toward disabled persons: An experimental study. *Rehabilitation Counseling Bulletin*, 1976, *19*(4), 572-579.

Felton, G. S. Changes in attitudes toward disabled persons among allied health paraprofessional trainees in an interdisciplinary setting. *Perceptual and Motor Skills*, 1975, *40*(1), 118.

255

Fenton, T. R. The effect of inservice training on elementary classroom teachers' attitudes toward and knowledge about handicapped children. *Dissertation Abstracts International*, 1975, *35*(9-A), 5966.

Forader, A. T. Modifying social attitudes toward the physically disabled through three different modes of instruction. *Dissertation Abstracts International*, 1970, *30*(9-B), 4360.

Friedman, R., & Marsh, V. Changing public attitudes toward blindness. *Exceptional Children*, 1972, *38*, 426-428.

Glass, R. M., & Meckler, R. S. Preparing elementary teachers to instruct mildly handicapped children in regular classrooms. *Exceptional Children*, 1972, *39*, 152-156.

Gottlieb, J. Improving attitudes toward retarded children by using group discussion. *Exceptional Children*, 1980, *47*, 105-111.

Granofsky, J. Modification of attitudes toward the physically disabled. *Dissertation Abstracts*, 1956, *16*, 1182-1183.

Guskin, S. L. Simulation games for teachers on the mainstreaming of mildly handicapped children. *Viewpoints*, 1973, *49*, 85-95. (Bulletin of the School of Education, Indiana University)

Halloran, J. D. *Attitude formation and change.* Leicester, Eng.: Leicester University Press, 1967.

Handlers, A., & Austin, K. Improving attitudes of high school students toward their handicapped peers. *Exceptional Children*, 1980, *47*, 228-229.

Haring, N. G., Stern, G. G., & Cruickshank, W. M. *Attitudes of educators toward exceptional children.* Syracuse NY: Syracuse University Press, 1958.

Hastorf, A. H., Wildfogel, J., & Cassman, T. Acknowledgement of handicap as a tactic in social interaction. *Journal of Personality and Social Psychology*, 1979, *37*, 1790-1797.

Hersh, A., Carlson, R., & Lossino, D. A. Normalized interaction with families of the mentally retarded to introduce attitude and behavior change in students in a professional discipline. *Mental Retardation*, 1977, *15*, 32-33.

Hovland, C. I., Janis, I. L., & Kelley, H. H. *Communication and persuasion.* New Haven: Yale University Press, 1953.

Jones, T. W., Sowell, V. M., Jones, J. K., & Butler, L. G. Changing children's perceptions of handicapped people. *Exceptional Children*, 1981, *47*, 365-368.

Koch, A. S. Changing attitudes toward blindness: A role-playing demonstration for service clubs. *New Outlook for the Blind*, 1975, *69*(9), 407-409.

Lazar, A. L., Gensley, J. T., & Orpet, R. E. Changing attitudes of young mentally gifted children toward handicapped persons. *Exceptional Children*, 1971, *37*, 600-602.

Lazar, A. L., Orpet, R., & Demos, G. The impact of class instruction on changing student attitudes. *Rehabiliation Counseling Bulletin*, 1976, *20*(1), 66-68.

McGuire, W. J. The nature of attitudes and attitude change. In G. Lindzey & E. Aronson (Eds.), *The handbook of social psychology* (Vol.3). Reading MA: Addison Wesley, 1968, 136-314.

Naor, M., & Milgram, R. M. Two preservice strategies for preparing regular class teachers for mainstreaming. *Exceptional Children*, 1980, *47*, 126-129.

Orlansky, M. D. The effects of two different instructional methods on student achievement and attitudes toward exceptional children in an introductory college course in special education. *Dissertation Abstracts International*, 1977, *38*(3), 1332A.

Rapier, J., Adelson, R., Carey, R., & Croke, K. Changes in children's attitudes toward the physically handicapped. *Exceptional Children*, 1972, *39*, 219-223.

Rusalem, H. Engineering changes in public attitude toward a severely disabled group. *Journal of Rehabilitation*, 1967, *33*(3), 26-27.

Sadlick, M., & Penta, F. B. Changing nurse attitudes toward quadriplegics through use of television. *Rehabilitation Literature*, 1975, *36*(9), 274-278.

Scheffers, W. A. Sighted children learn about blindness. *Journal of Visual Impairment and Blindness*, 1977, *71*, 258-261.

Schorn, F. R. A study of an in-service practicum's effects on teachers' attitudes about mainstreaming. *Dissertation Abstracts International*, 1977, *37*(9), 5762A.

Shaw, S. F., & Gillung, T. B. Efficacy of a college course for regular class teachers of the mildly handicapped. *Mental Retardation*, 1975, *13*(4), 4-6.

Shotel, J. R., Iano, R. P., & McGettigan, J. F. Teacher attitudes associated with integration of handicapped children. In G. J. Warfield (Ed.), *Mainstream currents*. Reston VA: Council for Exceptional Children, 1974, 91-97.

Siperstein, G. N., & Bak, J. J. Improving children's attitudes toward blind peers. *Journal of Visual Impairment and Blindness*, 1980, *74*, 132-135.

Siperstein, G. N., Bak, J. J., & Gottlieb, J. Effects of group discussion on children's attitudes toward handicapped peers. *Journal of Educational Research*, 1977, *70*, 131-134.

Skrtic, T. M. The influence of in-service on the attitudes and behaviors of regular classroom teachers toward mainstreamed learning disabled students. *Dissertation Abstracts International*, 1977, *37*(12), 7692A.

Soloway, M. M. The development and evaluation of a special education in-service training program for regular classroom teachers. *Dissertation Abstracts International*, 1976, *36*(7), 4425A.

Triandis, H. C. *Attitude and attitude change*. New York: Wiley & Sons, 1971.

Weinberg, N. Modifying social stereotypes of the physically disabled. *Rehabilitation Counseling Bulletin*, 1978, *22*, 114-124.

Westervelt, V. D., & McKinney, J. D. Effects of a film on nonhandicapped children's attitude toward handicapped children. *Exceptional Children*, 1980, *46*, 294-296.

Wilson, E. D. A comparison of the effects of deafness simulation and observation upon attitudes, anxiety, and behavior manifested toward the deaf. *Journal of Special Education*, 1971, *5*(4), 343-349.

Wilson, E. D., & Alcorn, D. Disability simulation and development of attitudes toward the exceptional. *Journal of Special Education*, 1969, *3*(3), 303-307.

Yates, J. R. A model for preparing regular classroom teachers for mainstreaming. *Exceptional Children*, 1973, *41*, 471-472.

Yerxa, E. *Effects of dyadic, self-administered instructional program in changing the attitudes of female college students toward the physically disabled*. (Doctoral Dissertation, University of Michigan, 1971) University Microfilms International, 1978.

Yuker, H. E. Attitudes of the general public toward handicapped individuals. *The White House Conference on Handicapped Individuals Workbook*. State White House Conference. Washington DC: U.S. Department of Health, Education and Welfare, 1976.

Zimbardo, P., & Ebbeson, E. B. *Influencing attitudes and changing behavior*. Reading MA: Addison-Wesley, 1970.